Digital Photography and Everyday Life

C000113734

Digital Photography and Everyday Life: Empirical studies on material visual practices explores the role that digital photography plays within everyday life. With contributors from ten different countries and backgrounds in a range of academic disciplines – including anthropology, media studies and visual culture – this collection takes a uniquely broad perspective on photography by situating the image-making process in wider discussions on the materiality and visuality of photographic practices and explores these through empirical case studies.

By focusing on material visual practices, the book presents a comprehensive overview of some of the main challenges digital photography is bringing to everyday life. It explores how the digitization of photography has a wide-reaching impact on the use of the medium, as well as on the kinds of images that can be produced and the ways in which camera technology is developed. The exploration goes beyond mere images to think about cameras, mediations and technologies as key elements in the development of visual digital cultures.

Digital Photography and Everyday Life will be of great interest to students and scholars of Photography, Contemporary Art, Visual Culture and Media Studies, as well as those studying Communication, Cultural Anthropology, and Science and Technology Studies.

Edgar Gómez Cruz is a Vice-Chancellor Research Fellow at RMIT, Melbourne.

Asko Lehmuskallio is Chair of the ECREA TWG Visual Culture and founding member of the Nordic Network for Digital Visuality.

Routledge Studies in European Communication Research and Education

Edited by Claudia Alvares, Lusofona University, Portugal,
Ilija Tomanić Trivundža, University of Ljubljana, Slovenia and
Fausto Colombo, Università Cattolica del Sacro Cuore, Milan, Italy
Series Advisory Board: Nico Carpentier, François Heinderyckx,
Denis McQuail, Robert Picard and Jan Servaes

ECREA

www.ecrea.eu

Published in association with the European Communication Research and Education Association (ECREA), books in the series make a major contribution to the theory, research, practice and/or policy literature. They are European in scope and represent a diversity of perspectives. Book proposals are refereed.

1 **Audience Transformations**
Shifting Audience Positions in Late Modernity
Edited by Nico Carpentier, Kim Christian Schrøder and Lawrie Hallett

2 **Audience Research Methodologies**
Between Innovation and Consolidation
Edited by Geoffroy Patriarche, Helena Bilandzic, Jakob Linaa Jensen and Jelena Jurišić

3 **Multiplayer**
The Social Aspects of Digital Gaming
Edited by Thorsten Quandt and Sonja Kröger

4 **Mapping Foreign Correspondence in Europe**
Edited by Georgios Terzis

5 **Revitalising Audience Research**
Innovations in European Audience Research
Edited by Frauke Zeller, Cristina Ponte and Brian O'Neill

6 **Radio Audiences and Participation in the Age of Network Society**
Edited by Tiziano Bonini and Belén Monclús

7 **Interactive Digital Narrative**
History, Theory and Practice
Edited by Hartmut Koenitz, Gabriele Ferri, Mads Haahr, Diğdem Sezen and Tonguç İbrahim Sezen

8 **Public Service Media in Europe**
A Comparative Approach
Edited by Karen Arriaza Ibarra, Eva Nowak and Raymond Kuhn

9 **European Media in Crisis**
   Values, Risks and Policies
   Edited by Josef Trappel,
   Jeanette Steemers and
   Barbara Thomass

10 **Digital Photography and**
   Everyday Life
   Empirical Studies on Material
   Visual Practices
   Edited by Edgar Gómez Cruz
   and Asko Lehmuskallio

Digital Photography and Everyday Life

Empirical studies on material visual practices

Edited by Edgar Gómez Cruz and Asko Lehmuskallio

Routledge
Taylor & Francis Group

LONDON AND NEW YORK

First published 2016
by Routledge
2 Park Square, Milton Park, Abingdon, Oxon OX14 4RN

and by Routledge
711 Third Avenue, New York, NY 10017

Routledge is an imprint of the Taylor & Francis Group, an informa business

British Library Cataloguing-in-Publication Data
A catalogue record for this book is available from the British Library

Library of Congress Cataloging-in-Publication Data
Names: Gómez Cruz, Edgar, editor. | Lehmuskallio, Asko, editor.
Title: Digital photography and everyday life : empirical studies on material visual practices / edited by Edgar Gómez Cruz and Asko Lehmuskallio.
Description: London ; New York : Routledge, [2016] | Series: Routledge studies in European communication research and education. | Includes bibliographical references and index.
Identifiers: LCCN 2015042827| ISBN 9781138899803 (hbk) | ISBN 9781138899810 (pbk) | ISBN 9781315696768 (ebk)
Subjects: LCSH: Photography–Social aspects. | Popular culture. | Photography–Digital techniques.
Classification: LCC TR183 .D55 2016 | DDC 770–dc23
LC record available at http://lccn.loc.gov/2015042827

ISBN: 978-1-138-89980-3 (hbk)
ISBN: 978-1-138-89981-0 (pbk)
ISBN: 978-1-315-69676-8 (ebk)

Typeset in Sabon
by Wearset Ltd, Boldon, Tyne and Wear

MIX
Paper from
responsible sources
FSC
www.fsc.org   FSC® C013604

Printed and bound by CPI Group (UK) Ltd, Croydon, CR0 4YY

Contents

List of figures   x

List of tables   xi

Notes on contributors   xii

Foreword   xv
RICHARD CHALFEN

Acknowledgements   xxii

Why material visual practices?   1
ASKO LEHMUSKALLIO AND EDGAR GÓMEZ CRUZ

PART I
Variance in use in everyday photography   17

1 'I'm a picture girl!' Mobile photography in Tanzania   19
   PAULA UIMONEN

2 'Today I dressed like this': selling clothes and playing for
   celebrity: self-representation and consumption on Facebook   35
   SARA PARGANA MOTA

3 Amplification and heterogeneity: seniors and digital
   photographic practices   52
   MARIA SCHREIBER

4 Illness, death and grief: the daily experience of viewing and
   sharing digital images   70
   REBECA PARDO AND MONTSE MORCATE

5 The Boston Marathon bombing investigation as an example of networked journalism and the power of big data analytics   86
ANSSI MÄNNISTÖ

6 Variance in everyday photography   98
KARIN BECKER

PART II
Cameras, connectivity and transformed localities   105

7 Photographs of place in phonespace: camera phones as a location-aware mobile technology   107
MIKKO VILLI

8 (Digital) photography, experience and space in transnational families: a case study of Spanish-Irish families living in Ireland   122
PATRICIA PRIETO-BLANCO

9 Visual politics and material semiotics: the digital camera's translation of political protest   141
RUNE SAUGMANN ANDERSEN

10 Linked photography: a praxeological analysis of augmented reality navigation in the early twentieth century   160
TRISTAN THIELMANN

11 Photographic places and digital wayfaring: conceptualizing relationships between cameras, connectivities and transformed localities   186
SARAH PINK

PART III
Camera as the extension of the photographer   191

12 Exploring everyday photographic routines through the habit of noticing   193
EVE FORREST

13 'Analogization': reflections on wearable cameras and the
   changing meaning of images in a digital landscape   209
   PAOLO FAVERO

14 Photo-genic assemblages: photography as a connective
   interface   228
   EDGAR GÓMEZ CRUZ

15 The camera as a sensor: the visualization of everyday
   digital photography as simulative, heuristic and layered
   pictures   243
   ASKO LEHMUSKALLIO

16 Is the camera an extension of the photographer?   267
   MARTIN LISTER

17 Outlook: photographic wayfaring, now and to come   274
   NANCY VAN HOUSE

   Index   284

Figures

2.1   'Tonight's outfit'; image posted by Sofia on her closet
      Facebook account   40
3.1   A picture provided by Bertl that was processed/finished
      to 'look good on the TV screen'   59
3.2   Picture provided by Sepp and Regina (faces pixelated)   62
4.1   The most important motivations for sharing images
      through Instagram, related to Alzheimer's   75
5.1   The themes of the *Boston Globe*'s Facebook posts and
      BAA's Twitter feeds   89
8.1   Pedro and Maria's 'circle of reference'   127
8.2   Homemade photo collage   129
8.3   Place-making event in transnational families   131
9.1   Citizen recording of police filming street clashes by the
      Brorson Church   141
9.2   Image used in reportage of police officers beating
      Christina Søndergaard   147
9.3   Framegrab of police leading arrested asylum seeker out
      of the Brorson Church   156
10.1 The Rand McNally Photo-Auto Guide, Chicago to
      Lake Geneva (1909)   161
10.2 Photographic Automobile Map, Chicago to Milwaukee
      (1905)   168
10.3 Photo-Auto Maps, New York to Chicago (1907)   172
13.1 Still from a videoclip taken with a GoPro camera   220
13.2 Photograph of a snail taken with a macro lens mounted
      on an iPhone 5   221
15.1 A minimum spanning tree based on a social network   256
15.2 Using navigational camera software in traffic   258
16.1 Andreas Feininger, 'The Photojournalist', 1951   269

Tables

8.1   Research design – breakdown of interviews and methods   126
15.1   An outline of the photographic process   251
15.2   Ways of creating simulative pictures resembling a photo   254
15.3   Ways of creating heuristic pictures   257

Contributors

Karin Becker is Professor Emerita in Media Studies at Stockholm University, and draws on a background in journalism, sociology and visual anthropology. Her research explores cultural histories and contemporary contexts of visual media practices – in the press, museum collections, private settings and, most recently, in public space. She is editor of 'Visual Frictions', a special issue of *Journal of Aesthetics and Culture* (2015), compiled from the Nordic Network of Digital Visuality, which she directed.

Richard Chalfen is Emeritus Professor of Anthropology, Temple University and currently Senior Reseacher at the Center on Media and Child Health, Boston MA. Long-term research focuses on participant media, home media, visual communication and visual cultures of modern Japan. His recent book is *Photogaffes: Family Snapshots and Social Dilemmas* (2012).

Paolo Favero is Associate Professor in Film Studies and Visual Culture at the Department of Communication Studies, University of Antwerp. A visual anthropologist, he has devoted the core of his career to the study of visual culture in India and Italy and presently conducts research on image-making practices in contemporary India.

Eve Forrest is a Research Fellow at Edinburgh Napier University. Her research interests are embodied photography, sensory media routines and phenomenology and specifically how these strands interweave within everyday image-making practices. Her current project focuses on opinion-making online, and how it is dispersed through various textual, verbal and visual forms.

Edgar Gómez Cruz is a Vice-Chancellor Research Fellow at RMIT, Melbourne. He has published widely on a number of topics relating to digital culture, ethnography and photography. His recent publications include the book *From Kodak Culture to Networked Image: An Ethnography of Digital Photography Practices* (2012). Current research investigates screen cultures and creative practices, which is funded through RCUK and Vice Chancellor research grants.

Asko Lehmuskallio is Chair of the ECREA TWG Visual Culture and founding member of the Nordic Network for Digital Visuality. As researcher at Universities of Tampere and Siegen, he specializes in visual culture, mediated human action and networked cameras. Recent books include *Pictorial Practices in a 'Cam Era': Studying Non-Professional Camera Use* (2012) and *#snapshot: Cameras Amongst Us* (co-ed., 2014).

Martin Lister is Professor Emeritus in Visual Culture at the University of the West of England, Bristol. His publications include the second edition of *New Media: A Critical Introduction* (2009), 'The Times of Photography' in *Time, Media and Modernity* (2012) and 'Overlooking, Rarely Looking, and Not Looking', in *Digital Snaps: The New Face of Photography* (2013). He is an editor of the journal *photographies*, published by Routledge.

Anssi Männistö is Senior Lecturer of Visual Journalism at University of Tampere. He has been actively researching new forms and tools of journalism, especially camera phones, tablets and web-videos. His doctoral dissertation in 1999 explored the Western images of Islam and the Muslims during the Cold War era.

Montse Morcate is an artist and photography professor at University of Barcelona. She is also coordinator of the centre *Francesc Català-Roca, espai de fotografia* in the same city. Her recent publications and art projects deal with the photographical representation of death, illness and grief. Currently, she is a Visiting Scholar at Columbia University and Scholar in Residence at the Morbid Anatomy Museum in New York City.

Sara Pargana Mota is a PhD student in the Department of Anthropology at the University of Coimbra (Portugal) and a research collaborator at the Centre for Research in Anthropology (CRIA). She has a PhD scholarship from the Portuguese Foundation for Science and Technology. Her dissertation is an ethnographic study that explores the plurality of practices related with digital photography in everyday life.

Sarah Pink is Professor of Design and Media Ethnography, and Director of the Digital Ethnography Research Centre at RMIT University, Australia, and Visiting Professor at Halmstad University, Sweden and Loughborough University, UK. Her recent books include *Digital Ethnography: Principles and Practice* (co-authored, 2016), *Digital Materialities* (co-ed., 2016) and *Doing Sensory Ethnography* (2nd edn, 2015).

Rebeca Pardo is a photographer and photography Professor at University of Barcelona and University Abat Oliba CEU (Barcelona). Her research and recent publications deal with the fields of self-referential visual representation of illness, grief and pain, and the relationship between memory, domestic images, identity and social exclusion in contemporary autobiographical visual narratives.

Patricia Prieto-Blanco is a doctoral fellow and part-time lecturer at the National University of Ireland, Galway. Her areas of expertise are visual methods of research and reception studies. She is an advocate of inter-disciplinary, participatory and practice-based research. Accordingly, her work has been both published and exhibited. Her latest article, 'The Digital Progression of Community Archives' was recently published in *Convergence: The International Journal of Research into New Media Technologies*, published by Sage.

Rune Saugmann Andersen is a post-doctorate at University of Tampere, doing interdisciplinary research on the visual mediation of security. His work has appeared in *Security Dialogue, Journalism Practice, European Journal of Communication* and *JOMEC Journal* as well as numerous edited collections. His research is available at saugmann.tumblr.com.

Maria Schreiber is a PhD candidate at the Department of Communication at the University of Vienna. She is part of an interdisciplinary project on 'Picture Practices' funded by the Austrian Academy of Sciences (ÖAW). Her research focuses on photo-sharing practices and digital media culture.

Tristan Thielmann is Professor of Science and Technology Studies at the University of Siegen in Germany. He holds a PhD in Media and Communication Studies and studied Experimental Media Art. His cross-disciplinary research explores the aesthetics, ethnomethods, histories and techniques of geomedia with a focus on wayfinding and mobile human–computer interaction.

Paula Uimonen is Associate Professor in Social Anthropology at Stockholm University. She specializes in digital anthropology and the anthropology of art, media and globalization. Her recent publications focus on mobile infrastructure in Africa (2015), visual identity in Facebook (2013) and digital media at an arts college in Tanzania (2012).

Nancy Van House is Professor Emerita in the School of Information at the University of California, Berkeley. In her research she addresses the changing world of visual media from the perspective of science and technology studies. She has published in journals that include *Visual Studies, Memory Studies* and the *International Journal of Human–Computer Studies*. She is also a published photographer.

Mikko Villi is the Director of the Communication Research Centre CRC at the Department of Social Research, University of Helsinki. His work is focused on themes related to media management, journalism, photography, new communication technology and new forms of communication, concentrating on mobile, visual and social media.

Foreword

Richard Chalfen

We live in an intellectually challenging time for witnessing, participating in and studying the emergence of new media, especially digital media immediately connected to problematic issues of visuality. Problematic concern lies within contexts of visual culture, human interaction, social relationships and competent participation in everyday life. Digital capabilities continue to contribute to camera-mediated sociality in different and more varied ways than initially expected. The pace of technological change has been impressive and begs the question: Have interests and abilities of the scholarly community kept pace in theoretical and practical ways?

Any review of the historical development of a research field suggests significant questions and faces important challenges when the subject matter of such a field is rapidly developing and changing, when definitions of such subject matter are either missing or being altered along the way and, third, when recognition and acceptance of academic attention to such subject matter are also in flux. In short, several dimensions or storylines must be included and simultaneously interwoven when constructing a dynamic assessment of such a field.

Fundamental questions

What consistencies and changes can be noted? First and foremost lies a neglected problem: what is the field being discussed and does this field have specific origins, themes, definitions, parameters and the like? Can we claim that this field is conceptually, methodologically, materially defined and unified? Or, is it possible to feel there is enough of a shared understanding about a hypothetical field that participants are able to contribute? Most importantly, what have researchers wanted to learn and know? The general answer for this last question is: *What do ordinary people do with their cameras and personal pictures, as part of everyday life?*

Nomenclature ambiguity

'What exactly is being studied?' Several commentators have cited instances of terminological confusion and shortcomings with nomenclature and the ambiguous use of certain labels. These include such moving targets as 'everyday', 'family', 'amateur', 'private' and 'public', 'home media', and 'vernacular', while some deride 'artistic' as the primary reference point for comparisons. Finally, as picture-taking changes from analogue to digital, some have even challenged the appropriate use of the term 'photographer'; the legitimacy of 'photography' and 'photographic' has been questioned, given the lack of chemically based processes and, as emphasized in the following chapters, a more expansive configuration of technologies, affordances/constraints, institutions and practices.

Multiple perspectives

The emergence of a shared and evolving understanding of everyday photography owes much to a growing diversity of academic perspectives. Our immediate attention is drawn to what is now recognized as the visual social sciences, including early studies in sociology, communication and anthropology, as well as folklore. Other contributions have been made by psychologists, historians, cultural geographers, family therapists and the like. Courses on personal amateur photography have emerged from such disciplines as English, Communication, Folklore, American Studies, History and Material Culture Studies, among others. A lot of attention is found in Information Science and Computer–Human Interaction (CHI), resulting in an increasingly rich and relevant bibliography of scholarly articles and references, further enhancing a field of study. History, for example, specifically the history of photography, has enlarged its scope to include multiple histories of photographic expressive forms, encouraging discussions of vernacular forms of snapshot activities and delving further into the emergence of everyday, at-home photographic practices. Interestingly, the humanities have played roles – even novelists, poets and song writers have contributed observations on the significance of everyday photography. In short, interests within different academic orientations have produced a broader range of questions, methodologies and insights.

One trend has been the slow acceptance of the scholarly study of everyday/non-professional photography. Early on, studies in home media were not a part of the canon and generally not an appropriate topic of academic inquiry. Perhaps the material was considered too trivial, too common and all too embedded in everyday life and, hence, taken for granted. However, much has changed since the first home media studies; the enthusiastic acceptance of digital technology, for everyday photography, is dramatically reflected in changing research questions and scholarship in general.

Approaching empirical work

First, we should acknowledge the interests of film and camera companies, their marketing firms and advertisers, who demanded empirical data prone to statistical results and analyses. The second source of potential influence is provided by the popular photography magazine industry, for example, the pages of *Popular Photography* and *U.S. Camera*, offering advice for making better pictures than family snapshots and avoiding the 'snapshot look' as much as possible. However, these sources seldom address the kinds of questions most relevant to social scientists and the problematic ways of working with these pictorial materials as sources of data.

More relevant is a growing range of research perspectives including paradigms and methods of study. Uneven attention was given to historical, philosophical, psychological, social, cultural or purely personal circumstances, with minimal attention to systematic empirical observation. In turn, we also find very uneven paths of academic attention to what ordinary people did, or currently do, with their cameras and pictures. Application of different approaches has been varied, for example, ethnographic description, content analysis, semiotic analysis, participant observation, discourse analysis, feminist approaches, etc. and spread across a growing number of disciplines and interests, all with varying value placed on including verbatim comments by family members and a greater respect for empirical approaches to field data.

Early empirical studies are rare, leaving much discussion of everyday photography in the form of personal reflections, mediations, narratives and explorations of such general questions as: *What do photographs mean? How do we understand the story of our lives through the pages of the family photo album? How do personal pictures exert a power to shape our personal memories and self-conceptions?* Less fieldwork-oriented observers chose to offer reflections on their own personal photographs, produced by the observer's family. Some accounts consisted of personal meanings of just a few images; initial intuitions and speculations were insightful and occasionally led to theoretical and philosophical discussion. The work of Roland Barthes and Susan Sontag provide two well recognized and frequently cited examples. Some accounts have used a sample-of-one (e.g. Barthes' 'Winter Garden Photograph') when an author preferred to reference his/her own picture collection as a 'spectator', speculating that everyone had the same or very similar pictures, feelings, understandings, and then went on to generalize from there. There was a reluctance to do fieldwork on everyday photography, to collect data or to apply replicable methods of examination, description and analysis to a collection of material.

An important exception is the empirical work done in France by Pierre Bourdieu. His field research included a blend of surveys, interviews and ethnographic data, and set the stage for asking what people do *with* their cameras and what pictures do *for* people who take and keep them. He attended to picture-taking habits and social functions of family photography in the aid of understanding social integration, social class and the French stratification system.

Scholarly attention to taking personal photographs seriously grew from the 1970s to recent decades, including the work of Julia Hirsch, Jo Spence, Gillian Rose, Marianne Hirsch, among others, all working with varying degrees of empiricism with analogue photography. Richard Chalfen offered a rare case of integrating questionnaires into his fieldwork. Early empirical work tended to focus on understanding the content of people's pictures and applying functional explanations for why people took these photographs and what such collections did for current and future family members. There was much less attention paid to the process underlying the production, use and display of such material. Early academic interests were much narrower than we see today, as abundantly illustrated in the chapters comprising this book. Historically, shifts in scholarly attention reveal that studies of what early family-related pictures *looked like* moved into questions about how ordinary people *enacted/practised* family photography – what family members did with their cameras and what their camera use did for family life, for social cohesion, kinds of interpersonal and cross-generational communication and the like.

Roles of cameras in everyday life

Other views emerge from considering changes in the roles that cameras and pictures played and how cameras became embedded in everyday life and, in turn, how digital cameras might be changing the home culture of ordinary people. Most would easily agree that dramatic changes have occurred in quantitative dimensions of camera possession, picture-taking frequency and the electronic display of personal photographs. Historically, examples of home media have been increasing in frequency and, in turn, steadily 'leaving home' as we find private pictures appearing in public zones of appreciation; facilitation of picture sharing has drastically increased the density of connectivity accompanied by a decline in the volume of printed personal pictures.

Everyone eagerly points out that digitization has clearly increased the number of cameras (and, of course, phones) per family unit. Even before camera phones, marketing reports indicated that numbers of both analogue and digital cameras, as well as frequency of picture-taking per household, had been growing. Digitization appears to have caused photography to be less compartmentalized in everyday life. There is no one 'family camera', primarily operated by Dad, just as no one person is assigned the role of family photographer. When the time comes to take a trip, family members are less likely to ask *Did you remember the camera?* or *Anyone buy some film?* Having cameras in the hands of all family members sometimes inspires the problematic and frequently cited question *When should I give my kid a cellphone?*

Second, camera appearance and use are no longer restricted to special occasions. In contrast, they are virtually carried everywhere, for potential use in 'non-traditional', newly 'photogenic' settings, events and activities. Any scene can be designated as 'photo-worthy' and will receive multiple recordings, multiple takes, from many people. Cameras are being called upon to see and 'capture' more of the world, of everyday life, than ever before. Indeed, more settings and topics are producing many instances of 'sousveillance' which, on occasion, are used as citizen photojournalism. Third, digital pictures seem to be more frequently accessed and referenced in everyday conversations, with fewer calls for 'getting out the family album'.

Perhaps the most dramatic change centres on a range of activities suggested by the younger members of families. Importantly, some scholars have refocused their attention from the pro-social norms of family-based adults and parents to occasionally anti-social habits produced by community-based younger people. Inspired by boundary-testing characteristics of adolescence, their ways of combining use of camera phones and the internet have, for instance, produced troublesome 'sharing' of photographs in instances of sexting and cyber-bullying.

Redirections for academic attention

My sense is that empirically based scholarship has been slow to keep pace with the rapid pace of emerging camera technology and, second, creative uses of such apparatus within everyday life. We are prompted to ask how changes associated with digitization require or result in altering scholarly directions or changes in research strategies, including methods of observation, inductive or deductive reasoning, quantitative and qualitative methodologies and the like. Just as digitization prompted the entrance of non-camera companies into photography, we also saw the appearance of new interests from different academic disciplines.

One theme that spans past, recent and hopefully future studies is how everyday photography functions as a mode of visual communication, one significantly embedded in visual culture. Some maintain a difference between the sporadic making of memories for long-term family uses (connected to analogue photography) and the more frequent recording and sharing of experiences for short-term individual uses (characteristic of much contemporary digital photography). Significantly, both instances involve participating in acts of visual communication, whether for interests of participants 'in the moment' or for shared memories of family members across generations.

Scholars will sense a need for new models of pictorial/visual communication for understanding the cultural underpinnings of what's happening, conceptually and practically, in terms of product, process and/or practice. Cross-cultural studies of home media can serve to avoid ethnocentric assumptions that prematurely homogenize constituencies, in this case the expanding universe of ordinary people acquiring a camera in their new mobile phone and taking increasing numbers of pictures as part of their everyday lives. Participant observation and ethnography will play important roles in such efforts, as nicely discussed in several of the following chapters.

One fear is that increased attention to schemes and patterns of affordances takes us away from fieldwork and empirical studies that reveal what people actually know about what *can* be done with their new equipment, in conjunction with or in contrast to what these same people are actually doing with such opportunities, to stretch their practices of personal photography in everyday life. In short, interest should persist on what ordinary people, both adult and especially young people, are experiencing with their new 'electronic possibilities', what they might know about algorithmic 'interference' and, in turn, what such changes might be doing to them. Clearly, a blend of these interests is apparent in the following collection of chapters.

This collection of chapters offers a productive approach along several dimensions, principally: (1) to multiple, often cross-cultural, applications of smartphones as just one example of modern camera technology, and (2) to new meanings of 'photography' based on enhanced understandings of process and procedures, in relation to the varied and multiple results of an imaging process or, as Edgar Gómez Cruz notes in his chapter, 'vernacular photography practices are increasingly becoming algorithmic and a source of metadata, while expanding their function as depictions and representations'. Editors Lehmuskallio and Gómez Cruz have presented us with a broad overview of some of the main transformations digital photography is bringing to everyday life, coupled with ways of productively thinking about and studying complex ongoing changes in an alignment of technologies, meanings, uses, institutions and practices, all central to evolving digital culture. As I initially stated, it is a very exciting time to be part of visual digital culture.

References

Barthes, R. 1981, *Camera Lucida: Reflections on Photography*. Hill & Wang: New York.

Bourdieu, P. 2004, *Photography: A Middle-Brow Art*. Stanford University Press: Stanford, CA.

Bourdieu, P. [1965]/1990, *Un Art Moyen*. De Minuit: Paris.

Chalfen, R. 1991, *Turning Leaves: The Photograph Collections of Two Japanese American Families*. University of New Mexico Press: Albuquerque, NM.

Chalfen, R. 1987, *Snapshot Versions of Life*. Popular Press: Bowling Green, OH.

Hirsch, J. 1981, *Family Photographs: Content, Meaning, and Effects*. Oxford University Press: New York.

Hirsch, M. 1997, *Family Frames: Photography, Narrative, and Postmemory*. Harvard University Press: Cambridge, MA.

Rose, G. 2010, *Doing Family Photography: The Domestic, the Public and the Politics of Sentiment*. Ashgate: Farnham.

Sontag, S. 1977, *On Photography*. Farrar, Straus & Giroux: New York.

Spence, J. & Holland, P. (eds) 1991, *Family Snaps: The Meanings of Domestic Photography*. Virago Press: London.

Acknowledgements

We would like to thank all the authors for their patience, effort and commitment in writing their contributions to this book. We are grateful for the chapters, our discussants, as well as the foreword and outlook, which all provide a sense of the kinds of meetings in which the idea for this book was born. In a way the book is a synthesis of the various meetings we've had with each other and with all of the authors; meetings focusing on mutual research interests.

The editorial work has been a joint effort, and it builds predominantly on work supported and made possible by research networks. We met originally at a seminar organized by the Nordic Network for Digital Visuality (NNDV) 2012 in Helsinki, later at a second seminar in Stockholm, and were provided with additional travel funds by NNDV for meeting both in Leeds and Helsinki to work on editing this book. The Communities and Culture Network+ in the UK allowed Edgar to travel to meet Asko in Berkeley, Edgar's work on this editing project, as well as supported part of the proofreading. The Academy of Finland project Mind, Picture, Image (MIPI) supported again Asko's work and part of the production costs. Maria Schreiber kindly provided production support from the Department of Communication, University of Vienna. As becomes evident, without the work conducted in research networks, this book would have never been possible.

We are particularly grateful for Claudia Alvares, Ilija Tomanić-Trivundža, Nico Carpentier and Colombo Fausto at ECREA for giving their trust to this project, for their helpful reviews, comments and support. We also want to thank Sheni Kruger and Natalie Foster at Routledge, as well as their colleagues, for their professionalism and guidance.

Asko wants to thank: Karin Becker and my fellow steering group members at NNDV for creating a very special framework in which to pursue this kind of work, Janne Seppänen for his continuous and encouraging support throughout this project, as well as Tristan Thielmann and Erhard Schüttpelz for continuing to aid and advance work on media practices in Siegen. Work on this book has been advanced during my time at UC Berkeley, University of Tampere, and University of Siegen, where a wide variety of colleagues have in enormous ways supported this work, though space does not allow me to thank everyone individually, I would like to give my sincere 'kiitos!'.

Edgar wants to thank: Helen Thornham for her ceaseless, endurable and vital support and wisdom, for her friendship, Rosie Wilkinson for her teachings and help with language limitations, Tom Jackson for the shared adventures during my time at Leeds. I want to thank Maria and Eve because they believed and were part of this dream since its inception, Sarah Pink for her trust (and for inviting me to be part of an exciting team in Melbourne) and to Leila, for her wonderful image, for her love.

Why material visual practices?

Asko Lehmuskallio and Edgar Gómez Cruz

Cameras are increasingly part and parcel of everyday life. They seem to be ubiquitous, used at social gatherings or when communicating over a distance, and are as well used for commercial, political and surveillance purposes. The possibility for networked connections, as well as the fact that cameras tend to capture digital files that can be modified, amended and combined with a variety of other digital technologies, has brought attention to the differences that can be found between 'classical' film-based photography and today's networked camera technology. The way we understand the camera, as part of a technology and as a tool, plays a crucial role in our understanding of photography.

Although a variety of differences can be found, many photo practices tend to continue along well-paved paths. Many families continue to take photos of graduations, birthdays, travels and of people important to them. Although the pictures taken can be shared over vast distances, shown on publicly available websites or used for a variety of other purposes, not all engage in the possibilities that digital photography affords. But, importantly, many do.

Today, in 2015, commercial video services such as Skype, Facetime and Hangouts are used by millions and millions of people, and photo-sharing sites such as Instagram and SnapChat, launched in 2010 and 2011 respectively, have hundreds of millions of users sharing over 40 billion photos (Instagram 2012). Cameras for using these and similar services are readily available and are embedded into a variety of devices, placed in mobile phones, laptops, wearable glasses and remotely controllable drones.

Arguably, the success of networked camera devices is tied to the *connected interactions* that they allow for. Business meetings, family gatherings, travels, weddings and online dating are only some of the potential instances for these connected interactions, mediated by camera devices and online services. In many cases, networked camera devices allow us to transcend the limits of our bodies, letting us share space mediated by computing networks and telecommunication infrastructures, in ways that exceed the narrow range of symbolic cues known from early computing interfaces.

By being able to provide, translate and transform these connected inter-actions, commercial service providers and manufacturers of digital camera devices play a crucial and powerful role in suggesting how people connect and interact with each other. Media scholars have long pointed to this con-nection, often maintaining that multinational companies distort social rela-tions, while at times suggesting that these relations are based on calculations of exploitation (Fuchs *et al.* 2011). These multinational com-panies are only one of many actors within the connected interactions that we deal with in our everyday lives: when something unexpected and terri-fying happens, the digital data collected to enable the sharing of important emotional moments of family life might become part of forensic databases. This is increasingly the case after acts of terror, such as the Boston Mara-thon bombings in 2013, when, in order to identify and capture the perpet-rators, all available data for analysis was requested, including snapshot photographs taken just before the bombings.

Already, these few examples provide support for recent calls to turn our focus away from images alone, to the complex entanglements they can be found in. Important academic work on photography has often focused on photographs as particular kinds of images, thinking, for example, about how photographic images relate to questions of journalistic evidence or artistic expression. In this book we propose to take a broader perspective on photography and to study it, empirically, as part of practices, ranging from the seemingly mundane ways in which families use digital photo-graphy to keep in touch to the politically unpredictable ways in which ver-nacular photography becomes part of forensic databases. Here, digital photography in everyday life is entangled with a variety of ways of being in the world, where neither the everyday nor photography can take clearly definable boundaries. We suggest that we could gain a broader understand-ing of digital photography by situating image-making processes in wider discussions about materiality and visuality, an emphasis visible in the title of this book, *Digital Photography and Everyday Life: Empirical Studies on Material Visual Practices*.

A need for practice-based approaches for studying digital photography

In the early stages of discussion on the impact of digital photography, many commentators stated that computer-generated photography did not refer to 'real events', as film-based photography was thought to do. The distinctiveness of photography seemed, for many, to lie particularly in pho-tography's ability to provide a trace of an event that really happened, and digitization seemed to question this connection. For example, for Batchen this meant that 'photography may even be robbed of its cultural identity as a distinctive medium' (Batchen 2002, p. 129). The questioning of digital photographs providing an indexical connection, tracing a resemblance to that depicted, opened increasing reflection on the particularities of digital photography. With sides taken for and against this claim, the debate helped, also, in reframing earlier understandings of photography. What became increasingly clear was that photography referred as a concept to various technologies for creating surface markings with light (Maynard 1997), and these technologies had always been changing. What had often been understood as 'photography' was just one of many possibilities for understanding processes of surface marking and their embeddedness in societal uses.

At more or less the same time as the digitization of photography seemed to call for new ways for thinking about photography and its various roles in everyday life, scholars who had long worked on images explicitly called for a pictorial or iconic turn (Boehm 1994; Mitchell 1994). These calls referred to the need to provide novel methods and theories for understanding the various roles pictures take, as well as taking the surplus value of images in their own right into account. This need has clearly been felt by a wide range of scholars, if we assess for example the amount of visual methods books published in the last 20 years (e.g. Banks 2001; Schulz 2005; Seppänen 2006; Margolis & Pauwels 2011; Rose 2011).

A broad variety of studies on pictures, images and visual culture have been published since then, but particularly noteworthy is how many scholars are interested, explicitly, in pictorial practices, focusing on the practices and interactions within which images become meaningful. W. J. T. Mitchell, who coined the concept of 'pictorial turn', has published on the 'lives and loves of images' (2005), whereas Hans Belting has provided an anthropology of images (2001, 2011), and books on cultures of the image (Mersmann & Schulz 2006), visual translation and cultural agency (Mersmann & Schneider 2009) and digital photographic practices (Larsen & Sandbye 2013) are just a few examples of this interest.

This 'practice turn' (Schatzki 2001; Reckwitz 2002) is visible in a variety of other fields as well. Approaches such as media anthropology (Rothenbuhler & Coman 2005; Ginsburg 2006; Bräuchler & Postill 2010), actor network theory (Latour 2005), non-media centric media studies (Krajina, Moores & Morley 2014), non-representational theory (Thrift 2008), a focus on media as practice (Couldry 2012) and novel work on media technologies (Gillespie, Boczkowski & Foot 2014), place particular emphasis on practices in studying media in general, and visual culture in particular.

For photographic theory, recent work (Schröter 2011; Van House 2011; Kember & Zylinska 2012; Lehmuskallio 2012; Rose & Tolia-Kelly 2012; Gómez Cruz 2013; Rubinstein, Golding & Fisher 2013) has underscored the benefits of practice-based approaches for going beyond previous understandings of photography, to account for the novel and often different ways in which digitally networked cameras are used. Although practice-based studies focusing on the various roles photography takes are increasingly growing, it is good to bear in mind that this is by no means mainstream for photography theory. As Martin Lister points out in this volume

> The act of finding meaning in a photograph is, of course, to engage with photography as representation. This, in turn (if it is not to be an innocent reading) inevitably entails a measure of academic discipline and methodology: the semiological scrutiny of images treated as texts with the aim of revealing or interpreting the meanings encoded within them. With regard to photography this is a developed practice that, over the last 30 years or so, became almost synonymous with photography theory.

As editors, our aim is to suggest a different approach. We want to emphasize the usefulness of taking a practice-based approach to studying digital photography in everyday life. We are particularly interested in *both* the visuality and materiality of photographic practices, maintaining that this approach, in its broadest sense, is helpful for understanding digital photography and the various roles it takes. We suggest that photography is tied to both ways of seeing and representing, as well as to ways of acting and performing. Photographic practices allow for different kinds of communicative actions from, for instance, text, speech or music, but they also offer different ways of experiencing the world. Photographic theory, engaging with photography as representation, needs to be *complemented* with practice-based assessments, especially as photographic technologies have become more complex.

Most of the texts in this volume are related to photography but they discuss it in relation to something else: to our experience of everyday life, the body, economic cultures, imagination, algorithmic cultures, surveillance, grief, communication, etc. This, indeed, signals something relevant in our discussion regarding photography, namely that we cannot speak, anymore, about a single main use of vernacular photography, a 'Kodak Culture', which Richard Chalfen (1987) identified as a particular cultural form of home-mode communication. The technological infrastructures for digital photography, as well as their uses, have become more varied and shifting theoretical interests help to highlight ever more relations that photography is part of.

The benefits of practice-based approaches, particularly those that have a focus on materiality

Practice-based approaches take many forms, as outlined in Reckwitz' (2002) influential article 'Toward a Theory of Social Practices'. In this text, Reckwitz generously combines a variety of approaches under the label of practice theories, suggesting that a range of authors, in their work on practices, share the idea that a 'practice' (*Praktik*) is a routinized type of behaviour which consists of several elements, interconnected with one other: forms of bodily activities, forms of mental activities, 'things' and their use, a background knowledge in the form of understanding, know how, states of emotion and motivational knowledge.

(p. 249)

It is this interconnection between various elements that becomes the focus of scholarly attention, to understand how individuals and groups behave and how they are able to share patterns of behaviour that make sense to them. As Reckwitz outlines, his general notion of practice theories has implications for understanding the role of the body, of knowledge, discourse and of social agents, and these differ from the purpose-oriented theoretical models of the *homo economicus* and the norm and value-based models of the *homo sociologicus*.

Whereas some tend to think of practice theory as a single, shared theoretical movement, it is important to emphasize that practice theories do not have one shared understanding of practice, or of agency within practices, for example. The understanding of practice developed by Bourdieu differs significantly, for example, from Latour's approach, and both ascribe agency in very different ways to the variety of interconnected elements within their respective understandings of practices.[1] It is also important to note the disciplinary differences in emphasizing practices. Whereas, for example, cultural anthropologists have a long history of focusing on the seemingly mundane ways in which people live and give meaning to their everyday lives, media and visual culture scholars have a much more recent interest in the practices in and around media use.

As editors, our shared interest is in understanding practices as being both part of social symbolization processes and materially mediated, which is why we opted for the subtitle *Empirical studies on material visual practices* for this volume. This is less out of an interest in following an orthodox programme, but has more to do with our curiosity regarding the complex entanglements that human bodies are involved in as they take up highly complex networked camera devices, in order to engage in everyday vernacular photography. This involves a shared interest in approaches that do not distinguish between stable entities, such as a camera and a person, but which help to refocus attention on how these are intertwined within particular kinds of constellations. This shift in focus, shared by a variety of other authors, does not provide us immediately with clear-cut answers regarding how digital photography and everyday life are entangled, but rather, at first sight, with questions that have to be taken up and studied empirically within very particular contexts.

Questions that arise relate to a focus on bodies, their respective media of action and the role images and visuality play in this constellation. For example, how does the phenomenological experience change as people take up cameras and the social role of photographer? What difference does it make that many cameras in use today are small 'action cams' that can be clipped to one's body? As cameras become increasingly networked, what is the actual material artefact that is taken up during photography? How is it stabilized as a particular assemblage and what is it envisioned that it will become? How does this coupling, interconnection and interfacing between bodies and material artefacts allow for novel kinds of constellations, as any part of this changes? What is the benefit of thinking about cameras as extensions of photographers or, the other way around, of photographers as extensions of self-activating networked cameras? What forms of sociality arise through these couplings? And where and when do the practices that relate to these questions take place?

These manifold questions are answered in chapters of this book, which are discussed in greater detail below. The questions themselves point to the importance of looking beyond mere representations for understanding digital photography in everyday life, namely to its material dimensions.

The role of visuality in digital photographic practices

Photographs, as images, obviously continue to be important; they provide an important reason for taking, sharing and using photography in the first place. A refocusing of attention on the materiality and embodied character of everyday practices needs to be complemented by a focus on images and visuality as key reasons for engaging in photographic practices. However, the importance of the image and what it refers to varies from context to context. For example, in the field of vernacular photography it is often the case that aesthetic quality or image sharpness are less important than using the camera as a way to create emotionally meaningful shared moments, by asking those depicted to hug each other, smile and provide other attributes of practices referring to having a good time (e.g. Frosh 2015). From the perspective of practice theories, images are thus meaningful as part of wider embodied practices. Earlier studies in visual culture studies and *Bildwissenschaft*,[2] especially those with a particular interest in pictorial practices, have been pivotal in underscoring the various roles that images play in our everyday lives.

Often, visual representations are of particular importance for understanding why they have been created and what kinds of forms of attention they might suggest. A focus on material practices should not let us forget that people use pictures because they continue to express and articulate relations in different ways from other modes of address. As, for example, Mitchell has repeatedly argued, images should receive particular attention because it seems so easy either to dismiss them as trivial or to fear the strong reactions they evoke. Careful visual analysis continues to be important for understanding our visual worlds. Practice-based assessments of digital photography are, more often than not, both material and visual, instead of only one or the other.

Questions that are addressed through this approach incorporate a broad range of reflection, such as why do particular images evoke strong affective reactions? How are images explicitly created in order to evoke particular kinds of responses? What kinds of changes can we see in regard to what counts as photographic images? How do these novel kinds of photographic visualizations invite us to attend to them? What kinds of novel entanglements do images allow for? Why does the mediation of images and practices related to them matter? And does it make a difference that there is an increasing amount of pictures used and distributed in everyday life? Answers to these questions, along with various others, are addressed in the chapters of this book. While empirical studies on how people actually use pictures tend to emphasize many non-representational aspects in relation to photography, careful examination of pictorial details is useful for providing an appreciation of why pictures are used instead of other means of expression.

Why should we focus on both material and visual practices?

Focusing contextually on material and visual practices helps us in reconsidering both photography (*What is it? How should it be understood, especially when taking digital forms into consideration?*), and everyday life (*What roles does digital photography take within everyday life?*). Digital photography, understood broadly, can thus be studied as a nexus that connects people in emotionally significant ways, as a family or as a group of friends, but, increasingly, also to current social and political movements. Increasingly, digital photographic technologies are becoming political actors, for example, by providing different perspectives on what has happened. It is difficult to imagine a world in which demonstrations, political conflicts or violent acts are not mediated through camera technology or the broader media logics imposed by using cameras. Because digital photo files carry metadata and can be combined with a variety of databases, their use for the purposes of modelling events which have taken place, or for predicting what might happen, is increasing. Digital photography provides for novel connections that differ, in their applications, from film-based photography. Networked cameras, in a way, invite for novel connections to be made.

This perspective enriches our understanding of the qualitative dimensions of everyday practices and takes into account the rich potential to act in complexly mediated constellations. Automation processes, algorithmic photography, metadata and big data are only some of the keywords recently used for describing changes in photography, and these need to be localized and situated. By suggesting to pay attention to both symbolic and material dimensions of pictorial practices, particularly in environments that are complexly and multiply mediated, we are not proposing one silver bullet, as the range of approaches within this book clearly show, but we do stress that we need to rethink how the increasing amount of networked cameras and digital imagery play a role in how we dream, desire, think, act and connect.

As Batchen has pointed out, the current debates about digital imaging are not only concerned with the possible futures of photography but with the nature of its past and present (2002, p. 143). As editors we suggest that instead of working towards a single and unique understanding of what photography is, it is more helpful at this point to open up our understandings of how photography is being used and therefore to what photography might be without defining it beforehand. This is especially important as some of those developing networked camera technology do not consider their work to deal with photography or visual culture at all. The complex sociotechnical assemblages that photography is part of are still in the process of stabilization, and might always remain unstable and restless (Seppänen 2014).

In opening up the idea of photography Maynard's (1997) work is one point of departure, helpful for considering it as surface markings created with light. Different elements of the process of surface markings with light become empirically relevant within sets of particular sayings and doings. We therefore suggest abandoning the efforts to map out one understanding of 'a' photography, and propose to create an alternative agenda. We suggest a focus on the practices, associations and connections afforded or shaped by photographic technologies. In order to underscore this approach, we chose as editors to write chapters questioning prevalent understandings of photographic images. Whereas Lehmuskallio shows how photographic visualizations today take a variety of forms, particularly simulative, heuristic and layered ones, Gómez Cruz argues that photographic technologies are increasingly used as imageless interfaces, as interfaces for photographs we never get to see.

Contents of the book

Most of the contributions in this volume show how photography is increasingly embedded in very different realms of everyday life. The work is based on empirical case studies, in order to accentuate both the diversity of uses, as well as the diversity of what digital photography might be. Due to the complexities underlying both everyday life as well as digital photographies, understanding their interconnection calls for interdisciplinary studies and transdisciplinary discussions. Our authors all combine work from various disciplines, while working at very different kinds of departments: media studies, anthropology, art, geography, communication studies, and science and technology studies.

The book has three parts: 'Variance in use in everyday photography', 'Cameras, connectivity and transformed localities' and 'Camera as the extension of the photographer'. Each of these parts has a discussant, a widely recognized expert in the field discussing the part's main ideas from her perspective. The book is complemented with a Foreword and an Outlook by distinguished scholars in the field.

In the Foreword, Richard Chalfen discusses ways in which scholars have historically approached vernacular, everyday photography. Whereas these early studies have not been very common in the fields of cultural anthropology, sociology or media studies, those who have found an interest in them include particularly influential figures such as Pierre Bourdieu and Luc Boltanski. Chalfen's own work has shown its relevance in time. After having worked with Erving Goffman, Sol Worth and John Adair, his work on *Snapshot Versions of Life* continues to have significant influence on scholars of visual communication. Chalfen notes how due to digitization, academic interests in everyday photography have taken new forms, resulting at times in nomenclature ambiguity, multiple perspectives and redirections for academic attention. As he notes, this book is an attempt to provide

> a broad overview of some of the main transformations digital photography is bringing to everyday life, coupled with ways of productively thinking about and studying complex ongoing changes in an alignment of technologies, meanings, uses, institutions and practices, all central to evolving digital culture.

In Part I, 'Variance in use in everyday photography' turns its attention to the importance of *who* connects to digital photography, *where* and in *which ways*. Several original innovative case studies are presented, to consider the different variations of use. Since empirical studies on the impact of digital photographic technologies tend to focus on Europe and the US, this part also pays attention to understanding how similar technologies are taken up in areas with significantly different technology infrastructures and social relations, such as Tanzania.

Uimonen presents an ethnographic inquiry about mobile photography in Tanzania with an emphasis on the multisensory materiality and relational sociality of mobile photographic practice. She describes how mobile phone cameras make it possible for people to explore and engage in photography in everyday life, thus constituting a relatively accessible entry point into forms of self-representation and self-expression considered to be 'modern'. She concludes that,

> since mobile phones are personalized artefacts, functioning like material extensions of the self, mobile photography also carries conflicting narratives of loss and control, which can be related to the materiality (phones) and immateriality (images) of mobile photography, within the broader context of cultural commodification.

Pargana Mota follows the discussion about self-representation in its current most trendy form: the selfie. She does so by studying ethnographically the so-called 'closet-shops' in Portugal by following the production, consumption and sharing of snapshots and self-portraits by a group of young Portuguese women who have created Facebook profiles in order to sell and trade their clothes. She explores how the practices of taking and posting selfies and pictures of clothes become central to the creation of an alternative fashion marketplace while these practices are also ways to claim individual presence and visibility. Her chapter both criticizes the logic of late capitalism that influences how her study subjects engage in self-branding practices and promotional cultures, while showing how these young women are able to navigate within the latter to counter the economic crisis they have to live in.

Schreiber again analyses a different age group in Austria. She studies the digital photography practices of a group of elderly people in their everyday lives with the aim of empirically exploring how the transition from analogue to digital might become relevant and to understand continuities and changes in their everyday photographic practices. Her findings show that photographic practices of seniors are amplified by digitization and are (or have probably always been) heterogeneous. Her chapter provides an important reminder of variance within different age groups using digital photography.

As photographic technologies are increasingly available, they are again used for practices that long remained in a variety of Western countries socially unacceptable, as Rebeca Pardo and Montse Morcate show. Depictions of illness, death and grief are increasingly to be found on blogs, photosharing and social network sites. Due to the possibility for connecting with digital technologies over space, these visual expressions provide for ways of articulating the strong and often difficult emotional burdens that those experiencing severe illness, or deaths of loved-ones, have. Sharing these visual expressions helps to create communities of support that can lend an affiliative look (Hirsch 1997) to those living through difficult moments in life, even if these communities are experienced only online.

The penultimate chapter of Part I takes a different direction from the earlier ethnographic inquiries by presenting a discussion regarding the use of images as active agents in a police investigation. Using the Boston Marathon bombings as a case study, Männistö engages with the Baudrillardian concept of fragmented hyperreality and proposes that: 'with the help of metadata enhanced mobile phone photos and new methods of analysis from fragmented pieces of information, something arose which I would like to call "hyperreliability"'. His chapter makes clear how vernacular photography might potentially become important evidence for forensic investigations, particularly as the possibility to collect, store and analyse large amounts of data has become both possible and socially expected, particularly so in times of crisis.

Karin Becker closes Part I with a discussion that suggests that a perspective that asks who connects to digital photography, where and in what ways, can help us understand how complex digital photographic technologies impact our ways of living together. She proposes two assumptions underlying that perspective: first 'that digital photography is not a single unified phenomenon but involves variation across many applications, practices and cultural settings; and, second, embedded in the notion of variation, that comparative research can contribute to this endeavour'.

Part II, 'Cameras, connectivity, and transformed localities' considers the ways in which our understanding of local presence is influenced by photographic technologies. Location-aware mobile technology, remote webcam connections, as well as virtual environments offering navigational cues for offline locations, all influence how we understand the kinds of activations possible over distance. The part shows how location-aware mobile technology enables the everyday sharing of 'place' in ways not possible before, attaching location information in both representational and non-representational ways. Importantly, as is shown, these representational forms themselves have at least a century-long history and are not as novel as some might think. Increasingly, though, the connections made with, and via, photographic technologies become ever more important for understanding the transnational, where connections bridging long distances are significant for people's everyday emotional lives.

In the first chapter, Villi focuses on the significance of place in visual mobile communication, in particular the use of camera phones in the mediation of place. The core notion of his chapter is that by communicating a photograph from the mobile phone immediately after capturing the image, it is possible to 'send the place' and mediate the communicator's presence in that place. In this sense, he proposes, that the communication of camera phone photographs is innately a location-aware form of mobile technology use. Villi's theoretical analysis is based on the results from a qualitative study focusing on the mobile photo-sharing practices of a group of Finnish camera phone users.

The sense of place is also the topic of Prieto-Blanco but in her case she unfolds an empirical investigation with Spanish-Irish families, trying to answer the question: How do transnational families use photographs? Her conclusions show that the studied families use photography to generate spaces of (inter)action to create realms of experience by both mediating presences and bestowing spaces with meaning. Prieto-Blanco suggests that the interaction with photographs across space contribute to the creation of bonds of affection, and ultimately intimacy, in spite of distances apart.

Image-making, place, agency and political action are the themes of Saugmann Andersen's chapter. By analysing videos taken at the eviction of the Brorson Church in Copenhagen, he states that the camera is a central but unstable non-human actor in contemporary political protest. He describes how the agency of the camera serves as a translator that substantially transforms political protest and reconfigures the conditions of possibility of effective political protest. At the same time, the agency of the camera itself is re-negotiated in political debate when powerful societal institutions such as governments and police forces make use of and comment upon the use of cameras in political protest.

Tristan Thielmann provides an important historical reading of navigational media nowadays commonplace in augmented reality applications. With the help of a close reading of navigational photo-auto guides published in the early twentieth century in the US, he shows how established navigational practices are embedded into novel media forms that are constantly edited in order to come up with inscriptions that can transcend time and place. These inscriptions, in order to be successfully applied to a variety of contexts, have to be abstract, mobile and combinable with others in order to become what Latour calls immutable mobiles. Interestingly, the representational strategies employed early on in these photo-auto guides had a relatively short lifespan, before they could be again seen in a variety of digital navigational apps.

Sarah Pink closes Part II with a comment on two concepts used in her work that could be useful to understand the relationship between connectivity, cameras and localities: place and wayfaring. She suggests that those concepts are useful to think 'about how digital photography is at once technological, virtual and material, often played out through human activity in the world, and also part of the actual environment in which we live and act'. She underscores the importance of thinking of photographs as being in particular places and part of movements, instead of relying on the idea that photographs would be of places. In this understanding, photographs are part of the ways in which everyday life is experienced and given meaning to, and not mainly external representations of something outside the pictures themselves.

Part III 'Camera as the extension of the photographer', the different authors discuss how, in the digital era, photography has become a key element to complex and multiply mediated assemblages that are not always related with image-making as such. This necessarily calls for reflections on photography that do not start or end with the photographic image per se. For example, in the text that opens the part, Eve Forrest, following phenomenological approaches by Seamon and Ingold, explores the concept of *noticing*, referring to 'how the photographer and their being-in-the-world is affected by the presence of the camera'. Based on a longitudinal ethnographic study of photographers based in North-East England, she concludes that 'noticing is a state awakened within the photographer; it is a form of rapture that can never be shaken off'. Noticing is a way of connecting one's body with technological equipment.

The other three texts in Part III take the camera, digital photography and imageless interfaces as a focus to explore ways in which changes in photographic technology challenge previous understandings of photography. Each text focuses on the material and visual elements that shape different assemblages in digital photography, calling for a broadened understanding of what 'photography' is in a digital age.

Paolo Favero challenges some of the early discourses on digital photography in two steps: first, he describes how the contemporary scenario of digital technologies is changing by describing some contemporary trends in the field of consumer digital technologies focusing on what he calls *analogization*, which is 'a process of materialization taking place within a digital environment'. Using Narrative and GoPro cameras as examples, he suggests that scholars need 'to bring the conventional tools of visual culture in touch with elements of digital and material culture and to move away from simplistic dualisms into a perspective that integrates the digital with the material (analogue) world'. Increasingly, digital tools are used to create analogical media.

Gómez Cruz suggests that digital photography is shaping different 'assemblages of visuality' from those of its photochemical predecessors. He suggests that it is important to understand 'photography as a process and as a technology', helping to move us in a different direction from which semiotic analyses of photographic images have tended to do. Gómez Cruz turns our attention to the exploration of the possible processes based on *photogenic practices*. By using QR codes as an example of these photogenic practices, Gómez Cruz discusses *images as interfaces* to show critically how digital photography is used within very different assemblages, assemblages that at times do not include the creation of photographs as visual images.

Based on fieldwork among developers of mobile and wearable camera technology, Lehmuskallio challenges the discursive pervasiveness of 'film-like digital photographs' and argues that a processual reconceptualization is necessary: to think about *cameras as sensors*, enabling a variety of surface markings with light of which only some resemble our earlier understandings of photographs. He suggests that problematizing the association between photography and a photograph is necessary to understand fully the variety of ends to which mobile and wearable camera technology is directed. Lehmuskallio does so by providing a processual outline of the photographic process. In particular, he focuses on the variety of visualizations created with digital photographic technologies, of which many are counterintuitive at first sight. Focusing on the referential character of photographic visualizations, he distinguishes between *simulative, heuristic* and *layered pictures* that are widely in use in mobile and wearable camera technology.

Martin Lister closes Part III with a discussion based on the title of the part: Is the camera an extension of the photographer, or rather the photographer an extension of the camera? He points at 'the turn away from a long dominant preoccupation with photography as representation' by acknowledging the emergence of a networked computational camera that shapes different kinds of relations with photographers than did previous cameras, while urging readers to keep in mind the insights that representational analysis has yielded. He explicitly underscores that a focus on practices does not mean that images would somehow lose their relevance as objects of study.

The book closes with an Outlook provided by Nancy Van House, a scholar contributing early on to studies on digital photography and everyday life. She pinpoints the importance of understanding the practices within which photographs are used. If used as part of social networking, it is clear that communicative, immediate uses of visual communication are often of importance for photo use, and it is particularly the variety of uses uploaded to a variety of social network sites that have been lauded as providing ever more people with a variety of points of view. Whereas photos have long been important for memory practices, the relative ephemerality of digital files may mean that these various points of view do not travel well over time, especially as older file formats cannot be accessed and archival practices continue to change. In reference to Freedberg and Mitchell she suggests that studying empirically the practices that people engage in may shed light on the *sine qua non* of image studies, namely the question 'Why are *images* so important?'.

The edited book provides readers with a wide array of case studies regarding digital photography and everyday life, each of which focuses both on visuality and materiality in analysis. Each chapter offers conceptualizations and exemplary analyses that can be taken up, applied and at times further developed with the help of additional material. Our hope, as editors, is that readers will enjoy the book as much as we do, as travel in words towards the complex entanglements in which digital photography can be found.

Notes

1 Reckwitz (2004) himself has discussed differences between Bourdieu's and Butler's approaches, and various other comparisons could be made.
2 Visual culture studies and *Bildwissenschaft* denote academic traditions working on images and visual culture, with some differences in the foci of publications and theoretical traditions. For a discussion, see Bredekamp (2003), Schneider (2008), Moxey (2008), Boehm and Mitchell (2009), Rimmele, Sachs-Hombach and Stiegler (2014).

References

Banks, M. 2001, *Visual Methods in Social Research*. Sage: London; Thousand Oaks, CA; New Delhi.

Batchen, G. 2002, *Each Wild Idea: Writing, Photography, History*. MIT Press: Cambridge, MA.

Belting, H. 2011, *An Anthropology of Images: Picture, Medium, Body*, trans. T. Dunlap. Princeton University Press: Princeton, NJ.

Belting, H. 2001, *Bild-Anthropologie: Entwürfe für eine Bildwissenschaft*. Fink: München.

Boehm, G. (ed.) 1994, *Was ist ein Bild?* Fink: München.

Boehm, G. & Mitchell, W. J. T. 2009, 'Pictorial versus Iconic Turn: Two Letters'. *Culture, Theory and Critique*, Vol. 50, pp. 103–121.

Bräuchler, B. & Postill, J. 2010, *Theorising Media and Practice*. Berghahn: New York; Oxford.

Bredekamp, H. 2003, 'A Neglected Tradition? Art History as *Bildwissenschaft*'. *Critical Inquiry*, Vol. 29, pp. 418–428.

Chalfen, R. 1987, *Snapshot Versions of Life*. Popular Press: Bowling Green, OH.

Couldry, N. 2012, *Media, Society, World: Social Theory and Digital Media Practice*. Polity Press: Kindle Edition.

Frosh, P. 2015. 'The Gestural Image: The Selfie, Photography Theory, and Kinesthetic Sociability'. *International Journal of Communication*, Vol. 9(2015), pp. 1607–1628.

Fuchs, C., Boersma, K., Albrechtslund, A. & Sandoval, M. 2011, *Internet and Surveillance: The Challenges of Web 2.0 and Social Media*. Routledge: New York.

Gillespie, T., Boczkowski, P. J. & Foot, K. A. 2014, *Media Technologies: Essays on Communication, Materiality, and Society*. MIT Press: Cambridge, MA.

Ginsburg, F. D. (ed.) 2006, *Media Worlds: Anthropology on New Terrain*. University of California Press: Berkeley, CA.

Gómez Cruz, E. 2013, *De la Cultura Kodak a la Imagen en Red: Una Etnografía Sobre Fotografía Digital*. Editorial UOC: Barcelona.

Hirsch, M. 1997, *Family Frames: Photography, Narrative, and Postmemory*. Harvard University Press: Cambridge, MA.

Instagram. 2012, 'Stats', viewed 18 October 2015, https://instagram.com/press/.

Kember, S. & Zylinska, J. 2012, *Life after New Media: Mediation as a Vital Process*. MIT Press: Cambridge, MA.

Krajina, Z., Moores, S. & Morley, D. 2014, 'Non-Media-Centric Media Studies: A Cross-Generational Conversation'. *European Journal of Cultural Studies*, Vol. 17, pp. 682–700.

Larsen, J. & Sandbye, M. (eds) 2013, *Digital Snaps: The New Face of Photography*. I.B. Tauris: London; New York.

Latour, B. 2005, *Reassembling the Social: An Introduction to Actor-Network-Theory*. Oxford University Press: Oxford; New York.

Lehmuskallio, A. 2012, *Pictorial Practices in a 'Cam Era': Studying Non-Professional Camera Use*. Tampere University Press: Tampere.

Margolis, E. & Pauwels, L. (eds) 2011, *The SAGE Handbook of Visual Research Methods*. Sage: London.

Maynard, P. 1997, *The Engine of Visualization: Thinking through Photography*. Cornell University Press: Ithaca, NY.

Mersmann, B. & Schneider, A. (eds) 2009, *Transmission Image: Visual Translation and Cultural Agency*. Cambridge Scholars Publishing: Newcastle.

Mersmann, B. & Schulz, M. (eds) 2006, *Kulturen des Bildes*. Fink: München.

Mitchell, W. J. T. 2005, *What do Pictures Want? The Lives and Loves of Images*. University of Chicago Press: Chicago, IL; London.

Mitchell, W. J. T. 1994, *Picture Theory: Essays on Verbal and Visual Representation*. University of Chicago Press: Chicago, IL; London.

Moxey, K. 2008, 'Visual Studies and the Iconic Turn'. *Journal of Visual Culture*, Vol. 7, pp. 131–146.

Reckwitz, A. 2004, 'Die Reproduktion und die Subversion sozialer Praktiken.

Zugleich ein Kommentar zu Pierre Bourdieu und Judith Butler', in K. H. Hörning (ed.) *Doing Culture: Zum Begriff der Praxis in der Gegenwärtigen Soziologischen Theorie*. Transcript: Bielefeld, pp. 40–54.

Reckwitz, A. 2002, 'Toward a Theory of Social Practices: A Development in Culturalist Theorizing'. *European Journal of Social Theory*, Vol. 5, pp. 245–265.

Rimmele, M., Sachs-Hombach, K. & Stiegler, B. (eds) 2014, *Bildwissenschaft und Visual Culture*. Transcript: Bielefeld.

Rose, G. 2011, *Visual Methodologies: An Introduction to the Interpretation of Visual Methods*, 3rd edn. Sage: London; Thousand Oaks, CA; New Delhi.

Rose, G. & Tolia-Kelly, D. P. (eds) 2012, *Visuality/Materiality: Images, Objects and Practices*. Ashgate: Aldershot; Burlington, VT.

Rothenbuhler, E. W. & Coman, M. (eds) 2005, *Media Anthropology*. Sage: London; Thousand Oaks, CA; New Delhi.

Rubinstein, D., Golding, J. & Fisher, A. 2013, 'On the Verge of Photography: Imaging Beyond Representation.' ARTicle Press: Birmingham.

Schatzki, T. R. 2001, 'Introduction: Practice Theory', in T. R. Schatzki, K. Knorr-Cetina & E. V. Savigny (eds) *The Practice Turn in Contemporary Theory*. Routledge: London; New York, pp. 1–14.

Schneider, N. 2008, 'W.J.T. Mitchell und der >Iconic Turn<'. *Kunst und Politik: Jahrbuch der Guernica-Gesellschaft*, Vol. 10, pp. 29–38.

Schröter, J. 2011, 'Analogue/Digital. Referentiality and intermediality'. *Kunstlicht*, Vol. 32, pp. 50–57.

Schulz, M. 2005, *Ordnungen der Bilder: Eine Einführung in die Bildwissenschaft*. Wilhelm Fink Verlag: München.

Seppänen, J. 2014, *Levoton Valokuva*. Vastapaino: Tampere.

Seppänen, J. 2006, *The Power of the Gaze: An Introduction to Visual Literacy*. Peter Lang: New York.

Thrift, N. 2008, *Non-Representational Theory: Space, Politics, Affect*. Routledge: Abingdon; New York.

Van House, N. 2011, 'Personal Photography, Digital Technologies, and the Uses of the Visual'. *Visual Studies*, Vol. 25, pp. 125–134.

Part I

Variance in use in everyday photography

1 'I'm a picture girl!'
Mobile photography in Tanzania

Paula Uimonen

'I'm a picture girl!' Jane exclaims, while charging her iPhone in her car. She bought the phone in 2012 so she could take 'nice pictures'. Similarly to most people in Tanzania, Jane does not own a camera, but she has had a mobile phone with camera since 2007. Jane likes to take pictures to preserve the memory, she explains to me, of special events or when she wears something that looks nice. Jane also takes pictures of her daughter, so she can 'see her growing up', including pictures of 'every birthday'. Jane keeps many photos on her phone and she often posts pictures online, through Instagram and Facebook. Jane is 33 years old and she lives with her daughter in Mwanza, the second largest city in Tanzania. Working as a sales executive, she earns a good living. Jane belongs to the urban middle class that can afford smartphones, but cameras are also becoming commonplace in simpler and cheaper phone models. In Tanzania, the mobile phone camera is the primary technology through which photographic practice is becoming widespread among the population at large.

This chapter focuses on mobile photography in Tanzania, with an emphasis on the multisensory materiality and relational sociality of mobile photographic practice.[1] Shaped by the materiality of the mobile phone, a personal artefact that embodies cultural expectations of modernity, mobile photography mediates the management of social relations, the performance of cultural identity and the creative agency of self-expression, while fuelling fears of exploitation and loss of control. On the one hand, mobile phone cameras make it possible for people to explore and engage in photography in everyday life, thus constituting a relatively accessible entry point into modern forms of self-representation and self-expression. On the other hand, since mobile phones are personalized artefacts, functioning like material extensions of the self, mobile photography also carries conflicting narratives of loss and control, which can be related to the materiality (phones) and immateriality (images) of mobile photography, within the broader context of cultural commodification.

The material presented here is based on a short period of ethnographic research in urban and semi-urban settings in Tanzania in June and July 2014, complemented with online observations in Facebook. Although limited in scope, this study draws on insights from ten years of ethnographic engagements in Tanzania, focusing on digital media (e.g. Uimonen 2012, 2013, 2015). In terms of interviews, this study is limited to five people, all of them women, which might carry a gender bias, leaving out male voices. These women are also young, aged 20 to 35, thus leaving out older voices. Moreover, all but one of the respondents belong to an urban or semi-urban middle class, so this analysis is not representative of the population at large. Indeed, while this short study shows interesting preliminary results, more research is clearly required to capture the complexities of mobile photography. The rapid spread of mobile photography in Africa offers a vantage point for scholarly analyses that can decentre the dominance of Western discourses on photography (cf. Behrend 2013, p. 13). This study can hopefully make a small contribution to such efforts.

Mobile modernity and photographic practice in Africa

In Tanzania, it is primarily through mobile phones that people have access to and ownership of a camera. In this cultural context, the convergence of digital technology, mobile media and photographic practice is particularly interesting, since mobile phone cameras signify the spread of what scholars refer to as amateur or personal photography, or vernacular photography, as discussed by Becker in this volume. While early research in the United States could use 'The introduction of camera equipment for anyone's everyday use' as a starting point for analyses of 'Kodak culture' and the 'home mode of pictorial communication' (Chalfen 2008, p. 4), in countries like Tanzania it is only through mobile phones that camera technology has become widespread among ordinary people (cf. Behrend 2013). Similarly to how mobile phones have brought access to telecommunications, bypassing fixed landlines, mobile phone cameras are spreading access to photographic technology, bypassing analogue and even digital cameras. According to official statistics, in March 2014 telecom penetration reached 63 per cent in Tanzania, primarily comprising mobile subscriptions (TCRA 2014). As in other parts of Africa, internet access is mainly through mobile networks, estimated to reach 15 per cent penetration in 2014.

The spread of mobile phone cameras is now catching the interest of scholars, although most of the research to date has been carried out in the Global North. Researchers have noted that mobile phone cameras support spontaneous image-making, expanding photo-worthy images to include the everyday (Van House 2011, p. 127). Through smartphones, mobile snapshots can be instantly shared in social media, serving as resources in online social interaction (Lee 2013), while photo messaging can be used to create a sense of mediated presence (Villi & Stocchetti 2011). The spread of mobile cameras, combined with mobile internet access, is contributing to the rapid increase in digital images and image-makers around the world; the ubiquitous presence of a 'camera at hand' (Van House 2011) shifting the focus of photography to the 'here and now' instead of 'then and there' (Knight 2013, p. 168). It has even been suggested that smartphones bring 'new photographic practices', centring on 'expression and dialogue', rather than 'recollection and recording' (Lee 2013, p. 185), while the 'distributed presence' enabled by new forms of visual communication is related to broader cultural transformations of individualization (Van Dijck 2008, p. 62).

Although mobile photography can enhance more impulsive and quotidian image-making practices, and while social media enable the instantaneous sharing and viewing of photographs, it is important to differentiate between social practices and technological affordances. Anthropological studies of digital media have clarified that the use of digital and mobile technologies depends on a variety of context-specific social and cultural factors (e.g. Horst & Miller 2012). Similarly, while the 'social functions' of photography tend to be rather similar around the world, especially when it comes to 'expression, identity and remembrance', they build upon cultural premises that can be profoundly different (Edwards 2011, p. 185). As shown in the material presented here, mobile photography in Tanzania builds on historically shaped photographic practices that both concur with and differ from what has been noted elsewhere. For instance, memory-making continues to be an important aspect of mobile photography, along with family relations, thus highlighting the characteristics of photographs as 'relational objects' (Edwards 2006). Mobile photography is also a 'relational practice' (Behrend 2013), as exemplified by the preference for pictures of the self taken by others, rather than selfies. Similarly, the performativity of photography continues to be a striking characteristic, building on cultural preferences for ideal selves rather than everyday snapshots (cf. Behrend 2013; Vokes 2012). Fears of loss of control over distribution are augmented by fears of exploitation, which build on historically shaped structural inequalities. These practices highlight the need to appraise mobile photography in different cultural contexts, paying attention to similarities as well as differences around the world. Indeed, as argued by Becker in this volume, from the perspective of vernacular photography, mobile photography can be approached as a 'visual dialect, with expressions, conventions and techniques that arise through social and cultural practice', which in turn are characterized by considerable variance around the world.

A growing body of research is examining photographic technology in Africa in relation to social change, but the advent of new media technology, such as mobile phones and the internet, is still relatively unexplored (Vokes 2012, pp. 14–15). Photography has a long history on the continent, as chronicled by scholars (see Peffer & Cameron 2013; Vokes 2012), but the impact of digital media remains an 'open and uneasy question', not least in relation to issues of identity and ownership (Peffer 2013, p. 26). Förster (2013) analyses online and mobile displays of portrait photographs in Côte d'Ivoire in terms of intermediality, thus stressing the interrelatedness of different media. Behrend (2013) draws attention to some of the threats and panic accompanying the rise of digital photography on the Swahili coast in Kenya, where an 'aesthetics of withdrawal' challenges the presumed universal appeal of visual digital media. Based on comprehensive ethnographic analyses of the historicity of photography, these studies illustrate the need to understand photographic practices in relation to the continuities and disruptions that digital media bring forth in specific cultural contexts in the interconnected 'global ecumene' (Hannerz 1996).

When it comes to mobile technology, it is worth recognizing mobile photography as a genre in its own right, rather than a subgenre of digital photography. Essentially, mobile photography refers to the practice of taking pictures with a mobile phone. But since the mobile phone is so much more than a camera device, it embodies much broader social and cultural processes. Unlike a digital camera, which has image-making as its sole function, the mobile phone is a multifunctional device that carries multiple layers of cultural meaning (cf. Horst & Miller 2006). Indeed, functioning like a material extension of the self, the mobile phone constitutes a multisensory artefact that features in most aspects of everyday sociality.

In a Tanzanian context, the mobile phone is associated with modern lifestyles – a highly desired artefact that embodies cultural aspirations for and expectations of modernity, especially ideals of mobility and connectivity (Molony 2008; Uimonen 2012, 2015). Mobile media have evolved into one of the most prominent features in local mediascapes (Ekström 2010), while mobile communication has become an integral part of the management of social networks, particularly family and kin, even among rural and urban poor populations (Stark 2013). Having a mobile phone is an important status marker and people tend to have the fanciest phone they can afford, dual SIM cards and cameras being some of the most sought out functions. Mobile infrastructure is visually manifest throughout urban and rural landscapes, thus influencing the very production and circulation of visual cultural forms, not least through commercial advertisements (Molony 2008; Uimonen 2015).

Relational objects for memory-making and family relations

'I'm proud of being a mother', Jane underlines, 'so I take pictures with my daughter'. Since Jane is busy with her full-time job, a young female relative helps look after her child when she is not in boarding school. Although Jane is not able to spend much time with her daughter, she is still one of the most important aspects of her identity, as evidenced in the many pictures she takes of her. Jane posts some of these pictures online, thus sharing visual memories of her daughter growing up.

Taking pictures as mementos, especially of family members, is a common feature of personal photography in general. Van House (2011, pp. 130–131) notes that personal photography with digital or mobile phone cameras can be categorized into four social uses: memory, relationships, self-representation and expressiveness. Memory work through images of relationships is very common, especially family members and life events, not least to give 'children a sense of history and membership in family' (ibid.). This diverts somewhat from Van Dijck's (2008, pp. 62–63) observation of a shift in the younger generation, whose 'photographic exchanges' of moments is replacing photographic memories of family, as a result of the growing emphasis on individualism at the expense of family. By contrast, the material presented here illustrates how new technologies retain the characteristics of photographs as 'relational objects' (Edwards 2006). Photographs are not just images but social objects that carry agency in the maintenance, reproduction and transformation of social relations, thus playing an active part in the making and articulation of histories (ibid., pp. 27–29). In the case of non-Western contexts like Tanzania, where individualism is less emphasized and where the family remains culturally significant, photography continues to be a markedly 'relational practice' (Behrend 2013).

Sauda's photographic practices, which centre on pictures of her family, illustrate the cultural significance of mobile photographs as relational objects. Sauda is 32 years old, married, with a five-year-old daughter. Her family lives in Bagamoyo, a small coastal town outside Dar es Salaam. Sauda often captures social relationships and social events with her mobile camera: pictures of birthdays, weddings and graduations, as well as religious events. Most of her pictures feature people she has close relationships with, especially family, but also friends. These are also the pictures that she sends through WhatsApp, to family members and friends.

Similarly to Jane, Sauda makes frequent references to her daughter when talking about her mobile photographic practices, which are distinctly relational. She takes pictures of Neema during her birthday or when she does something special, like dancing or playing drums. She shares some of these pictures through WhatsApp or Facebook. However, she also likes to keep them as memories of her daughter growing up, which she hopes to show her one day.

Sauda's habit of taking pictures of her daughter is expressive of her primary cultural identity, which, in a Tanzanian context, centres on her motherhood. In her everyday life Sauda is referred to as 'Mama Neema' (mother of Neema), her social identity defined through her relation to her child. Sauda's primary identity as Mama Neema is also evident in her profile and cover photos on Facebook, both of which depict her daughter. When Sauda talks of her husband, she refers to him as 'Baba Neema' (father of Neema), rather than 'my husband'. Similarly, rather than using their first names, she refers to her family members in terms of her relation to them: 'my mother', 'my sister', 'my brother', etc. Sauda's photographic practices are thus intertwined with the web of social relations that define her cultural identity, photographs of her family constituting relational objects that express her socially constituted self.

The circulation of family pictures ranges from *intimate* to *expansive* circulation. Far from being determined by technological capabilities, photographs are embedded in social relations, which determine the scope of how photographs are used to extend socialities beyond face-to-face encounters (Edwards 2006, pp. 33–34). While Sauda mainly shares photographs with her family, using the WhatsApp application on her phone, Jane shares photos through Instagram and Facebook. The applications differ in their scope, WhatsApp being limited to communication with individuals, while Instagram and Facebook cater to more extensive social networks. The choice of application can be related to differences in family composition. Sauda has a close-knit family, which she interacts with on a daily basis, while Jane is a single mother who lives far away from her kin and who interacts more with friends. Sauda's more *intimate circulation* is indicative of more immediate social ties, revolving around her family, while Jane's *expansive circulation* of mobile photographs can be related to the extended composition of her social relations, including a vast network of friends.

Online performance of selfhood and relational photographic practice

When it comes to self-representation, mobile photography mediates the performative dimensions of image-making as well as identity formation. It has been noted that all forms of photography in Africa have been influenced by 'local understandings of exhibition, comportment and display' (Vokes 2012, p. 9), with studio photography and other forms of portraiture often used to 'perform a vision of an ideal self' (Peffer 2013, p. 20; cf. Behrend 2013 and Borgatti 2013). This practice is by no means unique to African photography, since 'posing' and 'performance' are integral to photography in general, underlining its social agency (Edwards 2006, 2011). As noted by Van House (2011, p. 131), self-representation through personal photographs is not just a question of how we 'represent ourselves', but also how we 'enact ourselves'. In choosing what pictures to post online, people reflect on what aspects of their identity they wish to portray, thus underlining the reflexivity and interactivity of performance (Schieffelin 1998; Turner 1987; Uimonen 2013).

When posting pictures of herself online, Jane selects pictures where she poses for the camera, her performative act centring on her physical appearance, which builds upon local aesthetic ideals. Knowing that her 'African figure' embodies local standards of female beauty, Jane often shows her full figure from different angles, shifting her pose to accentuate her curves. Jane is often dressed in fashionable attire, her clothes and accessories colour coordinated, matched by elaborate hairstyles. The performative aspect of photography is evident in these carefully prepared poses, the very act of image-making constituting a reflexive construction of selfhood in relation to an imagined audience of viewers. Jane's potential audience is quite numerous; she has 554 followers in Instagram and 600 friends in Facebook.

Although Jane's online images tend to affirm local ideals of beauty and womanhood, sometimes her pictures provoke unexpected responses, illustrating the inherently 'interactive' and 'risky' aspects of performance (Schieffelin 1998, p. 198). Similarly to other performative acts, the online sharing of mobile photographs is a 'contingent process', the outcome of which hinges on the relationship between the performers and spectators in a given cultural context (ibid., pp. 197–198). One of the reasons why Jane posts pictures online is to get feedback: 'when I think I'm looking nice I want others to see'. She often gets a lot of appreciative comments, which makes her 'feel nice'. But not all comments are nice, Jane reflects. If she is 'wearing something short', some people reproach her, thinking she is 'selling' herself, or ask for her number. Not only do these responses divert from what Jane has in mind when posting pictures, but they are also indicative of gendered norms in visual culture. In the case of women's physical appearance, moral boundaries comprise a fine line between beauty and sexuality. A woman can show off her voluptuous curves, but if she reveals too much skin by wearing something short, she risks being treated like a sexual object.

The materiality of the physical environment serves as an important backdrop framing the online performance of selfhood through mobile photographs. Joan often poses with her car or with stylish furniture, in glamorous social settings or in the garden of her house. The materiality of these objects and places convey cultural aspirations for modernity, visual representations of a middle-class lifestyle associated with social progress and material affluence. Functioning as stages for the performance of selfhood, these physical spaces serve as reflections on Jane's multiple cultural identities. Whether she portrays herself as a single mother or a professional woman, Jane can display the multi-layered cultural identities of an urban woman, who follows fashion trends, lives in a modern house with stylish furniture and drives a car.

The carefully staged performance of an ideal version of the self is deeply entrenched in local forms of visual representation. In this cultural context, photography builds on cultural notions of public display that centre on visual ideals rather than social realities (Peffer 2013; Vokes 2012). If anything, the preference for presenting oneself as an accomplished social person, with the help of props and backgrounds that portray a better world, is one of the reasons why 'snapshot photography' has never evolved as a popular genre in East Africa (Behrend 2013, pp. 127–128). Instead of capturing everyday life with all its imperfections, mobile photography thus builds on photographic practices that privilege the visual performance of cultural ideals. The mobile phone itself plays an important role in keeping up appearances, an artefact that is used to display a model self (cf. Archambault 2013).

It is worth underlining that these visual performances of selfhood are not 'selfies', but retain photography as a relational practice. When Jane poses for the camera, someone else is taking the picture (often her sister, who she lives with). This is similar to the practices of other respondents in this study, as well as images that Tanzanian women post in Facebook, which are typically taken by someone else rather than selfies. This relational photographic practice differs from the popularity of more individualistic practices among young women in other places, indicating the contextual specificity and relational variation in 'selfie culture' (e.g. Miller 2014).

Creative agency and digital editing

Mobile photography facilitates creative image-making. The ease of use and constant presence of mobile phone cameras opens up more opportunities for artistic photography, encouraging people to 'see the world as a field of potential images' (Van House 2011, p. 131). Photographs can also be easily modified through editing software, thus enhancing creative agency in the performance of cultural identity. It has been noted that the endless potential for manipulation could make digital photography the 'ultimate tool for identity formation' (Van Dijck 2008, p. 67). In East Africa, creative manipulations of photographs have a long history, underlining the cultural ideals of perfection in photographic representation (Behrend 2013).

Trained as a visual artist, Nuri likes to take pictures of 'interesting things and places'. Nuri is 29 years old and works as a tutor at an arts college in Bagamoyo. She is not yet married but has been in a committed long-distance relationship for several years. Nuri has a Samsung S3, which she bought in the United States when visiting her boyfriend. Before that she had an LG smartphone, which had fast internet connectivity but not a very good camera, so she gave it to her sister. Nuri likes her Samsung, because it has the 'best quality in pictures and photos'. She has had a phone with a camera since 2006.

'Weird and unusual stuff' often catch Nuri's eye, the aesthetic qualities of which she captures with her mobile camera. As we flick through her mobile phone gallery, she shows me some of the pictures she has taken. A picture of a large snail, unusual since it is so big. A picture of rainbows over the ocean – a remarkable scene because two rainbows appeared at the same time, one arched above the other. A well-composed picture of a newly paved road, which used to have bumps but now looks nice.

Nuri's aesthetic sensibility is evident in the form and content of her photographs, capturing both mundane and extraordinary aspects of her daily life. Not only does she pay attention to what makes for a nice picture, but she also manages to visualize her everyday life, taking photographs of people, places and activities that form part of her social, cultural and professional life. Nuri's artistic talent is undoubtedly enhanced by her training in fine and visual arts, but it is the mobile phone camera that allows her to explore her skills in artistic photography on a daily basis.

Mobile artistic photography is enhanced by the creative use of editing functions. Nuri sometimes edits photos she posts online, changing the colour or using special effects to frame the picture. When Jane posts pictures of herself online, she often uses a photo grid. Through this photo editing application, she can post photo montages on Instagram and Facebook, mixing close ups and full figure images, or showing different poses from the same or different angles. The use of photo montage is a well established practice in many parts of Africa, displaying the individual in its 'multiple' form (Behrend 2013, pp. 167–169). Similarly to edited Facebook profile photos, these manipulated images can offer a more truthful depiction of the self, visualizing aspects of cultural identity that are not otherwise visible (Uimonen 2013).

Mobile materiality in display and circulation

The materiality of mobile phones affects the display and circulation of mobile photographs, thus highlighting some interesting features of mobile photography as a 'mode of visual communication' (see Chalfen in this volume). Since it is a storage device, the mobile phone is often used to display photographs, thus functioning as a mobile photo album. However, the phone can also be used for instantaneous sharing of images with distant others, serving as a material node in digital networks. The mobile phone thus acts as a socially distributed object in what Lehmuskallio and Gómez refer to as 'connected interactions' in their introduction to this volume. Far from constituting a loss of materiality, mobile photography thus offers new configurations of material practice, with the mobile phone replacing the materiality of the printed photograph, while mediating the circulation of immaterial digital photographs.

Sauda uses her phone to show her mobile photographs to family and friends. She reflects on a recent trip to Arusha when she took a lot of pictures. When she returned home she showed the pictures on her phone to her family and friends. The phone thus functioned as a photo album, containing memories of people, places and activities, which Sauda could use to share stories of her trip to people around her through multisensory narratives (cf. Edwards 2006). Reflecting the intimate circulation in her photographic practice, as discussed above, Sauda restricted the distribution of these photographs to her mobile phone, displaying them to a select number of people only. She did not post any photographs on Facebook.

For Nuri, mobile photography plays an important role in the management of her long-distance relationship with her boyfriend in the United States. When asked what she does with the pictures she takes, Nuri responded 'I just keep them [on the phone] and show my friends. Also, pictures that I think are interesting, I put on Facebook or Instagram to share.' Nuri has been on Facebook since 2008 and has over 100 pictures on her page. She started using Instagram in 2014, when she got her new phone, and has uploaded 33 pictures so far. However, her main use is 'sharing with my boyfriend', which she mostly does through WhatsApp.

'Michael and I like to share a lot of pictures of what we are doing', Nuri reflects, noting that photos are simpler to exchange than videos since they take up a lot of space. The pictures are often mundane photos of everyday life – a mediated exchange of images of their respective social worlds – thus reaffirming their social bond while bridging their spatial distance. This exemplifies the use of photo messaging for a greater sense of intimacy through 'mediated presence' and 'synchronized gaze' (Villi & Stocchetti 2011, p. 106). Nuri reflects how the exchange of pictures makes her 'feel more close' to her boyfriend, which 'makes the relationship more realistic'.

Normative boundaries and crazy pictures

Linda enjoys taking pictures with her mobile 'for memory', especially of her friends and of herself: 'just normal pictures', she concludes. Similarly to many young women in Tanzania, Linda did not complete secondary school. She is 20 years old and works in a low-paid service job in a local hotel in Kisesa, a semi-rural town outside Mwanza. Linda has a Tecno mobile with dual SIM cards – a cheap brand that is very popular among low income users. The phone has a camera but needs a memory card for storage, which she does not have. This is Linda's fourth phone since 2008, all of them given to her by others (mostly her parents). Her earlier phones also had cameras.

Similarly to Linda, Becky underlines that she takes 'just normal pictures'. These include pictures of her family (her children and herself), her parents and her friends, as well as pictures at work (she teaches at a college). Becky emphasizes that she does not take 'stupid pictures' or 'crazy pictures'. Becky is 35 years old, a mother of two children and lives in Bagamoyo.

The discourse of 'normal pictures' outlines the normative boundaries of photographic practice, which both influence and are being challenged by mobile photography. As Bourdieu (1991, pp. 131–132) reminds us 'there is nothing more regulated and conventional than photographic practice and amateur photographs'. Anthropological research has shown that notions of what is photo-worthy vary, depending on cultural context (e.g. Behrend 2013; Edwards 2011; Förster 2013; Pinney 1997; Vokes 2012). Historically shaped cultural ideals also influence mobile photography, shaping expectations of what constitutes 'normal' pictures.

In a Tanzanian context, mobile photography builds on and co-exists with commercial photography, which continues to be a common means to obtain photographs, especially in material form. As mentioned earlier, snapshot photography has never taken off in East Africa, since people prefer the staged performativity of photographic events. Studios can still be found in urban and semi-urban areas, offering ID photos and other services, while 'street photographers' attract customers in popular public places (cf. Behrend 2013). These commercial services offer professional photography (photo and video) for specific purposes (ID, passport, driver's licence), events (weddings, funerals, graduations) and places (historical sites, tourist spots). In addition to their professionalism, commercial photographers produce material objects (prints, DVDs), which distinguishes their practices from mobile photography.

Becky reflects on photography during the time of 'negatives' and how it was 'not easy to take photographs and print them', so people took it 'seriously'. Becky has an album with photos, mostly taken with analogue cameras and some pictures she took with her digital camera before it got stolen. The analogue pictures were taken by commercial photographers: 'it's like business: they take, you pay'. Becky used this service a lot in the past, thus following conventional photographic practice.

With mobile cameras, photography becomes mundane and ubiquitous: 'sometimes people take pictures every time – crazy pictures, stupid pictures – because it is easy to delete'. Becky's concern with excessive image-making highlights the ambivalence of changing photographic practices. What used to be restricted to photographic events can now take place anywhere and anytime, thus loosening social control over production. However, the ability to take an excessive amount of photographs is also associated with greater choice and control. Becky notes that one of the drawbacks of analogue photography was that you could not choose pictures; even if a picture was bad, you had to pay for it. With mobiles, 'you can play with it how you want, even take a picture 100 times', and if it is not nice, you can just delete it.

Fears of commercial and sexual exploitation

'Utaenda kuuza ulaya?' ('Are you going to sell it in Europe?') a man angrily shouts at me when I am taking a picture of a mobile phone stand near him. The notion that a *mzungu* (white person) takes photographs of people to sell the pictures overseas is common in Tanzania. This is also one of the main reasons why people dislike being photographed by unknown others, or insist on getting some money to have their picture taken. The concern with exploitative photography by cultural others is not without its historical justification, given the unequal relations between those taking pictures and those being photographed, dating back to colonial times (Strother 2013).

With the spread of digital photography, fears of exploitation are growing, which can be interpreted in terms of widening inequalities. A friend in Dar es Salaam, who is an accomplished amateur photographer, pointed out that he encounters more suspicion when using his camera, which he related to the growing display of photographs and photo exhibitions. Fears of photographic exploitation can be indicative of intensifying processes of cultural commodification, the production and circulation of digital images carrying narratives of social inequality. A person affluent enough to have a camera holds a social position associated with commercial power, the very ownership of photographic technology signalling power to transform images into commodities.

For women, mobile photography fuels fears of sexual exploitation. 'People use for good, some use it for bad. Maybe someone comes and says you look nice and want to take a picture, but maybe someone sent them and maybe they use it for bad purpose', Linda reflects, when I ask her about the benefits and drawbacks of mobile photography. Young women in particular are concerned about how their photographs might get used. I was told by a female friend that pictures of young women are sometimes taken in secret, manipulated on computers and circulated, often with sexual connotations. A respondent told me that in some instances a woman may agree to have sexually revealing pictures taken by her boyfriend, in privacy, but if the relationship ends badly, the pictures might get circulated. Intimate pictures can also be taken in secret. One interlocutor demonstrated, with her hands on her lap, how easy it is to take photos, while appearing to be doing something else with your phone. These fears echo concerns over pictures taken in secret in intimate situations and sold or circulated in Kenya, where mobile photography is creating worries of 'personal revelation, alienation, and indiscretion' (Behrend 2013, p. 243).

This fear of sexual exploitation can also be related to new forms of visual representation brought on by the commodification of culture. Over the last few years, sexually revealing photographs of young women have become more commonplace in Tanzania, often featuring in advertisements. Looking 'sexy' is an emerging aesthetic ideal that is commercially promoted, not least through beauty pageants sponsored by mobile phone operators (Uimonen 2012). As I have observed on Facebook, in photographs for their 'modelling portfolio', young women often display themselves in sexually provocative poses. While beauty pageants and photo modelling exemplify the agency of women in new forms of visual representation and popular culture (see Shipley 2013), they can also reify women as sexual objects in photographic practice, thus reducing their agency, while recasting them as sexual commodities.

Risk of theft and loss of control

The materiality of the mobile phone is a source of considerable concern, since phones are desirable artefacts that often get stolen. Nuri has had six phones stolen from her over the years, Becky had phones and a digital camera stolen and Linda lost several phones. Using the internet to store photographs can reduce the risk of loss, but this requires a smartphone. Jane uses her email account for storage, Sauda can store photographs on a flashdrive and Nuri keeps a selection of photographs on her computer. Even so, most of the time photographs are stored on the phone and the larger the storage capacity, the greater the number of photographs.

'If someone steals the phone, or I misplace it, also the pictures are gone and others can see them – later maybe even in the news', Becky reflects during our interview. What is at stake in the potential theft or misplacement of a mobile phone is not just the loss of personal photographs, but also the loss of control over their circulation.

This sense of vulnerability highlights the privacy of mobile photography as opposed to more public photographic practices. The mobile phone is a very personal possession and, as Becky reflects, it is more personal than a digital camera. She notes that pictures on a camera are often seen by others, but pictures taken on a mobile are often meant for personal consumption. This distinction between digital cameras and public circulation, on the one hand, and the more private uses of mobile photographs, on the other, is indicative of how mobile photography brings photographic practices into the private sphere. As in Kenya, mobile photography undermines the boundaries between the private and the public, thus intensifying the problem of controlling images of the self, especially in digital forms (Behrend 2013, p. 243).

The privacy of mobile phones is expressed in multisensory ways. A common way of personalizing the phone is through photographs of loved ones: Becky has a photograph of her daughter as background; Nuri has a photograph of herself with her boyfriend. It is also common to change ringtones, using popular songs, thus personalizing the sound of the phone. Some people modify the tactile feel of the phone: Sauda has a pink cover case for her smartphone. Above all, the phone is a personal belonging that is always present. People carry their mobile phones on their bodies, in hand or in pockets. Women, who usually wear dresses, keep their phones in handbags or in their brassiere. I was told that some women even have pockets sewn to their underwear for the safekeeping of phones. When people sit down and socialize, they often place their phones within easy reach. And, since phones are easily stolen, they are also kept close to the body at night, under the pillow or near the bed.

Since the mobile phone is such a personalized artefact, a material extension of the self, mobile photography carries conflicting narratives of loss and control. On the one hand, possession of a camera gives individuals control over image-making in everyday life. On the other hand, since mobile phones often get stolen, they also make individuals more susceptible to the loss of control over images. These conflicting tendencies can be related to broader social transformations, the digitally mediated constitution of modern subjects bringing a greater degree of control over new forms of self-expression, while mobile media also make individuals more vulnerable to the loss of personal artefacts containing their digitally constituted selves.

Conclusion

The multisensory materiality and relational sociality of mobile photography makes for complex interdependencies between digital technology and photographic practice. In Tanzania, mobile photography mediates new forms of self-expression while building on historically shaped photographic practices. Mobile photography is used for memory-making, with photographs functioning as relational objects, especially in the context of family. In the online performance of selfhood, mobile photography builds on cultural ideals of photographic representation while retaining photography as a relational practice. Through daily photo opportunities and digital editing, the creative agency of photography is enhanced, while the materiality of the mobile phone offers new forms of display and circulation. The ubiquity of mobile photography differs markedly from established commercial practices, loosening social control over photographic events while increasing individual choice and control. Meanwhile, fears of commercial and sexual exploitation carry narratives of social inequality and cultural commodification, while the risk of theft points to the vulnerabilities of mobile artefacts that serve as material extensions of the self.

Since mobile photography is spreading rapidly throughout Africa, more research will hopefully shed light on photographic practices in relation to mediality, modernity and social change. As mobile photography becomes more commonplace, it will undoubtedly offer valuable insights into changing meanings of selfhood and sociality in the context of global transformations that are as complex as they are diverse.

Note

1 I am grateful for the feedback from Helena Wulff and Andrew Mitchell at the Department of Social Anthropology, Stockholm University, and the constructive critique of three reviewers.

References

Archambault, J. S. 2013, 'Cruising through Uncertainty: Cell Phones and the Politics of Display and Disguise in Inhambane, Mozambique'. *American Ethnologist*, Vol. 40, no. 1, pp. 88–101.

Behrend, H. 2013, *Contesting Visibility: Photographic Practices on the East African Coast*. Transcript Verlag: Bielefeld.

Borgatti, J. 2013, 'Likeness or Not: Musings on Portraiture in Canonical African Art and its Implications for African Portrait Photography', in J. Peffer & E. Cameron (eds) *Portraiture and Photography in Africa*. Indiana University Press: Bloomington and Indianapolis, IN, pp. 315–340.

Bourdieu, P. 1991, 'Towards a Sociology of Photography'. *Visual Anthropology Review*, Vol. 7, no. 1, pp. 129–133.

Chalfen, R. [1987]/2008, *Snapshot Versions of Life*. Popular Press: Bowling Green, OH.

Edwards, E. 2011, 'Tracing Photography', in M. Banks & J. Ruby (eds) *Made to Be Seen: Historical Perspectives on Visual Anthropology*. University of Chicago Press: Chicago, IL, pp. 159–189.

Edwards, E. 2006, 'Photographs and the Sound of History'. *Visual Anthropology Review*, Vol. 21, nos 1–2, pp. 27–46.

Ekström, Y. 2010, '*We are like Chameleons!' Changing Mediascapes, Cultural Identities and City Sisters in Dar es Salaam*. Dissertation, Uppsala University.

Förster, T. 2013, 'The Intermediality of Portraiture in Northern C'ôte d'Ivoire', in J. Peffer & E. Cameron (eds) *Portraiture and Photography in Africa*. Indiana University Press: Bloomington and Indianapolis, IN, pp. 407–438.

Hannerz, U. 1996, *Transnational Connections: Culture, People, Places*. Routledge: London.

Horst, H.A. & Miller, D. (eds) 2012, *Digital Anthropology*. Berg: Oxford.

Horst, H. & Miller, D. 2006, *The Cell Phone: An Anthropology of Communication*. Berg: Oxford.

Knight, A. B. 2013, 'Performative Pictures: Camera Phones at the Ready', in J. M. Wise & H. Koskela (eds) *New Visualities, New Technologies: The New Ecstacy of Communication*. Ashgate Publishing Ltd: Farnham, pp. 153–170.

Lee, D.-H. 2013, 'Mobile Snapshots: Pictorial Communication in the Age of Tertiary Orality', in J. M. Wise & H. Koskela (eds) *New Visualities, New Technologies: The New Ecstacy of Communication*. Ashgate Publishing Ltd: Farnham, pp. 171–188.

Miller, D. 2014, 'Know thy Selfie'. Blog post, 1 April 2014, viewed 24 September 2015, http://blogs.ucl.ac.uk/global-social-media/2014/04/01/know-thy-selfie/.

Molony, T. 2008, 'Nondevelopmental Uses of Mobile Communication in Tanzania', in J. E. Katz (ed.) *Handbook of Mobile Communication Studies*. MIT Press: Cambridge, MA, pp. 339–352.

Peffer, J. 2013, 'Introduction: The Study of Photographic Portraiture in Africa', in J. Peffer & E. Cameron (eds) *Portraiture and Photography in Africa*. Indiana University Press: Bloomington and Indianapolis, IN, pp. 1–34.

Peffer, J. & Cameron, E. (eds) 2013, *Portraiture and Photography in Africa*. Indiana University Press: Bloomington and Indianapolis, IN.

Pinney, C. 1997, *Camera Indica: The Social Life of Indian Photographs*. University of Chicago Press: Chicago, IL.

Schieffelin, E. L. 1998, 'Problematizing Performance', in F. Hughes-Freeland (ed.) *Ritual, Performance, Media*. Routledge: London, pp. 194–207.

Shipley, J. W. 2013, *Living the Hiplife: Celebrity and Entrepreneurship in Ghanaian Popular Music*. Duke University Press: Durham, NC.

Stark, L. 2013. 'Transactional Sex and Mobile Phones in a Tanzanian Slum'. *Suomen Antropologi: Journal of the Finnish Anthropological Society*, Vol. 38, no. 1, pp. 12–36.

Strother, Z. S. 2013, ' "A Photograph Steals the Soul": The History of an Idea', in J. Peffer & E. Cameron (eds) *Portraiture and Photography in Africa*. Indiana University Press: Bloomington and Indianapolis, IN, pp. 177–212.

TCRA. 2014, *Quarterly Telecom Statistics*. Report prepared by Tanzania Communications Regulatory Authority (TCRA), March.

Turner, V. 1987, *The Anthropology of Performance*. PAJ: New York.

Uimonen, P. 2015, 'Number not Reachable: Mobile Infrastructure and Global Racial Hierarchy in Africa'. *Journal des Anthropologues*, no. 142–143, pp. 29–47.

Uimonen, P. 2013, 'Visual Identity in Facebook'. *Visual Studies*, Vol. 28, no. 2, pp. 122–135.

Uimonen, P. 2012, *Digital Drama: Teaching and Learning Art and Media in Tanzania*. Routledge: New York, http://innovativeethnographies.net/digitaldrama.

Van Dijck, J. 2008. 'Digital Photography: Communication, Identity, Memory'. *Visual Communication*, Vol. 7, no. 1, pp. 57–76.

Van House, N. 2011, 'Personal Photography, Digital Technologies and the Uses of the Visual'. *Visual Studies*, Vol. 26, no. 2, pp. 125–134.

Villi, M. & Stocchetti, M. 2011, 'Visual Mobile Communication, Mediated Presence and the Politics of Space'. *Visual Studies*, Vol. 26, no. 2, pp. 102–112.

Vokes, R. (ed.) 2012, *Photography in Africa: Ethnographic Perspectives*. James Currey: Woodbridge, VA; New York.

2 'Today I dressed like this': selling clothes and playing for celebrity

Self-representation and consumption on Facebook

Sara Pargana Mota

Introduction

Contemporary Western culture is marked by the rising ubiquity of the visual realm in everyday life. As Schroeder (2002, p. 3) points out

> we are exposed to hundreds of images every day. Not in church, or at museums – but all around us in advertising, on the Internet, on television, in newspapers, on billboards, magazines, buildings, radio, cable, t-shirts, credit cards, shopping carts, and cash register receipts. We live in a visual information culture. In no other time in history has there been such an explosion of visual images.

In a hyper-visual world, digital images pervade our lives, are tangled with our thoughts, desires, anxieties, passions, memories, loves and friendships, are part of our leisure and work activities and connect us to the world of consumption.

Nowadays, widespread images play a central role in many social and cultural aspects of life (Rose 2007). The digital turn has brought about an ever-growing mass and flow of digital media and images and has given a significant boost to the visibility and popularity of personal photography (Rubinstein & Sluis 2008), and its practices have become deeply woven into the dynamics of daily life. New technologies, apps and multiple digital visual platforms allow an unprecedented production, exhibition and distribution of personal photographs. The increasingly popular smartphone makes images instantaneous and pervasive, and facilitates the spontaneous photographing of the most mundane moments of everyday life. The countless personal pictures and everyday snapshots uploaded to social media platforms, for which Facebook can stand as a synecdoche, makes further apparent the increasing 'visual publicisation of ordinary life in a ubiquitous photoscape' (Hand 2012, p. 1).

The visual documentation of everyday life, from the most ritualistic to the most mundane, and the act of updating photographs to Facebook, to be uploaded, forwarded and shared while waiting for a 'like', a comment or feedback, are now commonplace. Such contemporary visual practices, as performed on Facebook, Instagram or Twitter, show the importance of photography as both a social act and an instrument of communication. These networked photographs have been designated as performative in everyday social practice and as intimately connected to presence and to 'common banality' (Petersen 2008). Ultimately, networked photographs now have the primary function of self-representation and identity formation, in opposition to the traditional use of photography as family representation and remembrance (Harrison 2002; Van Dijck 2008). They have been described as 'MeMedia' (Petersen 2008) in which individuals have become the focus of pictorial experience, affirming their individuality and personal ties and grooming their online identities through the practice of self-shooting.

The most popular type of self-representation in today's digital mediascape is the selfie, which can be regarded as a subgenre of self-portrait photography – something that has been around for a long time (Saltz 2014). Usually taken at arm's length or in front of a mirror using a digital camera, smartphone or tablet, and eventually posted online, the selfie has flooded social media sites and is now a well-established form of self-expression (Ardèvol & Gómez Cruz 2012). Although it has attracted a good deal of public notice and has been discussed in less formal arenas, such as blogs, the emergence of the selfie has hitherto received insufficient scholarly attention. For many, this photographic trend mirrors the narcissism endemic in Western society and is an indulgent practice adopted by celebrities or by ordinary and anonymous people.[1] Thus, as an article in the *Guardian* observed, celebrities such as Kim Kardashian and Justin Bieber have the same visual social media practices as their fans and have in common with them a 'grandiose exhibitionism, inflated self-views, superficial personalities and shameless self-promotion' (Chamorro-Premuzic 2014). Media commentators have condemned what they see as an increasingly exhibitionist and voyeuristic one-dimensional digital culture, characterized by a standardization of themes and poses. The selfie is particularly popular with young women and their use of these self-portraits has been critically analysed in the blogosphere. Some see selfies as a source of female empowerment. Alternatively, Sarah Gram's (2013) poignant analysis argues that the selfie is a 'ticket into the world of consumer capitalism', a form of gendered labour in which the body becomes a commodity within the economies of attention.

This chapter will focus on the production, consumption and sharing of snapshots and self-portraits by a group of young Portuguese women, who have created Facebook profiles in order to sell and trade their clothes. This kind of Facebook use has been occasionally mentioned (see, for instance, Miller 2011, p. 138) but not thoroughly examined. The aim of this work is not to examine the photographic images per se but to explore how taking and posting selfies and pictures of clothes, closets and bedrooms is central to the new fashion marketplace – given 'the postulate that consumption and vision are mutually constructing practices' (Fornäs *et al.* 2007, p. 82) – and how these practices are ways to claim presence and visibility. It will also analyse how social media and the photographic practices in which these women engage are inserted into processes of microcelebrity and self-branding, and so emerge as vehicles in a global labour market, characteristic of late capitalism. Further, this chapter will examine how the visual practices in which these women engage, although seduced by the charms of commercial image culture, open up a space for negotiations between creative forms of self-representation and the generalizations of mass media and celebrity culture, shaping how they understand themselves and their desires.

Outfit selfies, shopping-haul snaps and closet stories

Social networking sites are very popular in Portugal and are becoming increasingly central to people's everyday lives. The most popular of these is Facebook, with around 4.7 million users in Portugal (out of 1.2 billion worldwide). The premise of Facebook is that people use it to stay connected to friends and family, to discover what's going on in the world and to share and express whatever matters to them. Users can create public or semi-private profiles and share their personal interests and information about everyday life. Facebook is a highly visual environment and, with minimal effort, photographs and videos can be uploaded, shared and commented on within one's social network, thus fuelling social interaction and communication. Because photographic images are central to activity on Facebook, this is a fertile area for ethnographic research into practices and processes of meaning-making related to photography in everyday life. In the first instance, because of the sheer pervasiveness and diversity of these practices, research in this area makes apparent the amazingly creative ways people adapt new media platforms to their needs. This last point is very well illustrated by this investigation of the photographic practices and con-sumerist self-representations related to the use of Facebook as a space where young women sell, buy or swap clothes, shoes and accessories.

The financial difficulties experienced by many people in Portugal in recent years have boosted an already existing second-hand goods market, which is now expanding in physical space and on social media sites such as Facebook, where profiles of 'closet shops' or 'second-hand shops' are numerous and flourishing. More and more people buy and sell through Facebook since it is a platform where they already spend a significant amount of their time and where it's easy to upload a photo, write a description and respond to comments. There is also a feeling of trust generated by the buyer's ability to see what friends she has in common with the sellers and the instant social interaction that the platform enables.

The creators and owners of these Facebook closet profiles are mostly women aged 16 and upwards, with the majority being between 18 and 30. They come from different socioeconomic backgrounds and have diverse lifestyles and patterns of consumption. Some engage in these activities out of real need, as a way to solve urgent financial problems. They are selling their clothes so that they can pay the electricity bill at the end of the month. For others, and this is the case with many of the young women portrayed in this chapter, it is a hobby, albeit one driven by the need to reduce the excessive number of items in their wardrobes, and one that offers the opportunity of making a few euro along the way. These women have seen their families' income slightly reduced and are searching for ways of maintaining their fashion lifestyles, such as swapping clothes and thus acquiring new garments and renovating their wardrobes at zero cost.

The data for this chapter was gathered through ethnographic research conducted over a period of 12 months. For this purpose, a closet profile account was opened on Facebook. Within a few weeks of opening a 'closet shop' more than 1,000 friends had been added and dozens of friendship requests were being received every day. The cases portrayed and analysed in this chapter constitute a microcosm of fieldwork that encompassed participant-observation within a universe of thousands of Portuguese closets, ten face-to-face open-ended interviews and 15 online interviews.

Catarina,[2] a part-time freelance translator in her early thirties, has a closet shop on Facebook. She remembers that she discovered this world through a morning TV show on which a Portuguese actress and model announced that she was selling some of her clothes and accessories on Facebook. Catarina rushed to her computer, logged on, found the profile and within a few days the mailman had delivered a glamorous dress worn by a Portuguese celebrity. After spending weeks browsing through other closet shops and picking out fashion items for her wardrobe, she realized that this would be a great way to earn some extra cash and to de-clutter her overflowing wardrobe, thus making room for her new clothes, and so she opened her own shop. She already had a personal account on Facebook but opened a second account specifically for her shop. Catarina spends a great amount of her free time on her online boutique, although she uses it primarily to buy and sell and not for socializing. She has made some friendly connections through her shop but affirms the strictly instrumental purpose of the practice in which she is engaged.

Catarina notes

> You have to be camera-wise to be successful in your sales here. For example, you have to set up an attractive but neutral background, in order to get a nice colour contrast. The photo should be shot using natural light as photos with flash are awful. I see many people here posting crappy photos of their clothes for sale – blurry and dark shots, messy rooms in the background, clothes laid right on the floor (I wouldn't buy something that was dropped on a dirty floor, would you?). Poor quality photos are bad for this business; you have to be really appealing in your presentation.

Since entering the world of online shopping, Catarina uses her camera a great deal. She frequently lays clothes out on her bed and photographs the items she has for sale and also takes outfit selfies in front of the mirror. Clothing sells better when shown on the wearer but she tries never to show her face in these shots as she wants to maintain a certain distance from the 1,000-plus friends she has on her profile (the majority of whom are other closet shops). Every time she sells something she takes a photograph of the parcels before mailing them and then of the mail receipt as proof that she has sent them; she later posts these on her wall. She always asks for scans of bank invoices as proof that the client has paid for the goods.

Catarina says that 'taking and sharing these photos is very important to show how trustworthy one is'. She's proud of her feedback album of pictures of ready to send packages, especially after she holds auction sales and sells a batch of goods all at once. A photograph of a pile of parcels carefully set on top of her dining room table shows that she is a successful vendor. 'But this is really a time consuming activity', she sighs, 'you have to spend time burnishing your image here, like presenting your personal style in a trendy manner.' She has a shared album entitled 'Mine, just Mine', with photos of clothing and jewellery she has bought and is not selling, so that her customers can get an idea of her fashion sense and good taste.

Sofia is a 24-year-old unemployed psychology graduate who, like many young people in Portugal, still lives with her parents and has only very remote prospects of achieving financial independence. She considers herself to be a 'fashionable girl', and confesses that she is something of a clothes hoarder and an avid follower of those she considers to be 'fashion role models' on Facebook, Instagram, YouTube and fashion blogs. She loves watching television series like *Gossip Girl* and reality TV shows such as *Secret Story* (a version of *Big Brother*) and *Keeping up with the Kardashians*. Her new obsession is second-hand buying and selling on Facebook, an activity that she indulges in through her account, 'Sofia's Closet'. She doesn't really profit from her hobby as the money she earns is almost immediately spent on new clothes.

Sofia constantly uploads photographs of clothes she has up for sale on her wall and organizes them into albums: dresses, skirts, tops, knits, cardigans, accessories. Because she knows that many people are on a shoe-string budget, everything is priced at less than 20 euro. When she photographs the clothes laid out on her bed she pays particular attention to the bed itself, putting on her best pillows and bed cover, in an attempt to make her room resemble those portrayed in home décor magazines. However, what she really enjoys doing is shooting self-portraits, taking mirror outfit selfies wearing the clothes she intends to sell and also her favourite ensembles and outfits.

Whether or not they are for sale, Sofia often takes and uploads snapshots of her clothes, shoes and accessories. She also showcases, to her

Figure 2.1 'Tonight's outfit'; image posted by Sofia on her closet Facebook account showcasing a dress she bought earlier that day.

audience of nearly 2,000 friends, the purchases she made on her most recent shopping expedition – these could be called 'shopping-haul snaps'. She says that she was influenced by the American and British *beauty guru vloggers* she follows on YouTube. These young people have become micro-celebrities through their video makeup tutorials, beauty and fashion tips and for haul videos that ostensibly display their latest purchases. Unlike them, Sofia neither has five million followers, nor does she feel secure enough to express herself through YouTube videos. However, by sharing her outfit self-portraits and shopping-haul photographs on her wall, and getting that 'ego caress' that comes from the 'likes' and comments she receives, she can't avoid feeling glamorous and that she is a celebrity in her own small world. Commenting on a celebrity she follows, Sofia laughs and says that she tries to mimic Kim Kardashian's daily selfies on Instagram but instead of wearing designer brands like Kim she wears what she can afford (high street retail brands and even garments from her local Chinese clothing store).

Like Sofia, Ana is in her early twenties. She recently dropped out of university, having realized that she was taking the wrong degree, and still hasn't discovered what course she would like to pursue in the future. She is currently working part-time in a clothing retail shop. In the midst of her uncertainty, she is excited by her new discovery: closet shops. She has a lot of clothes for sale and has upgraded her wardrobe with some fabulous second-hand finds, mainly by swapping clothes with other closets shops, as her budget is tight. Her investment in 'Ana's Glam Closet' goes beyond selling and buying: she is passionate about showcasing her ever-expanding wardrobe and is continually snapping her best fashion pieces and different possible outfits with her smartphone in an attempt to portray her personal style. Ana curates a very visual closet. She has created a photographic catalogue that documents her different looks and ensembles. She has even printed some of these self-portraits and placed them on a board, thus making it easier for her to decide what to wear (the photographs on the board show outfits and combinations that worked well for her and so are guaranteed safe choices). She has also cut out images from magazines of celebrities she admires for their fashion sense and of outfits that inspire her. To some degree, Ana's photo board can be seen as an attempt to overcome the anxiety that is central to most women's relationship to fashion and clothes shopping (Clark & Miller 2002).

Ana sees 'Ana's Glam Closet' as a space in which she can improve her self-image and also perform and play with her femininity – a place she can use to share her self-portraits, discuss fashion finds and beauty tips and do things she would never share on her personal Facebook profile for fear of being criticized as superficial or shallow. She enjoys staging, taking (usually in front of the mirror) and posting selfies of her outfits before leaving home. These are always flattering self-portraits with carefully styled looks. She also likes to post photos of her freshly painted nails or of a new hairstyle. When in doubt about her look for a specific occasion she posts selfies of different outfits – sometimes while she's still in a shop fitting room – and asks her 5,000 friends which look she should choose and what accessories might be added. She says that she also gets inspiration from browsing through other closet shops, and perusing their outfit photo albums, and from following reality TV celebrities (onetime even finding herself plangently asking, on her wall, if anyone could help her find a fake fur jacket like that worn by a girl in an episode of *Secret Story*).

Consuming and playing for celebrity

Given that photographs are crucial to the marketing and consumption of fashion and beauty, it is not surprising that there is a continual visual frenzy on the Facebook profiles under discussion. Snapshots there give a glimpse of the richness of fabrics and colours inside the owner's closet or a new room decoration, clothes exhibited for sale, outfit selfies taken for the purpose of selling clothes, outfit selfies inside stores with soon to be pur-chased items, shopping-haul snaps, scans of bank invoices and mail receipts, parcels ready to be dispatched, photographs of newly polished nails and new hair-dos and celebrity photos or poses mimicking celebrity selfies. Every time I opened my research closet account I met with this seemingly endless visual medley of consuming practices, personal styles and playful identities.

The highly visual consumption and self-representation practices in which these young women engage are, to a certain extent, similar to tendencies that can be found on personal fashion blogs (Marwick 2011), where bloggers post pictures of themselves and their outfits on a regular basis, as well as in women's use of the webcam to broadcast their lives, as found in *Webcam-ming* (Senft 2008) and on the YouTube beauty community (Jeffries 2011).

In 'Conspicuous and Authentic', Alice Marwick (2011) examined fashion blogging, which she described as a subculture embraced mainly by young women who are both producers and consumers of fashion. These women 'participate in the global flow of consumption by buying goods (clothes, shoes, accessories, makeup, etc.), writing blog posts, and taking photographs which promote "fashion" as a concept' (ibid., p. 2). While rethinking conspicuous consumption theory in the light of the increasing visibility and mediation of consumer practices on social media, Marwick argues that, although fashion blogging clearly exposes acts of consumption to an audience, thereby increasing one's status, most fashion bloggers she interviewed were not merely passive consumers of commercial culture mes-sages. Moreover, their curation and display of clothing is not necessarily about signalling wealth or free time, but 'creative expression and origin-ality' (ibid., p. 3).

As is the case with the fashion bloggers investigated by Marwick, the self-imaging practices of the young women portrayed in this chapter are dynamic practices of consumption that are also deeply social and aesthetic. Like the celebrities they follow, they display and broadcast consumption through photographs but, even if many of the women behind the closet shops display their acquisitions, these are mostly financially accessible or second-hand clothing and the purpose is less to display wealth than to demonstrate how one can keep up with trends on a tight budget. Still following Marwick (2011), it is also not about signalling free time, although all the women I interviewed confessed to spending a lot of time browsing and shopping on other closet profiles, choosing outfits to display in their self-portraits, photographing looks and fashion apparel or attempting to snap the 'perfect selfie'. Their outfit selfies are staged in a manner that is conventionally most becoming and preferably with a currently trendy look. Unlike the bloggers portrayed by Marwick (2011), they seem to operate within the mainstream of commercial image culture. Marta, a 19-year-old student and owner of 'Marta's Bargain Closet', says

> I really like to see myself in my photos; I look different, in a good way. The other day I bought this stylish and classy jumpsuit in Zara's end of season sale and I really wanted to show it to my friends on my closet account, as it fitted me brilliantly. I think I saw Rhianna with a similar jumpsuit. I even put on a red lipstick and some sassy high heels before snapping a photo with my phone (my mother would kill me if I left the house dressed that way!). Anyway, I added some filters, and voilà, I really looked like a star. I got so many likes and comments! Everyone was asking me where I got that jumpsuit and telling me how amazing that look was!

Their practices within these spaces show that they want to represent themselves by crafting and showcasing their best visual selves, styled in a mainstream manner, with a detailed attention to their clothing, their bedrooms and their best expressions and most flattering angles. Many of the young women I interviewed commented that the act of documenting their outfits and acquisitions was something that celebrities (for instance, Kim Kardashian, empress of selfies and 'outfit selfies') also do.

Laura Jeffries' (2011) research on the American YouTube beauty community focused on the comments exchanged between 'YouTube Gurus' and their subscribers, within their tutorials and fashion/makeup-haul videos. For Jeffries, these female consumers' user-generated videos and the related comments exhibit a lack of resistance to 'the personal image landscape which has been designed by corporations and imposed through popular media' (p. 62). In a highly visually mediated and commodified world, entertainment and consumerism bring forth – from magazines, television, advertisements and social media – a flow of images, and the way many of the owners of the closet shops portray and mirror themselves is, like the YouTube beauty gurus referred to by Jeffries, strongly mediated by this torrent of images. Thus, they end up identifying with mass and celebrity culture and mimicking practices, postures and images derived from it or idealizing the appearances and lifestyles of prominent female celebrities. In this way, their self-imaging practices emulate the prevalent standards of female beauty promoted by popular media discourse.

Contemporary media has already been recognized as having a central role in the 'active process of identity construction and exchange' (Lister *et al.* 2009, p. 76), creating online spaces, like personal blogs or social networking profiles, that function as 'sites of self-presentation or identity construction through a bricolage of interests, images and links', in which there is an 'ongoing identity *performance*' (ibid., p. 268). Through their visual practices, these young women and their closet shops partake in this process of self-expression and identity construction. Their Facebook profiles are unique venues for the articulation of the self – an ever changing and flexible process that develops within an arena where visuality, communication and consumption prevail. As Kellner (1995, p. 233) points out, in mass consumption societies, in which media culture is a dominant force

> identity has been increasingly linked to style, to producing an image, to how one looks. It is as if everyone has to have their own look, style, and image to have their own identity, though, paradoxically, many of the models of style and look come from consumer culture, thus individuality is highly mediated in the consumer society of the present.

Our female closet shop owners present themselves back to themselves and to others by constructing, experimenting, performing, remixing and celebrating their digital self-images. Moreover, by reproducing normative forms of style, beauty and fame, their practices mirror the dominant ideology of the neoliberal system, which in turn translates into an ideology of consumption and desire for celebrity.

Graeme Turner (2010) argues that we live in a 'demotic turn', an epoch in which ordinary people are becoming protagonists in the narratives of global media culture. This is due to a combination of factors, including the ways in which reality TV shows fabricate instantaneous and ephemeral celebrities, the interactivity inherent to Web 2.0 and the entailed emergence of social networks and the general pervasiveness of celebrity in everyday life. One of the earliest examples of the possibility of anyone connected to the internet gaining unprecedented visibility was the phenomenon of 'camgirls'. In *Camgirls: Celebrity & Community in the Age of Social Networks*, Theresa M. Senft (2008) explored the phenomenon of 'camgirls': girls and women who use webcams to live-video-stream their lives. This kind of broadcasting functions as a vehicle for self-expression and community building, but, because of the engagement of 'camgirls' with their assumed audience, also brings forth concepts of microcelebrity and branded identities. For Senft, the interaction dynamics between the camgirls she studied and their audiences brings together the typical features of celebrification processes. She defines microcelebrity as 'a new style of online performance in which people employ webcams, video, audio, blogs and social networking sites to "amp up" their popularity among readers, viewers, and those to whom they are linked online' (ibid., p. 25). More recently, in 'Microcelebrity and the Branded Self', Senft redefined microcelebrity as 'the commitment to deploying and maintaining one's online identity as if it were a branded good, with the expectation that others do the same' (Senft 2013, p. 345). She comments that anyone who has an online profile may be engaging in practices that 'are part and parcel of microcelebrity' (ibid., p. 345).

From a perspective similar to Senft's (2013), Marwick and Boyd (2011) argue that microcelebrity can be understood as a set of performative practices that involve viewing the audience (friends or followers) as a fan base, and managing that audience is crucial for the amplification of popularity. In this process, self-presentation is carefully constructed to be consumed by others (traditional celebrities also operate in this way). Focusing on how celebrity is practised on Twitter by famous people, Marwick and Boyd observe the parallels between their practices and the practices of microcelebrity engaged in by non-famous people who use social media to create audiences and online status for themselves, as described by Senft (2008). They conclude by saying that

> even the famous must learn the techniques used by 'regular people' to gain status and attention online. Twitter demonstrates the transformation of 'celebrity' from a personal quality linked to fame to a set of practices that circulate through modern social media.
>
> (p. 156)

One of these practices and techniques is that of giving the audience the illusion of being backstage, to borrow Goffman's metaphor. Self-presentation in Facebook closet stores is played out in the private space of the bedroom, the closet and the bathroom mirror, where the frontstage and backstage co-exist simultaneously.

Visual and digital technologies have enabled the phenomenon of microcelebrity and have provided new tools and markets for celebrification, which can now be practised by all sorts of people. 'Camgirls', fashion bloggers, vloggers and Facebook closet shop proprietors all make use of the digital tools that they have at their disposal to access a new kind of visibility. In doing so, they present themselves in a way intended to be consumed by their audience and thus acquire a certain status. The networked self-portraiture practised by the women behind Facebook closet shops can also be considered as a tool for the promotion of celebrity, although on a smaller scale. Many of the women interviewed commented that when they are in front of the mirror, thinking about how to stage their portraits, they are already assuming an audience of their friends and followers. They know which self-portraits will attract the most likes and comments. For instance, Cristina, 25 years old, says her friends on her Facebook closet shop, with whom she shares that 'strange familiarity' (Senft 2008), always give her masses of feedback when she posts photographs of herself wearing recent clothing purchases. These, she proudly says, are often affordable clothes from major retailers, acquired second-hand in other closet shops or bought in her local gypsy market. So, every time she does offline or online shopping she will take a selfie and post it on her closet profile. She stands in front of the mirror holding her smartphone, which has a stylish case she bought from a Chinese retailer on Ebay (it has already caused a sensation on her Facebook wall) and complements her outfit. With her hand strategically resting on her hip she snaps her outfit selfie. Cristina knows these are popular photos that will be much commented on.

This research has focused on young women who have appropriated Facebook in order to engage in specific consumption practices, embracing, along the way, its expressive potentialities for self-imaging while playing with poses from fashion and celebrity culture. However, it is important to stress that the owners of these closet shops also use photography for commercial ends. Just as the activities they engage in in these spaces had the initial purpose of commercializing their clothes, so their networked self-portraiture practices are also strategies to gain a reputation and so increase sales.

Self-imaging practices, personal branding and the marketplace

Maria is 26 years old and works part-time as a waitress, to fund her studies for a master's degree. Maria is very active and on her closet shop profile she tries to create a visually appealing environment to increase sales. Every morning she tries to find interesting vintage and fashion photographs online, to post on her wall together with captions wishing a 'good morning' to her friends and followers. She showcases her clothes in a very theatrical and performative way, as if she was on a professional fashion shoot. She also has an album, 'My Closet', in which she posts photographs of her favourite pieces of clothing, varying from outfit selfies to stock photos of retail clothing. She uses photography as a tool to manage her image and her network of friends, and says that being very image-conscious has helped her create a really successful online shop.

> The best way to sell your clothes here is by selling an image of yourself as a fashionista and stylish woman, and having as many people as possible commenting on your photos. Even if they end up not buying the clothes you are showing, others eventually will.

Maria manages her Facebook boutique in an entrepreneurial way, like the YouTube vloggers whose practices have been explored by Burgess and Green (2009). By staging and performing their outfit selfies or their shopping-haul snaps, or even by remixing their personal photos with ones that come from the advertising, fashion or celebrity industries, the women behind closet shops are creating and managing a personal brand for others to consume, and by operating as consumable personas through their visual networked performances, they are recasting themselves as commodities, 'that is, as products capable of drawing attention, and attracting demand and customers' (Bauman & Lyon 2013, p. 32). They are 'simultaneously promoters of commodities and the commodities they promote. They are, at the same time, the merchandise and their marketing agents, the goods and their travelling salespersons' (ibid., p. 31). The dynamics of production are being replaced by a social dynamic played out by agents who are not simply consumers – they also emerge as producers of services and 'collaborators' in the conception of what is intended to be consumed and of how to consume it. In these prosumption processes (see Ritzer & Jurgenson 2010), Web 2.0 functions as a crucial instrument, affecting and reconfiguring the dynamic of the labour market. As Senft observes (2013, p. 348), 'in addition to serving as a marketplace, the internet contributes to a dynamic by which users frame themselves simultaneously as seller, buyer, and commodity'.

By visually curating themselves, their possessions and the goods they sell, female closet shop owners are also participating 'in the global flow of consumption' (Marwick 2011, p. 2). In other words, as authors and actors in these spaces of consumption and self-representation, they are also participating in the global market of commodities and services. They are one more element in the globalization machine, in the one-dimensional space where everything is bought and sold. Nevertheless, their practices are not only inserted into the global market, or merely located within the flow of commodities and services, but are developing in parallel with a far more complex movement: the entry of these young women into a specific global market – the immaterial labour market – a market of services, of skills and training, but also of creativity and self-fashioning. This conception of self-imaging practices of the Facebook closet shops is consistent with the approach taken by Alison Hearn (2008) in her analysis of the strategies of self-representation and promotion of marketable personas via social media. As Hearn (p. 201) points out, the contemporary 'reflexive project of the self' (Giddens 1991, p. 5) can be understood

> as a distinct kind of labour; involving an outer-directed process of highly stylised self-construction, directly tied to the promotional mechanisms of the post-Fordist market.... This 'persona produced for public consumption' reflects a 'self, which continually produces itself for competitive circulation' (Wernick 1991, p. 192) and positions itself as a site for the extraction of value.

All the individuals cited in this chapter reveal a universe in which the emerging practices are processes of microcelebrity and also processes of personal branding, which Hearn defines as 'the self-conscious construction of a meta-narrative and meta-image of self through the use of cultural meanings and images drawn from the narrative and visual codes of the mainstream culture industries' (2008, p. 198). The directed self-presentation strategies of the branded self are played out on social media profiles, in order to obtain cultural capital and material profit. They are also played out with others in mind. A practice of successive and multi-faceted mirrors that denies Sartre's famous assertion, 'L'enfer, c'est les autres', since here it is the other people who one wants to reach. The ground of the branded self is a space of tension in which everyone affirms themselves as commodities, subject to the gaze and the attention of others and provoking the desire of potential users or buyers. It develops within a logic of publicity in which everything that has the ability to capture attention is valued (Hearn 2008). This economy of attention, in which photography plays a prominent role (after all, an image is worth a thousand words), is well illustrated by the practices of many closet shop owners.

As has already been pointed out, the owners of Facebook closet shops use photography to sell or trade clothes and as a tool for social interaction and communication, for self-image management, in a constant effort to showcase themselves with the specific features of commercial image culture. In doing so, they seek to become microcelebrities and to stage scenarios that include and transmit all of these practices. Through their visual and consumption practices within their closets these young women of limited financial means, who are therefore outside the mainstream of mass consumption, acquire a way into this world of fashion, consumerism and visibility. The desire for such access has, in the context of Facebook closet shops, contributed significantly to the dynamics of production of outfit selfies, haul photographs and other self-imaging practices. This set of practices can be seen as being consistent with the logic of late capitalism, in which the immaterial economy is increasingly dominant. This tendency, allied to the economic crisis and to a shrinking labour market, has given a stimulus to self-branding practices (Hearn 2008; Senft 2013). As Senft (ibid., p. 349) argues, the process of labouring the self by facing outwards also makes apparent a contradiction of late capitalism:

at the very same time that job markets appear to be shrinking and exclusionary, cultural notions about notoriety, celebrity, and fame appear to be expanding and inclusive, thanks in part to the rise in relatively recent media formats such as reality television, talent-search shows, and personalized broadcast 'channels' on sites such as YouTube and MySpace

As Senft points out, on the one hand, we have more and more educated young people unemployed and struggling in an economy that does not provide jobs while, on the other, there is increasingly a sentiment in the younger generations that they have at their disposal a growing number of ways of promoting and projecting themselves outwards.

Conclusion

In a society marked by economic crisis and shaped by a neoliberal logic, with a labour market that is becoming ever more difficult to access, in which the younger generation is increasingly highly trained and yet has fewer financial resources, the internet has become an alternative way to find, or to try to find, what traditional means now refuse to provide: access to the markets. The young women who manage the Facebook closet shops profiles, with their curated portrayals and photographic postings, are crafting and adapting themselves to the demands of various markets. Not only are they collaborating in the dynamics of revaluation of the products they buy and sell, they are also defying the economic crisis and developing themselves as consumers, sellers and entrepreneurs, as designers, stylists and photographers, while gazing at and experimenting with their own performative femininity.

The photographic practices described in this chapter could be interpreted as narcissistic, vain or frivolous – the selfie phenomenon has been largely represented in this way by the mass media. However, it is more useful to say that they mirror the modes of living and being, of relating and desiring, of young women who, although on the periphery of the system, play, through their visual and self-branding practices, with the illusion of having that star quality of someone who is at its centre. The parallel markets of Facebook closet shops and networked personal photographs (outfit selfies, haul snapshots, etc.) that are generated and stimulated in that context are an act of courage and resistance in the face of the deepening of an economic crisis. They constitute creative and self-affirming practices: an empowerment that the crisis continually seeks to take from them and society tends to depreciate.

Notes

1 It should be noted that recent scholarly research on selfies has challenged this narcissism narrative. See the new special section of the *International Journal of Communication* on selfies, edited by Theresa Senft and Nancy Baym (Senft & Baym 2015).
2 The names of all informants and their closet Facebook accounts have been changed to protect the privacy of the individuals concerned.

References

Ardévol, E. & Gómez Cruz, E. 2012, 'Private Body, Public Image: Self-Portrait in the Practice of Digital Photography'. *Revista de Dialectologia y Tradiciones Populares*, Vol. 67, no. 1, pp. 181–208.

Bauman, Z. & Lyon, D. 2013, *Liquid Surveillance*. Polity Press: Cambridge.

Burgess, J. & Green, J. 2009, 'The Entrepreneurial Vlogger: Participatory Culture Beyond the Professional–Amateur Divide', in P. Snickars & P. Vonderau (eds) *The YouTube Reader*. National Library of Sweden/Wallflower Press: Stockholm, pp. 89–107.

Chamorro-Premuzic, T. 2014, 'Sharing the (Self) Love: The Rise of the Selfie and Digital Narcissism'. *Guardian*, 13 March 2014, viewed 25 September 2015, www.theguardian.com/media-network/media-network-blog/2014/mar/13/selfie-social-media-love-digital-narcassism.

Clarke, A. & Miller, D. 2002, 'Fashion and Anxiety'. *Fashion Theory*, Vol. 6, no. 2, pp. 191–214.

Fornäs, J., Becker, K., Bjurström, E. & Ganetz, H. 2007, *Consuming Media: Communication, Shopping and Everyday Life*. Berg: Oxford; New York.

Giddens, A. 1991, *Modernity and Self-identity: Self and Society in the Late Modern Age*. Polity Press: Cambridge.

Gram, S. 2013, 'The Young-Girl and the Selfie'. Blog post, 1 March 2013, viewed 25 September 2015, http://text-relations.blogspot.pt/2013/03/the-young-girl-and-selfie.html.

Hand, M. 2012, *Ubiquitous Photography*. Polity Press: Cambridge.

Harrison, B. 2002, 'Photographic Visions and Narrative Inquiry'. *Narrative Inquiry*, Vol. 12, no. 1, pp. 87–111.

Hearn, A. 2008, '"Meat, Mask, Burden": Probing the Contours of the Branded "Self"'. *Journal of Consumer Culture*, Vol. 8, no. 2, pp. 197–217.

Jeffries, L. 2011, 'The Revolution Will Be Soooo Cute: YouTube "Hauls" and the Voice of Young Female Consumers'. *Studies in Popular Culture*, Vol. 33, no. 2, pp. 59–75.

Kellner, D. 1995, *Media Culture: Culture Studies, Identity and Politics between the Modern and the Postmodern*. Routledge: London.

Lister, M., Dovey, J., Giddings, S., Grant, I. & Kelly, K. 2009, *New Media: A Critical Introduction*. Routledge: New York.

Marwick, A. 2011, 'Conspicuous and Authentic: Fashion Blogs, Style and Consumption'. Paper presented at the annual meeting of the International Communication Association, Boston, MA.

Marwick, A. & Boyd, D. 2011, 'To See and Be Seen: Celebrity Practice on Twitter'. *Convergence: The International Journal of Research into New Media Technologies*, Vol. 17, no. 2, pp. 139–158.

Miller, D. 2011, *Tales from Facebook*. Polity Press: Cambridge.

Petersen, S. 2008, *Common Banality: The Affective Character of Photo Sharing, Everyday Life and Produsage Cultures*. PhD Dissertation, Department of Innovative Communication, University of Copenhagen.

Ritzer, G. & Jurgenson, N. 2010, 'Production, Consumption, Prosumption: The Nature of Capitalism in the Age of the Digital "Prosumer"'. *Journal of Consumer Culture*, Vol. 10, no. 1, pp. 13–36.

Rose, G. 2007, *Visual Methodologies: An Introduction to the Interpretation of Visual Materials*. Sage: London.

Rubinstein, D. & Sluis, K. 2008, 'A Life More Photographic: Mapping the Networked Image'. *Photographies*, Vol. 1, no. 1, pp. 9–28.

Saltz, J. 2014, 'Art at Arm's Length: A History of the Selfie'. *Vulture*, viewed 20 November 2015, www.vulture.com/2014/01/history-of-the-selfie.html.

Senft, T. M. 2013, 'Microcelebrity and the Branded Self', in J. Hartley, J. Burgess & A. Bruns (eds) *A Companion to New Media Dynamics*. Wiley-Blackwell: Malden, MA, pp. 346–354.

Senft, T. M. 2008, *Camgirls: Celebrity & Community in the Age of Social Networks*. Peter Lang: New York.

Senft, T. M. & Baym, N. K. 2015, 'What Does the Selfie Say? Investigating a Global Phenomenon'. *International Journal of Communication*, Vol. 9, pp. 1588–1606.

Schroeder, J. 2002, *Visual Consumption*. Routledge: London; New York.

Turner, G. 2010, *Ordinary People and the Media: The Demotic Turn*. Sage: London.

Van Dijck, J. 2008, 'Digital Photography: Communication, Identity, Memory'. *Visual Communication*, Vol. 7, no. 1, pp. 57–76.

3 Amplification and heterogeneity
Seniors and digital photographic practices

Maria Schreiber

Introduction

Personal photography has always had and still has various social functions, such as social bonding, communication, demonstration of identity and the preservation and retention of memories (Sarvas & Froehlich 2011; Walser & Neumann-Braun 2013). It also serves the perpetual desire to represent, fix and transmit that which is seen in time and space (Lehmuskallio 2012, p. 74). However, the *means* by which bonding, representing and transmitting are practised are changing.

This chapter will take a closer look at the elderly and their ways of practising digital photography in their everyday lives. While a major part of the small body of research on digital (photographic) practices focuses on younger people and is often related to their use of social media platforms (Neumann-Braun & Autenrieth 2011; Van House 2011), older age groups, who grew up with analogue media, are under-researched. However, these groups could shed light on the complex entanglements of changes and continuities regarding the technological development of personal photography, as innovations have taken place throughout their lifetime.

Research on the digitization of personal photography indicates shifts from family to individual use, from memory tools to communication devices and from sharing (memory) objects to sharing experiences (Van Dijck 2008). Van Dijck states that 'the value of individual pictures decreases while the general significance of visual communication increases' (p. 62), which goes hand in hand with a 'widening range of photographable situations' (Schwarz 2010, p. 166). On the other hand, Pickering (2013, p. 207) notices a 'marked tendency to extrapolate only from the newer ways in which photo-images are used and deployed'. Researchers warn against 'stressing change, and in particular arguing that it makes for a major rupture with any antecedents' because possible continuities could be overlooked in terms of 'how the change itself may entail such continuities' (Keightley & Pickering 2014, p. 577; see also Van House 2011, p. 132). Digital photography clearly affords new possibilities (Larsen & Sandbye 2014, p. xxiii), but how those affordances are used, by whom and in which contexts and how different ways of engaging with the same affordance might evolve remains to be empirically investigated. Consequently, this research attends to the question of how digital photography and its affordances are meaningful to the practices of seniors, who were first introduced to digital media later in their lives.

The chapter draws on theoretical approaches that link material and visual practices and is based on a triangulation of observations of a computer training course, interviews with two Viennese couples who participated in the training course and a picture analysis of pictures that were provided by the couples. The aim was to explore, empirically, how the transition from analogue to digital might become relevant and to understand continuities and changes in their everyday photographic practices.

Based on the empirical results, two major findings can be shown: the photographic practices of seniors are amplified by digitization and are (or have probably always been) heterogeneous. I will show that seniors are often perceived by others as a homogeneous group of strangers to the digital world. However, when taking a closer look at their actual practices, it becomes clear that their experiences and actions with digital photography are diverse and often structured by implicit patterns that flow from analogue to digital. Digital technologies are not necessarily strange to them but, rather, seem to amplify and expand previously existing patterns to new dimensions.

Theoretical and methodological frame

Conceptualizing photography as practice

Consistent with a broader 'practice turn' in sociology (Reckwitz 2002) and media and communication research (Couldry 2004; Bräuchler & Postill 2010), conceptualizing photography as practice is necessary to understand the complex entanglements of humans, photographic technologies and visualities (Lehmuskallio & Gómez Cruz, in this volume). 'Practices' are defined as 'embodied, materially mediated arrays of human activity centrally organized around shared practical understanding' (Schatzki 2001, p. 2). This definition can help to unfold the relevant dimensions when researching photography: that is to say, photographic practices are complex in the sense that arrays of hardware and software, the *material mediation*, co-constitute them. Hence, both humans and artefacts have to be understood in their entangled, hybrid actions and agencies (Maynard 1997). A useful concept that sheds light on these entanglements is 'affordances',[1] which become relevant as a 'set of potential uses that facilitate, limit, and structure communication and action through these media. Affordances are materially founded in media as technological artifacts, are institutionally circumscribed, and are perceptually embodied by users and audiences' (Hjarvard & Petersen 2013, p. 5). The relevance of the *embodied human activity* points to the materiality and agency of the human body in any practice and emphasizes how incorporated experiences with cameras and computer technologies (e.g. how to zoom, click and scroll) are crucial to how practices are structured in varying ways. This research is, thus, aimed at *shared practical understanding* – the implicit, tacit layer of knowledge (Mannheim 1980) that is rooted in cultural and social experience and essential for *how* practices are structured. This is what Bourdieu (1987) called the *habitus*. These ideas call for a reconstructive methodological approach, such as the documentary method (Bohnsack 2008; Weller & da Silva 2011), which aims at the reconstruction of implicit knowledge that structures both practices and pictures. In reconstructing and interpreting the doings, sayings and 'showings' of a practice, the researcher seeks to explicate the implicit meanings, patterns and frames of orientation, reconstructing the meaning of an action in the social context of the participants. A reconstructive analysis of personal photography therefore has to change the perspective from questioning the 'what' to questioning the 'how', asking how digital photography becomes relevant within the lifeworld of the participants and how it is adopted, negotiated and routinized in relation to other practices.

A practice-oriented approach emphasizes the importance of implicit knowledge, embodiment and the relevance of artefacts in any human action. How the specificity of researching pictorial practices and visual artefacts can be respected theoretically and methodologically will now be briefly elaborated.

Conceptualizing photography as pictorial practice

Photographic practices are pictorial practices, and the visuality and materiality of the artefacts that are crucial within these practices have to be taken into account. Focusing on pictorial practices means drawing 'attention to the co-constitution of humans' subjectivities and the visual objects their practices create' (Rose & Tolia-Kelly 2012, p. 3) and asking how and what is made visible, with which media, in which context (Schade & Wenk 2011, p. 9). Visual and material dimensions are experienced simultaneously and both can become relevant for analysis, but they are rarely combined or related to each other in most research on photography. This chapter will, therefore, analyse the *relation and co-constitution* of both dimensions by analysing field notes, interview data and photos that were provided by the participants. For example, through a generic picture of a peach-coloured rose, we can gain access to the specific style and aesthetics that appeal to one of the participants; through the interview we understand how style, format and glossiness of the picture are intertwined with the HD-flatscreen on which it is meant to be shown.[2]

So far, the material dimension of photography has usually been analysed ethnographically, focusing on practices with the 'host' media, such as the photo album, Instagram, newspapers, etc. (Edwards 2009; Rose 2010).

How those practices and pictures are embedded in and co-constituted by specific contexts[3] also becomes relevant in this perspective. Whereas ethnographic approaches are prevalent in the Anglo-American research context on digital photography (Pink 2011; Van Dijck 2008; Van House 2011), German visual sociology stems from *Bildwissenschaft* and a tradition of art history and philosophy, which emphasizes the internal visual structure of images as meaningful starting points for empirical analysis. This approach, the analysis and interpretation of image 'content', is often criticized for its alleged arbitrariness and subjectivity, claiming that a diffuse, almost magical power seems to be ascribed to images (Wolff 2012), giving them their own agency (Stocchetti 2011). In fact, most German visual sociological approaches to the interpretation of images (Bohnsack 2008; Breckner 2010; Przyborski & Slunecko 2011; Przyborski & Wohlrab-Sahr 2013; Raab 2008) aim at a reconstruction of the social-visual construction of images. 'The composition of visual signs in an image is a result of social practices of image production and interpretation. The use of images ... *and* the ways realities are represented in an image are thus inherently social' (Burri 2012, p. 50). These approaches aim to reconstruct habitual patterns that are disclosed through/by the pictures in which

> the most trivial photograph expresses, apart from the explicit intentions of the photographer, the system of schemes of perception, thought and appreciation common to a whole group.... Adequately understanding a photograph ... means not only recovering the meanings which it *proclaims*, that is, to a certain extent, the explicit intentions of the photographer; it also means deciphering the surplus of meaning which it *betrays* by being part of the symbolism of an age, a class or an artistic group.
>
> (Bourdieu 1990, p. 6ff.)

This habitual, tacit (visual) knowledge structures our ways of producing and seeing images (Goffmann 1987; Warburg 1993). Visual conventions and habits of seeing are co-constituted by technical and material predispositions and specific visual practices and cultures, and they are sociohistorically and geographically contingent (Baxandall 1972). In short, they are conventions that evolve and change within specific historical and social contexts.[4] The importance of the interaction between internal and external images in becoming a subject in a specific sociohistorical situation is also emphasized in Belting's (2001) anthropological understanding of pictorial practice,[5] which grasps the subject formed through this interaction as collectively anchored and sociodemographically influenced. The aim of this research is to foreground a specific sociocultural-historical condition as a central theme and it puts forward the question of how seniors connect to digital photography in current circumstances,[6] – that is, how do they make photos visible, and what kind of photos?

Uncharted territory? Seniors and digital media

This study is interested in those who belong to a generation that did not grow up with digital media, vaguely defined as '60 and older'. 'Generations' are always constituted by distinction and conjunction at the same time (Mannheim 1990), making the label 'generation' a complex mixture of how others perceive a generation and how a generation perceives itself through collective experiences. Generations are grounded in the biological fact that people of different ages grow up at different historical points in time. Different media (technologies) are at hand while they grow up, but how this affects their everyday digital media practices remains to be empirically investigated. Intra- and inter-generational similarities and differences regarding habitual media practices can be reconstructed empirically and might be grounded in a 'naturalization' of media practice during youth, which could be a predisposition for the adoption of new media technologies throughout a lifetime (Schäffer 2003, 2006).

> Early impressions tend to coalesce into a natural view of the world. All later experiences then tend to receive their meaning from this original set, whether they appear as that set's verification and fulfilment or as its negation and antithesis.
>
> (Mannheim 1990, p. 373)

How this assumption holds true for the adoption of digital (photographic) media will be explored in this chapter. In any case, the notion of 'digital natives' as a tech-savvy generational collective (Prensky 2001) and 'immigrants' as the diametrical opposite has remained contested and criticized. To understand ICT as strongly shaping one generation and leaving everyone else behind is a technologically deterministic oversimplification that ignores the variety of ways in which media are used and the social contexts, processes and practices in which media use is embedded (Buckingham & Willet 2006; Hartmann 2005).[7] Additionally, what we actually know about so-called 'digital immigrants' is very little. Generation and age as relevant empirical determinants regarding digital media practices have primarily been included in quantitative studies on long-term changes in everyday media use (ARD/ZDF 2013; OECD 2013). There is a lack of differentiation in many statistics when it comes to older age groups, or they are reported 'as though it was a residual'[8] (Friemel 2016, p. 2). This becomes particularly tenuous as old age seems to be analysed from a mainly deficit-oriented perspective.[9] There is a general lack of qualitative studies and a particular lack of studies regarding the adoption of digital and networked media in old age (Schorb 2009, p. 327). At the same time, the 60+ population is growing larger and larger. Existing findings on the elderly are mainly concentrated on practices related to TV and radio, showing that retirement is often a break/disruption within media biographies and that there are a variety of ways in which media are integrated in everyday lives, dependent also on education, milieu, media biography, preferences, etc. (Schorb 2009; Doh 2011). As indicated by the few empirical findings that go into more depth, the heterogeneity of the lifeworlds of the elderly has to be taken into account. Lifecycle-specific experiences and developmental phases come into play when researching media practices of people of different ages, and factors, such as milieu and education, might also be decisive for how media practices are structured and embedded in their everyday lives.

Empirical example: seniors and digital photography

Access to the 60+ age group was gained through a photo editing training course that is specifically designed for seniors. The main aim of the course as stated in the description is to explain how to transfer pictures to a computer and how to organize, store and edit them. There is one trainer and nine participants, each working on a desktop computer.[10] I observed the course and asked the participants if they would be willing to be interviewed; two couples volunteered. They were interviewed in their homes and asked to provide pictures. The triangulation of observation, interview and picture analysis reflects the practical and pictorial dimensions of analysis that seem to be crucial for understanding photographic practices that have been outlined above. Data collection and interpretation are conducted within the framework of reconstructive social research (Bohnsack 2008; Przyborski & Wohlrab-Sahr 2013). In a brief ethnographic account, the structure and implicit guiding principles of the training course will be reconstructed and summarized. In a second step, interviews and pictures, textual and visual accounts of two couples who participated will be introduced as key empirical material, indicating findings on how digital photographic practices of this age group are heterogeneous and amplified by digitization.

Doing homogeneity: the photo editing training course for seniors

The heterogeneity of the participating seniors became obvious during the training course. The nine seniors differed very much regarding their preexisting knowledge and familiarity with hardware and software, with the tempo of the training being too slow for some and too fast for others. It became clear how embodied habitual knowledge is crucial for operating a computer when about half of the participants had problems with moving and double-clicking the mouse because they were used to the touchpads of their laptops at home. Downloading, storing and sharing photos are generally done with a computer that is located in their homes.[11]

Seniors sitting in front of the computer are perceived as extraordinary by others. This was clearly demonstrated by two incidents during the course. A professional photographer was searching for the motif of 'old woman in front of computer screen' and asked if she could take pictures in the course, but she was denied access. Later on in the course, a group of visitors to the training centre sneak-peeked into the room, creating a strange zoo-like situation for all those who sat inside.

A course setting with one trainer guiding nine participants through exercises does not allow for individual supervision. The training assumed analogue photographic practices and familiar artefacts, such as albums or shelves, as common frames of understanding for the group. The trainer explained practices of digital photo editing by referring, metaphorically, to analogue practices and spaces: folders on the desktop were described as equivalent to photo boxes on shelves and paper labels on those boxes became folder names. To show how pictures can be transferred into a folder, the trainer performed the transfer of photos in front of the wall where the desktop is shown with a projector. He 'grabbed' the projected pictures and 'shoved' them into a folder; with this little performance, he simultaneously imitated the movement of photo prints into a physical box and the movement of the mouse on the computer screen. He translated the practice from analogue to digital, emphasizing the hybridity of the digital software, which imitates analogue structures like folders and windows. The trainer played the role of a medium or intermediary between an analogue and digital world, which is further authenticated by his generational belonging as 40-something, hovering in between those that are generally perceived as digital natives and immigrants. The training is clearly guided by the presumption that translation from analogue to digital is necessary. The idea of the computer as a blackbox is not deconstructed, but reinforced through comments by the trainer about an anonymous mysterious 'they' who are responsible for the software being the way it is.

The observation of the training course showed that seniors were perceived and constituted as a homogeneous group by others and as needing translation help through the didactic structure of the course. The findings raise questions of how someone might be defined as digitally competent as well as who has the position and power to define this attribution, since it became clear that the seniors differed a lot regarding their familiarity with hardware and software and also regarding their expectations and aims. This became even more obvious when my next step led me into the homes and lives of two couples who participated in the course.

Anni and Bertl: snapping away and tinkering around

The first couple I interviewed were Anni (65) and Bertl (60+),[12] ex-partners who participated in the course together. They separated and re-married other spouses but are still friends and have a daughter together. Personal photography is a 'hobby' for both of them. They not only share a common interest in it, but it is also an important element of their interaction with each other, since Bertl mainly helped Anni in downloading and storing her pictures. He worked as a programmer and describes himself as very interested in 'tweaking and turning screws, no matter if these are software screws or other screws'.[13] Waiting to try out new technological stuff makes him 'feel itchy'. The relevance of this pattern becomes very clear in his description of his photographic practice, referring to how he uses different kinds of apertures and lenses and how he converts 'raw data' into other formats. He is proud of these skills and willing to share his knowledge. Amused, he recalls how the trainer in the course had problems trying to show how to correct red-eye, which was, in Bertl's view, caused by the poor quality of the free pre-installed software and the bad resolution of the picture the trainer used. He positioned himself as a technical expert and tinkerer who is not really interested in the particular motifs, in contemplating/gazing at his pictures or showing them to others. Once the tweaking and turning generated a picture that met his requirements, which means looking good in regard to focus, resolution and format on his TV screen, he was happy with the picture. The primary surface of presentation is his large digital TV screen, an interface that overtook the tube TV in terms of functionalities but might share the physical spot once occupied by the tube TV in the living room. Bertl doesn't like to develop photos on paper anymore as he is not happy with the poor quality of the results, which do not live up to his expectations or prearrangements. Having full control over post-processing is important to him. Only rarely does he print his grandchildren's photos to give them away. He does this at a trusted local shop, where Anni is also a regular.

Figure 3.1 A picture provided by Bertl that was processed/finished to 'look good on the TV screen'.

The picture is produced with the logic of the screen in mind regarding style, format and resolution. It remains digital but moves from the smaller screens of camera and computer to the bigger screen of the TV. The picture that Bertl provided shows a screen-oriented aesthetics, a rather generic motif: a close-up of a peach-coloured rose against a dark background. High resolution macro-shots of plants are commonly used as test screens for HD screens and Bertl's rose belongs to such an iconographic realm.[14] This normative, maybe even kitschy, style shows that Bertl's image of beauty is a rather generic one, which is framed by and framed for the material mediation of a digital HD flatscreen. His screen is not just any kind of flatscreen: 'everything is Sony, no question about that'. Sony, as a brand, points to high-end mass market products, but they are still mass market products and not products a professional would use. Looking at the structure of his practice, Bertl can be labelled as an ambitious amateur,[15] who reproduces mass-market aesthetics. Consuming and owning the appropriate equipment is an important part of being an amateur.

Anni's interest in photography is twofold. On the one hand, it is an artsy hobby. She loves taking pictures while strolling around and just snapping away. She mainly showed me photos of flowers, buildings, animals and landscapes. These pictures are not really intended to be shown, and even she is not very much interested in looking at them after she takes them and downloads them on to her laptop. On the other hand, pictures of her grandchildren have a totally different status.[16] She could not download and further process these digital pictures for quite some time. It was not until her friends demanded to see how her grandchildren were growing up that she felt the need to learn how to manage and transfer her digital photos. Now, she likes looking at how the grandchildren looked at different points in time and carries prints in a flip-through photo album with her.

Anni also keeps a box with analogue photos, which holds old pictures, mainly collected by her mother. Anni added her own pictures of family members to the box, which were mainly taken by Bertl. Anni is not too interested in order, continuity or systematization, and this is evident from the photos thrown together in a box to the non-existent file structure on her laptop. Still, she claims that she likes the haptic, material feeling of digging around in the box for memories and she avoids browsing photos on the laptop, the digital digging, which for her is an 'endless hassle with the mouse'. Both Anni and Bertl mention that they feel like they should spend time on dull duties, such as digitizing diapositives or systematizing file structures, now that they are retired and have time, but they avoid it. In this practice, photos are visual documents of the growing offspring, through which recognition from others – social capital – might be gained.

Being able to take photos for the sake of taking photos is amplified through digital photography, as it is easier to take more pictures, to 'snap away', like Anni does. She is not very interested in organizing, developing and sharing her pictures, except for the ones that track her grandchildren growing up. The course had differing implications for the ex-couple: while Bertl was reassured in his expert role, Anni wanted to learn how to transfer pictures from the camera and found it quite helpful, although these lessons would not have been sustainable without further, personalized support on her own laptop from Bertl. Neither share pictures online; they disapprove of the semi-publicness that is involved and Bertl clearly frames the practice of sharing experiences online as something typical for a different generation or age group: 'I am not 12 or 14 that I have to say my boyfriend kissed me or wanted to kiss me.'

Regina and Sepp: telling stories and rising standards

The second couple I interviewed, Regina (70) and Sepp (73), are married and have one son. They joined forces as a production team. Regina documents guided cultural trips, which she takes with two female friends; her husband, who does not like to travel, stays at home but is responsible for the digital post-production. Together, they decide what is left in the end-product, which is basically a mixture of movie and slideshows that are meant to be shown on the TV screen. They compose the dramaturgy, and the overall aim is that the product 'is not longer than "Universum"', which is a popular Austrian primetime format of 45-minute-long nature documentaries. Video clips, photos, text and voice-overs are included; digital photos are mainly used to emphasize specific locations or details, or when the video composition is not sufficient (for example a church window). The digital photo camera is also used as a mnemonic device, storing names of sights and streets for later use. While Sepp also cuts VHS videos by copying them from the camera to the tape with stop/play, he is pleased with the comfort and convenience of being able to move around clips with the editing software he uses.

What is clearly amplified by technological innovations is the professionalization and expansion of possibilities in their joint movie production or, as Sepp puts it, 'since she knows what I can do, her standards keep rising'. This includes among many other things, the audio track and all related practices: choosing music (he even bought CDs with ambient music); adding sounds; assembling the clips; recording voiceovers; adding special effects, such as a ringing clock to emphasize how early they had to get up to catch the plane. Regina's part in the post-production is that of a research and text editor. Using the travel agency's programme, guide books and internet research, she researches facts about the destinations to which she travelled. This practice also flows smoothly from analogue to digital. She now types her scripts in MS Word and not with a pen and paper. She collects bookmarks in the browser and leaflets in a folder, assembling the material in ring binders, which are labelled and neatly organized. She writes and times her voiceovers for the video and the couple records them together. They recently bought a microphone for this.

Sepp likes to tweak and turn screws, like Bertl, but he seems to be more interested in generating narrative continuity and assembling multi-medial stories than in technical perfection. One of the pictures he provided shows three women standing behind and next to a red car. It is obviously not a picture of their car but a random picture of their car's model from the internet, which he found and used as a building block for the missing picture of the part of the journey when he drove the ladies to the airport: 'this photo, for example, is fake. It does not exist. This is our car. I didn't have a photo anywhere [of the situation when he drove them to the airport], so I cut … the ladies out and put them in.' As he felt this situation was important to the narration of the journey, he (re)created it. He did the same with another picture (see Figure 3.2).

As the woman on the left with the red jacket was usually taking photos during the trips, she was never in the pictures herself. Sepp felt all three of them should be in this one, and he not only put her in the photo, he put

Figure 3.2 Picture provided by Sepp and Regina (faces pixelated).

her in a position that makes sense compositionally – he built a group scene, with his wife on top of the stairs. The group composition is complete, as the cut-out-and-paste figure on the left fills up an otherwise empty spot. All three women are turned towards the photographer, posing for the photo in front of a typical regional and cultural vehicle, showing us that they are travelling and 'conquering' foreign territories. Touristic photography, in particular, as shown in this picture, is 'intricately bound up with self-presentation and monitoring bodies' and shows 'desired togetherness' (Larsen 2005, p. 424), in this case, a togetherness that is achieved in the post-production.

Like Anni, Regina enjoys not having to worry about expensive film material. For Anni, 'snapping away' is in itself meaningful, but it seems to be crucial for Regina to have a broader variety of motifs and visual snippets with which the couple can work. She said,

> I know, now you can cut everything which is awesome. In former times we had movies where nothing has been taken away, where everything is on the film like I recorded it, because it was not possible in any other way, because there was no computer.

Throughout the movie production, the couple anticipates the future audience, which is mostly a group of interested friends. They make sure the product is self-explanatory, not too long, educating and fun. This strong orientation towards an audience points to a strong use of photography for doing and demonstrating a well-educated, bourgeois identity and a desire for cultural capital.

Their photographing and filming practices are amplified, and possibilities are expanded through digital technologies. Creating and framing togetherness as a group of friends and constructing an educative story are the main patterns that structure their photographic practice. Their common practice transcends the transformation from analogue to digital formats, in a sense that it is continuously framed by her urge to share with him what she has seen and by their creative co-production of movies. It was Sepp's idea that Regina start filming and taking pictures while she was travelling and she has now been doing it for 20 years. It is, therefore, a connecting hobby that resolves potential conflict regarding their diverging ideas about travelling.

Apart from their joint movie production, which is their main photographic practice, Regina and Sepp use their photo cameras for tracking change. They took a lot of pictures when their son was growing up and recently documented the renovation of their holiday home.

In analogue times they took diapositives, which they sometimes still look at with friends. They frame this practice as a collective amusement of looking at how people looked at a younger age and laughing about it as a group, which is in line with their other practices, that are clearly orientated towards building togetherness and showcasing and showing off in front of an audience. In contrast to the amusing ancient diapositives there are analogue pictures, which lost their worth soon after they were taken ('nobody would look at those now') or which are too generic to have long-lasting relevance ('Christmas, it's the same every year; there is a tree and everyone is standing around the tree'). Anni and Bertl made the same point.

Like Bertl, the couple was reassured of their expertise through the course. Asked about photographing with a phone, they said they preferred to stick with their well-rehearsed practice. They do not use cellphones with a camera function for photographing due to the poor resolution, but they took pictures of their contacts and added them to the address book because they said, 'when somebody is calling, the picture is easier to recognize than the name when you don't wear your glasses'. Here, the phone photograph is able to compensate their debilities of sight.

Conclusions

The interviews, as a second part of the empirical study, foreground the accounts of the participants through which their habitual photographic practices were reconstructed.

Diversity of modes of personal photography

The empirical data show strong variations regarding how photography becomes meaningful and how photographic practices are structured. Both case studies clearly show that there is not one, but many modes of personal photography, each related to a different set of meanings, themes, motifs and audiences. Pictures of (grand)children, for example, are strongly framed by the urge to keep track of their development and how they are growing up. Those pictures are very likely to be proudly shared with others. A sharing orientation is also prevalent when it comes to old diapositives, which serve as storage and triggers for long-term memories. These modes are strongly tied to photographs of those who are close to the participants. However, both couples have other major modes of photography. Regina and Sepp process her holiday pictures in a very specific way; there is a story to be told and information and knowledge about the destination that has to be mediatized. Their joint production is also a mode of reassuring them of their social status and their identity as a couple. The particular picture or snippet and its referentiality to reality is important and has to fit the story; if it does not, it will be made to fit. For Anni and Bertl, however, the playfulness of photographing and editing is practical: Bertl exploits technical possibilities and Anni enjoys snapping away without economic concerns. To them, the specific imagery of those pictures is irrelevant.

To conclude, personal photographic practices might be about communication, identity and memory (Van Dijck 2008; Sarvas & Froehlich 2011;

Keightley & Pickering 2014), yet we should further investigate how they might have various modes and specific functions that are entangled with particular habits and habitus, which are, for example, about storytelling for Regina and Sepp and about playfulness for Anni and Bertl.

Analogue and digital: amplification within continuities

In both case studies, the digitization of the technologies at hand and the pictures themselves amplify orientations that existed previously, but the range of technical and dramaturgical possibilities was expanded, economic limits were dissolved, and creation and manipulation were made easier and more convenient. All these changes alter concrete actions, but they do not revolutionize the practice. The implicit orientation, the practical understanding and patterns of practices remain constant. Digital technologies seem to add a new dimension to what has been done before, amplifying and reinforcing practices and challenging seniors to be more professional or more playful. The malleability of digital pictures (Lehmuskallio, in this volume) becomes relevant in Bertl's case as a form of technical gimmickry, while for Sepp, the possibility of creating a missing piece of a story is the prevalent orientation. Neither women are interested in these aspects. While this research uncovered diversity among the photographic practices of seniors, a possible gender imbalance in regard to technical playfulness as male domain is suggested by the material and should be explored in further research. The TV screen, a medium that accompanied this generation through their lives, remains important as an output device for digital photos. The screen has a defined space within the home and offers the possibility to show and present the product to a group of people, which is particularly important for Sepp and Regina and their educational or entertaining gatherings.

How can the outlined findings contribute to a better overall understanding of seniors and digital media? The habitual photographic practices of seniors seem to be as diverse and complex as all media practices. Both couples showed a strong affinity to photography, which manifests in varying ways. Some modes of photography are variably significant throughout the life cycle and may be related to having (grand)children, being able to travel or renovating a holiday home. Other practices seem to remain continuously important, such as snapping away aimlessly. 'Generation' does not seem to be a crucial conjunctive factor, and it is very likely that similar modes of photography could also be found in the photographic practices of people of different ages. Nevertheless, 'generation' becomes a distinctive factor in the participant's perception of intergenerational differences regarding familiarity with digital technologies. Except for Bertl, the participants present themselves as lacking fluency in some regards and they feel less competent compared to younger people (especially Regina and Sepp) but also to other people of their own age

(Anni). The findings suggest that the concept of digital natives and immigrants is not visible in the concrete doings, sayings and showings but might be a discursively produced common-sense construction that is grounded in a diffuse idea of competence and only becomes relevant by comparison to others. This should be further empirically challenged and analysed.

What also became clear is that the adoption of digital photography has amplified and expanded existing practices and may, thus, serve as emancipatory action for the elderly. Methodologically, a reconstructive approach proved to be helpful in understanding 'modification within continuity' (Keightley & Pickering 2014, p. 582) in the photographic practices of seniors and in carefully considering the heterogeneity of lifeworlds in which these practices are embedded.

Notes

1 This is elaborated in more detail, in terms of cameras and photography, by Lehmuskallio (2012, p. 61).
2 See the section on Anni and Bertl, below, for further elaboration of this example.
3 For example, a Flickr group (Gómez-Cruz & Ardèvol 2013), family photography (Durrant *et al.* 2009; Rose 2010) or locative practices (Hjorth & Pink 2013; Villi & Stocchetti 2010).
4 Nevertheless, some visual conventions and ways of seeing are more persistent than others (Goffman 1987) based on power relations (Schade & Wenk 2011) and visual orders (Silverman 1996).
5 As elaborated in regard to digital photographic practices by Lehmuskallio (2012, p. 30ff.).
6 Fieldwork in Vienna took place in early 2014.
7 While a lot of research takes the concept of digital natives and immigrants for granted, critics warn against 'the wider political and ideological agendas underlying the persistence of the digital native discourse in society' (Selwyn 2009, p. 375) or frame it as 'necessary illusion' (Sheely 2008, p. 914) that is needed to introduce new cultures of learning.
8 In a recent survey, Friemel (2016, p. 3) finds that 'the digital divide has grown old'. The major gap of usage lies between those who are 70+ and the rest of the population; every additional year of age decreases the likelihood of internet use, while higher education and income increase it (ibid., p. 11).
9 This has been pointed out by Schäffer (2006, p. 17).
10 It is, of course, a specific group of seniors who participate in such a course. Most of them at least have a basic interest in learning about new technologies or they feel they *should* be interested. The course is organized and sponsored by an Austrian network provider. Participation is free, but the waiting list is quite long.
11 Only one participant asked how to download photos to her computer from her smartphone. It remains to be investigated how the diffusion of smartphones (and the variety of affordances in one device) within older generations might alter digital photographic practices.
12 '60+' was all the information about his age he was willing to give.
13 All quotes from the interviews have been translated from German by the author.

14 A Google search for 'rose black background' generates very similar pictures.
15 Compare to Bourdieu (1990, p. 46ff.).
16 See also Keightley and Pickering (2014, p. 581).

References

ARD/ZDF. 2013, 'ARD/ZDF Onlinestudie 2013', viewed 10 June 2015, www.ard-zdf-onlinestudie.de.

Baxandall, M. 1972, *Painting and Experience in Fifteenth Century Italy: A Primer in the Social History of Pictorial Style*. Clarendon Press: Oxford.

Belting, H. 2001, *Bildanthropologie: Entwürfe für eine Bildwissenschaft*. Fink: München.

Bohnsack, R. 2008, 'The Interpretation of Pictures and the Documentary Method'. *Forum: Qualitative Social Research*, Vol. 9, no. 3, Art. 26, viewed 10 January 2015, http://nbn-resolving.de/urn:nbn:de:0114-fqs0803267.

Bourdieu, P. 1990, *Photography: A Middle-Brow Art*. Polity Press: Cambridge.

Bourdieu, P. 1987, *Die Feinen Unterschiede*. Suhrkamp: Frankfurt am Main.

Bräuchler, B. & Postill, J. (eds) 2010, *Theorising Media and Practice*. Berghahn: New York.

Breckner, R. 2010, *Sozialtheorie des Bildes: Zur Interpretativen Analyse von Bildern und Fotografien*. Transcript: Bielefeld.

Buckingham, D. & Willet, R. 2006, *Digital Generations: Children, Young People and New Media*. Lawrence Erlbaum Associates: Mahwah, NJ.

Burri, R. V. 2012, 'Visual Rationalities: Towards a Sociology of Images'. *Current Sociology*, Vol. 60, no. 1, pp. 45–60.

Couldry, N. 2004, 'Theorising Media as Practice'. *Social Semiotics*, Vol. 14, no. 2, pp. 115–132.

Doh, M. 2011, *Heterogenität der Mediennutzung im Alter: Theoretische Konzepte und Empirische Befunde*. Kopaed: München.

Durrant, A., Frohlich, D., Sellen, A. & Lyons, E. 2009, 'Home Curation versus Teenage Photography: Photo Displays in the Family Home'. *International Journal of Human–Computer Studies*, Vol. 67, no. 12, pp. 1005–1023.

Edwards, E. 2009, 'Thinking Photography beyond the Visual?', in J. J. Long, A. Noble & E. Welch (eds) *Photography: Theoretical Snapshots*. Routledge: London, pp. 31–48.

Friemel, T. 2016, 'The Digital Divide Has Grown Old: Determinants of a Digital Divide among Seniors'. *New Media Society*, Vol. 18, no. 2, pp. 313–331.

Goffmann, E. 1987, *Gender Advertisements*. Harper Torchbooks: New York.

Gómez-Cruz, E. & Ardèvol, E. 2013, 'Some Ethnographic Notes on a Flickr Group'. *Photographies*, Vol. 6, no. 1, pp. 35–44.

Hartmann, M. 2005, 'The Web Generation? Domestication, Moral Economies and Double Articulations at Play', in R. Silverstone (ed.) *From Information to Communication: Media, Technology and Everyday Life in Europe*. Aldershot: Ashgate, pp. 143–180.

Hjarvard, S. & Petersen, L. N. 2013, 'Mediatization and Cultural Change'. *MedieKultur: Journal of Media and Communication Research*, Vol. 54, pp. 1–7.

Hjorth, L. & Pink, S. 2013, 'The Place of the Emplaced Mobile: A Case Study into Gendered Locative Media Practices'. *Mobile Media and Communication*, Vol. 1, no. 1, pp. 110–115.

Keightley, E. & Pickering, M. 2014, 'Technologies of Memory: Practices of Remembering in Analogue and Digital Photography'. *New Media Society*, Vol. 16, pp. 576–593.

Larsen, J. 2005, 'Families Seen Sightseeing: Performativity of Tourist Photography'. *Space and Culture*, Vol. 8, no. 4, pp. 416–434.

Larsen, J. & Sandbye, M. (eds) 2014, *Digital Snaps: The New Face of Photography*. I.B. Tauris: London.

Lehmuskallio, A. 2012, *Pictorial Practices in a 'Cam Era': Studying Non-Professional Camera Use*. Tampere University Press: Tampere.

Mannheim, K. 1990, 'The Problem of Generations', in K. Mannheim, *Essays on the Sociology of Knowledge*. Taylor & Francis: London, pp. 163–195.

Mannheim, K. 1980, *Strukturen des Denkens*. Suhrkamp: Frankfurt am Main.

Maynard, P. 1997, *The Engine of Visualization: Thinking through Photography*. Cornell University Press: Ithaca, NY.

Neumann-Braun, K. & Autenrieth, U. (eds) 2011, *Freundschaft und Gemeinschaft im Social Web: Bildbezogenes Handeln und Peergroup-Kommunikation auf Facebook&Co*. Nomos: Baden-Baden.

OECD. 2013, *OECD Skills Outlook 2013: First Results from the Survey of Adult Skills*. OECD Publishing: Paris.

Pickering, M. 2013, 'Ubiquitous Photography'. *European Journal of Communication*, Vol. 28, no. 2, pp. 205–208.

Pink, S. 2011, 'Amateur Photographic Practice, Collective Representation and the Constitution of Place'. *Visual Studies*, Vol. 26, no. 2, pp. 92–101.

Prensky, M. 2001, 'Digital Natives, Digital Immigrants'. *On the Horizon*, Vol. 9, no. 5, pp. 1–6.

Przyborski, A. & Slunecko, T. 2011, 'Learning to Think Iconically in the Human and Social Sciences: Iconic Standards of Understanding as a Pivotal Challenge for Method Development'. *Integrative Psychological and Behavioral Science*, Vol. 46, no. 1, pp. 39–56.

Przyborski, A. & Wohlrab-Sahr, M. 2013, *Qualitative Sozialforschung: Ein Arbeitsbuch*, 4th edn. Oldenbourg: München.

Raab, J. 2008, *Visuelle Wissenssoziologie: Theoretische Konzeption und Materiale Analysen*. UVK: Konstanz.

Reckwitz, A. 2002, 'Toward a Theory of Social Practices: A Development in Culturalist Theorizing'. *European Journal of Social Theory*, Vol. 5, pp. 243–263.

Rose, G. 2010, *Doing Family Photography: The Domestic, the Public and the Politics of Sentiment*. Ashgate: Farnham.

Rose, G. & Tolia-Kelly, D. 2012, *Visuality/Materiality: Images, Objects and Practices*. Ashgate: Farnham.

Sarvas, R. & Froehlich, D. 2011, *From Snapshots to Social Media: The Changing Picture of Domestic Photography*. Springer: London.

Schade, S. & Wenk, S. 2011, *Studien zur visuellen Kultur: Einführung in ein transdisziplinäres Forschungsfeld*. Transcript: Bielefeld.

Schäffer, B. 2006, 'Die Bildung Älterer mit neuen Medien: Zwischen Medienkompetenz, ICT-Literacy und generationsspezifischen Medienpraxiskulturen'. *Bildungsforschung*, Vol. 3, no. 2, pp. 1–28.

Schäffer, B. 2003, *Generationen – Medien – Bildung: Medienpraxiskulturen im Generationenvergleich*. Leske+Budrich: Opladen.

Schatzki, T. R. 2001, 'Introduction: Practice Theory', in T. R. Schatzki, K. Knorr Cetina & E. von Savigny (eds) *The Practice Turn in Contemporary Theory*. Routledge: London, pp. 1–14.

Schorb, B. 2009, 'Erfahren und Neugierig: Medienkompetenz und höheres Lebensalter', in B. Schorb, A. Hartung & W. Rei mann (eds) *Medien und höheres Lebensalter: Theorie – Forschung – Praxis*. VS Verlag: Wiesbaden, pp. 319–337.

Schwarz, O. 2010, 'Negotiating Romance in Front of the Lens'. *Visual Communication*, Vol. 9, pp. 151–169.

Selwyn, N. 2009, 'The Digital Native: Myth and Reality'. *Aslib Proceedings*, Vol. 61, no. 4, pp. 364–379.

Sheely, S. 2008, 'Latour Meets the Digital Natives: What Do We Really Know', in *Proceedings from ASCILITE 2008*. Melbourne, pp. 908–916.

Silverman, K. 1996, *The Threshold of the Visible World*. Routledge: New York.

Stocchetti, M. 2011, 'Who Gets What When and How?', in M. Stocchetti & K. Kukkonnen (eds) *Images in Use*. Benjamins: Amsterdam, pp. 11–38.

Van Dijck, J. 2008, 'Digital Photography: Communication, Identity, Memory'. *Visual Communication*, Vol. 7, pp. 57–76.

Van House, N. 2011, 'Personal Photography, Digital Technologies and the Uses of the Visual'. *Visual Studies*, Vol. 26, no. 2, pp. 125–134.

Villi, M. & Stocchetti, M. 2011, 'Visual Mobile Communication, Mediated Presence and the Politics of Space'. *Visual Studies*, Vol. 26, no. 2, pp. 102–112.

Walser, R. & Neumann-Braun, K. 2013, 'Freundschaftsnetzwerke und die Welt ihrer Fotoalben: Gestern und Heute', in C. Wijnen, S. Trültzsch & C. Ortner (eds) *Medienwelten im Wandel*. Springer: Wiesbaden, pp. 151–166.

Warburg, A. 1993, *Mnemosyne-Atlas: Begleittexte zur Ausstellung Aby Warburg – Mnemosyne*. Daedalus: Wien.

Weller, W. & Da Silva, C. M. 2011, 'Documentary Method and Participatory Research: Some Interfaces'. *International Journal of Action Research*, Vol. 7, no. 3, pp. 294–318.

Wolff, J. 2012, 'After Cultural Theory: The Power of Images, the Lure of Immediacy'. *Journal of Visual Culture*, Vol. 11, pp. 3–18.

4 Illness, death and grief

The daily experience of viewing and sharing digital images

Rebeca Pardo and Montse Morcate

Introduction

The representation of grief, illness and death had an important photographic presence in America and Europe in the nineteenth century (Linkman 2011). Extensive research has been conducted, particularly on its presence in Western culture and the Victorian era, where the act of photographing the dying and the dead became one of the key elements of the mourning rituals, especially through post-mortem photography (Burns 1990; Ruby 1999; Batchen 2004). This practice continued throughout the twentieth century in many countries, merging with the various cultural idiosyncrasies involved and adapting itself with the arrival of the American way of death (Mitford 2000), a conception of death much more commercialized by the funeral industry that became more and more normalized, mainly in the industrialized countries and metropolitan areas. However, during the second half of the twentieth century as the authors previously referred to (among others) note, the images representing death and grief progressively fell into disuse. Many are the factors involved: a general laxity in mourning rituals in Western countries after the Second World War, the increase in life expectancy thanks to progress in science and medicine, which changed the relationship to death, etc. Although the practice has never completely disappeared, death, grief and illness started to be seen by many as non-appropriate aspects of life to be photographed within family territory.[1]

Photographic practices are changing, however, with the emergence of digital devices and sharing platforms (Lister 1995, 2013) – a phenomenon closely related to recent practices of consumerism and sharing.[2] These changes raise the question of what can be considered an appropriate photographic object – we suggest that death, grief and illness are returning as acceptable photographic subjects, with a remediated meaning to them (Bolter & Grusin 2000). This chapter explores some photography and sharing modalities related to illness, death and grief on Social Networking Sites (SNS), as a part of a long-standing and ongoing project about the online visual representation of these issues (Morcate 2013, 2014; Pardo, 2012, 2014a, 2014b).

Our findings suggest that image sharing on SNS is potentially developing and amplifying some practices which already exist, such as photographing illness, the dying and the dead. At the same time, our research
suggests that new practices, such as documenting the everyday nature of an
illness, are growing in importance. That leads us to consider images not
only as a memory device but also as a mediator between people, grief practices and sense of community. This chapter analyses how domestic and
intimate images of death, illness and grief are taken and/or shared by
common users. We suggest that digital image-taking and sharing through
social media help to normalize and offer visibility to the often hidden and
tabooed subject of certain kinds of illness and grief, providing the longed-
for awareness. By sharing these photos people often offer a very personal,
intimate and liberating way to express illness, death and grief that can
create a sense of community[3] within which to offer and receive support,
understanding and a release from isolation. We will exemplify this with
two case studies connected by processes of grief: one on Alzheimer's and
the second on memorialization online.

A note on method and ethics

We work with two case studies: one on self-referential representation of
Alzheimer's disease in SNS, by observing and collecting data from Flickr,
Instagram, Facebook, Twitter, Wordpress, Blogspot or Tumblr in
2013–2015, continuing a previous research project conducted in Barcelona
(Pardo 2013, 2014a, 2014b), and one on representation of grief and death
on two sites (a family photo memory site, *Dear Photograph*, and *Much
Loved*, a specific memorial site where images are shared to speak in a
straightforward way of grief and death (Morcate 2014)). The two sets of
data presented as the second case study were chosen for being representative of two very different ways of sharing digital images related to grief
and death through the internet on the mentioned sites. We conducted semiotic and textual analysis of the images and comments uploaded to these
sites between 2013 and 2015.

Being a delicate subject, the ethical discussion is crucial. We had the
consent of all the explicitly named participants to observe and use their
shared data in our research outcomes. When personal communication was
not possible, names were anonymized, in order to protect the privacy of
the owners of the photographs and the people whose memorial sites are
analysed.

Grief, illness and death in photography

It can be said that the representation of illness, death and grief in photography has been changing through the years and that it is culturally
contextual. From the open, proud production and exhibition of such

photographs to family members and acquaintances in the second half of the nineteenth century it eventually became an almost disgraceful private practice in the second half of the twentieth century. Therefore, photography, as a medium, has been able to shape and adapt itself to the different changes in attitudes towards death and dying and to some specific degenerative diseases since its invention, providing the caregiver and the bereaved the required and longed-for image for every situation and time (Morcate 2014; Pardo 2014a, 2014b; Morcate & Pardo 2013).

Grief is a complex concept that can be understood either as the manifestation of different reactions by the bereaved (Rosenblatt, Walsh & Jackson 1976) or as a pseudo-linear-staged (Kübler-Ross & Kessler 2010) or non-linear and more active process (Worden 2010), among many other interpretations. We focus here on grief understood as a process followed by a loss, which offers a wider meaning in which death is not the only cause. Thus, the bereaved takes an active role in finding meaning in a new context after the loss. In this sense, anticipatory grief, the grief usually present in case of a degenerative or terminal illness, and before death, is frequently portrayed. Artists were among the first to use imagery to deal with the grief often caused by the degenerative or terminal illness of a loved one or the artist him/herself (Morcate 2014; Pardo 2012, 2014a).

Susan Sontag (2005, 2007) states that to photograph is to participate in somebody's mortality and vulnerability. She said that photographs anaesthetize and that taking pictures is a social ritual, a protection against anxiety. This therapeutic value was proved by her long-time partner, photographer Annie Leibovitz, when she decided to take pictures of Sontag dying and dead as a comforting act and as a way of facing the reality of her death (Leibovitz 2009). This sort of reaction could now be found manifest not only in artists' work but commonly in digital photography. A continuing exposure of the loved one, online, by the bereaved might be a new mediatized death ritual in which we can expand his or her life and presence virtually. For example, in our interviews with Alzheimer's patients who have made self-referential images, people frequently reflect on how the camera mitigated the first stage of negation of the disease diagnosis. In self-referential works related with Alzheimer's, the authors frequently express their perception of the camera as a kind of shield that protects them from reality (Pardo 2012, 2013; Morcate 2014). Many of the interviewees mentioned that they take and share photos as a kind of agency against the malady (Pardo 2014a, 2014b). At the same time, most of them also expressed their sense of being taking care of (i.e. their legacy and memories) while photographing. So, there is also a therapeutic aspect in these kinds of projects (Spence 2005).

In our research through SNS we have found multiple examples of an interest in sharing images and also using them to gain visibility and awareness (claiming empathy surrounding the daily needs, grief and problems of the patients, the dying and their families). Through the data analysed we can suggest that, during some grieving processes, the sharing of domestic images portraying illness and death allow users to have the feeling of breaking the frequent isolation they live in and connecting with peers suffering in a similar situation. As an example, mental illness is part of one of the three forms of social stigma according to Erving Goffman (2006) and this idea can reinforce the necessity of connection and comprehension through SNS. As Goffman says, there is a necessity to make contact with a group within which there are no separations caused by stigma. Some patients who share their images comment that they share their stories to the world in the hope of making a difference, to erase offensive stereotypes, to talk to people like them and help themselves or to spread awareness.

In the changing landscape of digital photographic practices (Van House *et al.* 2005; Van House & Churchill 2008; Ito 2005) some boundaries are being shifted and our research shows that one of the most notable relates to the visual representation of disease, death and grief, which in the modern age has found a new scenario for visibility, in an explicit or veiled way, online. We present two examples, as case studies, of the use and sharing of digital imagery of grief, disease and death. Although limited in scope, these examples are suggestive of a normalization in the relationship between everyday photography and grief processes.

Case study 1: Alzheimer's and similar senile dementias

The representation of malady in the digital era is a truly interesting phenomenon in photography because it could signal a specific change in the subjectivity of the 'camera' and the meaning of sharing through social media. One important example is the practice of photographing mental maladies. The representation of mental health started in the nineteenth century when doctors used photography as illustrations for their scientific articles and books.[4] From that time on, the photographing of the insane became a catalogue of violent attacks, severe crises and other visible symptoms of madness. These images built an iconography of the insane as someone dangerous, violent and fearsome. In 1961,[5] a corpus of research offered a new pathway to seeing madness as a cultural product (Foucault 2010, 2011; Goffman 2001; Szasz 1994). Nevertheless, this representation, in the mass media, of mental health patients as dangerous and as an object of study for medicine was still present in visual representation throughout the twentieth century, through isolated documentary works about the precarious situation of mental hospitals. It was not until caregivers, patients and relatives had access to digital cameras, camera phones and SNS on a daily basis that an important change took place. In the last ten years we have seen an increasing visual presence of intimate images of Alzheimer's patients (frequently self-referential works) helping to change the representation of mental health in SNS to a more sensible and less violent iconography. Coincidentally, this is also the period in which digital cameras have changed our ideas of what is photo-worthy.

One Spanish example of this trend is the book *Pasqual Maragall Mira* (Maragall & García 2010) which published daily pictures taken with a mobile phone by Pasqual Maragall, a well-known Catalan politician,[6] while suffering from Alzheimer's. The images show him in quotidian situations, with family and friends, using smartphonography as a medium to fight against forgetting and his malady. The book is one of the actions Maragall and his family have made to bring awareness to this illness (as is the foundation created in his name to carry out research on Alzheimer's). While this is a well-known and reviewed project, there is also an increasing quantity of anonymous profiles on a lot of SNS that share personal or domestic images of Alzheimer's patients.

One of the most frequent practices in this context is the 'selfie', smiling and lovingly embracing or touching the Alzheimer's patient, who is usually sitting with vacant eyes. A lot of examples can be found just by searching for '#Alzheimers' or '#alzheimersawareness' on Instagram.

Another type of image which is widely shared is of volunteers' or caregivers' groups at shared meetings, talks or walks. These kinds of images are a clear illustration of the high value that support and socialization (family, friends, associations and support groups) have for patients and caregivers, and also of the importance of their struggle to give visibility and awareness to the problem. Usually the images are very similar to those of travels or excursions, with a group posing for the picture, but with purple T-shirts, posters, balloons or other awareness-raising materials. While we have found the same practice on several platforms, one of the most interesting sharing practices has been found on Instagram, probably because it is an SNS that not only facilitates the human encounter through images but also through the hobbies, concerns and interests that are photographed by the users (in Flickr, however, the focus is more on the photographs themselves, in their aesthetic or technical value).

As an example of the data collected, it is interesting to observe, in this graphic, how most of the tags used in Instagram relate not only to the illness, the geographical identification and the medical condition, but also to the constant needs that we have detected on other SNS and through other fieldwork: the importance of visibility, the way people interact and form associations, how people complain and provide support to others.

Therefore, apart from the peculiarities of each SNS and image/comment, most of the photographs are made by caregivers or relatives who want to identify those snapshots with the illness in order to give it visibility and raise awareness. For this reason, the use of tags is important to facilitate image searching.

Another means for sharing experiences of Alzheimer's is a blog. Once again, we find a relative, taking care of a loved one, who needs to explain the daily experience of the illness to help others and be helped (they usually

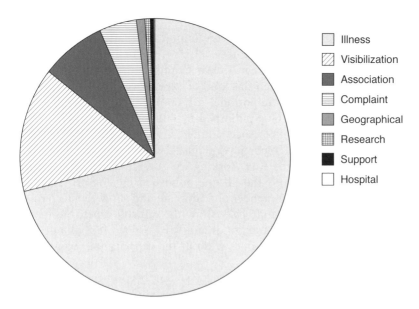

Illness

Visibilization

Association

Complaint

Geographical

Research

Support

Hospital

Figure 4.1 The most important motivations for sharing images through Instagram (on the basis of the hashtags used), related to Alzheimer's.

express their need to share experience and their gratitude for comments and understanding). The main objective of those blogs, as with the tags already commented on above, is sharing, support, to turn something visible and searchable and, finally, to raise awareness; in other words, connection and co-presence (Ito 2005). As an example, we can refer, among others sources, to *Diario de un Cuidador* (*Diary of a Carer*: Barredo 2013) and *Mi Vida con el Alzheimer* (*My Life with Alzheimer's*: Cordero 2013), the blogs of Pablo A. Barredo and Isabel Cordero, a son and a daughter care-givers of their mothers with Alzheimer's or *Ella, el Alzheimer y Yo* (*Her, Alzheimer's and Me*: Lucena Arevalo 2010)[7] the blog of Carmen Lucena Arevalo, who was the carer for her mother-in-law for eight years. In these cases, as in others, the blogs show the daily experiences of normal people who become long-term caregivers of relatives and need to share and to give visibility to the illness and their situation. In these blogs there are images, a few of which are personal. Sometimes they show images linked from professional sites, posters or awareness illustrations, but also a few domestic pictures of their caregiving and sometimes old family images. *Diario de un Cuidador* shows frequently sad, shadowed and lonely self-portraits of the carer, a son who left his work to take care of his mother full-time. This blog is also an example of the importance of the carer's situation and needs (MetLife 2006). The *ABC* Spanish newspaper (Ramón Ladra 2014) said that it had 287,000 followers on SNS and an audience for each post of 14 million people weekly all around the world. Pablo A. Barredo, as a result of closing his blog after his mother died, published the content as a book and has created an important platform online for anonymous and non-professional carers, which is the first foundation dedicated exclusively to carers. This is a clear example of the importance of co-presence and support through this kind of experience.

Another example of the importance of co-presence and support is represented by the personal blog published by Phillip Toledano from 2006 to 2010, to share his own experience, entitled *My Aging Father's Decline: A Son's Photo Journal*. As Toledano explains, the photos were taken over a three-year period, while he was working for some magazines on other projects. Once again, as with the photos published by non-professional photographers, the images are tender and intimate and show the deep relationship between father and son. They show the difficult times, the funny moments and, essentially, the strength of family love in the face of a degenerative malady that leaves loved-ones without the capacity for recognizing even themselves.

Nevertheless, all these blog experiences go far beyond the traditional intention of 'photographing to remember' and are surpassed by the dimension of the sharing, co-presence and connection with the community, that all of them recognize as being just as important as their own stories. It is impressive, for example, to note the data which Toledano gives in his blog about the reception of his pictures and project:

> After I began to publish these photos, I was surprised and overwhelmed by the way in which people interacted with my story. The site has been viewed by over 1.5 million people, and there are around 20,000 comments. I, personally, have gotten about 10,000 e-mails from people – lovely, honest, extraordinary e-mails. To me, in an odd way, all this is as important as my own story. It was entirely unexpected, and so helpful in dealing with the feelings of loss over my dad.

As in a hospital room or a funeral wake, perhaps the real need behind sharing pictures of times of grieving is for companionship, the need not to be alone with the pain and the grief. When it is not possible to have somebody with you, maybe mobile phones and SNS are a kind of door that can be opened to amplify your space to somebody who can be by your side with a deep feeling of connection ... virtually. It is important to emphasize that the two blogs with more images, in which these are either autobiographical or self-referential, are the most followed, with millions of visits and transcending the mere online sphere. We must stress that, in some way, people who have gone through similar experiences can identify with other carers and images of the bereaved. The fact that images are employed enhances the potential of mere text, strengthens the capacity to transport the viewer to the places and moments of the photographs, evoking sensations associated with the events represented and conjuring memories, feelings and emotions (Stelmaszewska, Fields & Blandford, 2008).

This visual interaction illustrates what Marianne Hirsch (2002) has called 'affiliative look': a 'Process in which we get involved in an alien family image and by means of which we adapt that image into our own family story' (p. 93). In this sense, domestic and family images are not only charged with more traditional values as information, memories and feelings, but, in the context of SNS, they are also shared to offer up a connection with the experiences and sensibilities of others more than to archive or preserve the moment. As Stelmaszewska, Fields and Blandford (2008) have said, these sharing activities provide bridges between contexts.

Likewise it can be said that the digital environment is changing some social customs and relationships with images in general and the representation of illness in particular, facilitating more humanized images of the daily experience of carers and patients. The public sharing of images is showing patients and relatives the power of domestic or quotidian images of their circumstances to bring awareness, to give visibility to their problems, to change the way they have been perceived and to make contact with others with the same problems. The same kind of practice has been observed not only with Alzheimer's disease, but also with other illnesses, such as diabetes and epilepsy. This suggests that all of these general practices relate to the contemporary experience of chronic illness rather than with the kind of illness portrayed.[8] In this sense, we suggest that photographic practices used during the progress of a degenerative illness are connected with contemporary photography of the dead and the dying, as they are immersed in anticipatory grief processes.

Case study 2: *Dear Photograph* and *Much Loved*

There seems to be an increasing interest in the relationship between current uses of photography and death (Brubaker, Hayes & Dourish 2013; Lagerkvist 2013; Massimi & Baecker 2010; Sumiala 2013; Walter *et al.* 2012). Grief related to death represents a more challenging and delicate subject and it is more difficult to find the practice openly and widely, for example using hashtags. Nevertheless, there are some platforms where this practice can be found extensively and we discuss two of them.

The first example is *Dear Photograph* (Jones 2011), a website created to share family photographs taken by amateurs. With a simple and effective slogan, Taylor Jones, the creator of the platform, announces his proposal: 'Take a picture of a picture from the past in the present.' The main purpose of this project is to observe the passage of time and evoke the past of the protagonist, who holds in his/her hand the original image. This allows us to see the background setting as it is in the present moment while allowing a visual regression to the past. Although not all the images shared are chosen because they depict relevant family memories, it is quite remarkable that about 25 per cent of more than 200 of the images analysed were related to grief. This percentage is based on the written statement that accompanies the re-photograph posted by the author, in which a reference to loss is made. However, it is plausible that other images are posted in order to commemorate the dead in a more subtle way.

Memory and grief are referred to in a very straightforward manner through the textual accompaniment, in which different types of grief can be easily detected. What makes photographs so powerful is the text, which uses the image as a reference or anchor point for the memory, to recall what are often deep memories or thoughts related to the person portrayed[9] and which might not be evident from the picture. The most numerous entries of this kind are due to the loss of a grandmother or grandfather (more than 15 images in our sample).[10] Images range from the late person's youth (in days gone by) to more recent images portraying him or her as an elderly person next to the grandson or granddaughter (usually from the time of the poster's childhood) underlining the relationship and bond between them through this picture, in an idealized way.

One of these images shows, in black and white, a young grandmother next to a little baby at the beach, with the caption '40 years ago she was the most beautiful grandma of the beach. The one who gave me the little self-confidence I have. She's been gone for one year now. I miss her' (posted 21 September 2013).

The grief for a mother, father or sibling is also represented, the last kind being the most touching, especially for the sense of the life cut short when a grown-up is holding the photograph of a child. One of these is the image of a lively little boy spreading his arms in what it seems the act of embracing the photographer on the other side of the camera (or the one who holds the picture in the re-photograph, the bereaved).

> Lovely brother … is now somewhere life is not the same as in earth. I hope when it will be my turn to die, he will open his arms like in this picture to show me the way, so I won't be afraid.
>
> (Posted 16 August 2013)

Dear Photograph offers a very hybrid place where memories are shared without distinction, so that sharing the picture of a much-loved dog seems absolutely appropriate, since this platform is not specifically about death or grief and nobody would question, in this sense, one post over another. In this sense, in the data collected, there is a significant presence of these kinds of grief, as more than 20 of the 200 (plus) images analysed are about these types of loss. One of them recalls the loss of a friendly faced dog one year after her death, which underlines the importance of the grief suffered by her owner:

> Dear Photograph, Today marks one year that she has been gone. I still miss her more than words could ever describe. I wish that I could have

cherished the moments we had together more, because I definitely took them for granted, looking back now. I just need to remember to keep breathing … and that breaks my heart. I love you … You'll always be by my side. Love.

(Posted 9 July 2013)

Interestingly enough, these pet posts have a considerable response by other users (even more than other types of loss), such as (bereaved #1) 'Oh man, this brought tears to my eyes. I dread that' or (bereaved #2) 'I lost my shorty 3yr ago it gets easier with time' (both as responses on the *Dear Photograph* Facebook page). Other examples go beyond the recalling of a family or personal memory and merge into collective and even historical memory such as images of the 9/11 attacks in the USA. One image, taken from a short distance of the twin towers, is captioned with the following text: 'Dear Photograph, I was astounded, but I hadn't had time to consider what I was seeing' (posted 14 September 2014). Every single image posted on *Dear Photograph* turns it into an open scenario where a new grief ritual takes place, thanks to the digital image and internet, enabling people to open up and talk about grief and death using memories. The retrieval, selection and exhibition online (many times through the digitization of old analogue print pictures) offers a new opportunity and a new audience to celebrate not only memory but also life, thanks to an open and empathic audience.

The other site we have analysed is *Much Loved*, probably one of the most popular tribute platforms online, and allows us to establish some constant characteristics regarding the use of digital images showing death and grief in the modern day.[11] Although most of the sites created by mourners show, publicly, typical family pictures, there are some differences depending on factors such as the age of the deceased, how the family wants to portray the deceased or even the cause of death. Tribute sites created for elderly people either tend to be scarce, with only one or two portraits of the deceased before his/her death or a brief review of the life of the deceased, in celebration. In the tribute site of B. T. (1923–2014) only a portrait showing him smiling at the camera is shown, in contrast to I. S. (1926–2014) with an extensive gallery of images of the lady posing with her relatives, most of which are recent photographs, not just to show the sunset of her life but also to highlight the company and love received from her family until the last day. Again, it is important to contextualize those pictures with the messages posted, which transform them from mere family snapshots into images of grief, such as with the dedication posted on 4 August 2014: '"Always on my mind, forever in my heart" keep visiting me in my dreams Nannygoats. Miss you so much, Love you to the stars and back xxxx.'

In order to understand the importance of images and text it is essential to pay attention to tributes dedicated to the youngest ones, the babies who were stillborn or died a few hours or days after their birth. In this group of memorial sites the most explicit images of death can be found, such as contemporary post-mortem portraits, of a type which would still be completely scandalous or inappropriate to publish outside a specific context like this. For many parents the acceptance of photography as a tool to help make it a little bit easier to say goodbye, and during the process of grief, is increasingly becoming accepted (Morcate 2013). On *Much Loved*, many examples of this kind can be found, showing different approaches in the way death is shown, whether explicitly or using visual metaphors.

The tribute site of baby J. D. (6–7 November 2013) is characterized by having a wide typology of images. The extremely short lifetime of the baby prevents his parents from composing a regular family album to commemorate him. As an alternative, the gallery is composed of very different styles of image in an attempt to register every single useful visual document able to generate a memory of the baby. A picture of the baby in the incubator portrays a strong sense of the medicalization of birth, showing a tiny J. D. intubated and fighting for life. Other images, in which the child is presumably already dead, resemble regular newborn family pictures, in which the mother and father pose for the camera while kissing their child. The gallery continues with a colour post-mortem portrait, in a more formal style, where only the baby is shown on a black background. More images, not showing the baby's face directly to avoid the full immediacy of death, are shared, such as one of the detail of the feet or one of the mother holding the baby's hand. Finally, some poetic images complete the gallery such as the one with the baby's fingerprints transferred on to paper, or that of the tombstone.

Another tribute site, dedicated in memory of M. and M. M. (no birth date) shows two little foetuses that lay over their mother's breast. Although they are stillborn foetuses, they are portrayed as beloved babies by their mother and the way to acknowledge their life and the parents' grief is using photography. The photograph has the ability to transform them into real people who have died too soon. Sharing those complex images online, especially using a tribute site, seems a good way for these people to make this reality visible to an open audience and an easy way to receive condolences and support or to interact with other parents who have suffered the same experience.

These are two of the numerous examples in which parents have taken advantage of the affordances of digital photography not only to generate mementos of their late sons but also as a way of sharing their grief in an open platform that allows their grief to be shared, recognized and be helpful to other people in their loss. Through the data analysed, we can observe that users tend to portray and talk openly about death and grief in memorial sites while they tend to use other more generic memory sites to pay homage to their dead, after the grieving process is over.

Conclusions

The data analysed demonstrates that, thanks to the internet, especially through SNS and other platforms such as blogs or dedicated sites, there is a significant increase in the visual presence of certain stigmatized illnesses and also of death. The characteristics of day-to-day sharing through the internet have influenced the kind of images generated, turning them into a more quotidian practice. These photographs are closer to domestic or familiar photography than to the more formal or professional images that are prevalent in other media. The fact that people are photographing and sharing implies a more humanized sense of the representation of both illness and death, changing what it was previously considered to be an exceptional way of representation. This is related to changing perceptions of what is worth photographing in the digital era and favours the integration of grief in daily visual experience.

Due to this more normalized use of images, it seems to be easier to connect with the experiences of others through the 'affiliative look'. The SNS, blogs and other websites facilitate encounters between peers and the mutual identification amongst a more empathetic audience, inclined to understand and eager to learn from each other's experiences, promoting connection and co-presence. This can generate a sense of community and togetherness. Thus, there is no longer a necessity to relegate grief to an intimate environment. Instead, there is a search for the most similar and empathetic company, this sometimes being strangers who would not have been connected in other circumstances and contexts. The case studies indicate that, depending on the platform, the audience and the kind of material shared changes, favouring the creation of specific communities and dynamics.

In all of the analysed websites and SNS we observe a relevant interrelation between images and texts. In those contexts, sharing images is usually the starting point for interactions that, depending on the site, can generate a comment, a 'like' or a textual/visual interchange as a response. The generalized use of text and tags with the images makes it possible to use search tools to facilitate searches and find mutual points of interest. The strong interaction with text also serves to provide context, which is especially important with certain domestic images whose unveiled significance is death or grief or to share medical experiences that can help other patients or relatives. These images and comments might also have a therapeutic value.

The increasing sharing of images such as these palliates the feeling of stigmatization and solitude and amplifies the awareness of these subjects. In this aspect, we have identified a different approach and/or goal in our fields of study. On the one hand, the purpose for many of those sharing images of stigmatized illnesses is not only to raise awareness but also to express a need for institutional and social help. On the other hand, many of those sharing images of grief and death pursue an aim of giving light to the history of the dead maintaining their legacy.

Finally, this analysis shows that the image in the digital context, due to its direct visual connectivity potential, transforms itself into a catalysing element for unresolved needs for support and understanding, leading to new practices and generating new virtual bonds and communities. This transcends previous uses of the images in other contexts and opens a new agenda for the study of photographic practices.

Notes

1 For a comprehensive overview of these factors see Batchen (2004), Burns (1990), Linkman (2011), Morcate (2014) and Ruby (1999), among others.
2 For a further reading on the subject see Van House *et al.* (2005), Van House and Churchill (2008), Van House (2011), Ito (2005), Okabe and Ito (2005), Kato (2005), Stelmaszewska, Fields and Blandford (2008).
3 For further reading on imagined and/or emotional communities see Anderson (2011) and Maffesoli (1990).
4 Dr Hugh Welch Diamond (1809–1886) has been considered the 'father of psychiatric photography', but there were other important doctors who took pictures, such as Désiré Magloire Bourneville (1840–1909) and Paul Regnard (1850–1927) (Bournville & Regnard 1878).
5 Several pertinent works were published in that year: *Folie et Déraison: Histoire de la Folie à l'Âgeclassique*, by Michel Foucault (2010 and 2011); *Asylums: Essays on the Social Situation of Mental Patients and Other Inmates*, by Erving Goffman (2001) and *The Myth of Mental Illness: Foundations of a Theory of Personal Conduct*, by Thomas S. Szasz (1994).
6 Pasqual Maragall was the 127th President of Generalitat de Catalunya, and as the Mayor of Barcelona from 1982 to 1997, helped to run the city's successful Olympic Games in 1992.
7 The content of this blog has also been published as a book entitled *Vivir sin Vivir* (*Living without Living*: Lucena Arevalo 2011) and some of the content is not available online at this time.
8 Some specific practices have been observed, depending on the kind of illness, but the analysis goes beyond the scope of this chapter.
9 See Barthes (2007) and Langford (2011) on the relation between text/oral narration and images as a way to recall family memories and/or grief.
10 The death of the grandmother or grandfather is probably more represented due to the age of the average user though this is merely a presumption, since no age information is provided.
11 Due to the impressive number of tributes hosted (more than 10,000 on the last day of access, December 2014) the analysis focuses on the sites open in 2013 and 2014.

References

Anderson, B. 2011, *Comunidades Imaginadas: Reflexiones Sobre el Origen y la Difusión del Nacionalismo*. Fondo de Cultura Económica: México.
Barredo, P. A. 2013, 'Diario de un Cuidador', viewed 2 September 2015, http://diariodeuncuidador.com.

Barthes, R. 2007, *La Càmera Lúcida*. Lleonard Muntaner: Mallorca.

Batchen, G. 2004, *Forget Me Not: Photography and Remembrance*. Princeton Architectural Press; Van Gogh Museum: New York; Amsterdam.

Bolter, J. D. & Grusin, R. 2000, *Remediation: Understanding New Media*. MIT Press: Cambridge, MA.

Bournville, D.-M. & Regnard, P. 1878, *Iconographie Photographique de la Salpêtrière: Service de M. Charcot*. Adrien Delahaye & Co.: Paris.

Brubaker, J. R., Hayes, G. R. & Dourish, P. 2013, 'Beyond the Grave: Facebook as a Site for the Expansion of Death and Mourning'. *Information Society: An International Journal*, Vol. 29, no. 3, pp. 152–163.

Burns, S. 1990, *Sleeping Beauty: Memorial Photography in America*. Twelvetrees Press: Altadena, CA.

Cordero, I. 2013, 'Mi Vida con el Alzheimer', viewed 2 September 2015, https:// mividaconelalzheimer.wordpress.com/page/3/.

Doka, K. J. 1989, *Disenfranchised Grief: Recognizing Hidden Sorrow*. Lexington Books: Lexington, KY.

Foucault, M. 2011, *Historia de la Locura en la Época Clásica I*. Fondo de cultura económica: México D.F.

Foucault, M. 2010, *Historia de la Locura en la Época Clásica II*. Fondo de cultura económica: México D.F.

Goffman, E. 2006, *Estigma: La Identidad Deteriorada*. Amorrortu: Buenos Aires.

Goffman, E. 2001, *Internados: Ensayos Sobre la Situación Social de los Enfermos Mentales*. Amorrortu: Buenos Aires.

Hirsch, M. 2002, *Family Frames: Photography, Narrative and Postmemory*. Harvard University Press: Cambridge, MA.

Ito, M. 2005, 'Intimate Visual Co-Presence', viewed 5 May 2015, www.itofisher. com/mito/archives/ito.ubicomp05.pdf.

Jones, T. 2011, *Dear Photograph*, viewed 5 May 2015, http://dearphotograph. com/.

Kato, F. 2005, 'Seeing the "Seeing" of Others: Conducting a Field Study with Mobile Phones/Mobile Cameras'. Paper presented at the T-mobile conference, Budapest Hungary, viewed 5 May 2015, www.hunfi.hu/mobil/2005/Kato_final. pdf.

Kübler-Ross, E. & Kessler, D. 2010, *Sobre el Dol i el Dolor*. Edicions 62: Barcelona.

Lagerkvist, A. 2013, 'New Memory Cultures and Death: Existential Security in the Digital Memory Ecology'. *Thanathos*, Vol. 22, pp. 8–24.

Langford, M. 2013, 'Contar el Álbum: Una Aplicación del Marco Oral-Fotográfico', in P. Vicente (ed.) *Álbum de Familia: [Re]presentación, [Re]creación e [In]materialidad de las Fotografías Familiares*. Diputación de Huesca – La Oficina: Madrid, pp. 63–82.

Leibovitz, A. 2009, *Vida de una Fotógrafa*. Editorial Lunwerg: Barcelona.

Linkman, A. 2011, *Photography and Death*. Reaktion Books Ltd: London.

Lister, M. (ed.) 2013, *The Photographic Image in Digital Culture: Second Edition*. Routledge: Oxford.

Lister, M. (ed.) 1995, *The Photographic Image in Digital Culture*. Routledge: London.

Lucena Arevalo, C. 2011, *Vivir sin Vivir: Ella, el Alzheimer y Yo*. Éride Ediciones: Madrid.

Lucena Arevalo, C. 2010, 'Ella, el Alzheimer y Yo', viewed 2 September 2015, http://ellaelalzheimeryyo.blogspot.es/.

Maffesoli, M. 1990, *El Tiempo de las Tribus*. Icaria, Barcelona.

Maragall, P. & García, C. 2010, *Pasqual Maragall Mira*. Blume: Barcelona.

Massimi, M. & Baecker, M. R. 2010, 'A Death in the Family: Opportunities for Designing Technologies for the Bereaved', in *Proceedings of the SIGCHI Conference on Human Factors in Computing Systems CHI* (April 2010), pp. 1821–1830.

MetLife. 2006, 'The MetLife Study of Alzheimer's Disease: The Caregiving Experience', viewed 5 May 2015, www.metlife.com/assets/cao/mmi/publications/studies/mmi-alzheimers-disease-caregiving-experience-study.pdf.

Mitford, J. 2000, *The American Way of Death Revisited*. First Vintage Books Editions: New York.

Morcate, M. 2014, *Duelo, Muerte y Fotografía: Representaciones Fotográficas de la Muerte y el Duelo Desde los Usos Domésticos al Proyecto de Creación Contemporâneo*. Unpublished doctoral thesis, University of Barcelona.

Morcate, M. 2013, 'Duelo y Fotografía Post-Mortem: Contradicciones de Una Práctica Vigente en el Siglo XXI', in A. Gondra & G. López (eds) *Imagen y Muerte*. Sans Soleil Ediciones: Barcelona, pp. 25–45.

Morcate, M. & Pardo, R. 2013, 'Grief, Illness and Death in Contemporary Photography'. Paper presented to Malady and Mortality: Illness, Disease and Death: Literary and Visual Culture Conference Congress, Falmouth University, Cornwall, 19–20 September.

Okabe, D. & Ito, M. 2005, 'Personal, Portable, Pedestrian Images'. *Receiver*, no. 13, viewed 5 May 2015, www.academia.edu/2717471/Personal_portable_pedestrian_images.

Pardo, R. 2014a, 'Self-Reference, Visual Arts and Mental Health: Synergies and Contemporary Encounters', in A. C. Sparkes, (ed.) *Auto/Biography Yearbook 2013*. British Sociological Association: Durham, pp. 1–21.

Pardo, R. 2014b, *Imágenes de la (Des)memoria: Narrativas Visuales Autorreferenciales del Alzheimer en Barcelona*. Unpublished MA thesis, University of Barcelona.

Pardo, R. 2013, 'Documentales Autorreferenciales con Alzheimer (O Cómo la Enfermedad del Olvido Impulsa la Recuperación Audiovisual de la Memoria y la Historia)', in *Actas Congreso Internacional Hispanic Cinemas: In Transición. Cambios históricos, Políticos y Culturales en el Cine y la Televisión*. UC3M: Madrid [CD-ROM].

Pardo, R. 2012, *La Autorreferencialidad en el Arte (1970–2011): El Papel de la Fotografía, el Vídeo y el Cine Domésticos como Huella Mnemónica en la Construcción Identitaria*. Unpublished doctoral thesis, University of Barcelona.

Ramón Ladra, J. 2014, 'Nunca Dudé en Dejarlo todo para Cuidar a mi Madre Enferma de Alzhéimer'. *ABC*, 19 September 2014, viewed 2 September 2015, www.abc.es/familia-mayores/20140919/abci-alzheimer-cuidador-actividades-201409161818.html.

Rosenblatt, P. C., Walsh, R. P. & Jackson, D. A. 1976, *Grief and Mourning in Cross-Cultural Perspective*. HRAF Press: Estados Unidos.

Ruby, J. 1999, *Secure the Shadow: Death and Photography in America*. MIT Press: Cambridge, MA.

Sontag, S. 2007, *Ante el Dolor de los Demás*. Santillana ediciones generales, Alfaguara: Madrid.

Sontag, S. 2005, *On Photography*. RosettaBooks: New York.

Spence, J. 2005, 'Apuntes sobre Fototerapia', in M. Dávila (ed.) *Jo Spence: Más Allá de la Imagen Perfecta: Fotografía, Subjetividad, Antagonismo.* MACBA, Barcelona, pp. 334–346.

Stelmaszewska, H., Fields, B. & Blandford, A. 2008, 'User Experience of Camera Phones in Social Contexts', in J. Lumsden (ed.) *Handbook of Research on User Interface Design and Evaluation for Mobile Technology.* Aston University: Birmingham, pp. 55–68.

Sumiala, J. 2013, *Media and Ritual: Death, Community and Everyday Life.* Routledge: London; New York.

Szasz, T. S. 1994, *El Mito de la Enfermedad Mental.* Amorrortu Editores: Buenos Aires.

Toledano, P. 2006, 'My Aging Father's Decline: A Son's Photo Journal', viewed 5 May 2015, www.dayswithmyfather.com/.

Van House, N. A. 2011, 'Feminist HCI Meets Facebook: Performativity and Social Networking Sites'. *Interacting with Computers*, Vol. 23, no. 5, pp. 422–429.

Van House, N. A. & Churchill, E. F. 2008, 'Technologies of Memory: Key Issues and Critical Perspectives'. *Memory Studies*, Vol. 1, no. 3, pp. 295–310.

Van House, N. A., Davis, M., Ames, M. G., Finn, M. & Viswanathan, V. 2005, 'The Uses of Personal Networked Digital Imaging: An Empirical Study of Cameraphone Photos and Sharing', in *Extended Abstracts of CHI 2005, ACM Conference on Human Factors in Computing Systems.* ACM: New York, pp. 1853–1856.

Walter, T., Hourizi, R., Moncur, W. & Pitsillides, S. 2012, 'Does the Internet Change How We Die and Mourn? Overview and Analysis'. *OMEGA*, Vol. 64, no. 4, pp. 275–302.

Worden, J. W. 2010, *El Tratamiento del Duelo: Asesoramiento Psicológico y Terapia*, 2nd edn. Ediciones Paidós: Barcelona.

5   The Boston Marathon bombing investigation as an example of networked journalism and the power of big data analytics

Anssi Männistö

Introduction

The Boston Marathon bomb attack in April 2013 has been described as 'the first atrocity to be covered in real-time for a mass audience in social media' (*BBC News*, cited in Allan 2014). Bombs that exploded on the final stretch of the running event killed several and wounded hundreds of people. The ensuing investigation of the attack highlighted the changing nature of news images and mobile social media in modern society. Mobile phone images and new social features of visuality proved to be essential for capturing the suspects.

In recent years, a number of studies have been conducted on how camera phones, social media, micro-blogging and user-generated content have become a powerful source of grassroots-level information in various crises and uprisings[1] (see Ali & Fahmy 2013; Allan 2014; Andén-Papadopoulos 2014; Brook 2012; Cottle 2011; Hermida 2010; Mortensen 2011; Murthy 2011; Van Leuven, Deprez & Raeymaeckers 2014; Wise 2013). These tools have fundamentally transformed and expanded the eco-system of news-making and reporting. In Boston, with the help of new analytical methods, it was possible to utilize photos that were taken long before the actual bombing took place, in order to piece together the event. According to Wall and Linnemann (2014), the reliance on public images came into full view during the 'crowdsourced' investigation of the Boston Marathon bombing.

Before the suspects in the Boston attacks could be tracked down, as they were, various types of camera and new social dimensions in photography were essential (see Männistö 2013; Allan 2014). In this chapter I will examine (1) the various roles that image-making and cameras performed, and (2) how the audience participated in the discussion of the images in Boston at different stages of the investigation. The analysis is done by studying data collected from social media sites and the feeds from some key institutions involved in reporting the Boston Marathon bombing. The data cover a period of six months after the attack.

Literature review

Verification of information is traditionally considered the cornerstone of journalism. Many studies have shown that professional journalists are worried about the reliability of citizen-created photos (Andén-Papadopoulos & Pantti 2013), while some others point out the growing tension in the changing relationship between professional journalists and citizen journalists (Allan 2014; Blaagaard 2013). In Boston, we see for the first time something completely new emerging: tweets and mobile phone photos were no longer just sources of, or channels for, information. More than that, mainstream media, as well as investigators of the crime, were using tweets and mobile phone photos to verify the facts and photos taken by others. This development was enhanced by extensive and groundbreaking use of big data analysis by the police (see Ackerman 2013).

Theoretically, this chapter contributes to the growing interest in the shift to 'networked journalism' (Andén-Papadopoulos & Pantti 2013) and to 'new patterns of information gathering' (Mortensen & Kristensen 2013). As an example of networked journalism, we see in Boston, for example, that journalists rapidly discovered from Twitter the first photos of the attack and asked for permission to publish the photos from the person who tweeted them. In the same manner, the police released pictures of the suspects on Twitter first (leading to almost instant recognition of the suspects) and officers used Twitter in real time to update the public about the proceedings of the manhunt. These actions heralded new qualities in information gathering.

These and other findings strengthen earlier notions of Twitter as an 'awareness system', highlighting the emergence of new journalistic conventions (Hermida 2010; Vis 2013). It may even appear that the term 'awareness system' might not be enough in some cases. Sheller (2015, p. 17) argues, in the context of the Boston Marathon attack, that the tethering of a television production to a single production crew on location, or a distant newsreader in a studio, make it uncompetitive in the race to get ambient news instantaneously from every direction. Author James Gleick described his media habits when he followed the Boston news, stating that

> During the drama of the Boston manhunt and car chase, it never occurred to me to turn on the TV. The screen I needed was on my iPhone, where I followed the tweets of newspaper reporters running through the streets.
>
> (Dowd 2013)

In Boston, the traditional media was already at the scene covering the race, and thus was able to use its own material together with crowd-sourced material in its reporting of the attack. Contrary to this, the January 2015 terrorist attack, in Paris, on the *Charlie Hebdo* newspaper was, in a way, a 'Twitter-only' moment. The fight between the terrorists and the police, and the cruel execution of one officer, was recorded in detail, from different vantage points, by eyewitnesses with mobile phones. That material was immediately sent to Twitter. As in Boston, the manhunt in Paris lasted two days. In the end, in both cases, the traditional media was kept away from the area the police had surrounded. It seems that during those moments we were occasionally witnessing not broadcast-led but Twitter-led news reporting.

We may argue that, as a result of the investigation of the Boston attack, our understanding of the role of mobile phone photos changed and this may affect the famous Baudrillardian notion of fragmented hyperreality. The ever increasing amount of media channels and flow of information made Jean Baudrillard describe the postmodern universe as 'one of hyper-reality in which entertainment, information, and communication technologies provide experiences more intense … than … everyday life' (see e.g. Kellner 2007). Under these conditions, Baudrillard thought individuals would flee from the 'desert of the real' for the ecstasies of hyperreality. In this technologically bound universe, subjectivities are fragmented and lost (ibid.). For Baudrillard (cited in Mitra 2013, p. 35), 'the real is not only what can be reproduced, but that which is always already reproduced. The hyper real.' According to Baudrillard, people live in the 'hyperreality' of simulations in which images, spectacles and the play of signs replace the concepts of production and class conflict as key constituents of contemporary societies. Baudrillard expressed particular concern about the flood of visual imagery and the exhausting impact of entertainment and communication technology, which he predicted would give rise to a fragmented hyperreality (Kellner 2007).

The various roles of images and the use of social media in the Boston bombing investigation

The Boston Marathon bombing is a textbook example of how social media plays an integral part in the reporting of a contemporary event. Social media acts as a constant, active generator, distributing information and serving as a channel for communication for various agents before, during and after the actual event. These dynamics, during the first days after the Boston bombing, are examined in this chapter, in detail, through the viewpoint of three actors: law enforcement, traditional media and unofficial investigators. All the actors were conducting their own investigations to find out the course of events before the explosions and they all used social media for crowd-sourcing data and for giving feedback or information to the audience.

Primary sources for the study are posts to social media by two organizations: the Boston Athletic Association (BAA), the organizer of the running event, and the *Boston Globe*, the leading local newspaper in the area. The research period is from 15 April to 10 October 2013. From that period, all

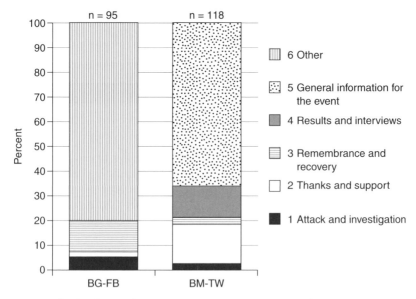

BG-FB = *Boston Globe*'s Facebook posts 16 April to 15 October 2013
BM-TW = BAA's @bostonmarathon tweets 15 April to 15 October 2013

Figure 5.1 The themes of the *Boston Globe*'s Facebook posts and BAA's Twitter feeds.

the Facebook posts by the *Boston Globe* and the Twitter feed from @bostonmarathon (published by the BAA) were collected for analysis (see Figure 5.1).[2] Adding to this material for the quantitative study, I have scanned through a variety of other accounts, such as Twitter feeds by the *Boston Globe* and the Boston Police Department (@bostonpolice) as well as the Facebook site of the BAA.

On marathon day, 15 April, before the explosions, the BAA sent dozens of tweets using its Twitter handle @bostonmarathon, clarifying some details of the arrangements and conveying the general mood during the marathon. In the same manner, the *Boston Globe* followed the progress of the event in real time on Twitter. Half an hour prior to the explosions, a photo showing four young men dressed in comical clothes and cheerfully running in the marathon was posted to Twitter with the hashtag #bostonmarathon. The caption stated:

> Quite possibly the best #BostonMarathon photo we've seen so far.
> (Shepard 2013)

So, when the explosions took place, the marathon event was already being widely reported through social media. Due to this, the first photos of the explosions were seen immediately on Twitter, Instagram and other social media channels. One of the first photos of the attack was published one minute after the explosions and appeared on the *Boston Globe*'s Twitter feed. At that point, the sender, Georges Scoville, was unsure of what had actually happened

> I think a bomb just went off in Boston. Can't tell. Can smell smoke. Emergency vehicles everywhere.
>
> (Scoville 2015)

At the same time, another spectator, Steve Silva, posted a tweet with a link to a photo he had just taken in the middle of the chaos. Within half an hour, he was asked by various journalists for permission to publish those photos.

The BAA was already actively using its Twitter feed to deliver official information for the runners and their supporters before and during the marathon. When the explosions occurred, the feed stayed in a professional mode. Only a few tweets that were directly related to the explosions were published. Instead, the majority of tweets offered more general information, such as where to find personal belongings or that the official after-race party was cancelled. It is noticeable that the BAA's Twitter feed was not used for sending photos of the attack. Similarly, the Boston Police Department did not publish photos of the explosions in its tweets. Instead, it sent out dozens of tweets giving updates on the investigation.

Traditional media reported comprehensively on the investigation. In the case of the *Boston Globe*, its Facebook site acted as an integral part of its news workflow. The newspaper communicated intensively with its audience through Facebook, which can be seen, for example, in the content of the *Boston Globe*'s Facebook posts during the 14 days following the explosions, all of which dealt with the attacks or their investigation. It was only after two weeks that other topical themes overtook the attacks. However, the attacks appeared again on 28 May, six weeks after the explosions, when the *Boston Globe* published a photo on its Facebook site showing bombing victim Jeff Bauman, who was going to throw the opening pitch of the Boston Red Sox home game. This post gained 6,018 comments and 1,196 shares, both numbers being among the highest in this six-month research period.

Simultaneously with the reporting by the traditional media, both the official investigation by law enforcement and various unofficial investigations by active groups and individuals on the web began.[3] A day after the attack, on 16 April, investigators turned to crowd-sourced photographs and videos in order to hunt down the perpetrators (Zhang 2013a). The FBI received more than 2,000 tips and sifted through more than ten terabytes of data. The data included surveillance footage collected by city cameras, local businesses, gas stations, media outlets and spectators who volunteered to provide cell phone videos and photos (Serrano & Bennett 2013).

Several online communities were attempting to identify the attackers behind the bombings by crowd-sourcing publicly available photographs from the scene (Zhang 2013b). This activity produced both results and excesses. Some self-styled detectives published photos in which they had tagged potential suspects, who in the end proved to be innocent. The same also happened in the traditional media. The *New York Post* took one of these wrongly tagged photos and ran it on the front page with the headline: 'Bag Men: Feds seek these two pictured at Boston Marathon' (Zhang 2013c).

This phase in the flow of news, marked by false rumours or unconfirmed information, has been typical in crisis reporting. In Boston, this phase of limbo lasted only two days. As soon as 18 April, the FBI was able to publish the confirmed photos of the suspects. The police asked their audience for help with several tweets like this:

> Do you know these individuals? Contact boston@ic.fbi.gov or 1-800-CALL-FBI.
>
> (Boston Police Department 2013a)

When the FBI published the photos of 'possible suspects' on the internet, the public quickly provided crucial tips, leading to the discovery of the identity of the suspects. The arresting of the suspects progressed when a victim of a carjacking called police and the thieves were identified as the alleged bombers. Police officers were able to track the vehicle using the victim's iPhone and the car's Mercedes satellite system (Henry 2013). One suspect managed to escape but officers were able to locate him in a certain neighbourhood of the city. Then, one of the most intensive manhunts in recent US history began and police roped off the area and began to search the neighbourhood house by house.

In this phase of the investigation the police were updating Twitter, in real time, about the progress of the search. We might describe this action by the police as giving information to the audience via social media. The police used specific hashtags, such as #CommunityAlert, #MediaAdvisory and #Wanted. In these tweets, the public was told to 'stay indoors' and 'not to answer door unless instructed by a police officer' (Boston Police Department 2013b). One new phenomenon that occurred was that the police gave a strong media alert (#MediaAlerts)

> WARNING – Do Not Compromise Officer Safety/Tactics by Broadcasting Live Video of Officers While Approaching Search Locations.
>
> (Boston Police Department 2013c)

This warning received much attention and generated a heated debate on Twitter. Some tweeters were sympathetic towards these demands, while others were opposed to these kinds of restrictions. An example of the latter viewpoint is a tweet by Egodram (@JL_Chadbourne)

@Boston_Police Do forgive me, but people DO have a right to film police.

(Chadbourne 2013)

At the end of the operation, with the help of a helicopter-mounted infrared camera, the suspect was found hiding in a boat. Directly after the capture, the Boston Police Department sent out a tweet

CAPTURED!!! The hunt is over. The search is done. The terror is over. And justice has won. Suspect in custody.

(Boston Police Department 2013d)

This tweet gained 133,000 retweets, which is almost ten times more than any other tweet in that week for the feed @bostonpolice.

Cameras were present also in the final episode of the manhunt. People living near the spot where the suspect was captured filmed the raid and immediately put the material on the web. Thus, in the end, the police were mainly using social media for giving feedback and information, while the audience was witnessing and publishing the actions of the police.

The power of big data analytics

When the speed and effectiveness of the Boston investigation is compared to some previous investigations, the contrast is stark. At the 1996 Atlanta Olympics, an explosion in a park killed one person and injured more than 100. People became frustrated as the criminal investigation seemed to stumble. Gartner (2013) emphasized two factors that exist today that were in their infancy in 1996, in Atlanta, which dramatically assisted the Boston investigation: one is the revolution in mobile imaging and the other is the availability of big data analysis.

The investigation showed a glimpse of what big data and data analytics can do. The main goal of any big data project is to pull insights from large amounts of data with the help of powerful computers (Konkel 2013). In Boston, the computers helped to analyse large amounts of visual data. This included the use of biometric tools such as facial recognition (Ackerman 2013). By feeding thousands of cell phone, media and security camera images into massive computers capable of sorting faces, times and locations, authorities were able to put together a comprehensive picture of the comings and goings of individuals near the running event (Gartner 2013).

During the Boston investigation the authorities and the media were interested in different kinds of photos. Traditionally, for the media, the most valuable photos have been 'a moment after the explosion' type of scenes. However, in this case, the authorities were more interested in collecting photos that were taken hours before the attack and also from locations further away than the actual site of the bombings (Vänskä 2013).

The investigation benefited from the ability of making a *continuous* visual narrative from thousands of *separate* photos. Using images of the event from different angles and moments, captured by hundreds and thousands of people, the investigators were able to create a three-dimensional photo narrative. This enabled the identification of where all the spectators of this large event were positioned at a certain point in time. Photos and videos taken by different spectators, from different vantage points and angles, helped investigators cross-check people they thought were suspicious (Ackerman 2013).

Lauren Grabbe, a freelance contributor to *Wired* magazine, was one spectator who was photographing near the Boston Marathon finish line about 90 minutes before the bombs went off. One panoramic photo Grabbe took with her camera phone caught the FBI's interest. The photo showed a lot of people, what they were wearing and where they were positioned. The FBI analysed this and other photos using biometric tools such as facial recognition. With this data, investigators assembled an understanding of what normal behaviour at the marathon looked like. This helped to narrow down the people that just did not fit the pattern (Ackerman 2013).

As a consequence of the success of big data image analysis in Boston, it may be possible that in forthcoming years many people might be faced with requests from the police for photos that may help to solve crimes committed years or decades ago. Even ordinary tourist photos might prove to be valuable, should they contain faces of possible suspects.

Conclusions: from hyperreal to hyperreliability?

The rapid spread of camera phones during the past ten years has changed the production, distribution and availability of photos. Consequently, the overwhelming influx of images (and videos) has affected our lives and lifestyles in many fundamental ways. The notion of a public sphere, for example, has changed forever as unlimited amounts of potentially active cameras surround almost every situation. When something tragic happens, as in Boston, mobile phones are ready and on the spot to record and distribute the images. With the same devices, people can participate immediately in the debate on social media sites and they take on the roles of active sources for networked journalism.

Camera phones have also brought rich metadata as a standard feature of digital photos. Various sensors are included in high-end camera phones, such as GPS, gyroscope, electronic compass and accelerometer. These sensors enable contextual information to be stored in the metadata of an image file. This flood of metadata may be valuable in situations where the reliability of a photo is under question or when its weight as evidence is evaluated under a 'social microscope' of social networks and blogs, or by law enforcement. Metadata rich mobile phone photos may also be used to verify the veracity of other photos depicting the same event.

In the investigation of the Boston Marathon bomb attacks, a large number of photos and videos were used to generate a consistent narrative of reality and its actors. The fragmented reality became police evidence, that could be used to track down the perpetrators. The effectiveness of big data analysis, which targeted crowd-sourced photos and videos, combined with an active audience, willing to discuss the contents of images, might challenge the famous notions of fragmented, hyperreal conditions made by Baudrillard.

One element in Baudrillardian thought is that the flood of visual imagery and the exhausting impact of entertainment and communication technology would give rise to a fragmented hyperreality. In Boston, an opposite trend was emerging. With the help of metadata enhanced mobile phone photos and new methods of analysis from fragmented pieces of information, something arose which I would like to call 'hyperreliability'. The flood of visuality was no longer something that would drown out the meanings. Contrary to this, the more photos and videos taken by different people, in different locations and at different times, the better for the investigation and for the results. This is the essence of the term 'hyperreliability'.

Notes

1 According to Ali and Fahmy (2013), in the case of the uprisings in Iran, Egypt and Libya, the work of citizen journalists provided a powerful source of news for the rest of the world. However, it also provided a valuable resource for traditional media that had the ability to pick and choose stories that fit their organizations' routines.
2 As all the posts from the day of the attack, 15 April, have been removed from the *Boston Globe*'s site, the analysis started on 16 April.
3 For many years there have been numerous communities on the internet focusing on scrutinizing the photos. These communities have been successful in revealing fraud, for example intentional manipulations. One of the most famous examples of this is the revelation of the manipulations related to the Lebanon war in 2006. This scandal led the news agency Reuters to introduce its very strict rules concerning news photo manipulation (see Winslow 2006; Schlesinger 2007).

References

Ackerman, S. 2013, 'How This Photo of Boston Marathon Gives the FBI a Bounty of Data'. *Wired*, viewed 2 October 2015, www.wired.com/2013/04/boston-photograph.

Ali, S. R. & Fahmy, S. 2013, 'Gatekeeping and Citizen Journalism: The Use of Social Media during the Recent Uprisings in Iran, Egypt, and Libya'. *Media, War and Conflict*, Vol. 6, no. 1, pp. 55–69.

Allan, S. 2014, 'Witnessing in Crisis: Photo-Reportage of Terror Attacks in Boston and London'. *Media, War and Conflict*, Vol. 7, no. 2, pp. 133–151.

Andén-Papadopoulos, K. 2014, 'Citizen Camera-Witnessing: Embodied Political Dissent in the Age of "Mediated Mass Self-Communication"'. *New Media and Society*, Vol. 16, no. 5, pp. 753–769.

Andén-Papadopoulos, K. & Pantti, M. 2013, 'Re-Imaging Crisis Reporting: Professional Ideology of Journalists and Citizen Eyewitness Images'. *Journalism*, Vol. 14, pp. 960–977.

Blaagaard, B. B. 2013, 'Shifting Boundaries: Objectivity, Citizen Journalism and Tomorrow's Journalists'. *Journalism*, Vol. 14, no. 8, pp. 1076–1090.

Boston Police Department. 2013a, 'Do You Know These Individuals? Contact boston@ic.fbi.gov or 1-800-CALL-FBI (1-800-225-5324), Prompt #3.' Twitter, 18 April 2013, 2:46 p.m., viewed 26 October 2015, https://twitter.com/bostonpolice/status/325002310369542144.

Boston Police Department. 2013b, '#CommunityAlert: Residents of Watertown asked to Stay Indoors. Do Not Answer Door unless Instructed by a Police Officer.' Twitter, 19 April 2013, 12:43 a.m., viewed 26 October 2015, https://twitter.com/bostonpolice/status/325152560849756160.

Boston Police Department. 2013c, '#MediaAlert: WARNING – Do Not Compromise Officer Safety/Tactics by Broadcasting Live Video of Officers While Approaching Search Locations.' Twitter, 19 April 2013, 10:14 a.m., viewed 26 October 2015, https://twitter.com/bostonpolice/status/325296472117620736.

Boston Police Department. 2013d, 'CAPTURED!!! The Hunt is Over. The Search is Done. The Terror is Over. And Justice has Won. Suspect in Custody.' Twitter, 19 April 2013, 5:58 p.m., viewed 26 October 2015, https://twitter.com/bostonpolice/status/325413032110989313.

Brook, P. 2012, 'Photographs are No Longer Things, They're Experiences'. *Wired*, 15 November 2012, viewed 2 October 2015, www.wired.com/rawfile/2012/11/stephen-mayes-vii-photography/.

Chadbourne, J. L. 2013, '@Boston_Police Do Forgive Me, but People DO Have a Right to Film Police. http://reason.com/archives/2012/04/05/7-rules-for-recording-police … How goes Catching the Bomber?' Twitter, 19 April 2013, 10:22 a.m., viewed 26 October 2015, https://twitter.com/JL_Chadbourne/status/325298478739779584.

Cottle, S. 2011, 'Media and the Arab Uprisings of 2011: Research Notes'. *Journalism*, Vol. 12, no. 5, pp. 647–659.

Dowd, M. 2013, 'Lost in Space', *New York Times*, viewed 10 October 2014, www.nytimes.com/2013/04/24/opinion/dowd-lost-in-space.html?_r=1&.

Gartner, S. S. 2013, 'Big Data could Uncover Clue on Marathon'. *USA Today*, viewed 26 October 2015, www.usatoday.com/story/opinion/2013/04/16/boston-marathon-and-big-data-column/2087145/.

Henry, J. 2013, 'M-B Tech led Cops to Bostons Suspects' Car', viewed 29 April 2013, www.autonews.com.

Hermida, A. 2010, 'Twittering the News: The Emergence of Ambient Journalism'. *Journalism Practice*, Vol. 4, no. 3, pp. 297–308.

Kellner, D. 2007, 'Jean Baudrillard'. *Stanford Encyclopedia of Philosophy*, viewed 26 October 2015, http://plato.stanford.edu/entries/baudrillard/.

Konkel, F. 2013, 'Boston Probe's Big Data use Hints at the Future'. *The Business of Federal Technology*, viewed 26 October 2015, http://fcw.com/articles/2013/04/26/big-data-boston-bomb-probe.aspx.

Männistö, A. 2013, 'Trust Rethought: Digital Image after Boston'. *Backlight Photo Festival 2014*, viewed 26 October 2015, http://backlight.fi/archive/BL14/anssi-mannisto-trust-rethought-digital-image-after-boston/.

Mitra, A. 2013, 'Mapping Narbs', in J. Macgregor Wise & H. Koskela (eds) *New Visualities, New Technologies: The New Ecstasy of Communication*. Farnham: Ashgate, pp. 27–40.

Mortensen, M. 2011, 'When Citizen Photojournalism Sets the News Agenda: Neda Agha Soltan as a Web 2.0 Icon of Postelection Unrest in Iran'. *Global Media and Communication*, Vol. 7, no. 1, pp. 4–16.

Mortensen, M. & Kristensen, N. N. 2013, 'Amateur Sources Breaking the News, Meta Sources Authorizing the News of Gaddafi's Death: New Patterns of Journalistic Information Gathering and Dissemination in the Digital Age'. *Digital Journalism*, Vol. 1, no. 3, pp. 352–367.

Murthy, D. 2011, 'Twitter: Microphone for the Masses?'. *Media, Culture and Society*, Vol. 33, no. 5, pp. 779–789.

Schlesinger, D. 2007, 'The Use of Photoshop', viewed 26 October 2015, http://blogs.reuters.com/blog/archives/4327.

Scoville, G. 2013, 'I Think a Bomb Just Went Off in Boston. Can't Tell. Can Smell Smoke. Emergency Vehicles Everywhere.' Twitter, 15 April 2013, 11:53 a.m., viewed 26 October 2015, https://twitter.com/stackiii/status/3238716660757 29921.

Serrano, R. A. & Bennett, B. 2013, 'Possible Pressure Cooker Bomb Believed Hidden in Black Backpack'. *Los Angeles Times*, viewed 26 October 2015, http://articles.latimes.com/2013/apr/16/nation/la-na-nn-boston-bombings-pressure-cooker-0130416.

Sheller, M. 2015, 'News Now: Interface, Ambience, Flow, and the Disruptive Spatio-Temporalities of Mobile News Media'. *Journalism Studies*, Vol. 16, no. 1, pp. 12–26.

Shepard, M. 2013, 'I Think a Bomb Just Went Off in Boston. Can't Tell. Can Smell Smoke. Emergency Vehicles Everywhere.' Instagram, 16 April 2013 at 2:22 a.m., viewed 26 October 2015, https://instagram.com/p/YIaw3cAWSE/.

Van Leuven, S., Deprez, A. & Raeymaeckers, K. 2014, 'Towards More Balanced News Access? A Study on the Impact of Cost-Cutting and Web 2.0 on the Mediated Public Sphere'. *Journalism*, Vol. 15, no. 7, pp. 850–867.

Vänskä, O. 2013, 'Paljastaako Bostonin Pommittajan näin Yksinkertainen Tekijä?' *Talouselama*, viewed 26 October 2015, www.talouselama.fi/uutiset/paljastaako+bostonin+pommittajan+nain+yksinkertainen+tekija/a2180628?s=r.

Vis, F. 2013, 'Twitter as a Reporting Tool for Breaking News: Journalists Tweeting the 2011 UK Riots'. *Digital Journalism*, Vol. 1, no. 1, pp. 27–47.

Wall, T. & Linnemann, T. 2014, 'Staring Down the State: Police Power, Visual Economies, and the "War on Cameras"'. *Crime Media Culture*, Vol. 10, no. 2, pp. 133–149.

Winslow, D. R. 2006, 'Reuters Apologizes over Altered Lebanon War Photographs'. *NPPA*, viewed 26 October 2015, https://nppa.org/news/2156.

Wise, J. M. 2013, 'Introduction: Ecstatic Assemblages of Visuality', in J. Macgregor Wise & H. Koskela (eds) *New Visualities, New Technologies: The New Ecstasy of Communication*. Farnham: Ashgate, pp. 1–5.

Zhang, M. 2013a, 'Boston Marathon Bombing Investigators Using Crowdsourced Photographs', viewed 26 October 2015, http://petapixel.com/2013/04/17/boston-marathon-bombing-investigators-using-crowdsourced-photographs/#QByMit5jv wfRiQ8w.99.

Zhang, M. 2013b, 'Reddit and 4chan Working to ID Boston Bomber Using Available Photos', viewed 26 October 2015, http://petapixel.com/2013/04/18/reddit-and-4chan-working-to-id-boston-bomber-using-available-photos/#68vmUQyrtrc 6CoO6.99.

Zhang, M. 2013c, 'NY Post uses Photo of Innocent Teen as Boston Bombing Cover Photo', viewed 26 October 2015, http://petapixel.com/2013/04/19/ny-post-uses-photo-of-innocent-teen-as-boston-bombing-cover-photo/#Kh8fXcKT2lpvk vzM.99.

6 Variance in everyday photography

Karin Becker

The aim of this chapter is to suggest ways that a perspective that asks *who* connects to digital photography, *where* and *in what ways* can help us to understand how complex digital photographic technologies impact on our ways of living together. There are at least two assumptions underlying this perspective: first, that digital photography is not a single unified phenomenon but involves variation across many applications, practices and cultural settings; and, second, embedded in the notion of variation, that comparative research can contribute to this endeavour. Digital photography is often laden with a third assumption, namely that its technologies have broken with previous applications and practices, transforming everyday photography into a new phenomenon, barely recognizable within the old frameworks of photography as a medium. Twenty years ago, Martin Lister (1995) pointed to how the rhetoric surrounding new image technologies had constructed the notion of their 'newness', resulting in false dichotomies and oppositions between 'photography' and the digital image that blocked systematic interrogation of digital practices as negotiations with photographic cultures from the past or elsewhere. This rhetoric of novelty and transformation persists, and with it the necessity to reflect upon and critique the language used to characterize digital technologies. Variation is implicit in the questions of *who*, *where* and *in what ways* these technologies impact ways of life, inviting comparative research across time, place and cultural experience.

Three of the studies in this part of the book scrutinize forms of photographic practice by people who are often assumed to be beyond the 'digital divide' due to their age, nationality or economic vulnerability. Selecting a group of Austrian seniors, as Maria Schreiber has done, suggests that they use digital technologies in ways that may diverge from the practices of younger cohorts, so-called 'digital natives'. Indeed, she finds that seniors do draw on patterns and practices familiar from analogue photography, but show a proficiency and playfulness as they adapt these to digital media. Despite their innovative practices, most of her informants saw themselves as less 'fluent' in digital technologies than younger people, which suggests that inter-generational differences are a 'discursively produced common-sense construction ... grounded in a diffuse idea of competence'. Paula Uimonen's research is based on ten years of experience investigating digital practices in Tanzania, particularly among young people. In this chapter, she looks at young urban women's uses of cell phones for personal photography, and how they 'enact' themselves through self-representation. Interestingly, the 'selfie' is not part of these women's practice. Uimonen traces the 'relational sociality' of their mobile photography, including the mobile phone as a material object that affords new forms of editing, display and circulation of images. She also notes the women's fear and vulnerability, knowing that their pictures may fall into the wrong hands, not least because of the high rate of theft of mobile devices. Sara Pargana Mota's chapter investigates a particular set of practices involving fashion, presentation of self and entrepreneurship among Portuguese women who have created 'closet profile accounts' on Facebook, to sell and trade clothes. Against the backdrop of the economic downturn, and despite their limited financial means, these women have created an entry into the world of fashion, consumerism and visibility, a form of 'microcelebrity' for themselves.

Instead of examining the practices of a group, Anssi Männistö takes his point of departure in an event, the Boston Marathon bomb attack in 2013, and considers how mobile phone images and the possibilities for connectedness in real time, through social features of digital media, were instrumental in apprehending the suspects. What becomes evident in Männistö's study is how, under extraordinary circumstances, 'everyday' practices can quickly be transformed and used instrumentally for other purposes. Authorities carried out a 'crowd-sourced' investigation that generated huge amounts of visual data but that nevertheless proved somewhat difficult to control. During the pursuit, for example, the police requested that no live video of officers approaching search locations be 'broadcast', which was debated heatedly on Twitter. The 'revolution' (as Männistö calls it) in mobile imaging, together with big data analysis (including biometric facial recognition), enabled a rapid investigation of the bombing to take place.

So, what is meant when these photographic practices are characterized as belonging to the realm of the 'everyday'? The term is broader than 'amateur' or 'family' or 'domestic' photography, and can be seen to challenge the ways these earlier terms framed understandings of photography as a binary practice situated between public and private life (Slater 1995). Photography is *both* a professional and a leisure activity, and when focused on the 'family' quickly becomes implicated in perpetuating a particular social construction while obscuring the commercial interests and marketing strategies that have mutually constructed this genre (Bourdieu [1965]/1990). As the studies in this volume make abundantly clear, any border that may have previously existed between public and private photography has become increasingly blurred. The perspective of the 'everyday' invites a critical interrogation of distinctions drawn between private and public domains of daily life, including when they infringe upon each other. It permits us, following Slater (1995), to examine how photographic practices 'mediate' between public and private spheres.

I have previously proposed the term 'vernacular' as a more accurate characterization of the patterns and practices that arise as people combine these new and old tools and platforms when making, editing and distributing photographs in the contexts of their daily lives (Becker 2002). 'Vernacular' includes the everyday without excluding those special, unusual or 'historic' occasions that people use their own image-making devices to capture. Vernacular photography rests on the notion of a visual dialect, with expressions, conventions and techniques that arise through social and cultural practice. The vernacular is dynamic, building on tradition and, at the same time, breaking new ground, often drawing on forms of popular and public culture, both visual and non-visual. While inviting a bottom-up perspective on everyday photography, a vernacular perspective takes into account how practices are shaped by the affordances and constraints of technology and by the commodification of image-making and circulation as globalized phenomena.

To the extent that vernacular imagery, whether digital or analogue, is understood as representing the experience of an ordinary person, it also carries an aura of authenticity without the veneer of professionalism or instrumentality associated, for example, with commercial or press photography. This is not the same as claiming that vernacular photographs are more 'real' or 'true'; it does assume, however, that the vernacular is more closely tied to the photographers' lived experience. Recent research in press photography indicates that readers' beliefs in a photograph's authenticity may be enhanced when it is known to be the work of an amateur (Andén-Papadopoulos & Pantti 2011; Williams, Wahl-Jorgensen & Waddle 2011). The amateur image is understood as raw and direct, giving it value as a report direct from the scene. This is especially true when the photograph portrays a traumatic event and the photographer lacks the professional experience that would enable him/her to 'compose' an image under such circumstances. The vernacular photograph is understood, in the first instance, as an expression from a participant's perspective, from inside the event. This can explain why the Boston authorities were so eager to locate and analyse spectators' photographs from the bombing, as Männistö recounts. It also has been the case when photographs of historic and traumatic events by non-professionals have become part of the larger or collective memory (Becker 2015; Zelizer 2002). However, 'authenticity', in this sense, can also explain the value of photographs from domestic settings that cross other genres of public photography, including fashion (as Pargana Mota's subjects demonstrated with their 'closet profiles' on Facebook) or their appearance in the fine arts, as Karen Cross (2012) and others have noted.

This further points towards these photographs as 'relational objects', following Edwards (2006), and to perspectives that include embodiment and performance as aids to understanding the ways they are made and used. In my own research, I have drawn on performance and folklore studies' analysis of cultural 'enactments' and 'speech events' to gain insights into vernacular photography and where emergent dimensions of multi-semiotic modes of meaning can be taken into account (Geertz 1973). A cultural enactment assumes a public or audience who is, in turn, making a qualitative assessment of the 'performance' (Bauman 1977; Kirshenblatt-Gimblett 1998; Becker 2001). A performance perspective thus directs our inquiry into interactions among participants and situates participants (including the audience) in time and space, while also structuring individual and group identities (Becker 2001; Kirshenblatt-Gimblett 1998). The forms of microcelebrity Paragana Mota identifies among her Portuguese subjects, drawing on Senft (2008), provides a clear example. The performance of photography is not, in the first instance, visual, but physical and multisensory, as a way of situating one's self in the world.

More than a set of technologies of visual representation, photography is 'a constitutive type of (visible) action within the social world' (Frosh 2001, p. 43). From this perspective, taking and displaying pictures becomes a 'performance of representation', that is, an enactment of social knowledge of photographic practices and of the networks of power and creativity that arise within the nexus of photographers, viewers and those who are photographed. Photography is, in this sense, 'a manifest performance of the power to make visible' (ibid., p. 43; Becker 2015).

Reflexivity is central to photography as a cultural performance and is critical to understanding how these practices relate to the everyday. Compared with the discourses and material practices that compose everyday life, performances are often stylized and self-reflexive enactments, that comment on and transform that which is taken for granted, making it visible and available for reflection (Becker 1995). Photography, in all its manifestations, is inherently a reflexive practice, both for its practitioners and for those who study it.

Having now argued for a perspective that takes variance in everyday digital photography as culturally based and performative, what are we to do with its technologies? First, as suggested in the introduction to this chapter, researchers need continually to remind themselves that a 'new' platform or format is not in itself 'transformative'. Examining *who* uses it, *where* and *in what ways* must also include critical attention to the rhetoric of novelty and transformation in which technologies quickly become embedded, and how this discourse forms and informs research. As the studies in this volume demonstrate, established research initiatives can blind us to alternative explanations regarding who is using new technologies, where and in what ways. The newly retired generation of 'silver surfers', who now have time to establish fluency in digital media practices, the young Taiwanese involved in creative techno-swapping and who began watching television as they married and had children, or research on the

Iranian 'Facebook revolution' that remains ignorant of how the under-ground exchange of cassette tapes of Ayatollah Khomeini contributed to processes of social change a generation ago – these are only a few of the examples illustrating the importance of challenging and revising established discourses of digital media's transformative power (Christensen & Morley 2014; Sreberny-Mohammadi & Mohammadi 1994).

The lesson here is that research focusing on a single 'new' medium or platform tends to disregard the ways these practices draw upon and mix with other media, as well as other social practices. Miller and Madianou have introduced the concept of 'polymedia' to account for the commingling of a variety of media technologies in the communication practices among transnational families, and where 'media are mediated by the relationship as well as the other way round' (2012, p. 148). Just as a single 'new' medium is rarely, if ever, transformative per se, people interact with media in many different ways. As important as it is to avoid the media-centric perspective that would privilege a single medium as accounting for interaction and change, we must not forget the particular affordances of each specific medium, in order to understand just how they contribute to the polymedial and social mix of communication. In her writing about 'screen practices', Friedberg pointed to the movie screen, the TV screen and the computer screen as having specific histories and characteristics, 'at the same time that the types of images one sees on each of them are losing their medium-based specificity' (2003, p. 346). Maintaining a balance between considerations of the histories and cultures of specific media practices and applying these critically to contemporary digital photography – whether techniques or platforms or social applications – is the greatest challenge facing research on everyday or vernacular photography and its impact on our ways of living together.

Finally, research must address the power relations built into the inter-connectedness of digital imagery. Nearly two decades ago, Sarah Kember pointed to the 'lie of safety' in surveillance photography; despite its promise of security, its aim was the protection of property (Kember 1998, p. 13). Today, academic discourses of surveillance still primarily address rhetorically oriented macro-perspectives, yet, in the experiential and onto-logical realm of the 'mediatized everyday' addressed in this volume, sur-veillance is just as likely to be horizontal and continuous, at the level of everyday use. Christensen and Janson (2013) introduce the term 'interveil-lance' to describe this banal form of everyday surveillance, where the flow of digital images across platforms such as Facebook and Instagram, with their metadata, would also be implicated. This is the level at which Uimo-nen's subjects express concern over being exposed through their own digital photography practices and Männistö's study is a case study of how quickly and effectively these 'personal' photographs can be redirected and deployed in the interest of law enforcement and the state. Even when digital practitioners claim a lack of concern over these forms of (potential) control and their misuse, these ubiquitous structural affordances and constraints are integral to how photographic technologies impact on our ways of living together. They should, therefore, be written into current research agendas.

Yet, are these structures truly 'ubiquitous' or is this, again, part of the rhetoric of digital technologies? Today, there are growing numbers of 'digital refugees' who, for any of an entire range of reasons, live some portion, or even their entire daily lives, outside the realm of online communication. They may be trying to avoid pursuit or censorship, they may lack resources or knowledge, or they may be striving to retain their independence in the face of the pressure towards the interconnectedness that characterizes daily life for many people today. The 'digital refugee', like the vernacular photographer, is not a unified category, but is part of the variance we find as we extend our gaze across this expanding landscape of photographic practices. When we ask *who* connects to digital photography, we will find that some people do not. Their practice, even as an absence, cannot be excluded from our research purviews. Quite the contrary: when we come upon gaps in a cultural practice we had taken for granted as something 'everybody' does, we are on the edge of what may well prove to be the most interesting and challenging insights into its significance. Digital refugees are therefore important keys to understanding, ontologically and experientially, the impact of digital photographic technologies on contemporary social life. A full perspective on variance in everyday photography demands their presence.

References

Andén-Papadopoulos, K. & Pantti, M. (eds) 2011, *Amateur Images and Global News*. Intellect Press: Bristol.

Bauman, R. 1977, *Verbal Art as Performance*. Waveland Press: Prospect Heights, IL.

Becker, K. 2015, 'Gestures of Seeing: Amateur Photographers in the News'. *Journalism*, Vol. 16, no. 4, pp. 451–469.

Becker, K. 2002 'Fotografier: Lagrade Bildminnen' (Photographs: Archived Visual Memories), in K. Becker, E. Bjurström, J. Fornäs & H. Ganetz (eds) *Medier och Människor i Konsumtionsrummet* (Media and People in the Space of Consumption). Nya Doxa: Nora, Sweden.

Becker, K. 2001, 'Creative Culture as Life Form', in P. F. Snickars (ed.) *Culture, Society and Market*. Swedish National Council for Cultural Affairs: Stockholm, pp. 79–90.

Becker, K. 1995, 'Media and the Ritual Process'. *Media, Culture and Society*, Vol. 17, no. 4, pp. 629–646.

Bourdieu, P. [1965]/1990, *Photography: A Middle-Brow Art*. Stanford University Press: Stanford, CA.

Christensen, M. & Jansson, A. 2014, 'Complicit Surveillance, Interveillance, and the Question of Cosmopolitanism: Toward a Phenomenological Understanding of Mediatization'. *New Media and Society*, Vol. 17, no. 9, pp. 1473–1491.

Christensen, M. & Morley, D. 2014, 'New Media, New Crises, New Theories? An Interview with David Morley'. *Popular Communication*, Vol. 12, no. 4, pp. 208–222.

Cross, K. 2012, 'Photography and "the Cult of the Amateur"', in J.-E. Lundström & L. Stoltz (eds) *Thinking Photography: Using Photography*. Centrum för Fotografi: Stockholm.

Edwards, E. 2006, 'Photographs and the Sound of History'. *Visual Anthropology Review*, Vol. 21, nos 1–2, pp. 27–46.

Friedberg, A. 2003, 'The Virtual Window', in D. Thorburn & H. Jenkins (eds) *Rethinking Media Change: The Aesthetics of Transition*. MIT Press: Cambridge, MA; London.

Frosh, P. 2001, 'The Public Eye and the Citizen-Voyeur: Photography as a Performance of Power'. *Social Semiotics*, Vol. 1, no. 1, pp. 43–59.

Geertz, C. 1973, *The Interpretation of Cultures: Selected Essays*. Basic Books, Harper: New York.

Kember, S. 1998, *Virtual Anxiety: Photography, New Technologies and Subjectivity*. Manchester University Press: Manchester.

Kirshenblatt-Gimblett, B. 1998, *Destination Culture: Tourism, Museums and Heritage*. University of California Press: Berkeley, CA.

Lister, M. 1995, 'Introduction', in M. Lister (ed.) *The Photographic Image in Digital Culture*. Routledge: London, pp. 1–28.

Miller, D. & Madianou, M. 2012, *Migration and New Media: Transnational Families and Polymedia*. Routledge: London.

Senft, T. M. 2008, *Camgirls: Celebrity & Community in the Age of Social Networks*. Peter Lang: New York.

Slater, D. 1995, 'Domestic Photography and Digital Culture', in M. Lister (ed.) *The Photographic Image in Digital Culture*. Routledge: London, pp. 129–146.

Sreberny-Mohammadi, A. & Mohammadi, A. 1994, *Small Media, Big Revolution: Communication, Culture and the Iranian Revolution*. University of Minnesota Press: Minneapolis, MN.

Williams, A., Wahl-Jorgensen, K. & Waddle, C. 2011, '"More Real and Less Packaged": Audience Discourses on Amateur News Content and their Effects on Journalism Practice', in K. Andén-Papadopoulos & M. Pantti (eds) *Amateur Images and Global News*. Intellect Press: Bristol, pp. 193–210.

Zelizer, B. 2002, 'Finding Aids to the Past: Bearing Personal Witness to Traumatic Public Events'. *Media, Culture and Society*, Vol. 24, pp. 697–714.

Part II

Cameras, connectivity and transformed localities

7 Photographs of place in phonespace

Camera phones as a location-aware mobile technology

Mikko Villi

Introduction

Verbal mobile phone communication is mostly confined to locations that have no intrinsic relationship to the act of communication; the content of communication is mostly determined by the participating subjects, not by the physical location in which the communicators reside. When talking or texting on the mobile phone, one does not necessarily have any indication of the location of the other communicator. By contrast, when communicating with photographs, there is often an essential connection between the physical setting and the act of communication. The photograph is, after all, captured in a definite location and, with the aid of the mobile phone, the photograph can be shared right from the spot immediately after capture. By using a camera phone photograph, one can 'send the place', visually mediating one's local presence. The main argument of this chapter is that camera phone photographs accentuate the significance of location in mobile communication, from being mere points of communication into being individual places, places with identity.

In this sense, the sharing of camera phone photographs is a predecessor to, for example, such mobile applications as Swarm[1], which enable the easy sharing of location and also emphasize the significance of the location where the use of the mobile phone occurs. An important contribution of the chapter is, then, in shedding light on such location-based networked interactions in mobile communication that existed before smartphones with global positioning system (GPS) receivers were introduced to consumers. A goal of the chapter is also to build a theoretical link between camera phone photo communication practices and novel location-aware mobile technologies. *Location-aware technologies* consist of devices that are able to locate themselves via a GPS, Wi-Fi or the triangulation of radio waves, and therefore can provide users with location-specific information (de Souza e Silva & Frith 2012, p. 6). *Locative media* can be defined as a term that is used to capture the diverse array of location-aware technologies and practices (Wilken & Goggin 2015, p. 4). Importantly, as already noted, photography is also a strongly location-aware form of communication, although it has not generally been studied in relation to locative media.

The concepts of place and location often seem to overlap in discourse on both location-aware mobile technologies and photography. Also, in everyday language, the two words are commonly used rather synonymously. Adriana de Souza e Silva (2013, p. 119), notes how the term *location* has received sparse scholarly attention when compared to its correlate *place*. For the purposes of this chapter, it is necessary to distinguish the two and offer a specific definition of place (see also Pink in this volume). First of all, location can be considered to be a place deprived of meaning (Cresswell 2004). Location refers merely to the position of a person or thing and is, thus, less culturally and socially encompassing than place (Wilken & Goggin 2015, pp. 2–3), which is all-pervasive in the way that it informs and shapes everyday lived experience (Wilken & Goggin 2012, p. 6). *Place* does not refer only to a point on a map but rather arises in the dynamic interrelatedness of things (Malpas 2012, p. 28) and is, thus, about more than just physical geography (Hjorth 2012, p. 140). Not all places even have fixed geographical coordinates. For example, heaven and hell are places but cannot be located (de Souza e Silva & Frith 2012, p. 10).

Place is a networked, dynamic and meaningful entity and a psycho-social construct that includes social relations (Gordon & de Souza e Silva 2012, p. 90; Gibson, Luckman & Brennan-Horley 2012, p. 123). In a sense, the relation between location and place can be outlined by comparing location to the concept of 'non-place', as coined by Augé (1995). Certain locations, such as motorways, airports and aeroplanes, hotel chains, leisure parks and shopping malls are physical places but at the same time they are non-places. Augé (pp. 77–79) explains that a place which cannot be defined as relational, historical or concerned with identity is a non-place.

A useful concept in examining the mediation of place in both mobile communication and photography is 'mediated presence' (Villi 2015). Mediated presence is not a clearly articulated theoretical model, but rather a conceptual theme describing the use of telecommunication technology for being in contact with one another over physical distance – being socially present despite being physically absent. A photograph, too, can mediate presence, as it embodies the possibility of the object, place or person in the photograph being present for the viewer. In the context of camera phone communication, these two dimensions of presence are conjoined, as presence is mediated by images over distances by utilizing a telecommunicative connection.

Re-localization of mobile communication

The popularity of *location-based services* – services and media of communication that are functionally bound to a location (Wilken 2012, p. 243) – is an interesting trend in mobile communication, as it is in striking contrast to a central theme in the discourse on mobile communication, namely the liberation from location in communication. In telephone communication, mobility is nowadays more of a premise than an added value. A popular notion has been that, when people become immersed in the 'mobile media sound bubbles of communication' (Bull 2005, p. 178), the places they pass through in their daily lives increasingly lose significance (Meyrowitz 2005, pp. 25–27; Geser 2004, p. 36; Ling 2008). It is true that the mobile phone does have the capacity to disrupt a user's connection to place and co-present others. However, at the same time, it can connect the user to (even previously unknown) others in that place and to the place itself (Campbell 2013, p. 11).

In contrast to many of the views presented in the first decade of the century, mobile phone use is now increasingly bound to a location. Rather than directing someone towards 'absent presence' – as in indicating a state where one is physically present, yet at the same time absorbed by a techno-logically mediated world elsewhere (Gergen 2002, p. 227) – mobile tech-nologies actually work as interfaces to locations. The technologies also foreground the importance of locations – as places – in our social and net-worked interactions. Therefore, due to the increasing use of location-aware technologies, location becomes paramount to social interaction and spatial construction, and locations are filled with a wealth of digital information (de Souza e Silva & Frith 2012, pp. 8, 14, 102, 169).

Mobile devices can help strengthen users' connections to their surround-ing location, rather than removing them from it. Location-based services have become an elemental component of mobile communication. By using the mobile phone's location-aware capabilities, users can annotate loca-tions, find other people in the vicinity and access information connected to specific locations (de Souza e Silva 2013, p. 117; Humphreys 2013). When people attach visual or other information to locations they share their memories and understandings of those locations, along with the physical coordinates (Özkul 2015, p. 102). According to what Gordon and de Souza e Silva (2012) call 'net locality', location is becoming the organizing logic of our networked interactions. Net localities include an increasing amount of location-based information that is not only attached to places but also becomes an intrinsic, dynamic part of those places. Through the increasing use of location-aware technologies, locations acquire renewed interest and meaning (de Souza e Silva & Frith 2012, p. 10). 'De-localized' mobile communication is 're-localized' (Licoppe & Heurtin 2002, p. 101), either automatically or as a consequence of the intentional activities of the user. This re-localization represents a new awareness of location in medi-ated communication.

The re-localization of mobile communication can be accomplished in various ways. In a verbal call, re-localization can be achieved by providing information on the caller's location during the phone call. 'Location talk' has been an obvious feature of mobile communication. For this reason, much research into mobile technologies has addressed issues focusing on location and place (Laursen & Szymanski 2013, p. 315). Nowadays, smartphone apps offer a multitude of localization services, ranging from Swarm to Find My Friends. The users of Swarm can even 'collect places' when checking in takes precedence over movement (Gazzard 2011, p. 416).

Camera phone users, for their part, are localized by the photographs they communicate. In its most simple form, the physical location is appended by automatic geotagging of the photograph by embedding metadata received from the phone's GPS chip. In mobile phone photography and such smartphone apps as Instagram, geotagging is increasingly the default, rather than a choice (Hjorth & Pink 2014, p. 40). Naturally, photographs also communicate the location by the contents of the photograph itself.

Mediated presence

Photographic re-localization is closely connected to the concept of mediated presence. In general, mediated presence is enabled by the various teletechnologies – television, radio, telephone and the internet. Mediated presence is not about direct physical co-presence but, instead, about presence that is communicated through a medium. Users of mobile communication technology are not present by any physical means, but merely connected to one another in another location by using a communication device. Mediated presence emulates the experience of actually being in a remote location or with a remote other.

Licoppe (2004, p. 135) states that telecommunication technologies are used in mediated relationships to substitute or compensate for the rarity of face-to-face interactions and the absence of others. Therefore, the aspect of *tele* in communication can actually be equated with absence. 'The essence of tele-presence is that it is anti-presence' (Manovich 1995). Mobile phone communication is about technologically mediated sociability (Schroeder 2010, p. 83; Jensen 2013, p. 26; Ito & Okabe 2005, p. 263) in times of absence (Haunstrup Christensen 2008, pp. 435, 446). Mediated presence, thus, captures the most salient trait of mobile communication: the possibility for close communicative engagements among distant agents, a form of absence in which proximity can be established and preserved through mediated communication. The fundamental ambivalence of telecommunication media consists of their usability as tools for both presence and absence: they can induce a feeling of presence and facilitate absence (Villi & Stocchetti 2011, pp. 102, 104).

Similarly, a photograph conveys the presence of the absent one, the object or person captured in the photograph. Photography exemplifies the epistemological dialectic of presence and absence (Lister 2007, p. 353). Actually, as Sonesson (1989, p. 73) writes, 'The whole point of photography is to offer us vicarious perceptual experience, that is, the illusion of having seen something without having been present at the scene.' A photograph gives presence to absence. Sontag (1977, pp. 16, 155) asserts that a photograph is both a 'pseudo-presence' and a 'token of absence', a surrogate possession of a cherished person or thing.

In the presence mediated by a photograph, of great importance is the indexical relation between the photograph and the object or location photographed. The index ties the photograph to the location. Barthes ([1981]/2000, pp. 76–77, 80, 87) notes that every photograph is a certificate of presence, 'literally an emanation of the referent'. The fact that the photographed object has been there is the essence, the 'noeme' of photography. As its name translates from Greek, the photograph has been 'written with light' (Batchen 1999, p. 101). Photographs are 'images produced as a consequence of being directly affected by the objects to which they refer' (Batchen 2004, p. 31). A photograph is not only an interpretation of the real but also a trace, something directly stencilled off the real. There is always a presumption that something exists in the location, or did exist, which then is depicted in the picture (Sontag 1977, pp. 5–6, 154).

What the mobile phone adds to the locally rooted, indexical presence is the contemporaneous aspect of communication. The mobile photograph, sent and received in a matter of minutes, is not rooted to the location where the photographer was, say, two weeks ago, but where he or she is at the moment of communication. The novel element of telecommunication affects the way a photograph can mediate the being of the object or person in the image. A conventional photograph mediates it from *there-then* to the *here-now* (Barthes [1977]/1991, p. 44), as for example, when a photographic print is here in front of my eyes (present), but at the same time the situation depicted in the photograph is already gone (in time) – the person photographed might even be dead. By contrast, a photograph sent forward from a camera phone immediately after capture can form a connection between *there-now* and the *here-now* (Villi 2015).

A dividing line can be drawn between mediated presence as the sense or the illusion of 'being there' and 'being there together' – between 'physical presence' and 'social presence' (IJsselsteijn *et al.* 2000; Schroeder 2005, p. 342). For the major part, mobile communication can be described, essentially, as using a medium to be with another, providing a social presence. More often than having a sense of the place, the users experience the sense of being with another (Biocca, Harms & Burgoon 2003, pp. 456, 458). However, with the mobile photograph, it is possible also conveniently to send the place and give the other a sense of being there. The photograph does not necessarily need to express photographic skills or quality, as its function is more in the communicative use of the photograph. The 'visual little nothings' of everyday life, photographs of and from mundane places, serve well in establishing a connection and communicating one's presence. Sending the place forms a part of 'visual chit-chat' (Villi 2012), as people communicate about themselves and their whereabouts with a steady stream of photographs, such as is exemplified by the selfie culture. Visual chitchat or small-talk can be a valuable communicative activity, even if it consists of repetitive and superfluous photographs. Photographs enable phatic interpersonal communication about place (Sutherland 2012, p. 165). These conventions follow largely from the practices of mobile communication, where often the act of calling or texting counts at least as much, if not more, than what is said.

'Phonespace' and 'photospace'

In relation to place and location, it is essential to discuss space as well. Here, I utilize *space* in the sense that Massey (2008) defines it: space is the product of the simultaneous existence and interrelations of people. I adapt this notion of space to 'telecommunicative space', where the interrelations do not occur between co-present people, but rather between people connected via telecommunication media. The concepts of telecommunicative space and social presence describe very much the same thing. Thus, people reside in a physical location, but at the same time they can act in a telecommunicative space, for example when talking on the telephone. Castells *et al.* (2007, pp. 171–178) point out how mobile communication redefines places as a space of communication; places act as points of convergence in communication networks and they are subsumed into the space of flows.

The space of the telecommunicative connection can also be labelled as 'phonespace' (Hulme & Truch 2005, p. 466). People spend an increasing share of their daily lives in the phonespace. A growing proportion of social interactions are mediated; they occur with mostly verbal representations of others, rather than through co-present face-to-face encounters (IJsselsteijn, van Baren & van Lanen 2003). For many users, mobile communication can be perpetual rather than consisting of only temporal excursions into the telecommunicative space. Ito and Okabe (2005, p. 264) conclude that by using mobile communication, people can experience a sense of a persistent social space. Thus, the phonespace is a constant space, but the physical locale keeps on changing. With increasing mobile internet connections, phone communicators move between online and offline, surrounded by people and things, while also traversing social networking sites and other online elements. For them, places are, in fact, both online and offline places through these movements (Hjorth & Pink 2014, p. 45). Mobile media mesh located place and networked space (Richardson & Wilken 2012, p. 184).

Like location, the telecommunicative space, as such, has no identity. It obtains its value and importance from the fleeting and ephemeral, yet meaningful, acts of communication that take place (or perhaps I should say 'take space') in the communicative space. Many 'real places' (e.g. traditional meeting places such as cafés) – places of active presence – can actually turn into non-places when people engage in mobile communication with those who are absent and thereby transform their physical locales into socially meaningless places. Mobile communication can transform non-places into telecommunicative spaces and places into non-places. However, through the use of both location-based services and photographs in mobile communication, both places and non-places can acquire new location-related meanings. First, many places become locations – that is, the locational aspects of many places acquire relevance (de Souza e Silva & Frith 2012, p. 10). Second, many non-places, or the 'in-between places', are no longer contexts for just killing time. The temporal presences in these non-places have become key moments where new forms of visuality and sociality are generated through camera phone photography and the digital co-presence enabled by mobile media (Hjorth & Pink 2014, pp. 42, 45). For example, on Swarm, users are deliberately marking locations, such as airports and railway stations, as places of identity by sharing them with others. This identity is then extended through the social network attached to Swarm (Gazzard 2011, p. 408).

Sending the place

In the following, I will present observations and perceptions from a study that I carried out with a group of Finnish camera phone users. For the study, I utilized qualitative in-depth interviews, interviewing eight subjects individually. The sampling procedure for the interviewees was purposive and consisted of searching for exemplary informants – people who have shared photographs from their mobile phones. The interviews lasted, on average, one-and-a-half hours, and they were recorded and transcribed.

I used a semi-structured model for the interviews and presented a set of questions to all of the interviewees. The dialogue during the interviews was staged according to a thematic, topic-centred structure, which also provided a context for unexpected themes to develop (Mason 2002, pp. 62–63). The interviewees could continue their thoughts along new lines, and they were asked to elaborate on certain themes that seemed interesting and to express reflective and critical views. The study proceeded, from analysis and coding of parts of the data set, to developing a holistic understanding of the practices and views expressed by the interviewees. By applying thematic analysis, I classified the interview material based on a study of the previous literature on camera phones and mobile communication. I was also open to themes that emerged from the analysis or originated with the informants, but the analysis was predominantly theory based.

I will use pseudonyms when referring to the interviewees. They formed a quite knowledgeable group when it comes to photography and, in that sense, they were not representative of the general population. None of them were professional photographers. They were interested in taking and communicating with photographs, which, however, seems to be quite common nowadays, as is demonstrated by the popularity of posting photographs on Instagram and Facebook. A significant proportion of the population in developed countries – and increasingly in developing countries as well – are potential photographers, as they have access to a camera in their mobile phone. In this sense, I suggest that individuals without specialist knowledge in photography can and do use their camera phones for mediating presence.

Kasper (aged 21) was specializing in digital multimedia in his college studies. He had previously worked as a photographer at a local newspaper and had also taken promotional pictures for music bands. Lotta (aged 21) was specializing in digital multimedia as well. She was a habitual photographer, describing her habits as 'taking pictures for fun, from parties and different occasions'. Like Kasper and Lotta, Joakim (aged 23) was specializing in digital multimedia. For him, photography was a hobby and he usually carried both a stand-alone camera and a camera phone with him. Mikael (aged 21) was a student of media culture. He had studied photography a bit but had not published photographs. Anja (aged 55) worked at a college as the director of a study programme. She took pictures of family and nature, as well as travel photographs. Kjell (aged 52) was a programme director. He photographed regularly, several days a week, and had also developed photographs by himself. Ulla (aged 35) was a teacher in the media technology department. She had the habit of building pictorial archives. She had archived plants and, at the time of the interview, was archiving photographs of VW Kleinbuses. Bengt (59) worked at a college as a research coordinator. He took a lot of pictures when travelling but also photographed his grandchildren when he met up with them.

The idea of mediating one's contemporaneous presence in a certain location by sending photographs has also been introduced in several other studies on camera phones. Even before the introduction of multimedia messaging (MMS) there were predictions that the 'sending of place' and the experience of 'being there' would become possible through camera phones (Kopomaa 2000, p. 96). In *Mobile Image*, a pioneering book on camera phones (Koskinen, Kurvinen & Lehtonen 2002, p. 78), it was concluded that digital images are used to share one's visually mediated experience, often in a very concrete way: 'Look, I am at a café with my friends! My, what a mountain of dishes I have to do! Now I am abroad, now I am parachuting!'

In 2005, Scifo (p. 373) wrote

> the camera phone enables the multiplication of connections between different physical and social spaces, rather than the weakening of a 'sense of place' – even though mobile communication is often cited as contributing to the processes of disembedding experience from local contexts.

With its new visual potential, mobile technology emphasizes forms of experience that are strongly rooted in physical locations. The camera phone enables 'the doubling of place', or the translocation of place. In photographic communication, the place or situation is transformed into the content of the communication itself (ibid., pp. 364–365).

In the study by Kindberg *et al.* (2005, p. 46), a subject described the photographic connection as 'telepresence', in that it made his absent girl-friend feel as if she were 'here to see it' (for similar views, see also Counts & Fellheimer 2004; Gai 2007, p. 205; Kondor 2007, pp. 27–28). One con-clusion of Kindberg *et al.* (2004, p. 12) was that

> Unlike text messaging, many of the images sent to absent friends and family were in fact visual evidence or proof of something having had occurred … Proof of being somewhere or experiencing some event could be made more potent by showing when something was happen-ing as well as what was happening.

Absence of the other motivates the communication of photographs (Rose 2003, p. 11).

In my study, the relation between photographs and place came up clearly in the discussion with the subjects. Joakim noted that by sending camera phone photographs one can 'prove that you are somewhere', in a 'certain situation'. Photographs are not independent of place (Pink 2011, p. 9). According to Mikael, the reason for sending photographs might be that 'It has been something funny you want to show some friend or you want to say *hi!* from a ski resort.' He described sending many photographs portraying himself in specific places that acted as (indexical) proof of his presence there. For Mikael, the camera phone 'brings maybe a new dimen-sion to visual communication; you can send them [the photographs] wher-ever you are'. As for Bengt, he explained, 'With this camera phone it is more to show where you are and what you do, and there is not so much aesthetic value in that picture.' For him, a photograph can also act as an invitation or wish for the other to 'join' the place, as in 'I wish you were here.' According to Hjorth and Pink (2014, pp. 42, 45), 'Camera phone practices provide new ways of mapping place beyond just the geographic: they partake in adding social, emotional and psychological dimensions to a sense of place.' Locations become 'somewheres' through photographs.

The difference between text messaging, in mediating presence, and photographs was obvious. For example, during his trip to Japan, Joakim ended up in the middle of an enormously big crowd, and thus a photo-graph which says *hey check out the number of people and I'm standing right in the middle of them* would have been more effective than a text message sent from the same situation. Mikael observed that 'Maybe the photograph helps to put the text in place and time, that now I am here and doing this, and this is the place where I am, whereas text messages are only, like, they could come from anywhere.' This relates to how camera phone picture-taking and sharing can be viewed as part of a broader process of 'emplacement' (Hjorth 2015, p. 24).

Based on their descriptions, it is easy to notice how many of the photographs sent by the interviewees resemble postcards, especially ones sent during holidays. Kjell explained how he can send an 'instant postcard' with his camera phone: 'I want to say what I am doing now, this is my moment.' Bengt had bought a camera phone for his lady friend just before she went on a trip to Egypt, so that they could send photographs to each other. He had also sent photographs to his daughter from a trip to Italy and, in general, most of the photographs he had sent were from trips. Bengt explained that 'The longer the distance, the bigger reason there is to send [photographs]. You send postcards; these are instant postcards.'

Ulla described how she had sent a photograph to a friend from the hospital after breaking her leg. The photograph of the leg, all wrapped up, communicated, 'Greetings from hospital.' However, of the subjects in the study interviews, only Ulla explicitly stated that she did not feel like she was mediating her presence in a certain place through the photographs that she communicated from her camera phone. She rather liked to share what she was seeing. This can be regarded as an example of the use of mobile photographs as a form of television, or rather 'tele-vision'. This follows the meaning of *television* as 'vision at a distance'.

An aspect related to the communication of photographs as tele-vision is the 'synchronous gaze' (Villi 2015; Villi & Stocchetti 2011). Photographs do not necessarily represent face-to-face telecommunication; that is, the photograph does not inevitably include the face of the person sending the photograph. However, to achieve a sense of mediated presence, one does not have to see the other person, but rather feel that they are sharing the same view. This type of mediated presence is common to mobile communication in general. Ito (2004) makes an important point, in that the metaphor in text messaging is side by side, in contrast to the face-to-face modality of a telephone conversation. What mobile photographs add to the side-by-side presence of text messaging is the aspect of visual perception. A photograph offers both an interpersonal, shared experience and a common view to the same world through the photograph.

The idea of the synchronous gaze surfaced in several of the study interviews. The use of the verb 'to show' was exemplary of this in the descriptions of the camera phone communication practices. Joakim remarked that '[With a photograph] you can show unusual or strange things happening at the moment they happen, and you can send a picture of that to a friend or somebody: *hey, something like this happened right now.*' Bengt commented

> I think that those [photographs] I would send from the phone have to do with what's going on, the feeling which is there; there is a connection that *I'm here now watching this* ... I can take a picture and show that *hey, now this is going on ... share the experience.*

Lotta noted

> A text message is a simple way just to say one thing you have to say, and if you put a photo in it, it's probably because it is something fun or good-looking, like a view or something; you want someone to see what you are seeing [in the place].

Conclusion

In this chapter, my intention has been to join the study of camera phone photography with the discussion on location-aware mobile communication. Based on studies focusing on the communication of camera phone photographs, including my own qualitative study, it can be claimed that there is often a connection between the physical setting and the act of photographic communication. The 'phonespace' is appended with visual peeks into the changing locations of the communicators. The 'photospace' – the telecommunicative space of camera phone communication – is thus more location-bound than the phonespace.

The main argument of the chapter is that photographs can emphasize the relationship between mobile communication and location by incorporating the location to the communicative act. The sender of the photograph can provide a visual notion of her or his existence in a certain location, the *I am here now*. The indexicality of the photograph serves as the guarantee of presence. Thus, the location is not just a point of communication and mobile communication is not only about engagement in the phonespace. Accordingly, photographs communicated from a mobile phone can provide, in addition to social presence, the sense of being together, also physical presence, the sense of being there. The photograph re-localizes the act of communication. This is in contrast to verbal mobile phone communication, where the actual location of communication often has very limited significance and is not necessarily known to the other communicator. The location is often mainly manifested only as background noise.

When using the camera phone to capture and communicate a photograph, one's presence in the place can be the purpose and motivation for the act of communication, similarly to when a user checks in on Swarm. Communicating a photograph and mediating presence by checking in are both examples of location-aware networked interaction. Interestingly, the GPS features in mobile phones, that enable many location-based services' applications, can further amplify the physical location in photographs, as when photographs are supplemented with location-related metadata. In Augmented Reality (AR) applications, the camera apparatus in the phone is given an additional role when, in addition to capturing images of places, it mediates location-based information to the user. When utilizing AR applications, the camera is a window – not a window to another place, as in tele-vision, but a window loaded with local information. In this sense, the screen in the camera phone is not only a viewfinder but also an 'information finder'.

Location-aware mobile technology forms a context within which to explore new and old models of communication, connection and communality. Mobile and networked interactions do not occur only in the phonespace, but they are also increasingly connected to the physical location. The camera phone is one of the first location-based applications in mobile communication and certain practices of photographic communication act as a forerunner for the location-aware technologies, services and mobile apps that have been introduced in recent years. In my view, the concept of mediated presence particularly serves as a valuable framework for studying the practices that are emerging in the field of locative media. Naturally, mediated presence does not relate to all forms of location-based mobile use, but clearly it relates to the use of Swarm, for example, and other apps that emphasize the sharing of place. A check-in can act as authentication of one's 'present presence' and, at the same time, links the users to their friends or followers. Very much in the same way, a photograph, communicated from the place photographed, can authenticate the contemporaneous presence of the communicator, share the place and establish a connection.

Note

1 In 2014, Foursquare introduced the spin-off app Swarm to include the check-in feature previously offered by the Foursquare app.

References

Augé, M. 1995, *Non-Places: Introduction to an Anthropology of Supermodernity.* Verso: London.

Barthes, R. [1981]/2000, *Camera Lucida: Reflections on Photography.* Vintage: London.

Barthes, R. [1977]/1991, *Image, Music, Text.* Essays selected and translated by Stephen Heath. Noonday Press: New York.

Batchen, G. 2004, *Forget Me Not: Photography and Remembrance.* Princeton Architectural Press: New York.

Batchen, G. 1999, *Burning with Desire: The Conception of Photography.* MIT Press: Cambridge, MA.

Biocca, F., Harms, C. & Burgoon, J. K. 2003, 'Toward a More Robust Theory and Measure of Social Presence: Review and Suggested Criteria'. *Presence*, Vol. 12, no. 5, pp. 456–480.

Bull, M. 2005, 'The Intimate Sounds of Urban Experience: An Auditory Epistemology of Everyday Mobility', in K. Nyíri (ed.) *A Sense of Place: The Global and the Local in Mobile Communication.* Passagen Verlag: Vienna, pp. 169–178.

Campbell, S. W. 2013, 'Mobile Media and Communication: A New Field, or Just a New Journal?'. *Mobile Media and Communication*, Vol. 1, no. 1, pp. 8–13.

Castells, M., Fernández-Ardèvol, M., Linchuan Qiu, J. & Sey, A. 2007, *Mobile Communication and Society: A Global Perspective.* MIT Press: Cambridge, MA.

Counts, S. & Fellheimer, E. 2004, 'Supporting Social Presence through Lightweight Photo Sharing On and Off the Desktop', in *CHI 2004, April 24–29, 2004, Vienna, Austria*. ACM: New York, pp. 599–606.

Cresswell, T. 2004, *Place: A Short Introduction*. Blackwell: London.

De Souza e Silva, A. 2013, 'Location-Aware Mobile Technologies: Historical, Social and Spatial Approaches'. *Mobile Media and Communication*, Vol. 1, no. 1, pp. 116–121.

De Souza e Silva, A. & Frith, J. 2012, *Mobile Interfaces in Public Spaces: Locational Privacy, Control, and Urban Sociability*. Routledge: New York.

Gai, B. 2007, 'A Local Study of the Camera Phone: The Usage Pattern and Beyond', in G. Goggin & L. Hjorth (eds) *Mobile Media 2007: Proceedings of an International Conference on Social and Cultural Aspects of Mobile Phones, Media and Wireless Technologies*. University of Sydney: Sydney, pp. 198–207.

Gazzard, A. 2011, 'Location, Location, Location: Collecting Space and Place in Mobile Media'. *Convergence: The International Journal of Research into New Media Technologies*, Vol. 17, no. 4, pp. 405–417.

Gergen, K. J. 2002, 'The Challenge of Absent Presence', in J. E. Katz & M. Aakhus (eds) *Perpetual Contact: Mobile Communication, Private Talk, Public Performance*. Cambridge University Press: Cambridge, pp. 227–241.

Geser, H. 2004, *Towards a Sociological Theory of the Mobile Phone*. University of Zurich: Zurich.

Gibson, C., Luckman, S. & Brennan-Horley, C. 2012, '(Putting) Mobile Technologies in Their Place: A Geographical Perspective', in R. Wilken & G. Goggin (eds) *Mobile Technology and Place*. Routledge: New York, pp. 123–139.

Gordon, E. & de Souza e Silva, A. 2012, 'The Urban Dynamics of Net Localities: How Mobile and Location-Aware Technologies are Transforming Places', in R. Wilken & G. Goggin (eds) *Mobile Technology and Place*. Routledge: New York, pp. 89–103.

Haunstrup Christensen, T. 2008, '"Connected Presence" in Distributed Family Life'. *New Media and Society*, Vol. 11, no. 3, pp. 433–451.

Hjorth, L. 2015, 'Intimate Cartographies of the Visual: Camera Phones, Locative Media, and Intimacy in Kakao', in R. Wilken & G. Goggin (eds) *Locative Media*. New York: Routledge, pp. 23–38.

Hjorth, L. 2012, 'Still Mobile: A Case Study on Mobility, Home, and Being Away in Shanghai', in R. Wilken & G. Goggin (eds) *Mobile Technology and Place*. Routledge: New York, pp. 140–156.

Hjorth, L. & Pink, S. 2014, 'New Visualities and the Digital Wayfarer: Reconceptualizing Camera Phone Photography and Locative Media'. *Mobile Media and Communication*, Vol. 2, no. 1, pp. 40–57.

Hulme, M. & Truch, A. 2005, 'Social Identity: The New Sociology of the Mobile Phone', in K. Nyíri (ed.) *A Sense of Place: The Global and the Local in Mobile Communication*. Passagen Verlag: Vienna, pp. 459–466.

Humphreys, L. M. 2013, 'Mobile Social Media: Future Challenges and Opportunities'. *Mobile Media and Communication*, Vol. 1, no. 1, pp. 20–25.

IJsselsteijn, W., de Ridder, H., Freeman, J. & Avons, S. E. 2000, 'Presence: Concept, Determinants and Measurement'. *Society of Photo-Optical Instrumentation Engineers (SPIE) Conference Series*, Vol. 3959, pp. 520–529.

IJsselsteijn, W., van Baren, J. & van Lanen, F. 2003, 'Staying in Touch: Social Presence and Connectedness through Synchronous and Asynchronous Communication

Media', in *10th International Conference on Human–Computer Interaction*, 22–27 June 2003, Crete, Greece, viewed 26 October 2015, www.academia. edu/996928/Staying_in_touch_Social_presence_and_connectedness_through_synchronous_and_asynchronous_communication_media.

Ito, M. 2004, 'Personal Portable Pedestrian: Lessons from Japanese Mobile Phone Use'. Paper presented at the *Mobile Communication and Social Change, the 2004 International Conference on Mobile Communication*, 18–19 October 2004, Seoul, Korea.

Ito, M. & Okabe, D. 2005, 'Technosocial Situations: Emergent Structuring of Mobile E-mail Use', in M. Ito, D. Okabe & M. Matsuda (eds) *Personal, Portable, Pedestrian: Mobile Phones in Japanese Life*. MIT Press: Cambridge, MA, pp. 257–276.

Jensen, K. B. 2013, 'What's Mobile in Mobile Communication?'. *Mobile Media and Communication*, Vol. 1, no. 1, pp. 26–31.

Kindberg, T., Spasojevic, M., Fleck, R. & Sellen, A. 2004, 'How and Why People Use Camera Phones'. Consumer Applications and Systems Laboratory, H&P Laboratories, Bristol, viewed 22 August 2010, www.hpl.hp.com/techreports/2004/HPL-2004-216.pdf.

Kindberg, T., Spasojevic, M., Fleck, R. & Sellen, A. 2005, 'The Ubiquitous Camera: An In-Depth Study of Camera Phone Use'. *IEEE Pervasive Computing*, April to June 2005, pp. 42–50.

Kondor, Z. 2007, 'The Mobile Image: Experience on the Move', in K. Nyíri (ed.) *A Sense of Place: The Global and the Local in Mobile Communication*. Passagen Verlag: Vienna, pp. 25–34.

Kopomaa, T. 2000, *Kännykkäyhteiskunnan synty* (Birth of the Mobile Information Society). Gaudeamus: Helsinki.

Koskinen, I., Kurvinen, E. & Lehtonen, T.-K. 2002, *Mobile Image*. Edita: Helsinki.

Laursen, D. & Szymanski, M. H. 2013, 'Where are You? Location Talk in Mobile Phone Conversations'. *Mobile Media and Communication*, Vol. 1, no. 3, pp. 314–334.

Licoppe, C. 2004, '"Connected" Presence: The Emergence of a New Repertoire for Managing Social Relationships in a Changing Communication Technoscape'. *Environment and Planning D: Society and Space*, Vol. 22, pp. 135–156.

Licoppe, C. & Heurtin, J.-P. 2002, 'France: Preserving Image', in J. Katz & M. Aakhus (eds) *Perpetual Contact: Mobile Communication, Private Talk, Public Performance*. Cambridge University Press: Cambridge, pp. 94–109.

Ling, R. 2008, *New Tech, New Ties: How Mobile Communication Is Reshaping Social Cohesion*. MIT Press: Cambridge, MA.

Lister, M. 2007, 'Photography, Presence, and Pattern', in J. Elkins (ed.) *Photography Theory*. Routledge: New York, pp. 350–358.

Malpas, J. 2012, *Heidegger and the Thinking of Place: Explorations in the Topology of Being*. MIT Press: Cambridge, MA.

Manovich, L. 1995, 'To Lie and to Act: Potemkin's Villages, Cinema and Telepresence', in *Ars Electronica 1995 catalog*, Linz, Austria, viewed 7 October 2015, www.manovich.net.

Mason, J. 2002, *Qualitative Researching*, 2nd edn. Sage: London.

Massey, D. 2008, *Samanaikainen Tila* (The Concurrent Space), collected and translated by M. Lehtonen, P. Rantanen & J. Valkonen. Vastapaino: Tampere.

Meyrowitz, J. 2005, 'The Rise of Glocality: New Senses of Place and Identity in the

Global Village', in K. Nyíri (ed.) *A Sense of Place: The Global and the Local in Mobile Communication*. Passagen Verlag: Vienna, pp. 21–30.

Özkul, D. 2015, 'Location as a Sense of Place: Everyday Life, Mobile, and Spatial Practices in Urban Spaces', in A. de Souza e Silva & M. Sheller (eds) *Mobility and Locative Media: Mobile Communication in Hybrid Spaces*. Routledge: New York, pp. 101–116.

Pink, S. 2011, 'Sensory Digital Photography: Re-Thinking "Moving" and the Image'. *Visual Studies*, Vol. 26, no. 1, pp. 4–13.

Richardson, I. & Wilken, R. 2012, 'Parerga of the Third Screen: Mobile Media, Place, and Presence', in R. Wilken & G. Goggin (eds) *Mobile Technology and Place*. Routledge: New York, pp. 181–197.

Rose, G. 2003, 'Family Photographs and Domestic Spacings: A Case Study'. *Transactions of the Institute of British Geographers*, Vol. 28, no. 1, pp. 5–18.

Schroeder, R. 2010, 'Mobile Phones and the Inexorable Advance of Multimodal Connectedness'. *New Media and Society*, Vol. 12, no. 1, pp. 75–90.

Schroeder, R. 2005, 'Being There Together and the Future of Connected Presence'. *Presence: Teleoperators and Virtual Environments*, Vol. 15, no. 4, pp. 339–344.

Scifo, B. 2005, 'The Domestication of Camera-Phone and MMS Communication: The Early Experiences of Young Italians', in K. Nyíri (ed.) *A Sense of Place: The Global and the Local in Mobile Communication*. Passagen Verlag: Vienna, pp. 363–374.

Sonesson, G. 1989, *Semiotics of Photography: On Tracing the Index. Report 4 from the Project 'Pictorial Meanings in the Society of Information'*. Lund University: Lund.

Sontag, S. 1977, *On Photography*. Farrar, Straus & Giroux: New York.

Sutherland, I. 2012, 'Connection and Inspiration: Phenomenology, Mobile Communications, Place', in R. Wilken & G. Goggin (eds) *Mobile Technology and Place*. Routledge: New York, pp. 157–174.

Villi, M. 2015, ' "Hey, I'm Here Right Now": Camera Phone Photographs and Mediated Presence'. *Photographies*, Vol. 8, no. 1, pp. 3–22.

Villi, M. 2012, 'Visual Chitchat: The Use of Camera Phones in Visual Interpersonal Communication'. *Interactions: Studies in Communication and Culture*, Vol. 3, no. 1, pp. 39–54.

Villi, M. & Stocchetti, M. 2011, 'Visual Mobile Communication, Mediated Presence and the Politics of Space'. *Visual Studies*, Vol. 26, no. 2, pp. 102–112.

Wilken, R. 2012, 'Locative Media: From Specialized Preoccupation to Mainstream Fascination'. *Convergence: The International Journal of Research into New Media Technologies*, Vol. 18, no. 3, pp. 243–247.

Wilken, R. & Goggin, G. 2015, 'Locative Media: Definitions, Histories, Theories', in R. Wilken & G. Goggin (eds) *Locative Media*. Routledge: New York, pp. 1–22.

Wilken, R. & Goggin, G. 2012, 'Mobilizing Place: Conceptual Currents and Controversies', in R. Wilken & G. Goggin (eds) *Mobile Technology and Place*. Routledge: New York, pp. 3–25.

8 (Digital) photography, experience and space in transnational families

A case study of Spanish-Irish families living in Ireland

Patricia Prieto-Blanco

Far away and still so close

When I left my home country 11 years ago I had already lived far from home for three years but still within the boundaries of the Spanish state and culture. Going abroad was something different for me and it meant a bigger change for my family as well. Back then, phone calls abroad were very expensive and, from my home in rural Spain, almost nobody had an internet connection. A few months after my arrival in Germany I sent my sister a couple of photographs from my first adventures in North Rhine Westphalia, which she printed and hung on the wall of my old bedroom. When I went back to Spain the following Christmas, I found the photographs. I can still feel the emotion that overwhelmed me when I encountered those images back home: my two worlds had been brought together by my little sister.

Today I am in two WhatsApp family groups: one populated by my mum, my sister and several aunts, uncles and cousins – my mother's side of the family; the other one includes my dad (my parents have been divorced since I was 14 years old), my cousin and my sister. If I don't look at my phone during the day, by evening time I usually have about 30 unread messages from both groups, most of which are photographs. My sister has a young toddler and she is determined to share her mothering experience with me, my dad and my mum, the four of us living in different places. My niece has seen me in person only three times in the past two years, but uncountable times face-to-face via Skype – she knows that when the computer is left on my sister's living room sofa and facing her play area there, her aunt in Ireland, with a now-funny accent, is waiting to play with her on the screen. The place we share is created thanks to the ubiquity of digital technology. A photograph of my sister and I rests on my sister's mantelpiece. About a month ago my niece realized that the person on the computer screen and the person in the photograph are the same: her favourite (and only!) aunt. She still needs to make this connection with me as a person in the flesh. I'm also in a long-distance relationship with my partner, who lives in the UK, and we interact with each other almost constantly through the day. For four years we have sent each other photographs of our morning coffee and of digital kisses before bed at night. We even have virtual date-nights, stream-watching TV shows together while chatting on WhatsApp or Skype.

At present, many of us are actively contributing to a redefinition of social boundaries, involving private and public spaces, on one hand, and public displays of affection on the other hand (Chalfen 2012, pp. 165–210). We take *selfies*, photograph our lunches and use cameras as note-taking devices. As our lives play out before us, we choose to give a visual account of our intimate moments, anticipating the reaction of our family and friends. We share these snapshots immediately with them, some of whom live far away from us, thereby establishing ephemeral connections. As discussed by Villi in this volume, often these fleeting communicative acts provide non-places and telecommunicative spaces with relevance and value. Digital photographs are shared as both objects and as experiences (Van Dijck 2007, p. 114) in photospaces[1] and possibly beyond. Seemingly, we want to interact across distances and so we create third spaces[2] in order to do so.

However, photography has always been a tool used by families to remain in touch, despite temporal or spatial distances. Sometimes, the sense of touch is literally embedded in the photograph by means of adding hair or other objects, such as dried flowers, textiles, etc. (Batchen 2004, p. 74). At other times, photographs are creatively transformed into utilitarian objects of affection that are meant to be touched – pillows and bracelets, mugs and mouse pads. With regard to their representational and material qualities, these objects are made to last – we want to remember and be remembered by the images upon them, and to interact with them on a daily and casual basis, as part of our everyday lives. Conversely, Snapchat pictures are intended to last a maximum of ten seconds, fulfilling an (arguably) newly emergent social desire for impermanent photographs – specifically impermanent social representations – which fit within the context of the fleeting, immediate, visual conversations in which we take part everyday via digital technologies and social media. As Van Dijck has pointed out: '[A] younger generation seems to increasingly use digital cameras for "live" communication instead of storing pictures of "life"' (2007, p. 58). Snapchat illustrates the way in which photography is used and understood today. Technology has drifted further and more easily into people's lives, to the degree that our active, daily lived experiences – our friendships and familial ties, affinities and affections – are mediated by technology to a massive degree.

In her fieldwork investigation, Gillian Rose (2014) identified a significant development related to new technologies. When the participants sent photographs as email attachments to their friends, they were expecting an exchange of snaps to follow. The reciprocity was thereby perceived as more important and valuable than the photographs themselves (ibid., pp. 83–84). Digitally networked cameras (Lehmuskallio 2012, p. 14) have transformed the way we communicate with photographs. On one hand, this development signals a possible enhancement of the communicative function of photography as an area of further study. On the other, the lives, whereabouts and, in summary, what we do and what happens to family photographs arises as a theme to be closely examined. It is especially felt that people's lived experiences need to be further examined as they seem to have been altered by new camera technologies.

Studying (digital) family photography implies looking primarily at non-professionally made, distributed, stored and received media outputs, particularly photographs (as opposed to video or audio recordings, although both of these are becoming almost as pervasive, due to technology improvements in social media, and are also ripe for study). By taking a 'non-media-centric media studies'[3] approach (Moores 2012), this chapter explores photography from a holistic perspective, where contextual conditions are accentuated in line with complementary works carried out in social sciences (Stumberger 2007; Pink 2011b; Harper 2012). Furthermore, this approach means working in an interdisciplinary manner, both at the level of theory and at the level of methodology. Inherent to this is the need to analyse media through the contexts within which they operate, as opposed to scrutinizing their particularities and specificities in isolation. Also, the urgency of bringing everyday life into the equation of researching media uses, and accompanying practices, is the core idea brought up by Moores in his re-definition of media studies as a discipline (2012, pp. 11, 50, 103–110).

At present, research in this area seeks to adhere to this novel conceptualization of the discipline. The underlying belief is that media research benefits from a collaborative approach, which takes anthropological and social inquiry into account. 'For the "message" of any medium or technology is the change of scale or pace or pattern that it introduces into human affairs' (McLuhan 1964, p. 10).[4] Consequently, digital photography is used, here, metonymically and stands for the ongoing cultural, social and technological transformations that are impacting on the pragmatics of photography in general and of family photography specifically. An intrinsic human need to produce pictures hides behind family photographs, along with the desire to communicate better, and to be able to share our perceived reality with others. It is in this sense that, situated at the core of this project, is the idea of mediation 'as a particular and unique enhancement or performance – in short a repetition – of structure that risks always transforming the media and the actors' (Lanzeni 2014) and the understanding of photography as a medium.[5] It is against this background that the question of how transnational families use photographs can be posed. The answer might throw some light on how particular uses of the photographic image are unlocked in a context of digital and locative media.

An ethnographic approach to transnational family photography

This chapter has been extracted from a larger doctoral project, in which the impact of digital technologies on telecommunication (processes and strategies) in the precise spatial setting of Spanish-Irish families[6] living in Ireland was researched. The present chapter concerns the empirical investigation done in relation to the following research question: how do transnational families use photographs? Of particular interest were those photographs displayed in order to be openly viewed in the participants' family homes. The project was framed within the conceptual lens of visual sociology (Pauwels 2010; Harper 2012) and a narrative inquiry approach guided the fieldwork. Moreover, the three axes of research of the narrative approach – temporality, sociality and place (Clandinin & Huber 2010) – coincided with the leading research question and its theoretical implications: the understanding of family photography as a practice and of photographs as objects.

This research seeks to provide a sample of honest, respectful and insightful ethnographic research on family photography. Giving participants a voice by allowing their stories to unfold is of key importance as it acknowledges how, given this subject matter, research and personal life interweave progressively. Families were asked to construct actively their contributions to the project together with me, as a researcher, which occurred in several ways. Families chose which photographs and other photographic objects (such as mugs, key rings, etc.) to share with me as a researcher, as well as the appropriate time to share them. Families also had access to all photographs taken during the fieldwork and either approved or dismissed them for further academic use. From December 2012 to July 2014, 11 families participated in the study, two of which dropped out. Due to the constraints of this publication, this chapter presents visual examples of one family only, although four of them inform the analysis. They are all married couples with children and have been living in Ireland for between seven and 20-plus years.

The methods put in place, the position of the researcher (also a Spanish migrant living in Ireland) and the ethical implications serve to provide the necessary critical distance for the analysis as well as to introduce a second key question in this chapter: how can we discuss personal photography without placing something of ourselves into the text? This text intends to offer a provisional answer.

Transnational families and digital (family) photography today: practices and places

During our first meeting, families were asked to produce a visual representation of their 'circle of reference' using colour cardboard on a black

Table 8.1 Research design – breakdown of interviews and methods

Time	Day 1 information session	Day 2 (carried out 1 or 2 weeks after first interview)	Day 3 (carried out 4 to 6 weeks after second interview)	Days 4 to 6 (carried out with a lapse of time of 4 to 6 weeks between each interview)	Day 7 (carried out approx. 6 months after the last follow-up)
Location	Neutral venue	Neutral venue	Participant's home	Neutral venue	Neutral venue
Expected duration	30 minutes	30–45 minutes	45–60 minutes	3–30 minutes, every 6 weeks	30 minutes
Notes for participants	Discover what the research project is about and what your participation would involve.	Bring 3–5 photos that you have already shared with distant family members. We will discuss them. The interview will be audio-taped. The photographs will be copied.	Talking about where you display family photographs at home. Interview will be audio-taped. Places of display of family photos will be photographed. Some of the photographs you have shared with distant family members will be copied.	Talking about when, what, why you photograph and how you select photos to be shared with distant family members. The interview will be audio-taped. Dates of when photographs were taken and when shared will be recorded. Some of the shared photographs will be copied.	Talking about when, what, why you photograph and how you select photos to be shared with distant family members. The interview will be audio-taped. Dates of when photographs were taken and when shared will be recorded. Some of the shared photographs will be copied.

background. Participants themselves were represented by a pink card marked with an 'X'. They freely chose how to distribute the strips of cardboard to represent the configuration of people whom they rely on, whom they share photographs with and whom they share photographs with on a regular basis (at least once a month). This exercise was helpful for two main reasons. First, it allowed me to have a clear insight into the personal relationships of the participants and the hierarchy of those relationships. Second, this visualization provided an opportunity for a first engagement with issues of audience and control. For example, although the colour pink was chosen to represent 'people whom the families share daily life with', participants equated this with family. Similarly, the colour blue was associated with friends, even though the line given was 'people whom they do not share daily life with but who are close'. The keyword for green was acquaintances and for brown was pets, and neither was modified by participants. The negotiations of categories that took place during the exercise were also taking place at the level of distribution of photographs.

Both Maria and Pedro pointed out a flaw in this method: there was no room for in-between statuses or dynamics. Although I use the word 'circle', this doesn't mean that everyone in it is equally distant from the centre. In fact, quite the opposite is true. Maria and Pedro wanted to clearly show how some 'people who are close but whom they didn't share daily life with' actually felt like family, and therefore more as 'people whom they share daily life with'. In this context 'daily' didn't literally mean every single day. Participants perceived it more in terms of affective bonds. Maria and Pedro created hybrids by adding strips of pink to some blue tokens, in order to mark significant friendships. Later, during the second interview, when we were discussing whom they would send photographs

Figure 8.1 Pedro and Maria's 'circle of reference' (source: photograph by Patricia Prieto-Blanco).

to which were taken in more intimate places, such as the bath or the bedroom, this hybridization came up again.

MARIA: It depends, if they [their children] are au naturel or in their pyjamas...
PEDRO: That is true, if the children are naked, for example. I do not like to send photos of the children naked via internet. From the waist up, that is ok. I mean, if they are in the bathtub and you can't see it, ok. And I am careful that they are not exposed. But it gives me the creeps, you know. And then those photos in which ... So it is somebody's name day and you go to sing to her/his bed and everybody is in their pyjamas and they have bad hair and so on, well I might send those photographs to parents and siblings and that is it.
MARIA: And to one very good friend. Yes, somebody who knows me but not the neighbour.

Thus, media usage turned out to be different when sharing photographs with people they had qualified as pink, from when sharing photographs with people they had qualified as blue. These negotiations that occurred during the exercise, and were reproduced when talking about media usage, could be read in terms of kinship-making. Franklin and McKinnon (2005) stress the twofold character of kinship: inclusion and connection as well as exclusion and rupture. The circle of reference and the subsequent representation of photo-sharing circles and habitual photo-sharing circles offer a visualization of these processes of inclusion and exclusion. Although in the first instance inclusion and exclusion are referred to photographic exchanges only, as we will see below – and in line with previous work in the area of family photography (Hirsch 1981; Slater 1991; Hirsch 2008; Rose 2010) – family photographs articulate belonging and are tools of socialization. Weston (1997) proposes commitment as a category to explore kinship and family formation, a factor that is present in the narratives below. As they unfold, we will see that continuity, which can be interpreted as the commitment of keeping in touch, is a seminal factor of the photographic practices of transnational families. Smart and Shipman (2004) elaborate a bit further by highlighting cultural and historical variations evaded by Beck and Beck-Gersheim's individualization thesis (2002). They empathically relate these differences with 'the experience of migration, transnationalism and geographical distance' (Smart & Shipman 2004, p. 506).

This theoretical argument has recently found resonance in work with transnational families and their use of multiple media (Madianou & Miller 2012). As mentioned above, media pragmatics in diasporic communities is an under-researched area (Ponzanesi & Leurs 2014), especially in Europe. This chapter aims to go some way towards filling the existing gap. Contemporary debates on kinship and family led Gabb to conceptualize family 'as an ongoing and interactive process which is contingent upon the mutual understandings of family members and is moreover contingent and negotiable rather than normatively defined' (2004, p. 5). Also, what family is, results from an ongoing process of negotiation and commitment, responding to individual and collective situations of proximity, distance and propinquity.

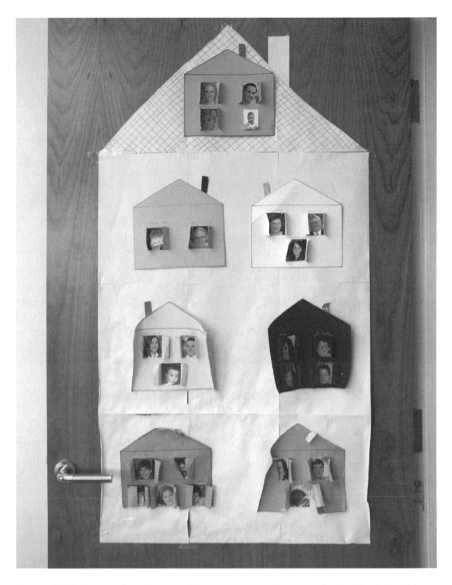

Figure 8.2 Homemade photo collage (source: photograph by Patricia Prieto-Blanco).

MARIA: We don't do this now very often. This was more for when she was one year old or one-and-a-half years old and she started to recognize people. Right now it is more Skype. She asks me to call XY.

PEDRO: But, for example, now her aunt is going to come [for a visit]. Her aunt [is coming] from Slovakia in two weeks. So the latest by next week, we will start telling her *You know what, your auntie XY is coming*. And even if they talk in Skype, they won't be talking that often. But the photograph ... we show her the photograph at least once a day before she goes to sleep. And then when the aunt is here you realize that she is sort of familiar with her, she knew who was coming.

Interestingly, we can see how, in the excerpts above, a sense of agency is associated with photographs.

But the photograph ... we show her the photograph at least once a day before she goes to sleep. And then when the aunt is here you realize that she is sort of familiar with her, she knew who was coming.

Photographs are a tool, an instrument that allows Pedro and Maria's daughter to become familiar with her geographically distant relatives. As new media environments are gradually incorporated into the routines of everyday life (Miller 2010, p. 108), such as the house collage and the Skype calls, they are constituted into places, which are continuous with pre-existing ones (Moores 2012, pp. 6–8). Pedro and Maria's family collage represents and constitutes a place. The extended family, as the institution it still is, defines and contours the locale (Agnew 2011) of the home place for Maria, Pedro and their children. The collage is part of the ideal setting where everyday activities take place. Moreover, the collage itself, with its multiple photographs, enables everyday participation in place-related affairs (ibid., pp. 23–24). Social solidarity, collective action and a sense of belonging is produced and partly negotiated through the collage.

Other families also use photography to overcome space. A case study example is Celia. Despite living in Ireland for over 20 years, she has never missed Spain. However, since becoming a mother she finds photography very important in order to incorporate her relatives into her children's everyday lives, and vice versa. Although Celia referred to her children most of the time when talking about the photographs, some of the examples below give an account of how the images are also relevant to herself, for her own relationship with her family in Spain. Celia brought up her cousin in relation to the first photograph we looked at together in her kitchen. Her cousin had lived at Celia's, in Ireland, for over nine months. During that period their relationship strengthened greatly and ever since they have kept in touch regularly, mainly through phone messaging. Celia said:

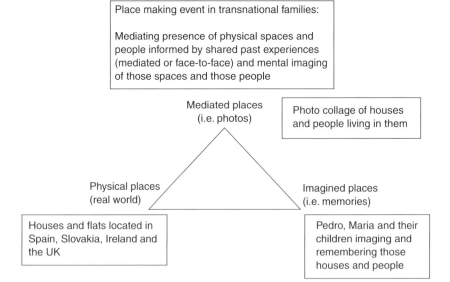

Figure 8.3 Place-making event in transnational families (sources: based on Pink's (2011) and Rose's (2010) definitions of practice and Jensen and Waade's (2009) image culture and the production of place. Images and moving bodies 'are both emergent from and implicated in the production of, the event of place' (Pink 2011a, p. 9)).

> It's been four years since [she lived with us]. Four years of relationship really…. I send her loads of photos, mostly of the kids so that they have a relationship. I like to keep her posted on our day-to-day lives. For example, I have also sent her photos of the recent snowfall.

When I asked Celia to elaborate more on the outcomes of the exchange of photographs with her cousin, she told me, 'A dialogue always takes place after sending photographs', but it doesn't necessarily entail more pictures. 'It depends. For example, another day I was a bit *I don't know how* [Spanish way of saying one has the blues] and she sent me a photograph blowing me a kiss.'

Yessica also talked about how photographs contribute to transform her house into a home. She has a large number of photographs on the walls of her living room and on the mantelpiece because, 'We spend ninety percent of the time here…. And I like when people come to visit, well, because I am a woman … I don't know, walls without pictures are lifeless.' However, she keeps a very special photograph on the door of her fridge, stating, 'This is one of the last photographs I have of my dad and I think this is the last photo of my son with his grandfather.' Instead of treating the photograph as a precious object and placing it in a shrine, Yessica likes to see her father through the day, every day, and allow her children to become familiar with their grandfather, even after his death. When I asked what the differences were between the photographs on the wall of her living room and the photographs on the door of the fridge, she told me,

> I can always change the photographs on the fridge, but these ones are permanent. They have dust on them, but I am not going to change them.... They were made like that, that moment was like that for a reason and so I like that they should remain.

At the same time, although she suggested that she could always change the photographs on the door of the fridge, during the 18 months of fieldwork the photograph of her father remained there only, on the fridge door. Only when I visited her for the last time, just before they moved back to Spain and after they had packed already, was the photograph gone. The fridge looked very bare.

As evidenced so far, contemporary photographic practices mix analogue with digital, as well as rather durable carriers, such as paper, with rather ephemeral ones, such as digital files. Underneath this variety lies the versatility of digital technologies, which allowed Pedro and Maria's relatives to visit their new apartment in Ireland virtually and enables their daughter to see her aunt live on the screen every now and then. But, as Pedro implied himself, the collage of houses fulfils a different need. The printed photographs are a constant presence in the house. The materiality offers not only durability but also stability, a crucial factor when it comes to socializing Pedro and Maria's children into the larger family unit. In this context, a working definition of materiality is that it is a synergy of subject, place and material, always embedded in concrete sociocultural and historical contexts. In transnational families, face-to-face interactions and real-time mediated ones, via Skype and similar software, take place often. However, printed photographs have provided members of transnational families with a constant presence of their (extended) family in their daily lives. They literally see them every day and often, as they enter and leave the living room. One could argue that these tangible photographs transmit a sense of ontological security because, as analogue objects, they exist in the world – they are concretely present and constantly visible for Pedro, Maria and their children.

Several decades ago, Chalfen noted that there was no obvious intention to 'publish' mediated message forms produced within the home mode of communication (Chalfen 1998, p. 216). However, at least among younger generations, things seem to be shifting. Gala used her camera phone in order to share her daughter's prom evening preparation immediately with her relatives in Spain, and to thereby enable their participation in the event. 'But, this one has circulated. This one has been received by my cousin, my mother ... through my brother.' Gala continued telling me about the photograph of her daughter's prom evening preparation:

I think it was via Whatsapp because they live in a different place and my mother was going crazy, 'Please, send them!', so he [her brother] sent them.... He sent them to my cousin and then they met [her mother and her cousin] so that she saw them.

As she continued explaining, her daughter had a different approach to the photographs. 'Mine no, but other ones taken by the thousands of people attending it are, in fact, in Facebook.... Even the ones she took herself', Gala said.

The circulation of the photographs shared was something that was seemingly difficult to control for these four families. Facilitated by the use of social networks, email and image/text message services, they tried to contain the spread by sharing the images privately in closed groups. For example, Yessica used to upload her photographs to a Facebook group until she started to feel that she was losing control about who had access to the photographs. Worrying about privacy settings and overwhelmed by the lack of transparency of the site, she stopped uploading photos to the site. Instead, she started using WhatsApp and persuaded her mother to buy a smartphone and start using Skype.

Transnational families constantly renegotiate their feelings of affection and intimacy (Shome 2011) and audio-visual media seem to play a fundamental role in this process. For example, Gala's Spanish family was invited to be present at her daughter's prom ball evening preparation and Celia's cousin comforted her with a visually mediated kiss, which she in turn shared with me the day after she received it. These two examples are part of ongoing transient conversations, which visually mediate the presence of those who are physically distant. When distance as *punctum* is not transitory but practically permanent, and fleeting acts of communication do in fact constitute the most frequent and enduring communicative interactions among family members, recentness might play a part.

The concept of *affordances* (Gibson 1979), applied to the realm of networked cameras and mediated presence, reinforces Spadola's understanding of medium and mediation (see Note 5) in that objects are explored with references to users and context of use. The continuous negotiation of real and perceived affordances of digital and locative visual media is a core part of how place is shared over distance and presence is authenticated. The experience of the user is not determined by the affordances of the object, however the object is endowed with meaning through the experience of the user, which is always located, always emplaced. Cameras might not take photos on their own, but neither can we produce photographs without adequate technologies. Material mediations 'do not determine embodied actions, nor symbolization processes – but it surely seems to have an effect on them' (Lehmuskallio 2012, p. 49). Affordances are opportunities for action. Actions are transformations of perceived realities and are always mediated. By participating in acts that adhere to conventions, these become necessary and part of reality.

If media settings are perceived – or constituted – places (Moores 2012, pp. 8–25), then place becomes places. Furthermore, the process of habitation inherent to space becoming place, to the house becoming home, to interaction across distances being an affective and intimate experience, becomes crucial. These communicative spaces are ubiquitous and immediate and can be temporarily inhabited by nomadic world citizens (Belting 2001). Their proliferation seems to respond to the need to communicate in time and over space rather than over time in the same space, although the four families all expressed an innate desire to share experiences in face-to-face situations. As expressed by Yessica, 'Technology is great but you never know what tomorrow might bring. It is good to sit down and share the photographs. My son and I have done it. It is different. It is very different.'

A few final thoughts

The extension of home places beyond the house, and the generation of third spaces of interaction, seems to be of crucial importance for transnational families, even if only because face-to-face situations among distant family members are not commonplace for them. Rose has recently made the case that the digital does not have a significant impact on photographic practices of families and, instead, digital techniques are qualified as being 'only better' for snapshot photography (Rose 2014). However, her observations did not result from a new engagement with current users and neither did she work with transnational families. While Rose states that stepping up into the digital world of photography was not a priority for the families she worked with, the opposite is the case for transnational families or digitally connected migrants (see references above to the work of Madianou in the Philippines and the UK, and Ponzanesi's research in Europe). They are early adopters of technology, which they use to overcome the physical separation from their loved ones. This is not just a simple matter of doing better snapshot photography, as Rose puts it (ibid.), but a crucial change in the social function of the medium, because the incorporation of photography into the everyday changes its pragmatics. Connecting, talking and sharing experiences, 'remotely but immediately', are prominent keywords associated with the use of digital photography by transnational families. This is not to say that memory-making and celebration – as older keywords linked to the practice in seminal works (Bourdieu & Boltanski [1965]/1993; Langford 2001; Hirsch 2008) – have dissolved. They are just sharing relevance with the newer ones.

The photographic practices of these transnational families illustrate two contemporary phenomena of digital photography: the search for immediacy and the growing need to overcome space. The first argument developed in this chapter is that the act of sharing photographs is an event by which third places of familial interaction are generated. This mediated production of place brings people together, as it is a way of temporarily obliterating physical distance. The acts of mediating interactions in these third places of familial interaction could be described as 'tele-cocooning'. A tele-cocoon is: 'a zone of intimacy in which people can continuously maintain their relationships with others, who they have already encountered, without being restricted by geography and time' (Habuchi 2005, p. 167). As an event, the act of sharing photographs gives rise to mediated third places of familial interaction. This mediated production of place is a strategy for the temporary erasure of distance and for the enactment of ephemeral connections. These mediated third places of interaction could be described as 'tele-cocoons'. Note that Habuchi refers only to the development of relationships that had already started in face-to-face interactions, however, as exemplified above. Connections across space can also be created when tele-cocooning.

PEDRO: I think that then, don't you [addressing Maria]? Well there is a time when children are afraid of strangers in general and she [Pedro's daughter] was less afraid of her family. I think that somehow, in the same way as she [Maria] was saying before that, her family perceived this house as a familiar place, her family was more familiar to her [their daughter] because she had already seen them [Maria assents].

Digital photographs, when shared, contribute to create a collective sense of togetherness. Moreover, they are intrinsic enablers of interactions between people across space, which in turn contribute to the strengthening of intimate bonds in spite of physical distances. Therefore, these photographic practices and their outcomes contribute to the socialization of children into larger family units, as we have seen. Furthermore, kinship can also be negotiated and extended through photographic practices (Bourdieu & Boltanski [1965]/1993, p. 38; Chambers 2001, p. 89). Recall, here, when Maria contrasted her good friend with a neighbour, in the context of sharing more intimate visual depictions of family life, such as photographs taken in the bath or of people in pyjamas.

Sharing photographs, and the exchanges this fosters, can be seen as a response to the ephemeral nature of the connections we established via digital means, such as camera phone photography. However, as a pair, the ephemeral and photography have a long history together. Evanescence and its representability are the subject matter of photographic media. Fixing moments in time and embalming them to be retrieved later are classic functions ascribed to the medium. As an extension of man, photography is said to prolong human memory. Following Villi (this volume), fleeting communicative acts are fundamental for the emergence of third places of interaction. However, while the collage of houses is permanently on Maria and

Pedro's living room door, and is thus part of their home environment (they see it every day), Celia's photo-kiss is temporary, uncertain and at the same time linked to a very specific experience and moment in time. The printed photographs of the collage are instruments of remembrance and memory and, as such, there is a quality of certainty to them. The photo-kiss is an instrument of immediacy and experience, and, as such, is rather temporary. By embedding networked images in a never ending conversation or dialogue, a sense of continuity, certainty and security is imbued in them. The socialization process fostered by networked images doesn't cease, it is just interrupted, under the promise that it will be resumed soon. Thus the act of sharing photographs with people you care about is as important as what they depict.

Such exchanges of photographs contribute to create a sense of family, of togetherness (Rose 2010, pp. 43–45). In this way, the content of the photographs exchanged becomes less relevant than the actual act of exchange. We use anything we have at hand to establish and renew the *phatic*[7] communion that opens up a space for further and deeper interaction. Both Celia's photo-kiss and Gala's prom night camera phone photographs can be considered as *phatic* acts and testimonies of *mediated presence*.[8] Photographic practices of transnational families can be understood as mechanisms of disclosure of intimacy and formation of intimacy (Jamieson 1998, pp. 2, 159). The photographic practices of transnational families are essentially a series of repeatable and customary acts, whereby affect is mediated and places of intimate interaction are constructed.

Notes

1 Although Villi defines the term 'photospace' as 'the telecommunicative space of camera phone communication', he also points out that other networked cameras – devices used in order to produce pictures that 'can be shared, shown and archived with the aid of a vast array of interoperable software operations' (Lehmuskallio 2012, p. 14) – entwine photography and telecommunication. Thus, both 'photospace' and visually 'mediated presence' are not confined to the mobile phone only.
2 In her long-term study of middle-class mothers in the South of England, Gillian Rose found evidence of a generation of stretched spaces through photographic practices. She argues that the familial home is extended beyond the house by photographic means and that photographic objects are crucial in the production of domestic space (Rose 2003, pp. 9–15; Rose 2010, pp. 41–58). Although Rose talks about space, both Sarah Pink's work and Agnew's conceptualization of place and space – as discussed below – suggest that these third spaces are actually third places in which the sense of belonging is mediated through the photographic image.
3 This conceptual approach locates media studies as a discipline equally concerned with the particularities of media themselves, on the one hand, and the complex dynamics between media, institutions, technology and politics on the other (Moores 2012, p. 108). The 'non-media-centric media studies' lens builds upon previous work in the area of audience studies (Kuhn 2010), cultural geography (Morley 2007) and media studies as such (Couldry 2002).

4 For some readers it might seem contradictory that McLuhan is brought up right after advocating for a non-media-centric approach towards media studies. The intention behind this, however, is to remember that McLuhan was the first theorist to embark on an anthropological investigation of media by, admittedly, on the one hand, setting media in the centre of historical development, but, on the other, by always interrogating media and technologies in the context of human development. In his work, he prioritized the analysis of the relationships between human beings and media: media as extensions of ourselves, thus his study of media was the study of human development. Since, for McLuhan, the kernels of media are neither the content of messages nor communicative instances, it is the entanglement between human beings and media systems that comes to the fore. The newness of the non-media-centric approach is to acknowledge the need for and productivity of a synergetic understanding of media studies as a discipline (see above).

5 In a contribution to the mailing list discussion 'Medianthro', Emilio Spadola, drawing on Morris, Derrida and his own fieldwork, defined medium as any structure of communicative possibility including kinship and ritual structures (Lanzeni 2014). His understanding of communication, mediation and medium emphasizes the prosthetic qualities of technology (in consonance with McLuhan's line of thought) and the possibility of future that is thereby opened.

6 The concept of family is inherent to sociocultural and historical contexts. As such, it is in constant evolution. In Ireland, the concept of family has been the object of agitated public and political debate for the past 20 years. The political discussion about the family started out by implicitly accepting the UN definition of family in 1994 (Éireann 1995). The debate culminated with the recent incorporation of diverse forms into the legal definition of family (Department of Justice and Equality 2013).

   During this time, several studies (Daly & O'Leary 2004; Martin 2005) carried out among the Irish population revealed people's assumptions, expectations and conceptualizations of family. The popular meaning of family in Ireland accentuates the feeling of belonging as essential for a family to be considered as such. However, belonging can be achieved through blood ties, formal or informal kinship and can be stretched beyond particular households (Daly & O'Leary 2004, pp. 22–28). As a reflection of the increasing non-Irish national population, diversity within the family emerged as a topic in these studies too. In nine years, the percentage of non-Irish national residents changed from 5.8 per cent in 2002 to 12 per cent in 2011 (CSO 2012), transforming Ireland very rapidly into an immigration country. Belonging is also paramount for migrants' family identity, as Watters (2009) explains. Accordingly, belonging is located at the core of the definition of family in this study with Spanish-Irish families.

7 The *phatic* is a mode of human action that affords a community to be formed through the performed communicative act (Wulff 1993, pp. 142–144). It both assumes and creates a social relationship of contact. The phatic fulfils a subjective and thus variable need, on the one hand, and an intersubjective or constant on the other, the latter being where the tacit knowledge resides (Jakobson & Bogatyrev 1980). In turn, phatic acts are essentially mimicable, reproducible because they conform to pre-existing conventions and they are performed within a certain community of participants (Austin 1975, pp. 96–98): the 'phatic community'. A 'phatic community' is pro-actively established under common circumstances by attending well-known rules and responds to the objectivity of the situation and to the subjectivity of the participants. It is formally constituted in a vis-à-vis (*gegenüber*) of roles. However, the face-to-face situation, as well as customary types of behaviour, can be mediated/simulated when it comes to visual telecommunication and mediated presence. Just as in Wulff's example of television (1993, p. 151), 'phatic communities' can be established over space.

8 As argued by Villi (in this volume), 'Mediated presence is not a clearly articulated theoretical model, but rather a conceptual theme describing the use of telecommunication technology for being in contact with one another over physical distance – being socially present despite being physically absent.'

References

Agnew, J. 2011, 'Space and Place', in D. Livingstone & J. Agnew (eds) *The SAGE Handbook of Geographical Knowledge*. Sage: London; Thousand Oaks, CA; New Delhi; Singapore, pp. 316–330.

Austin, J. L. 1975, *How to do Things with Words: The William James Lectures delivered at Harvard University in 1955*. Oxford University Press: Oxford.

Batchen, G. 2004, *Forget Me Not: Photography and Remembrance*. Van Gogh Museum and Princeton Architectural Press: Amsterdam; New York.

Beck, U. & Beck-Gersheim, E. 2002, *Individualization: Institutionalized Individualism and its Social and Political Consequences*. Routledge: New York; London.

Belting, H. 2001, *Bild-Anthropologie: Entwuerfe fuer eine Bildwissenschaft*. Wilhelm Fink Verlag: München.

Bourdieu, P. & Boltanski, L. [1965]/1993, *Eine Illegitime Kunst: Die Sozialen Gebrauchsweisen der Photographie*. Suhrkamp Verlag KG: Frankfurt am Main.

Chalfen, R. 2012, *Photogaffes: Family Snapshots and Social Dilemmas*. Dog Ear Publishing: Indianapolis, IN.

Chalfen, R. 1998, 'Interpreting Family Photography as Pictorial Communication', in J. Prosser (ed.) *Image Based Research: A Source Book for Qualititative Researchers*. Falmer Press Ltd: London; Philadelphia, PA, pp. 214–234.

Chambers, D. 2001, *Representing the Family*. Sage: London; Thousand Oaks, CA; New Delhi.

Clandinin, D. J. & Huber, J. 2010, 'Narrative Inquiry'. *International Encyclopedia of Education*. Sage: Thousand Oaks, CA, pp. 1–23.

Couldry, N. 2002, 'Mediation and Alternative Media, or Relocating the Centre of Media and Communication Studies'. *LSE Research Online*, viewed 26 October 2015, http://eprints.lse.ac.uk/7354/.

CSO. 2012, 'Irish Census 2011: Profile 6. Migration and Diversity', viewed 7 October 2015, www.cso.ie/en/census/census2011reports/.

Daly, M. & O'Leary, O. 2004, 'Families and Family Life in Ireland: Challenges for the Future'. Report of Public Consultation Fora, viewed 26 October 2015, www.welfare.ie/en/downloads/iyf2004.pdf.

Department of Justice and Equality. 2013, 'Children and Family Relationships Bill 2013: Briefing Note', viewed 26 October 2015, http://goo.gl/AjjpEs.

Éireann, D. 1995, 'Definition of Family'. *Ceisteanna – Questions: Oral Answers*, Houses of the Oireachtas, viewed 26 October 2015, http://debates.oireachtas.ie/dail/1995/02/14/00012.asp.

Franklin, S. & McKinnon, S. 2005, 'Introduction: Relative Values: Reconfiguring Kinship Studies', in S. Franklin & S. McKinnon (eds) *Relative Values: Reconfiguring Kinship Studies*. Duke University Press: Durham, NC, pp. 148–149.

Gabb, J. 2004, 'Reviewing Intimacy'. *Journal of Sex Research*, Vol. 42, no. 1, pp. 3–12.

Gibson, J. J. 1979, *The Ecological Approach to Visual Perception*, 1986 edn. Houghton Mifflin: Boston, MA.

Habuchi, I. 2005, 'Accelerating Reflexivity', in M. Ito, D. Okabe & M. Matsuda (eds) *Personal, Portable, Pedestrian: Mobile Phones in Japanese Life*. MIT Press: Cambridge, MA; London, pp. 165–182.

Harper, D. 2012, *Visual Sociology*, Routledge: London; Thousand Oaks, CA; New Delhi; Singapore.

Hirsch, J. 1981, *Family Photographs*, Oxford University Press: Oxford.

Hirsch, M. 2008, 'The Generation of Postmemory'. *Poetics Today*, Vol. 29, no. 1, pp. 103–128.

Jakobson, R. & Bogatyrev, P. 1980, 'Folklore as a Special Form of Creation'. *Folklore Forum*, Vol. 13, no. 1, pp. 1–21.

Jamieson, L. 1998, *Intimacy: Personal Relationships in Modern Societies*. Polity Press: Cambridge.

Jensen, J. L. & Waade, A. M. 2009, *Medier og Turisme*. Systime Academic: Aarhus.

Kuhn, A. 2010, 'Snow White in 1930s Britain'. *Journal of British Cinema and Television*, Vol. 7, no. 2, pp. 183–199.

Langford, M. 2001, *Suspended Conversations: The Afterlife of Memory in Photographic Albums*. McGuill-Queens University Press: Montreal.

Lanzeni, D. 2014, 'Media Futures'. *Media Anthropology Network European Association of Social Anthropologists (EASA) Discussions*, pp. 1–20, viewed 26 October 2015, www.media-anthropology.net/file/discussion_media_futures.pdf.

Lehmuskallio, A. T. 2012, *Pictorial Practices in a 'Cam Era': Studying Non-Professional Camera Use*. Tampere University Press: Tampere.

McLuhan, M. 1964, *Understanding Media: The Extensions of Man*. McGraw-Hill: New York.

Madianou, M. & Miller, D. 2012, *Migration and New Media: Transnational Families and Polymedia*. Routledge: London; New York.

Martin, F. 2005, 'The Changing Face of Family Law in Ireland'. *Judicial Studies Institute Journal*, Vol. 5, no. 1, pp. 16–41.

Miller, D. 2010, *Stuff*. Polity Press: Cambridge.

Moores, S. 2012, *Media, Place and Mobility*. Palgrave Macmillan: Basingstoke; New York.

Morley, D. 2007, *Media, Modernity and Technology: The Geography of the New*. Routledge London; New York.

Pauwels, L. 2010, 'Visual Sociology Reframed: An Analytical Synthesis and Discussion of Visual Methods in Social and Cultural Research'. *Sociological Methods and Research*, Vol. 38, no. 4, pp. 545–581.

Pink, S. 2011a, 'Amateur Photographic Practice, Collective Representation and the Constitution of Place'. *Visual Studies*, Vol. 26, no. 2, pp. 92–101.

Pink, S. 2011b, 'Multimodality, Multisensoriality and Ethnographic Knowing: Social Semiotics and the Phenomenology of Perception'. *Qualitative Research*, Vol. 11, no. 3, pp. 261–276.

Ponzanesi, S. & Leurs, K. 2014, 'On Digital Crossings in Europe'. *Crossings: Journal of Migration and Culture*, Vol. 5, no. 1, pp. 3–22.

Rose, G. 2014, 'How Digital Technologies do Family Snaps, Only Better', in J. Larsen & M. Sandbye (eds) *Digital Snaps: The New Face of Photography*. I.B. Tauris: London; New York.

Rose, G. 2010, *Doing Family Photography: The Domestic, the Public and the Politics of Sentiment*. Farnham; Burlington, VT: Ashgate.

Rose, G. 2003, 'Family Photographs and Domestic Spacings: A Case Study'. *Transactions of the Institute of British Geographers*, Vol. 28, no. 1, pp. 5–18.

Shome, R. 2011, '"Global Motherhood": The Transnational Intimacies of White Femininity'. *Critical Studies in Media Communication*, Vol. 28, no. 5, pp. 388–406.

Slater, D. 1991, 'Consuming Kodak', in J. Spence & P. Holland (eds) *Family Snaps: The Meanings of Domestic Photography*. Virago Press Limited: London, pp. 49–59.

Smart, C. & Shipman, B. 2004, 'Visions in Monochrome: Families, Marriage and the Individualization Thesis'. *British Journal of Sociology*, Vol. 55, no. 4, pp. 491–509.

Stumberger, R. 2007, *Klassen-Bilder: Sozialdokumentarische Fotografie 1900–1945*. UVK: Konstanz.

Van Dijck, J. 2007, *Mediated Memories: Personal Cultural Memory in the Digital Age*. Standford University Press: Stanford, CA.

Watters, J. 2009, 'Migrant Networkscapes: Spatialising Accounts of Migrants' Social Practices'. *Translocations: Migration and Social Change An Inter-Disciplinary Open Access E-Journal*, viewed 26 October 2015, www.trans locations.ie/docs/v07i01/Vol%207%20Issue%201%20-%20Peer%20Review %20-%20Migrant%20Networkscapes,%20Watters.pdf.

Weston, K. 1997, *Families We Choose: Lesbians, Gays, Kinship*. Columbia University Press: New York.

Wulff, H. J. 1993, 'Phatische Gemeinschaft/Phatische Funktion: Letikonzepte einer Pragmatischen Theorie des Fernsehens'. *Montage A/V*, Vol. 2, no. 1, pp. 142–163.

9 Visual politics and material semiotics

The digital camera's translation of political protest

Rune Saugmann Andersen

In the hand of the police officer is a digital camera. You can see the photo. But is it an actor?[1] That question informs my writing in this chapter. I use videos taken at the eviction at the Brorson Church in Copenhagen, from one of which the framegrab in Figure 9.1 is taken, to investigate the agency of digital cameras in political activism. In doing so I explore three themes in greater detail: first, I zoom in on the agency of the camera as a translator which substantially transforms political protest and reconfigures the conditions which make possible effective political protest by tying such effectiveness to the semiotics enacted in online and mass media remediation of visual media content. Second, I turn to the instability of camera agency. I ask how the agency of the camera itself is re-negotiated in political debate when powerful societal institutions, such as governments and

Figure 9.1 Citizen recording of police filming street clashes by the Brorson Church (source: screen capture from video, viewed 18 November 2014, www. youtube.com/watch?v=PrTviRZujgU&feature=youtube_gdata_player).

police forces, make use of and comment upon the use of cameras in political protest, enacting the camera along a continuum of credibility from a weapon of deception to a neutral agent of truth. Finally, I consider the indirect agency of cameras in protest by looking at how the parties involved in the confrontation anticipate and prepare for the conflict to be filmed and choose strategies that will be likely to produce visual translations that benefit them. There is a sort of Heisenberg principle at work when cameras become part of protest infrastructure.

The chapter argues that the camera is a central but unstable non-human actor in contemporary political protest. It charts the material and semiotic networks enabled and inhibited by the camera as the key semiotic inscription device that connects the corporeal materiality of political protest (including the networks of force that go into producing and repressing protests) to the digital materiality of media content (including the networks of media institutions, norms, and economies, journalists and professional political actors that produce everyday political debate).

Introduction

Images of political conflicts have, in the past decade, been portrayed as increasingly essential to the logic and meaning of conflict. Studies have shown how both authorities and protesters depend on visual mediation and shape their strategies for physical confrontation with an acute attention to the visual mediation that a conflict will generate.

To take but a few examples from the perspective of international politics, the discipline within which I usually write, visual media concerns have been shown to have shaped both the understanding of and resistance to the Guantanamo camp (van Veeren 2010), to direct our understanding of HIV and Aids (Bleiker & Kay 2007) and to be deeply involved in the strategies used in the 2003 Iraq war (Campbell 2003a). Laura Shepherd (2008, p. 213) argues that

> The 'war on terror', as a response to the events of 11 September 2001, was in part communicated by and made meaningful through visual representation. These representational practices are discursive practices [and] construct an intelligible reality that then itself acts as a referent for the construction of meaning.

Similarly, a large body of literature has investigated how amateur photography is increasingly vital to our understanding of far-away conflict (see, for example, chapters in Andén-Papadopoulos & Pantti 2011). What neither the works in international relations, nor the works engaging with citizen mediation of conflict have done a lot of so far, however, is to take a material semiotic approach and investigate how the omnipresence of cameras – the precondition for the citizen photography that has been extensively studied – changes not only the mediation of a conflict, but also the conflict itself.[2] Apart from this, considerations of material semiotics (Law 2009 coins this more precise name for what is also called 'actor network theory') are strangely absent from international relations and security studies – even from their so-called 'visual turn', which came as an after-effect of the visual turn in social sciences (Campbell 2003b; Möller 2009, 2005). Material semiotics are only recently being considered in conjunction with visualities as interesting analyses engage the technologization of security management through, for example, airport scanners (Bellanova & Fuster 2013), drones (Walters 2014) and assemblages of technologies and standard operating procedures (Schouten 2014).[3]

At the start of the War on Terror, David Campbell pointed out how visual media strategies targeted at and inspired by Western mass media became key to the design of operations in the Iraq war (2003b, p. 63). The concerns in this chapter are similar, in that it is about how political conflict is not only made meaningful through visual representation that acts as a referent, an 'intelligible reality', but in how the practices of translation and mediation involved structure how a political conflict is produced, including the expectations and strategies of parties to such conflict. Rather than focusing solely on the discursive structures of meaning-making, as Campbell does, the present contribution highlights the material transformation effected by the camera's translation of corporeal conflict into digital images – in that way it is more similar to Kennedy's contribution.

The translation done by the camera – rendering a political confrontation as a digital visual artefact – is by no means a passive recording. This chapter proposes to see the camera as the central inscription device that transforms political confrontations, translating the corporeal, spatially and temporally situated materiality of political confrontation in three crucial ways, that will be explored.

First, the digital images captured with the help of technologies omnipresent at contemporary political protests are not bound to appear in a certain time and space, as the protest itself is. The camera, therefore, translates the materiality of the protest, making image-borne protest bound to different material and semiotic networks and different space–time logics to a non-filmed corporeal political confrontation. Second, the depiction made by the camera enables the political locus of a conflict to be dispersed from the space of the physical confrontation itself to a mediaspace where logics of remediation and representation trump logics of physical force, but it does not guarantee it. The resources relating to the visual media networks in which the conflict also takes place supplement the resources, logics and objectives of violent political encounter. However, the question of which resources and logics become of prime importance is one that cannot be predetermined but one that is negotiated in an assembled space of violent political conflict, produced by the translation of the camera. Third, and finally, the camera has a kind of indirect agency through how the parties to the confrontation anticipate and prepare for the political conflict to be filmed, choosing conflict strategies that will be likely to produce visual translations in line with their goals for the conflict.

This analysis combines the representational and non-representational (material) semiotic approaches to the camera – much along lines recommended by Lister, later in this volume. Even if the development of digital video mediation technologies is central to the way in which the camera currently translates political protest, the approach developed here is not one of technology per se but one which emphasizes the sociotechnological entanglements that produce everyday political reality. As such, the exact camera and media technology is not at the core of my argument – the core is the camera's rendering of protest in images that can be circulated in media. This is possible with different camera and mediation technologies, even if the advent of digital imaging technologies and media networks makes it much more likely to happen. One of the most important aspects of this advent of digital technology is social, as digital image technologies have changed the social norms of visual news mediation to break photojournalists' monopoly on representing crises (Andersen 2012; Andén-Papadopoulos & Pantti 2013; Kristensen & Mortensen 2013). While the specific mediation and image production technologies matter, the technological specificity of, for example, image sensors (Lehmuskallio, in this volume) and algorithms (Gómez Cruz, ibid.) is less central to my argument here.

Before I analyse how each of the three aspects of visual translations of political conflict play out in practice in the Brorson controversy, I provide a short sketch of the confrontations. It is to this task that we now turn.

Background – the Brorson conflict

The translation practices studied here relate to the violent conclusion of a protracted political conflict taking place in Denmark in 2009. Throughout 2009, debate had been going on about whether Denmark should forcefully repatriate the many Iraqi asylum seekers who had fled the war in Iraq but had been denied refugee status in Denmark. In May 2009, Danish immigration authorities decided that a group of 282 Iraqi asylum seekers were to be repatriated to Iraq – either by leaving voluntarily with a sum of money and a 'repatriation plan'[4] or, if not leaving voluntarily, to be deported and left to their own means. By late May, most of the refugees had gone underground, a few had taken the voluntary repatriation offer and about 60 individuals publicly took refuge[5] in a church – first in Vor Frue Kirke (Church of Our Lady), the cathedral in central Copenhagen, and from late June in the much smaller parish church, Brorson Church in Nørrebro, a multicultural and renowned leftist neighbourhood in Copenhagen.

On 13 August 2009, the Copenhagen police carried out a search of the church with the aim of finding able-bodied male individuals, sought for forced repatriation. As the police operation started shortly after midnight on 13 August, protesters gathered outside the church and engaged in civil disobedience actions, trying physically to block the police from removing the asylum seekers by forming human roadblocks across the streets near the church. The Copenhagen police responded with force to these roadblocks, searched the church, arrested the 19 male adults found in it and took them to a special prison for asylum seekers, in Ellebæk, to await deportation. The confrontations between police and protesters lasted till around 4:30 a.m.

A number of videos – taken by bystanders, protesters and the police authorities, during street battles and inside the church – make up the visual translation of the confrontations that I engage with in this chapter.

The camera as an inscription device: visual translation of protest

This section elaborates the translations that the camera performs on political protests when these are captured in digital image formats, focusing on how the changes to the materiality of the protest alters the networked character of the protest.

This move begins with us seeing the camera as an inscription device and then considers the differences between the materialities of political protest before and after the camera's translation. In *Laboratory Life*, Latour and Woolgar define an inscription device in terms that are readily applicable to the work done by the digital camera and its associated digital mediation systems, arguing that 'an inscription device is any item of apparatus or particular configuration of such items which can transform a material substance into a figure or a diagram' (1979, p. 51).

The translation performed by this inscription device is understandable through *La Trahison des Images*, Magritte's famous artwork that W. J. T. Mitchell (1994) rightly calls a pictorial theorization, a theory of representation that is painted rather than written. The painting depicts a pipe and the words 'this is not a pipe'. It speaks, thus, of the material difference between the visual representation and that which is depicted – Magritte allegedly encouraged anyone doubting the transformed reality of the pipe to 'just try to fill it with tobacco' (Spitz 1994, p. 47).

Drawing on Michel Serres, John Law uses the difference between reality and representation pointed to by Magritte to elaborate how our efforts to know the world through representations of it is an active and transformative act: '[S]ince no two words *are* equivalent, translation also implies betrayal: *traduction, trahison*. So translation is both about making equivalent, and about shifting' (2009, p. 144). Returning this thought to visual translations and to our topic here, we may say that the visual recording of political protest both translates and betrays the physical encounter. The camera translates physical protest into a visual archive, but also transforms or betrays the physical protest that it depicts, introducing new dynamics that arise from the protest-as-image, not from the protest-as-street-confrontation. A pipe that is good for smoking may not look like a pipe at all; a picture that 'is' a pipe is worthless for smoking. When the omnipresence of cameras translating face-to-face experience into images means that political protest blends these two realities – its manifestation as a meeting between people in a specific time and place, and its manifestation as images of this meeting – protest dynamics become an assemblage of altogether different sets of logics. While the logics of the street confrontation would include temporally and spatially localized factors, such as numbers of protesters and of police, goals of police and protesters, unity of purpose and tactics in both camps, etc., the logics of protest imagery is tied not to localized achievement of goals in a specific space, but to logics of spread, remediation and representation. Understanding this transformation is the core step of this chapter and it is the foundation for the subsequent parts of my argument. The remainder of this section explores the idea of different logics by pointing to the meaning and importance attributed to a single instance of camera-recorded police brutality during the violent Brorson confrontations.

Translating the cast: an unlikely main character

Christina Søndergaard was not a core organizer of the protests at the Brorson Church, nor one of the Iraqi asylum seekers that the confrontations were supposedly all about. Yet, due to a spectacular instance of visually recorded police violence performed on her body, she became the unlikely, possibly unwilling and unprepared spokesperson for those resisting the forced repatriation of Iraqi asylum seekers.

The morning after the Brorson confrontations, a video of a young woman being struck eight times with a police baton was widely circulated online and quickly spread to mass media. Here, the woman seen suffering in the video became the topic of numerous interviews and news pieces. Newspapers used online opinion polls to engage consumers, asking them to judge the appropriateness of the police conduct in the light of the video. Søndergaard, the woman in the video, was the most sought-after interviewee of the day, questioned about how her suffering felt, about her experience of police brutality, in live current affairs TV programmes.

While news and current affairs programming on TV focused on the female protagonist in a spectacle of gendered suffering, tabloid newspapers followed up by attributing gendered and sexualized connotations to the spectacular violence, such as naming Søndergaard 'the baton girl' (Harder 2009).

The massive focus on this single, random episode – a young woman with a distinctively Danish look, who is being brutalized by a policeman – is a view of the confrontation encouraged by the translation of the camera.

Figure 9.2 Image used in reportage of police officers beating the young woman Christina Søndergaard (source: screen capture from video, viewed 12 November 2014, http://ekstrabladet.dk/nationen/article4165808.ece).

Rather than a political confrontation about the forced removal of bodies from the church to the prison, the visual translation of the conflict redistributes what is important in the conflict. In the assemblage of visual archives and news media logics, the sensible becomes not the political stake of the conflict but the spectacular gendered or sexualized violence.

The video of Søndergaard, arguably, has a high degree of what we may call 'remediability' – the ability to be continuously remediated in online and mass media – since a young woman suffering police brutality nicely fits the requirements of a Danish mainstream news media operating in a competitive environment, increasingly using citizen footage and struggling with demands for cheap and fast production (Kristensen & Mortensen 2013; Lund 2002). The format of online protest video easily and cheaply adapts to the news format, and the format itself carries a symbolic weight independent of its content, a weight that makes it attractive to remediate for both media and political actors (Andersen 2013).

While the publicity is secured, in Søndergaard's case, with the widely remediated video and follow-up stories, and she thus becomes a key node in the Brorson network, her case is a poor articulation of how a refugee politics devoid of care for individuals inflicts suffering in the pursuit of political goals. The woman herself points to as much when she states in interviews that 'I think it is a far more serious crime to deport people to a country in which they risk being killed' (Hansen and *TV2 News* 2009, sec. 2:15), attempting to shift the discussion back to the political project in which she inscribes her suffering. Yet, the most prominent result of the visual translation of the Brorson conflict, the image of Søndergaard, does not provide clear visual signifiers evoking the refugee issue, but rather translates the conflict into a debate about police operational conduct, one that is far removed from asylum politics. I shall return to this question in the last section where I discuss how the anticipated presence of cameras changes protester and police tactics. For now, I just point to the political displacement that takes place as Søndergaard's beating becomes the symbolic image of the confrontation, even if it is a rather poor symbol of the violence of refugee politics devoid of care for asylum seekers.

By altering perception from lived and localized experience to the portable reality of photographic and video archives, the camera fundamentally changes how political protest is made and made (in)efficient. The knowledge of camera translation, likely to, for example, encourage the representation of political conflicts as single moments of spectacular violence, transforms the protest itself, as participants anticipate it and their strategies reflect that the materiality of a confrontation is not merely about the physical superiority of force in a spatially and temporally delimited conflict. As participants are aware that a confrontation is mediated by the camera's translation, for most of the individuals and institutions in the network that make up the confrontation, the taking into account of the 'unconscious optics' revealed in this translation become a prime concern.

However, before we turn to that argument, the second part of this analysis introduces a measure of uncertainty: while cameras record, translating lived realities into digital images, it is not fixed, once-and-for-all, what these digital images *are* in politics. Returning to the example of Magritte's pipe, what is at stake here is whether an image will be understood politically as a pipe (i.e. a form of access to an everyday reality rather than a depiction) or as a painting (a depiction without any connection to the object it depicts).

The instability of the camera – how networks co-produce the agency of depicting political protest

The preceding argument points to how digital imagery changes the networked character of political conflict – supplementing face-to-face sociality with a media sociality. The second argument I want to make has to do with the make-up of the digitally mediated sociality around political protest, and with the logics of political protest in this form of networked sociality. The empirical section of this argument explores how the intervention of key political actors in the network built by digital images of the Brorson protest changes the meaning of and status attributed to the images.

We already saw that the translation of political protest could change the key protagonists of a protest movement, away from those with key positions in the network of the face-to-face encounter and towards those who come to occupy key positions in the digital visual network (such as the woman, Christina Søndergaard, from the Brorson protests). Yet, sheer exposure is not enough to make a political protest successful in the digital media sociality, as Christina's indication of her own inability to symbolize the violence of refugee politics demonstrates. Rather than the camera being a translation device that decisively transforms protest in a one-off act, the camera performs an unstable translation without a pre-determinate effect. This is because the transformation of a political protest into an archive of digital images says little about the political life of these images, since this political life is determined in the political actor network that the protest both performs and performs in as it is transformed into images. Specifically, it is not up to the camera to determine whether the images produced are seen as politically meaningful or not, as documents which demand political thinking and response or as media consumer entertainment. We express this by saying that the camera's translation is the condition of possibility for a protest's digital media life, but the actual reach of that extension is determined not in the act of producing digital images of protest, but in subsequent networked acts taking place around these images.

This aspect of the translation performed by the camera is concerned with how the networked character of political confrontation is reconfigured when the camera adds visual mediation to the already complex assemblage of actors, institutions and discourses making up corporeal protest, making contemporary political protest an assemblage of media and direct action logics. An assemblage has been characterized as designating 'a host of different phenomena and processes working in concert' (Haggerty & Ericson 2000, p. 608), and it is exactly this working-in-concert that is at stake in this section. An assemblage can also be thought of as an actor-network (Law 2009, p. 146), a network that is material-semiotic in the sense that its elements, both human and non-human, define and shape each other. Where the first aspect of translation was about how the camera interprets and shapes face-to-face protest, this second aspect is about how the network of actors and media change and interpret the camera and the images it produces.

The basic idea is that the political performativity of protest image is a network effect produced in the assemblage of digital images, political actors and on- and offline political news media. This thought flows from the idea that '[i]n a material-semiotic world all actions, including those of great men, are relational effects' (Law 2009, p. 145). In this line of argument, the translation of a protest or conflict into a digital archive – visual or audiovisual – reconfigures the ways in which it performs in larger societal networks and thereby what it does and what the protest does. The digital image travels (in its translated form of protest-as-image) by online visual media and news media; both of which are central for the network established between a protest or conflict and mainstream political debate. However, simply being a digital visual artefact, an image with a specific framing, focus and sets of omissions and highlights, does not say much about its political performativity. More important is how the protest images perform in the networks they enter into and co-construct, and the factors that influence this performance. The idea that networks determine the outcome lead Latour, in a famous statement, to reject the notion that Pasteur was a 'great man', arguing instead that he was positioned in a network that allowed great things to be done and thereby allowed his actions to become those of a great man (Law 2009, p. 145).

Similar lines of thinking can be found in Cook's (2005) work on how governing in a media-saturated democracy is best characterized as a co-production in which both news institutions and political actors are essential, and in which the assembled effect of the networked acts made in both spheres characterizes political governance. In the Brorson context we may use this literature to think about how sheer access to the visual reality of a protest might not be enough for the images of protest to enter political debate. Just as the sheer number of people does not determine success in a face-to-face protest, political logics play into the media life of protest images. Most prominently, the powerful and extensive networks of official politics influence the networks formed around a protest or conflict. This is often sought by ensuring the participation of political institutions (trade unions, interest organizations, etc.) and professional politicians in protests, but it can also be accomplished by these institutions or individuals engaging with and remediating protest images (on the idea of remediation, see Bolter & Grusin 2000; I develop a take on protest image remediation in Andersen 2012).

The remainder of this section looks more closely at how the political performativity of the images from Brorson is co-produced by the network around them, interrogating how this idea plays out in practice. The section describes how the political life of protest images can reconfigure *what* the camera does when translating protest. The translation in which the camera renders protest as an archive of images – taken by professionals as well as citizens – enables the protest to draw on the media networks of news and online political debate, but it is the networks that make sense of the image archive, rather than the camera itself. The event I use to interrogate this idea is a situation when powerful institutions introduced and endorsed visual mediation of the Brorson confrontations, allowing for scrutiny of the political performance before and after this intervention.

'This video proves it': image performativity as network effect

When the Copenhagen Police carried out the search of the Brorson church, a debate had been going on for months about the fate of the refugees hiding in Brorsons Kirke. Thus, there was from the outset a large and well-established network around the confrontation. This consisted of an ad-hoc non-governmental organization (NGO), Kirkeasyl (Church Asylum) created to support the asylum seekers, loose networks of activists who had formed text-messaging chain networks and pledged to block the eviction, Copenhagen Police and its spokespersons, professional politicians opposing and supporting the eviction and repatriation, mainstream news media and freelance journalists and photographers expecting confrontations. It is thus no surprise that the morning after the forced eviction of the church, the confrontations were prominent news. This network paved the way for the video of Christina Søndergaard becoming the main focal point, relating a debate about the conduct of the Copenhagen Police during the confrontations as the main post-confrontation debate. Yet after two days of relatively intensive coverage, in which both professional and citizen photographers' images were illustrating events, media interest dropped markedly, with only a few news pieces published after 14 August.

Subsequently, only the church minister, pastor Per Ramsdal, was able to keep the occurrences on the national agenda, speaking out about how he had experienced riot-clad police officers and frightened Iraqis in his church when he was woken up by the noise from the eviction. Over the following weeks the descriptions of events given by the pastor, illustrated by but not carried by video clips and images filmed by protesters and support group, continued to disturb the narrative of a 'perfectly executed operation' laid out by police spokespersons (Clemmensen & Drevsfeldt 2009). This controversy led the Copenhagen Police to publicly assert, on 19 August, that the pastor of the church was deliberately misrepresenting events (Hansen 2009), an assertion that, again, expanded the media network around the events, yet did so without severely undermining the pastor.

As the trouble with the pastor continued, the Copenhagen Police released their video surveillance tapes from the operation on 30 August. This publication broke a tradition of only using police surveillance tapes in court, in training and for investigation (Copenhagen Police 2011). Following a careful media strategy, the police published the tapes exclusively through private broadcaster *TV2* and right-of-centre tabloid *BT*. Such picking of outlets is a standard tool in media management strategies, designed to ensure that the source has a good idea of the kind of treatment the materials will receive (Cook 2005), thus providing some degree of control over how they will be framed and the narrative they will be promoted in relation to.

The publication of police surveillance video was accompanied by statements by government spokespersons, annoyed by the priest's criticism of the refugee policy. 'Minister: Priest Lying' (*BT* 2009) was the headline of a video showing the Minister of Justice reviewing the surveillance tapes on the day of their broadcast (ibid., 01:30). Such endorsement both framed the surveillance tapes and ensured that they became front-page news. Later, the Minister of Integration, responsible for the deportation order the police were carrying out, delivered both the strongest condemnation and the strongest endorsement of video as truthfulness, claiming that 'it is a bold lie that the police escalated the situation. *And this video proves it*' (Clemmensen 2009, my italics).

The nationalist Danish People's Party – staunchly anti-immigrant, anti-refugee and the parliamentary base of the government – called for an official investigation of the priest (Ritzau 2009a). After two weeks of dying interest in the case, the media network was dramatically expanded by the participation of top-level government officials, sending the Brorson controversy back on to the front pages of newspapers and back into the prime slots of news programming.

However, the intervention of government officials to authenticate the truth-telling power of videos and expand their reach had an interesting effect on the actor-network around the Brorson case. While the visual archive of the protest had played a part in the debate since the eviction of the church, the strong endorsement of video by top officials altered the network configuration. Following a material semiotic logic, in which network elements give meaning to each other, what happened here was that the agency of video images was re-configured. Hitherto, video had mainly been used as illustration of news narratives, such as police violence or the execution of the search, but the intervention of top government officials re-imagined video images as neutral carriers of truth. The success of this endeavour re-inscribed – at least temporarily – the identities of the police and government officials (truth-tellers), protesters (exaggerating claims of brutality, as the police video did not contain much police violence) and the priest (liar/manipulator). It also positioned images as central to the network, as they became the nodal point around which questions of truth are negotiated.

The re-imagination of images as indisputable evidence allowed activists and journalists to exploit the centrality of video, however, rather than being marginalized by it. Soon, already forgotten videos from the Brorson night re-surfaced as evidence of police manipulation. A series of videos depicted policemen with video recording devices outside the church, policemen who would appear to be recording confrontations that were not to be found in the police surveillance video (Gjerding, Geist & Clemmensen 2009; Ritzau & *information.dk* 2009; Rømer 2009). Whereas these videos, with the exception of the one of Søndergaard, had not been very powerful in questioning the police claims that no unnecessary violence was used, the new positioning of video and images as a central arbiter of truthfulness now allowed videos – such as the one shown in Figure 9.1 at the beginning of the chapter – to contradict police claims.

Underlining the strength of digital images in the new network configuration, the police chiefs' repeated denials of possessing more footage were brushed aside by the same videos that had been powerless in testifying to police brutality. Yet, as the configuration of the debate placed high value on video rendered as evidence, the police leadership was forced to take these claims seriously. This is evident in the beginning of the press release announcing the 'newfound' footage: 'The Copenhagen Police have been presented two video clips from the Internet that would show two policemen video photographing' (Københavns Politi 2009). The visual evidence, not the repeated verbal articulations of the same arguments, is invoked as decisive.

Striking, in comparison, are the vain efforts by journalists to confront the police without the help of visual evidence: extensive questioning of police management about what was meant by their shifting and contradictory explanations, including the demand for an explanation or investigation of the false and misleading claims made by police management and spokespersons, achieved little beyond entertaining headlines.[6] The Brorson pastor was brushed aside when raising similar issues, as was the Police Union. While the visual translation of political conflict is thus not universally powerful – it failed to sustain a meaningful debate about either police violence or refugee policy in the weeks after the eviction – it can, when placed centrally and configured as evidence by the material semiotic of a network in which it participates, be a formidable power. It paints a dynamic picture of the political performativity of images, showing that the question of whether images are able to draw marginalized voices into a debate and enable these to question powerful institutions.

Recent scholarship has shown how the prominence of amateur images change how journalists articulate and understand key media institutions, those concerned with objectivity, journalistic professionalism and self-understanding that Andén-Papadopoulos and Pantti group as journalistic ideology (2013, p. 961; for the understanding of such beliefs as media institutions, see Cook 2005). This section locates such change less squarely with amateur images themselves, arguing that the roles of images and journalists alike is negotiated in the complex assemblage of political and media dynamics that protest images exist in. However, the following section extends Andén-Papadopoulos and Pantti's argument, in a sense, detailing how the expectation of networked amateur images change not only journalistic ideology but also how such expectations are changing the strategies of protesters and security governance authorities.

Anticipating visibility

The last aspect of the agency of the camera in relation to political protest that I wish to point to here is the indirect agency that stems from the anticipation of visual translations of political conflict. As noted above, the prevalence of amateur visual translations of crisis have been seen to change the ideology of media professionals, key actors in the networks of conflict mediation (Andén-Papadopoulos & Pantti 2013). However, media actors are far from the only category of actors undergoing change as they become part of visual protest assemblages. This section explores how police and protesters' anticipation of the agency of visual translations of political conflict can be seen in their preparations for the Brorson conflict.

With intense public debate preceding the search of the Brorson Church, the police operation came as a surprise to no one. Even if the precise timing and tactics were kept secret, the situation and the media reverberations it would generate could be and were anticipated by both police and activists. This section briefly explores the anticipatory moves of, first, protesters and then police.

The strategies of activists opposing the forced repatriation anticipated camera translations of the protest in two ways. First, visuality and visibility were central to the efforts of activists helping the asylum seekers. As well as a nursery and food, activists provided the asylum seekers with a less ordinary 'refugee camp' kind of help: a media team, taking care of procuring maximum exposure of their double refuge – filming the everyday life of the group and making a public point of being constantly on the ready with video cameras inside the Brorson Church to prevent a 'dark' police operation. Ensuring that the eviction would be filmed was also a way of ensuring that it would be debated. As multiple scholarly works over the last years have documented, 'previously marginalised individuals can now narrate the events themselves and become recognised not only in social media but also in the global and national mainstream media' (Andén-Papadopoulos & Pantti 2011, p. 354). This investigation probes this claim in the traditionally elite-focused domain of security politics.

Second, activists not affiliated with the Kirkeasyl network, set up to help asylum seekers, had publicly pledged to use street protests to try to block any police action, organizing text-messaging networks to alert activists if the church refuge was broken (Larsen 2011). This set the scene for almost certain clashes between protesters and police. This strategy both alerted news media in advance of the protest and promised to deliver dramatic images with high newsworthiness (Cook 2005). The strategies of the creation of an ad-hoc NGO with a media team, the creation of a double refuge and the promise of direct action by radical protesters were, thus, from the beginning laced with elements that would render the visual imprint of the conflict appealing to news media and give activists some degree of control over the visual imprint of an eviction of the Brorson Church.

The Copenhagen Police, likewise, anticipated visual translations of the conflict in their strategies. First, they videotaped the operation, second, they entered the church not in riot gear but in short-sleeved shirts and soft hats and, third, they chose only to arrest able-bodied males. The second and third of these strategies became major talking points after the confrontations (Ritzau 2009b; Steen & *TV2 News* 2009).

First, however, the police strategy to film the arrests and the confrontations: this strategy resulted in the large amount of footage that would later become the turning point around which the agency of protest images was re-negotiated. In research interviews the police officers responsible for the Brorson operational planning were clearly attentive to a preventive effect of video documentation – that it would limit disobedience and violence against the police by easing its prosecution and punishment (Copenhagen Police 2011).

Second, instead of entering the church wearing protective gear the police were kitted out in short-sleeve shirts and soft hats in the summer night. This strategy also works in and through the visual imprint of confrontations. Immediately after the first critiques of the operation, both police spokespersons and government ministers made much of the short sleeves and soft hats, using the images as an immediate visual rebuke of those arguing that the police were acting with a brutality inappropriate for dealing with non-violent protest and vulnerable asylum seekers (*BT* 2009; Hansen 2009; for a critical reaction, see Rehling 2009). In using the images as a visual back-up for talking points, and doing so fast, forcefully and from a wide array of governmental speaking positions, the official enactment of 'soft hats as proof of peaceful police' shows an awareness of the visual translation of the conflict.

Third, the police followed a strategy of only arresting the one-third of the asylum seekers who were able-bodied men. The police explained the strategy as the result of 'humanitarian concerns' (Steen & *TV2 News* 2009) and a presumption that the rest of the asylum seekers would follow on their own (Copenhagen Police 2011). This is somewhat at odds with the police explanation of the operation as the last resort with regards to those individuals who were in breach of the repatriation order. Following the heated debate, police planners could reasonably expect a number of images of police confronting protesters as well as arresting, and perhaps violently subduing, the targeted asylum seekers. Visible traces of an operation targeting only able-bodied men would, indeed, be viewed very differently in the securitized immigration and refugee debate in mainstream Danish media from images of a similar situation involving police officers handcuffing, physically restraining and forcefully subduing women and children. As Campbell (2003b, p. 59) puts it, 'the emotional value of feminised victims,... and official appreciation of all these factors, can all be located in recent coverage'. By ensuring that visual translations of the protest would be depicting police officers in short sleeves and soft hats facing upset Middle Eastern-looking men, this strategy enacts a version of the refugee debate compatible with the view that Danes must be protected from immigrants, rather than images emphasizing the vulnerability of asylum seekers. And, indeed, the initial news coverage of the arrests did feature images of defiant-looking men rather than vulnerable women, as shown in the framegrab in Figure 9.3.

Tales of translations and network effects

This chapter has explored the potential of viewing images of political protest as a translation effected by the digital camera and its associated mediation systems; a translation that (re)makes political conflict as an assemblage of logics from the spatially and temporally defined street confrontation, and logics from the temporally and spatially flexible digital mediasphere, where protest fragments can be experienced independently of time and space. The chapter has shown how viewing protest as an assemblage of the political logics found on the street level and on the digital media level, can help us think about changes to the distribution of roles, goals and strategies enacted in political confrontations (who the protagonists are and what the goals of the parties in a confrontation might be). It has suggested that the camera, viewed as an inscription device, is central as it translates the 'reality' of the conflict into fragmented video-bites and snapshots, and makes it possible for these to traverse by digital media. It has reviewed confrontation strategies to show that this is not an abstract and purely theoretical insight, but rather one that is shared by the actors who engage in political conflict and understand it as a material relation in

Figure 9.3 Framegrab of police leading arrested asylum seeker out of the Brorson Church (source: screen capture at 00:21a.m. from video illustrating Hansen (2009), viewed 9 November 2014, http://nyhederne.tv2.dk/article.php/id-24441636:politi-pr%C3%A6st-lyver-om-rydning.html).

which the camera translates a spatially and temporally bounded conflict into digital visual archives that can extend through media networks. The positioning of actors in networks and the viewing of their action in terms of network effects they engender is certainly of value in thinking about issues such as how ordinary people, media professionals and media themselves act on the translations of political protest performed by the camera.

Notes

1 I am paraphrasing, here, the introduction to Law and Mol's study of the agency of sheep in relation to animal disease and responses to it. I draw a lot of inspiration from this piece, not least the separation of questions of agency from questions of intentionality (Law & Mol 2008, p. 58).
2 The exception to this is Kennedy's work on soldier photography, which engages with soldiers' quotidian camera use to argue convincingly that digital cameras bring a mundane dimension to the war zone as soldiers capture routine and exceptional moments and, as part of everyday practices, share them with people who are not in the battlefield (Kennedy 2009).
3 For a good discussion of materiality in international relations and security see Aradau *et al.* (2014, ch. 4).
4 The 'repatriation plans' were later ridiculed, as absolutely none of the plans had any correspondence to the lives Iraqis were able to live in the ongoing civil war. Three years after the repatriation, none of the asylum seekers had heard of the organization supposed to help them and the Danish Foreign Ministry evaluated the programme as a disaster (Amnesty International 2012; Geist *et al.* 2010).
5 The supporters of those taking public refuge in the church invoked a contested tradition of 'church refuge'. According to those who invoke the tradition, individuals can seek refuge in the arms-free space of the Church to avoid persecution. This tradition was reported in the Danish media as being somewhat dubious: a centuries-old but non-codified tradition; some asserted that the tradition never existed. Beyond controversy, however, is that the governing councils of Brorson and Vor Frue churches, the parochial church council (consisting of and elected by members of the local parish), invited the Iraqi refugees to stay in the church during the time they were there.
6 To give an example: 'According to the fifth explanation from the police, the fourth explanation was a lie' (Gjerding & Geist 2009).

References

Amnesty International. 2012, 'Irakere sendt Hjem til Tomme Løfter'. Amnesty.dk.

Andén-Papadopoulos, K. & Pantti, M. 2013, 'Re-imagining Crisis Reporting: Professional Ideology of Journalists and Citizen Eyewitness Images'. *Journalism*, Vol. 14, pp. 960–977.

Andén-Papadopoulos, K. & Pantti, M. 2011, *Amateur Images and Global News*. Intellect: Bristol; Chicago, IL.

Andersen, R. S. 2013, 'Citizen "Micro-Journalism": How #IranElection Was Exploited in Politics and Newspaper Stories', in R. Berenger (ed.) *Social Media Go to War: Rage, Rebellion and Revolution in the Age of Twitter*. Marquette Books: Spokane, WA, pp. 335–353.

Andersen, R. S. 2012, 'Remediating #IranElection: Journalistic Strategies for Positioning Citizen-Made Snapshots and Text Bites from the 2009 Iranian Post-Election Conflict'. *Journalism Practice*, Vol. 6, no. 3, pp. 317–336.

Aradau, C., Huysmans, J., Neal, A. W. & Volkner, N. (eds) 2014, *Critical Security Methods: New Frameworks for Analysis, New International Relations*. Routledge: Abingdon; New York.

Bellanova, R. & Fuster, G. G. 2013, 'Politics of Disappearance: Scanners and (Unobserved) Bodies as Mediators of Security Practices'. *International Political Sociology*, Vol. 7, no. 2, pp. 188–209.

Bleiker, R. & Kay, A. 2007, 'Representing HIV/AIDS in Africa: Pluralist Photography and Local Empowerment'. *International Studies Quarterly*, Vol. 51, no. 1, pp. 139–163.

Bolter, J. & Grusin, R. A. 2000, *Remediation: Understanding Bew Media*, 1st edn. MIT Press: Cambridge, MA.

BT. 2009, 'Minister: Præsten lyver'. BT TV.

Campbell, D. 2003a, 'Representing Contemporary War'. *Ethics and International Affairs*, Vol. 17, no. 2, pp. 99–109.

Campbell, D. 2003b, 'Cultural Governance and Pictorial Resistance: Reflections on the Imaging of War'. *Review of International Studies*, Vol. 29, pp. 57–73.

Clemmensen, L. 2009, 'Brorson-Optagelser er Politiets Imagepleje'. information.dk.

Clemmensen, L. & Drevsfeldt, S. 2009, 'Politiet: Alt Forløb Perfekt'. information.dk.

Cook, T. E. 2005, *Governing with the News*, 2nd edn. University of Chicago Press: Chicago, IL.

Copenhagen Police. 2011, Research Interview with Copenhagen Police Operational Planner, Mogens Jensen.

Gjerding, S. & Geist, A. 2009, 'Ifølge femte forklaring fra politiet var fjerde forklaring løgn'. Information.

Gjerding, S., Geist, A. & Clemmensen, L. 2009, 'Også Politiets Fjerde Forklaring var Forkert'. information.dk.

Geist, A., Geist, E., Gjerding, S. & Aagaard, C. 2010, 'Da de svarede sunni, blev de skudt'. Information.

Haggerty, K. D. & Ericson, R. V. 2000, 'The Surveillant Assemblage'. *British Journal of Sociology*, Vol. 51, no. 4, pp. 605–622.

Hansen, J. L. 2009, 'Politi: Præst lyver om rydning'. tv2.dk.

Hansen, J. L. & TV2 News. 2009, 'Kirkerydning: Vil klage over slag'. TV2 News.

Harder, T. 2009, 'Knippel-Pigen Bliver Meldt til Politiet'. Ekstra Bl.

Kennedy, L. 2009, 'Soldier Photography: Visualising the War in Iraq'. *Review of International Studies*, Vol. 35, no. 4, pp. 817–833.

Københavns Politi. 2009, Københavns Politi: Pressemeddelelse vedrørende Københavns Politis Videooptagelser ved Brorsons Kirke.

Kristensen, N. N. & Mortensen, M. 2013, 'Amateur Sources Breaking the News, Metasources Authorizing the News of Gaddafi's Death: New Patterns of Journalistic Information Gathering and Dissemination in the Digital Age'. *Digital Journalism*, Vol. 1, no. 3, pp. 352–367.

Larsen, B. 2011, *Kirkeasyl : en Kamp for Ophold*. Frydenlund: Frederiksberg.

Latour, B. & Woolgar, S. 1979, *Laboratory Life: The Social Construction of Scientific Facts*. Sage: Beverly Hills, CA.

Law, J. 2009, 'Actor Network Theory and Material Semiotics', in B. S. Turner (ed.) *The New Blackwell Companion to Social Theory*. Blackwell, Oxford, pp. 141–158.

Law, J. & Mol, A. 2008, 'The Actor-Enacted: Cumbrian Sheep in 2001', in L. Malafouris & C. Knappett (eds) *Material Agency*. Springer: Boston, MA, pp. 57–77.

Lund, A. B. 2002, 'Fra Nyheder til her- og Derheder', in F. Esman (ed.) *Nyhedskriterier I Det 21: Århundrede*. DR Multimedie, Copenhagen, pp. 84–199.

Mitchell, W. J. 1994, *Picture Theory: Essays on Verbal and Visual Representation*. University of Chicago Press: Chicago, IL; London.

Möller, F. 2009, 'The Looking/Not Looking Dilemma'. *Review of International Studies*, Vol. 35, no. 4, pp. 781–794.

Möller, F. 2005, 'Friction and Discomfort: Visual Representations and Security Policy'. New Directions in Peace and Conflict Research, CPS Working Papers 2005.

Rehling, D. 2009, 'Løgn og Videobånd'. Information.

Ritzau. 2009a, 'Pia K: Ramsdals løgne skal undersøges' Kristeligt Dagbl.

Ritzau. 2009b, 'Politiet: Vi forsøgte med Dialog'.

Ritzau & information.dk. 2009, 'Politiet Filmede også uden for Kirken'. information.dk.

Rømer, M. 2009, 'Politiet: Vi har flere Optagelser'. Ekstra Bladet.

Schouten, P. 2014, 'Security as Controversy: Reassembling Security at Amsterdam Airport'. *Security Dialogue*, Vol. 45, no. 1, pp. 23–42.

Shepherd, L. J. 2008, 'Visualising Violence: Legitimacy and Authority in the "War on Terror"'. *Critical Studies on Terrorism*, Vol. 1, no. 2, pp. 213–226.

Spitz, E. 1994, *Museums of the Mind : Magritte's Labyrinth and other Essays in the Arts*. Yale University Press: New Haven, CT.

Steen, L. & TV2 News. 2009, 'Derfor gik Kvinder og Børn Fri'. TV2 News.

Van Veeren, E. 2010, 'Captured by the Camera's Eye: Guantánamo and the Shifting Frame of the Global War on Terror'. *Review of International Studies*, Vol. 37, no. 4, pp. 1721–1749.

Walters, W. 2014, 'Drone Strikes, *Dingpolitik* and Beyond: Furthering the Debate on Materiality and Security'. *Security Dialogue*, Vol. 45, no. 2, pp. 101–118.

10 Linked photography

A praxeological analysis of augmented reality navigation in the early twentieth century

Tristan Thielmann

Introduction

Although augmented reality navigation appears, at first glance, to be something completely new, it is in fact based on a very old cultural technique. Virtual travel through pre-recorded spaces can be traced back at least to 1905, which saw the first attempt at capturing the residential streets of select routes in photographs. The idea was to make them available as 'photo-auto guides', with superimposed textual and pictographic route instructions. Moreover, these guides were designed as 'social media', with empty lines under each photograph allowing the preservation of photo-related memories. The navigation instructions were layered within a series of photographs, as if arrows had been drawn in the dust of the streets. Therefore, while 'texting and driving' with photo-auto guides, the viewer is in a first-person navigational experience. This permits the viewer to wander through the depicted space, moving deeper into the frame and exploring off-screen space.

This chapter presents a material analysis of linked location-based photographs by looking at their mode of navigational practice and form of production. In doing so, we follow the recursive trajectory of photo-auto guides, which had their heyday between 1905 and 1912 (Ristow 1964, p. 622).

Theoretical grid position

Performative cartography and operative images

Photo-auto guides can be characterized by their integration of very different media: the interplay between landscape photography, textual instructions, road maps and inscribed direction signs, combined and unified through the medium of a book (see Figure 10.1).

The operability of this medium is therefore characterized by a hybrid of four already established navigational practices: (a) virtual travel by pinpointing on landscape photographs, (b) following verbal logs of routes,

Figure 10.1 The Rand McNally Photo-Auto Guide, Chicago to Lake Geneva
(1909) as an open book; photo nos 19 to 22 of the paragraph 'Return
from Lake Geneva to Chicago'.

(c) following a diagrammatic map of a route with the eyes or a finger and
(d) inking lines that trace the route of an automobile journey on a white
sheet or printed map.

This inscribed complexity may be one of the reasons for the fact that
photo-auto guides have yet to be the subject of an in-depth analysis, in the
field of cartography, in science and technology studies, or in media studies.
Photo-auto guides have led a rather more marginal existence as 'boundary
objects' (Star 1989). Another barrier to the study of route guides is the traditional propensity of cartographic theory, media theory and histori-
ography, to focus on the end-products of the mapping process – and
therefore on an understanding of route sketches as artefactual maps –
rather than on the process as a practice in itself.

However, according to Rundstrom (1991, p. 6) it can be argued that
any kind of map is a trace of an ongoing accomplishment that 'situates the
map artifact within the mapmaking process', *and* at the same time 'places
the entire mapmaking process within the context of intracultural and inter-
cultural dialogues occurring over a much longer span of time'. This implies
two consequences: from a praxeological perspective, the study of carto-

graphic and navigational practices is constantly blurring the distinction traditionally made between map makers and map users, whilst taking into account their different skills, knowledge and agency. From a genealogical perspective and by referring to W. J. T. Mitchell, this leads to the argument that maps are inevitably 'redirected to the history and anthropology of the image' (Harley 1989, p. 8).

In the course of this discussion, Christian Jacob's (1996) influential call for an extensive study of the culture of map use has reached the field of media studies, as demonstrated in processive concepts such as 'performative cartography' (Verhoeff 2012) or 'operative images' (Krämer 2009). According to Krämer, operative images are situated in the intermediate field between map, notation and diagram. They can be characterized by (a) their flatness (a two-dimensional spatial layout and order that cause synoptic concurrence), (b) their directionality, (c) their graphism (particularly lines that draw a distinction), (d) their syntacticality (whereby images are not only viewed, but have to be read) and (e) their referentiality (with respect to exteriority). All these characteristics can be applied to the operative photos discussed here.

The object of this investigation is photography that is turned into layered operative imagery through inscriptions (see also Lehmuskallio in this volume). These 'graven images' (Mukerji 1983; Latour 1990, p. 34) are operative in two ways: on the one hand, the presented photographs have been subjected to operative changes through information being embedded in their surface; on the other hand, the photographs were taken and compiled in such a way that they became part of an operative practice: the practice of autonavigation.

One component in the practice of autonavigation is following the traces of route sketches, which the photo-auto guides include in an enclosed book section. Mappings of this kind have a difficult status in cartography, as they are located on the border between printed, and therefore timeless, maps on the one hand, and ephemeral manuscript maps on the other. American road mapping is a perfect example of this kind of boundary work. It reveals a number of examples that lie on the cusp between unfinished intermediary cartography and the endpoint of a mediation process: a finished spatial representation. These boundary objects include the wide range of route guides that were published in the USA at the start of the twentieth century (Akerman 2006).

During the 1900s, route logs were published by motor clubs and a host of semipublic and private organizations. In some cases, these collections of logs were accompanied by simple diagrammatic maps of the routes they described. The standard work of this kind was published by the Automobile Blue Book Company; its first volume came out in 1901. In 1906, the *Automobile Blue Book* gained the endorsement of the American Automobile Association (Ristow 1946, p. 400). These guides provided hundreds of detailed mile-by-mile verbal logs of recommended routes for travel between major cities. The photo-auto guides discussed here also belong to this category of published itineraries of intercity routes. The log collections reached the end of the road, so to speak, as soon as travel bureaus began offering customized route plans and American oil companies distributed free road maps (Akerman 2000, p. 35). Hand-inked lines tracing a pro-posed route on printed sheet-maps were superior to augmented reality navigation, as they could be further personalized and were more flexible to use.

Akerman reveals the different roles and functions fulfilled by the inscribed road maps. Above all, they served as records of past routes, revealing 'the traveler's pride in these trips and their affection for their memory' (ibid., p. 32). It is no surprise that the photo-auto guides took this route-logging function into account and contained a memo field for personal entries. In addition, it was not unusual, at the start of the twenti-eth century, for institutional inscribers, as well as individual inscribers, to be involved in the map-making process.[1] The published photographs super-scribed with arrows can also be understood as such pre-consumer annota-tions, revealing the intermediary and ephemeral status of the routes they set forth.

Mediation theory

The actor network theory (Latour 2005) included a mediation theory developed by Bruno Latour (Thielmann & Schüttpelz 2013) that can be used as a basis for the analysis of navigation practices with the aid of photo-auto guides. In his studies in navigation and the sociology of tech-nology, Bruno Latour traces the linking of people, artefacts and signs via mediators, delineating the logistics that make changes of scale possible. Seen from a media studies perspective, this enables the formation of a praxeological media genealogy founded on the concept of mediation, by drawing on the analysis of chains of media translations, as well as on the tracing of cumulative technological developments.

In the studies of science and technology, this chain of operation follows a deflation strategy that always leads to 'a small window through which one could read a very few signs from a rather poor repertoire' (Latour 1990, p. 22). These inscriptions, as he calls them, 'have the properties of being *mobile* but also *immutable, presentable, readable* and *combinable* with one another' (p. 26). The more artificial and abstract the inscriptions, the greater their capacity to be associated with others and thus to approach reality more closely. The degree of similarity also serves as an index in a chain of association, which leads, seemingly unavoidably, to standardiza-tion and institutionalization within 'centres of calculation' (Latour 1987, p. 215ff.).

In his book *Science in Action*, Latour illustrates the accumulation of knowledge within centres of calculation by an analysis of knowledge gained through mapping and surveying – explaining how implicit local knowledge becomes the universal knowledge of cartography. In order to accumulate knowledge within centres of calculation 'you have to go and to come back *with* the "things" if your moves are not to be wasted. But the "things" have to be able to withstand the return trip without withering away. (Latour 1990, p. 26)

With regard to photography, this means: 'What should be brought into the picture is how the picture is brought back' (ibid., p. 25).

The central image-theoretical assumption is not to understand inscriptions as isolated references. Operative images are situated at the beginning, in-between or at the very end of a long series of transformations (Latour 2014). Location-based photography therefore has to be interpreted in contrast to the punctured trace, the course (of action) from which they are taken. In other words, performative cartography or operative geoimages are never only mimetic. If they were, no wayfinding process would be possible (November, Camacho-Hübner & Latour 2010). The fact that we are dealing with 'migrating images' that arrive and depart (Mitchell 2004), very much within the sense of picture theory, is revealed in a highly specific manner based on the inscribed photographs that are listed in the photo-auto guides published by Rand McNally.

Analysis of photo-auto guides between 1905 and 1909

Groundwork

At the start of the twentieth century, Rand McNally & Company was one of the first automobile road map publishers (Ristow 1964, p. 622) and therefore also a centre of calculation, very much in the sense of Latour's use of the term. The company had made its name in the nineteenth century, mainly by printing timetables and guides for railroads. Based on the experience of printing the *Railroad Guide*, which was a route map for a single railroad, the son of the company founder, Andrew McNally, apparently had the idea of producing corresponding route maps for automobiles (Santi 1998). These were route guides leading to and from Chicago, site of the company's headquarters. H. Sargent Michaels produced the first 'Photographic Automobile Maps', from which the name of these guides originates, in 1905. The Newberry Library archive in Chicago has the Rand McNally & Company records for the years from 1856 to 1996 and stores an entire series of these 'photographic runs', as the photo-guides were also entitled.

According to a Rand McNally advertisement, there were 27 different 'Photo-Auto Guides for Motorists' in 1909. Of these guides, seven guides will be the object of analysis:[2]

- *The Rand McNally Photo-Auto Guide Chicago to Milwaukee – Milwaukee to Chicago (Kilbourn Route)*. Chicago, IL/New York: Rand McNally 1909 (© H. Sargent Michaels 1905) [C-M/M-C 1909].
- *The Rand McNally Photo-Auto Guide Chicago to Lake Geneva – Lake Geneva to Delavan – Delavan to Beloit. Returning from Lake Geneva, via Channel Lake, Lake Catherine, Lake Marie, Antioch, Loon Lake, Cedar Lake, Deep Lake, Lake Villa, Grays Lake, Libertyville, Half Day, and Highland Park*. Chicago, IL/New York: Rand McNally 1909 (© H. Sargent Michaels 1905) [C-LG/LG-C 1909].
- *The Rand McNally Photo-Auto Guide Chicago to Cleveland – Cleveland to Chicago*. Chicago, IL/New York: Rand McNally 1909 (© G. S. Chapin 1907) [C-C/C-C 1907].
- *Photo-Auto Maps New York to Chicago – Albany to Saratoga Springs, Saratoga Springs to Albany – Toledo to Detroit, Detroit to Toledo – South Bend to Indianapolis, Indianapolis to South Bend*. Chicago, IL/New York: Rand McNally 1907 (© G. S. Chapin 1907) [NY-C 1907].
- *Photo-Auto Maps Chicago to New York, New York to Chicago – South Bend to Indianapolis, Indianapolis to South Bend – Toledo to Detroit, Detroit to Toledo – Albany to Saratoga Springs, Saratoga Springs to Albany*. Chicago, IL/New York: Rand McNally 1907 (© G. S. Chapin 1907) [C-NY/NY-C 1907].
- *Photographic Automobile Map Chicago to Lake Geneva – Lake Geneva to Delavan – Delavan to Beloit. Returning from Lake Geneva, via Channel Lake, Lake Catherine, Lake Marie, Antioch, Loon Lake, Cedar Lake, Deep Lake, Lake Villa, Grays Lake, Libertyville, Half Day and Highland Park*. Chicago, IL: H. Sargent Michaels 1905 [C-LG/LG-C 1905].
- *Photographic Automobile Map Chicago to Milwaukee. Also Intermediate Points Highland Park, Waukegan, Kenosha, Racine*. Chicago, IL: H. Sargent Michaels 1905 [C-M 1905].

Methodologically, we will approach the observation of the photo-auto guides in reverse order, both at the historiographic and praxeological levels, in order to find inscriptions that are 'able to withstand the return trip', as Latour (1990, p. 26) describes it.

In the following, we are attempting to make visible the recursive chains of operation. This is because, in particular, the historical reverse observation of the photographs of the return journey reveals which portions of route information are of relevance in navigational practice – which objects 'have the properties of being *mobile* but also *immutable*, *presentable*, *readable* and *combinable* with one another' (ibid.).

Case and comparative analysis

The 27 photo-auto guides published by Rand McNally were mainly new editions of H. Sargent Michaels copyrighted versions from 1905. This also applies to the first two examples discussed here: [C-M/M-C 1909] and [C-LG/LG-C 1909].

Trace 1

The preface to the *Rand McNally Photo-Auto Guide Chicago to Milwaukee – Milwaukee to Chicago* [C-M/M-C 1909] states that there are at least six different routes that can be taken to get to Milwaukee:

> The selection herein made is the best possible route. The 'Shore,' 'Green Bay,' 'Howell,' 'New,' 'Loomis,' and 'New Chicago' are all good in places under favorable weather conditions. The one selected is not a macadamized boulevard, by any means; it has its good and bad spots the same as all the others, though the bad ones are not as numerous as in following any single one of the above-named routes. After heavy rains the one given recovers more quickly than the others. Also one of the principal reasons for selecting the entire route as photographed was that the people and horses are more familiar with automobiles, reducing that source of danger and delay, and as a rule, favors are readily granted.
>
> [C-M/M-C 1909]

The decisive criteria for the choice of route are given as enjoyment of the drive, road condition, shortness of the route and the lowest possible danger due to railroad and streetcar crossings. The selection of the route is not made for technical reasons alone, but is also based on social reasons: the authors assumed that automobiles would be better tolerated on the Kilbourn Road route than on the others. Assumptions about the expected density of traffic are clearly already integrated into the production of these guides. The maps and the photographic series arranged in them are therefore not cases of a pure representation of a physical infrastructure, but are already sociotechnical representations.

The photo-auto guide comprises 26 photos for the journey to Milwaukee and 23 photos for the journey back to Chicago (98.8 miles each). The return journey features fewer pictures. It is evidently assumed that the users have already travelled along the route – that the photographed and practically experienced return journey are congruent.

All photo-auto guides are structured in more or less the same way. The front section features a photographic run of the outbound journey, with a numbered photographic run in the back section for the return journey.[3] The numbered photographs correspond to the numbers on seven 'outline maps' that are found in the middle of the guide.[4]

In all of the photo-auto guides, the route starts and ends at a hotel. The photographs of the forks in the road for the return journey are essentially the same, but are taken from a different perspective.[5]

In this special guide version [C-M/M-C 1909], the inscribed arrows fit into the background landscape, as the arrows were drawn on the photographs as if they were directional instructions that were visible in geographical space. The arrows and the names of destinations that are occasionally inscribed are integrated into the landscape in perspective.

The photos were taken either at eye-level or from above to allow for inscribing the arrows as centrally as possible and with the least possible distortion in perspective. The roads are generally empty in this edition, with neither people nor other vehicles. Clearly, the photographer was working towards creating a space that was as open and uniform as possible for the inscriptions.

Bridges, canals, rivers, viaducts, railroad and streetcar lines, as well as forks in the route, are entered into the route sketches. The route sketches only show what is visible when the driver is on the route (see Figure 10.2, overleaf). They do not map a territory beyond a designated route. This means that the route sketches simply duplicate the information that can also be gleaned from the photos and the figure legends.

Even if no scale is given in the route sketches, the line drawings still attempt to convey the different distances between the locations where the photos were taken. However, this uniformity of scale only refers to the individual sketch on each single page of the guide. The map scale is reduced when longer distances are covered between cities, so that the route can be depicted. Drivers may therefore switch to a new scale when turning the page.[6]

Some pages show two or three segments of the route in parallel, though they are to be followed one after the other. The individual pages can therefore not be read as an imaginary stringing together of a route, as was common in military cartography in the nineteenth century, when reconnaissance led to the depiction of the visual history of a campaign (Engberg-Pedersen 2011, p. 40ff.). The spatial fragments of campaigns that also develop a narrative differ from the route maps discussed here in that they are aimed at visualizing the terrain and are constrained by an absolute spatial construction.

In the event that there is no change in direction, the illustrated route is compressed. The medial translation thus develops its own spatial temporality. The basis for the visual depiction is the travel time that has been completed. Route elements in the city that are covered at lower speed are illustrated in more detail; only rough sketches are provided for cross-country routes that are covered at greater speed. The illustration of the route thus uses a relational scale and not an absolute scale.

On the outbound journey, the route sketches are read from the bottom upwards. The medium is thus tailored towards being read in the direction of travel. On the return journey, the same route sketches are followed in

WINNETKA SIGN

No. 13

TO AVOID HUBBARDS HILL

Winnetka water tower, turn to the left and go west to railroad tracks then north.
Some parts of this road are not very good in continued wet weather.

Figure 10.2 Photographic Automobile Map, Chicago to Milwaukee (1905) with
photo nos 12 and 13 from the first section, and an associated route
sketch from the section in the back.

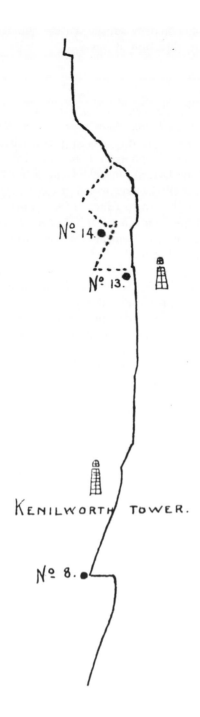

Figure 10.2 Continued.

the opposite direction, from top to bottom. The practical use on the return journey is thus hampered by substantial difficulties, as the maps must be read opposite to the direction of travel.

Trace 2

The *Photo-Auto Guide Chicago to Lake Geneva – Lake Geneva to Delavan – Delavan to Beloit. Returning from Lake Geneva* [C-LG/LG-C 1909] is also a new edition of the H. Sargent Michaels copyrighted version from 1905. It contains 38 photos for the route from the Stratford Hotel in Chicago to the Hotel Denison in Lake Geneva (84.1 miles) and ten photos for the route from Lake Geneva to Beloit (35.1 or 35.3 miles). The return journey from Lake Geneva to Chicago (82.9 miles) is depicted in far less detail than the outbound journey, with 22 inscribed photos. The 29.2-mile stretch from image no. 22 (Central Ave) back to the Stratford Hotel does not have a single additional photograph. This demonstrates that this photo-auto guide was designed for daytrips 'that can be made in one day, up and back' (from the Preface). Prior knowledge of the route, based on the outbound journey, is a precondition.

In addition, the route instructions for the entire route, including all changes in direction, are summarized on one page in continuous text. Furthermore, this photo-auto guide provides an overview of all photos, giving details on the distance that remains to be covered after the photo has been passed. The previous guide gives the total accumulated route underneath the photos. That is missing here. Instead, there are four maps at the end of the guide that show the roads along the numbered plots of land that are grouped around the lakes. What this reveals is that roads in many parts of the country followed the line fences of farms and were located, as a general rule, for the benefit of the property owner, not for the benefit of the travelling public (Dods 1911, p. 3). It is a reminder that road traffic was never regarded as a national responsibility in the US, but was managed by the counties and cities (Reid 2014, p. 151ff.).

Comparative analysis of Traces 1 and 2

It is notable that the first 9.6 miles of the photo-auto guide from Chicago to Milwaukee and the guide to Lake Geneva are essentially identical. Some of the inscribed photographs are therefore found in both guides.

Even though the initial stretch ought to be identical, the route that is given is slightly different.[7] This reveals a navigation problem that is typical for US conditions: cities are planned in quadrants, such that one is always moving along either a North–South or East–West axis and can never lose one's sense of direction. Accordingly, the cardinal directions play a central role in the photo-auto guides. Typical instructions on the photos read 'To Left, West' or 'To Right, North'. The cardinal directions are also important because the photo-auto guides did not use a uniform pictorial language that would always show the subjective perspective of the motorist. They do attempt to ensure that the driver and camera perspectives are identical, but this principle is not maintained in every photo.

On the return journey, there is a series of photos (nos 6–8, 13–21; photos 9 to 12 are missing from the copy) in which the same automobile is depicted with the same driver (see Figure 10.1). The automobile is always in exactly those places that show which route must be selected. Apparently, the photograph was composed such that the decision on which direction to take is visualized through imagery. The arrows, thus, simply emphasize the information conveyed by the image, which could also be gleaned from the unaugmented photograph.

However, conceptual flaws resulting in heterogeneous imagery crept in and must have caused confusion in navigational practice. The flaws stem from the fact that the third-person over-the-shoulder perspective was not maintained throughout the photo series.[8] In some pictures the photographed automobile is *approaching* the viewer, while in others the arrow points *towards* the user. In these images, it appears as if one would have to reckon with oncoming traffic, or as if the photo has been taken from the opposite direction. This runs counter to the majority of the other 'graven images', where the driver's perspective matches the one shown in the picture.

On one page, five route segments were drawn. They provide a confusing image of the route that is divided into different stretches, corresponding to photos 1 to 14. This points to the conclusion that the wayfinding procedure was designed entirely on the basis of the proposed photo navigation. But, either way, it would have been difficult to follow both elements – the photo route *and* the route sketch – as the two different navigational aids were bound in the one book and would have required turning pages back and forth. A reciprocative practical approach is recognizable here in the 1907 edition.

Trace 3

In addition to the H. Sargent Michaels copyrighted version, Rand McNally also marketed a Gardner S. Chapin series of photo-auto maps. These include the *Photo-Auto Maps New York to Chicago* [NY-C 1907], published in 1907 (see Figure 10.3). They contain 796 photos for the route from New York to Chicago, 56 photos for Albany to Saratoga Springs – Saratoga Springs to Albany, 32 photos for Toledo to Detroit – Detroit to Toledo and 94 photos for South Bend to Indianapolis – Indianapolis to South Bend. Chapin dedicated his guide to the national highway from Chicago to New York. At the time, he thought that this highway would render his photo-auto maps obsolete.

No. 519

HIGHLANDS

Turn LEFT, West.   Next turn two and three-tenths miles.

Memo ....

....

....

....

....

No. 518

Turn RIGHT, North.   Road-house on left.   Next turn two and three-tenths miles.

Figure 10.3 Photo-Auto Maps, New York to Chicago (1907) with photos from the section 'South Bend to Chicago', and an associated route map from the plate section.

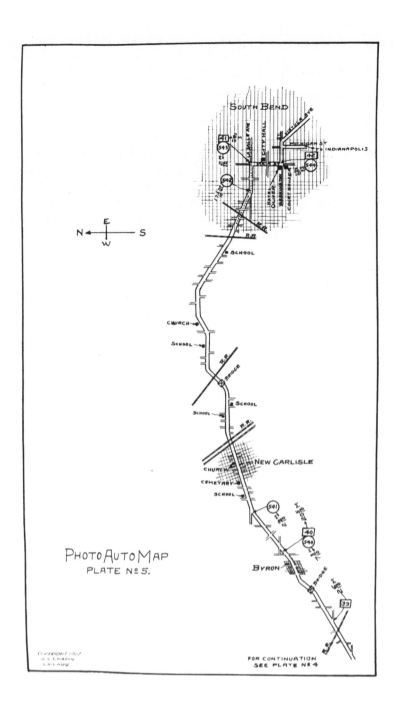

Figure 10.3 Continued.

In contrast to the guides designed by H. Sargent Michaels, the Chapin guides included instructions on how to navigate in practice. These instructions explained that the route map formed the basis of the driver's navigation. This point is also implied by the different derivations and variants of the 'photographic maps' (also in the title).

> The best way to use the Photo-Auto Maps is to follow the route by the topographical map and refer to the photographs only to make sure that you are turning at the right place. Use your meter at all times to get the distances between turns. The distances given between turns will vary with different machines, as a slight difference in size of tires, different conditions of the roads and many other things tend to vary the register. Three meters were used and an average taken to get the distances given.... This map is not drawn to scale, but is made to show the turns to the best advantage. Where turns occur close together the map is enlarged, so do not judge distances by the appearances of the map. Go entirely by the meter readings. Distances between closest points only are given to insure the smallest variations. The distances given are the average obtained from three different makes of speedometers and a re-check by the Warner Auto-Meter.
>
> [NY-C 1907]

The route maps – no longer just sketches as in H. Sargent Michaels' guides – are the central navigational instrument in the instructions. They provide the most reliable information, with the aid of a speedometer, on where to turn off (what direction the driver must take). It is therefore no surprise that the photo-auto guides carry a series of advertisements for speedometer companies. The New York to Chicago edition, for example, contains an advertisement for a Jones speedometer that could simultaneously be used as an odometer. 'It places at the instant command of the motorist in the most convenient manner, with unquestionable permanent accuracy, a means for the determination of the distances cited on the Road Maps', the advertisement states in the photo-auto maps for that edition. A Jones advertisement in the photo-auto guide for Chicago to Cleveland – Cleveland to Chicago states: 'By means of the Odometer you can compute the distance cited on the maps.'

If we look at H. Sargent Michaels' original third photographic run, it becomes evident that this linked odometric practice indicates a navigational transition that Rand McNally copied more or less exactly in 1909.

Trace 4

In contrast to Rand McNally's photo-auto guide (see Trace 1), H. Sargent Michaels' *Photographic Automobile Map Chicago to Lake Geneva – Lake Geneva to Delavan – Delavan to Beloit. Returning from Lake Geneva*

[C-LG/LG-C 1905] contains images of four additional traffic signs that refer to speed limits. Such additional information was avoided in the Rand McNally versions, because each photograph was inherently integrated into the serial structure, in order to signal a turning. No photograph was shown so long as the driver did not need to deviate from the selected cardinal direction or road.

It was different in H. Sargent Michaels' photographic automobile maps. His photographic runs, at least occasionally, provide hints for the driver to remain on the same route ('continue north', 'keep on northeast', 'keep ahead'). In addition, the first edition contains a 'List of Holders of Property Surrounding Delavan Lake'.[9] The names in this list are numbered and these numbers can also be found on the enclosed maps, such that it is not only possible to get to specific people, but also to identify the owners of the roads that the driver is on. This makes it clear that this photo-auto guide is not just a route guide. It contains a directory of towns that can be reached in the lakes region if one leaves the central route, for example, 'Lake Marie. Two miles west from Photo No. 12, return.' However, the places that can be reached along and off the route are not marked as possible destinations on the photographs or on the route maps. The directory amounts to a potential network whose point of emergence lies in the photos themselves. These unmapped target points are either between photographs (e.g. 'East Delavan, Wis. Between Photo 3 and 4, Lake Geneva to Beloit') or in a specific cardinal direction away from the photographs (e.g. 'Fort Sheridan. One mile north of Photo No. 19').

From a praxeological perspective, it is notable here that this potential network is not composed of the places or points on a map, but of situated landscape photographs. It is only when the photographs are studied in situ that it becomes clear which cardinal direction to follow. The photograph alone is insufficient to derive the cardinal direction. A user is wholly restricted to the designated routes when the photographic automobile maps are used as a virtual travel guide. Other locations can only be reached by moving into uncharted territory in a specific direction, starting from the photographs.

Trace 5

Based on the reverse approach to the analysis, we now reach the original version underlying all the photo-auto guides. The brief description of the photographic run in Series A, from Chicago to Milwaukee [C-M 1905], is sufficient to highlight significant differences between the 1905 and 1909 designs of the route guides. The following is noted at the start of the original version published by the H. Sargent Michaels Company: 'Containing a carefully compiled series of photographs of ALL TURNS and landmarks … along the most picturesque and pleasant route' [C-M 1905]. Meanwhile, the Rand McNally photo-auto guides offer '[a] series of photographic reproductions of all turns and intersecting cross roads, with arrows point-ing to the right road. Giving distances between turning points, and outline maps of the entire route' [C-M/M-C 1909].

The 1905 edition also contained distance data. However, these were slightly more hidden in the continuous text in the figure legends. Further-more, not all photographs indicated distances between turning points. Rand McNally standardized (at least in [C-M/M-C 1909]) the instructions for directions in the figure captions based on the template provided by Gardner S. Chapin in 1907. The descriptions of the images were substan-tially more detailed in H. Sargent Michaels. We can therefore state that it is thanks to Rand McNally that some of the characteristics in the original were completed and unified.[10]

Comparative analysis of Traces 5 and 1

A comparison of the 1905 and 1909 versions of the route from Chicago to Milwaukee reveals that the majority of the inscribed photographs are the same. Rand McNally simply adopted them. However, the figure legends are fundamentally different in design. The point of origin in the Series A photographic run is also the Stratford Hotel – epically entitled 'the start of the right road' by H. Sargent Michaels, and technocratically as '0 Miles' by Rand McNally. However, the original version [C-M 1905] also con-tains information like 'The management of the Stratford Hotel extends to all autoists the accommodation of its spacious waiting rooms whether guests or not', while an advertisement for the hotel is placed under the photo in the Rand McNally version.

In 1909, uniform reference is made in the figure legends to left or right turns that must be taken. Cardinal directions are occasionally also men-tioned in parentheses. Conversely, the 1905 H. Sargent Michaels version mainly refers to the cardinal direction that is to be followed ('turn north', 'keep on northeast', etc.). This was necessary simply for the reason that the depiction in the first-person perspective was not yet uniformly implemented and cardinal directions were therefore the only option for providing clear information on the route. Simultaneously, this required the perceptual judgments on the part of the drivers to follow 'the truth-value of an under-lying non-token-indexical spatial proposition' (Gell 1985, p. 279).

The Rand McNally guides therefore represented a praxeological optimi-zation, as fewer navigational skills were needed to use them. There was no requirement for orientation based on geographical directions. In addition, the original makes clear that the separation of advertisements and route information, as well as the separate designation of the distances that had been completed, form part of the standardization of the later Rand McNally editions. At the same time, the inscribed photographs lose their uniform quality, because Rand McNally re-uses a number of the pictures, while also adding new ones.

Drawing traces together

Mode of navigational practice

Let us now turn the recursive chain of operation round and move in the direction of travel again. By following the development of the photo-auto guides, it becomes clear that the standardization pertains mainly to the media methods, i.e. the organization and production structure of the different individual media. A process of abstraction can be diagnosed that highlights the information regarded as important to navigational practice. This includes the distance completed (in miles) and the non-token indexical directional instructions (e.g. 'Turn right', 'Barn on right') at the start of the figure captions.

Furthermore, a more uniform design process is to be detected in the production and selection of the photographs. To use Latour's and Ivins' terminology, the aim is to produce 'optical consistency' (Ivins 1973; Latour 1990, p. 27ff.) through a uniform camera position and image composition. From 1907 on, the newly taken photos were oriented based on the first-person perspective of the automobile driver navigating in practice. In contrast, uniformity is neglected in the inscription of the arrows.

In 1905, a total of 52 photos were required for the route from Chicago to Milwaukee. In 1909, only half this number was needed for the same distance. Instead, the Rand McNally edition also features photographs of the return journey. The media-practical experience therefore results in the separation of important from unimportant information, while simultaneously increasing the scope of the information regarded as important. In addition, this had the favourable effect on navigational practice that fewer pages needed to be turned in the later editions. The strategy of deflation therefore refers to the reduced scope of the illustration of a route (both in images and in text) and to the production of optical consistency through the use of a standardized and situated practice of geovisual sensing.

In contrast, the route sketch is characterized by an accumulation of information. In the 1905 original, we can read the individual pages of the route sketches as an imaginary stringing together of a route. Only the route is shown, without intersecting crossroads. Turning points are indicated based on landmarks that are marked on the photographs and on the sketches; even alternative routes are entered into the sketches (see Figure 10.2, route sketch on the right). In the 1909 Rand McNally edition, however, orientation is based on the unambiguousness of *one* path that can also be read bidirectionally. The medium of the outline map therefore gains in practical diversity and in multiple interpretations. Information is shifted from the photographs and figure legends into the route sketches.

Within the meaning of Latour's approach, we cannot simply refer to a general deflation strategy, but must note that inscriptions move from one medium into another when seen from a genealogical mixed media perspective. This is a result of the fact that the photo-auto guides are increasingly decoupled from the form of their production over the course of their development. In the following, we will investigate the question of how far, based on visual analysis, conclusions can be drawn as to the form of production of the photo-auto guides.

Form of production

The route sketches depicted in the first photographic automobile maps ([C-LG/LG-C 1905] and [C-M 1905]) in 1905 still reveal the form of their production. They lead us to assume that they were produced in the same way as the route logs published by the Automobile Blue Book Company. It is therefore no accident that Akerman (2006, p. 170) describes the photo-auto guides as a variant of the Blue Book model. The automobile therefore served as an instrument for the production of the relevant route guides.

Based on the different ways in which the arrows were inscribed, we can see that the augmented photos were used in different photo-auto guides. Interestingly, however, this does not apply to the figure legends and route sketches. Different photographs were allocated to identical route segments. Ready-made routes were therefore not resorted to, but each photo-auto guide was given a newly surveyed route. The interchanging of the photographs allows us to assume that the images of the road forks were subsequently added to a route that was recorded. The mapping and surveying of the route was therefore probably not interrupted by taking photographs of it.

The very rudimentary route sketches in the 1905 original appear to be drawn in one flourish with a pen, without stopping the stroke. They do not depict any crossroads, but only occasional bridges and railroad crossings. This corresponds to the method described by Dods, in 1911, for the production of the road sketches for the Blue Book series:

> For the most part the early maps consisted of nothing more than lines drawn between towns and were gotten out without any accurate knowledge of the territory through which they ran as to road directions and conditions.... In England and in France, where nearly all roads are macadam and have been for years, it is possible to issue maps which will not go out of date for years. Maps also are made practical in these countries because of the thorough manner in which every road is signboarded. In this country the people are just beginning to realize the value of good roads and although the movement is general, it will be years before the standard touring routes will be so improved a map can be made with almost absolute assurance that for a few years at least it will remain the accepted route.
>
> (p. 2)

The roads themselves were constantly changing, so there was uncertainty about routing. As the roads, as well as the vehicles moving about on them, were mobile, and therefore no 'immutable mobiles' could be generated, how could knowledge be gained? It was difficult with established epistemic methods, and so the publishers took up a new idea. To produce these maps, cars were sent out to gather the information for route directions. In each car was a sketch maker who had to be able:

1 to record 'all route matter in the form of a sketch showing in their proper relation to the road being traveled all intersecting roads, landmarks, schools, churches, railroad crossings, telephone poles, etc.' while driving in a moving car on rough roads;
2 'to imagine himself traveling above the road in a flying machine as it were, looking down, in order to get an accurate idea of the angle at which two roads intersect' (ibid., p. 4).

So there was already a combination of real-time recording and an envisaged planimetric a-perspectival view, something digital mapping companies are still trying to accomplish with GPS survey cars today.

> This sketch method not only saved time and gave data from which the route could be written in both directions ... Another very important feature about this method is the fact that absolutely nothing is left to memory. Even a stranger who never covered a mile of the route could take one of these sketches and knowing the symbols could read it now or a year hence.
>
> (Ibid.)

The photographic automobile maps from 1905 demonstrate exactly this production practice at the level of their reproduction. The producer's skill in drawing a line on the paper, in real time and on a bumpy surface, overlaps with the user's skill of keeping the automobile on the correct course. A modus of continuous movement applies both to the practice of drawing and of driving.

In 1907, this symmetric construction of action on paper and on the road was further differentiated, as the scale of the route inscribed in this way is not uniform: 'Where turns occur close together the map is enlarged' [NY-C 1907]. In this respect, the photographic run manifests the same lack of uniformity in scaling for the route as the purported 'topographical map'. The route is reduced to the nodal points where action is required and reveals the topological and, simultaneously, the topographical structure (see Figure 10.3, right).

Individual central locations are given particular emphasis and appear at a larger scale than the scale corresponding to the topography. The inhomogeneous scale of the map guides the eye towards the infrastructural nodes.

The fact that the cartographic scale changes, based on the level of detail in the terrain and the affordances for turning off, is essentially due to the drawing practice of the automobile linehaul. This variation in scaling is already visible in the original edition, but is not implemented with as much sophistication, or as consistently, as in the 1907 edition.

The guide designed by Gardner S. Chapin reveals less about the methods involved in map production. The route sketches are tailored to the user's navigational practices and no longer to the discoverer's wayfinding practices. An aesthetic-semiotic adaptation process has taken place. The photos, text and drawings of the route now provide hardly any different information, but are becoming congruent with regard to content. The criterion defining the difference – the emergence of media specificity – is now provided simply by the different forms of representation.

The important information was separated from what was unimportant, at a photographic level, in the course of decoupling the medium from its production. The sky is always cropped in the version copyrighted by Gardner S. Chapin, in order to focus the image fully on the road. Where H. Sargent Michaels still covered photos of artefacts (buildings, telephone poles, etc.) in their entirety – making these visible as route signs – the peripheral infrastructure is reduced to a backdrop in 1907. The picture frame often cuts buildings in half (see Figure 10.3, left).

The photos taken by H. Sargent Michaels in 1905 are shown in the normal landscape format,[11] while the photos in the 1907 version appear in the 'cinemascope' format of 21:9. Cinemascope creates an even stronger movie-like appearance and supports the impression of a sequence shot being printed out by the photo-auto guides. This modus of continuous movement is not only inscribed into the map-drawing praxis and automobile driving practice, but also into the aesthetic impression of the photographs themselves. At the same time, the 21:9 format provides more space for other information on each page of the book. The spatial gain was used to insert a memo field under the figure caption, thus making at least two lines, and occasionally up to 13 lines, available for personal notes.

The number of lines in the memo field is entirely dictated by the remaining available space, dependent on the length of the text describing the route that is to be taken, and also on whether only one photo, or two, is placed on the page. An active appropriation is desired. However, this is also a secondary design property – or rather, more of a stopgap. The photo-auto guides examined here contain no personal entries. Even so, their openness to user inscriptions is an important indication of the change in mediality of the photo-auto guides. Above all, the sheets with lines are an expression of an adaptation to the medial form of the book.

The ongoing standardization of the guides is apparent in the design properties introduced by Gardner S. Chapin. These were incorporated into the new design in the guides copyrighted by H. Sargent Michaels. The new editions of the guides published with changes in 1909 were, indeed, entirely in the style of the 1905 version; however, isolated newly added photographs reflect the knowledge of a potential subsequent inscription. They were designed to create as much space as possible for the arrows to be inscribed. This implicit photographic knowledge was not yet present in the first photographic automobile maps.

Conclusion

The linking in the image diagnosed in this chapter is to be found at different levels and can be viewed as applicable to all navigational applications in augmented reality that have appeared since the photo-auto guides. There is a semiotic linking of map, photo and text that results in an exchange of inscriptions between these three elements. This network points in different directions:

1   On the one hand, it points in the traditional reading direction. There is an indexical connection between the photographic runs and the route sketches, which are not adjacent to each other but are located in different chapters of each guide. This creates a linking of information that is given at the front and the back – whether on different pages of a book or between layers of geo-referenced information on a display.

2   In addition, there is a semiotic exchange between the crucial information given in the image and in the figure caption. This network structure is not spread over multiple pages, but on a single book page – handed down to iconography.

3   At the level of the image itself, the inscribed arrows create a network level that refers to the physical environment. This is a case of using signposts that connect the real and virtual worlds to each other (November, Camacho-Hübner & Latour 2010). The sequentiality of the photographic runs harbours the promise that all turns or all nodes in the road network are depicted that need to be passed through to reach the destination. For this reason, the placing of the landscape photographs in sequence already has both mimetic as well as navigational qualities.

What makes the photographic automobile maps so special is the fact that the network is not depicted by a map. Quite the opposite – the illustrated route is really only understood to be a sketch of a route that lays no claims to completeness or even objectivity that would be found beyond a subjective perspective. Leaving the route lines is not even intended. The networking is happening in the image, between images and between image and text, as well as in the text itself. The inter- and intramedial exchange is even more intense because there is, as yet, no form of depiction that would be capable of precisely representing the complexity of navigation on *one* display level.

This changes substantially with the photo-auto maps produced in 1907 and their more detailed and frayed cartographic representation. The development of the route sketches from 1905 through 1907 to 1909 shows that more and more practical knowledge is transmigrating from the photography into its mapping. Photo-auto guides therefore demonstrate quite clearly that topographical maps successively spread along route sketches. What can be observed historically over several centuries is here focused on a cartographic developmental process spanning only a few years.

Simultaneously, the problem with photo-auto guides was, among other things (e.g. the absence of scalability), their lack of optical consistency, as they were not in a position to follow an abstraction process and create 'immutable mobiles'. Photo-auto guides therefore thwart Latour's media-genealogical observation: the more artificial and abstract the inscriptions, the greater their capacity to be associated with others and thus to approach reality and practical affordances more closely (1987, p. 242).

The 'immutable mobiles' are not limited to the history or development of a medium (in this case, the medium of the map), but move from one medium into another. Therefore, multiple chains of operation must be investigated. As demonstrated by this study, the 'immutable mobiles' are not founded in the map itself, but in the apodemics – the methodologicization of travelling (Stagl 2002) – on which pathfinding is based.

In the event that we are 'holding the focus steady' (Latour 1990, p. 24) on the representation of a route *and* the route instructions, the following forms of networking can be diagnosed:

1   networking on the mimetic level as medial doubling (a re-presentation) of the road infrastructure;
2   networking on the medial-navigational level (in the book, between layers);
3   networking on the situated-navigational level, through the practical life that fluctuates between medial and physical experience;
4   networking on the virtual-navigational level, through the reader's travel experience, imagined as an armchair traveller;
5   networking on the mental-navigational level, through the conceptual navigation within the image that is indicated by the arrows (and created through the first-person perspective). Both together create an 'avenue through space' (ibid., p. 27), allowing the viewer to wander through the depicted space.

The excess of navigational levels permits 'bypassing the mimetic interpretation given of maps' (November, Camacho-Hübner & Latour 2010, p. 587). Even so, navigation cannot be reduced to any one of the medial, situated, virtual or mental levels. This stabilizes the navigational practice, but is also simultaneously the reason why praxeological research of lived, hybrid and multi-modal interactive space is so difficult. The sequential depiction in the medium of the book, however, allows us to gain analytical access to the complexity of navigational processes, which is complicated in digital applications by the black-box nature of software processes. Digital route guides in augmented reality do not reveal the form of their production in a self-evident way.

As Lehmuskallio (in this volume) shows in his analysis of 'layered pictures', augmentation is not only a specific form of visualization, but an immediate media-specific way of enabling a situated decision-making process. In our case, such 'thick visualizations' (Hochman & Manovich 2013) involve crawling through the database of the photographed auto trail by using the old cultural technique of flipping through pages. Thick visualizations are not, and never were, dependent on digital computing power.

Moreover, this analysis of 'graven images' reveals that there is a sense of mobility and user-generated operability within layered image-space, which challenges our inherited definitional assumptions of location-based photography. It can be argued that the digitization of photography within augmented reality applications has only rematerialized 'handy' chains of mediation. The analysis of seven photo-auto guides that are over 100 years old, and their analogue photographs augmented with geoinformation, show a form of online/offline space complexity that does not lag behind that provided by digital photography.

Linked location-based photographs existed long before the age of digital computing. Even so, photo-auto guides only existed for a short period. Their end was heralded in 1910, once maps were issued as supplements to many road books (Ristow 1964, p. 622). They simply became impractical. Photo-auto guides became quite bulky for certain routes; some ran to over 1,000 pages and became difficult to consult while travelling. The thrill of speed also contributed to their demise. Increased motorcar speeds minimized the value of location-based photographs and detailed descriptive notes. In 1912, Rand McNally discontinued the supply of photo-auto guides. It will be interesting to observe whether the current augmented reality navigation applications survive for longer than the brief period of seven years during which photographic automobile maps and photo-auto guides existed.

Notes

1 For example, on the maps they distributed, hardware chains like the Minnesota Retail Hardware Association used orange dots to mark towns belonging to the association (Akerman 2000, p. 29ff.).
2 [C-M/M-C 1909] and [C-LG/LG-C 1909] are copies from the Library of Congress, Washington, DC. The other guides are from the cartographic collection in the Hermon Dunlap Smith Center for the History of Cartography at the Newberry Library in Chicago, IL. I thank James R. Akerman for his help and support.

3 Subsequent exceptions to this concept are also entered into later on in this chapter.

4 One or two 'outline maps' are missing from the tattered copy from the Library of Congress, at least on the PDF scans.

5 This does not apply to two photos (photos nos 2 and 8 from Milwaukee to Chicago). These are the only photos where the arrows are inscribed in the opposite direction on the return journey. The same photo was used as for the outbound journey, with only the arrows being changed.

6 A similar process takes place with current navigation systems: if there is a sequence of several bends or turning points, then the user is zoomed into the map, and when a greater distance is covered without changing direction, the navigation system zooms out and shows a smaller scale on the map.

7 The turning is after a different block in photos nos 2 and 5 in the Milwaukee guide, and after 2, 3 and 6 in the Lake Geneva guide.

8 The third-person over-the-shoulder perspective is, nowadays, the default mode in open world games such as *Grand Theft Auto* (see Chesher 2012).

9 This list of landowners was apparently dropped from the Rand McNally version. However, it is also possible that the list is simply missing from the PDF scan of the copy from the Library of Congress.

10 However, this does not apply to [C-LG/LG-C 1909] and [C-LG/LG-C 1905], as the two are almost identical.

11 Although in the 16:10 format instead of the 16:9 format that is standard today.

References

Akerman, J. R. 2006, 'Twentieth-Century American Road Maps and the Making of a National Motorized Space', in J. R. Akerman (ed.) *Cartographies of Travel and Navigation*. University of Chicago Press: Chicago, IL, pp. 151–206.

Akerman, J. R. 2000, 'Private Journeys on Public Maps: A Look at Inscribed Road Maps'. *Cartographic Perspectives*, Vol. 35, pp. 27–47.

Chesher, C. 2012, 'Navigating Sociotechnical Spaces: Comparing Computer Games and Sat Navs as Digital Spatial Media'. *Convergence: The International Journal of Research into New Media Technologies*, Vol. 18, no. 3, pp. 315–330.

Dods, J. P. 1911, 'Advancement in Art of Pathfinding'. *Motor Age*, Vol. 20, no. 6, pp. 1–6.

Engberg-Pedersen, A. 2011, 'Die Verwaltung des Raumes: Kriegskartographische Praxis um 1800', in S. Siegel & P. Weigel (eds) *Die Werkstatt des Kartographen: Materialien und Praktiken visueller Welterzeugung*. Fink: München, pp. 29–48.

Gell, A. 1985, 'How to Read a Map: Remarks on the Practical Logic of Navigation'. *Man (N.S.)*, Vol. 20, no. 2, pp. 271–286.

Harley, J. B. 1989, 'Deconstructing the Map'. *Cartographica*, Vol. 26, no. 2, pp. 1–20.

Hochman, N. & Manovich, L. 2013, 'Zooming into an Instagram City: Reading the Local through Social Media'. *First Monday*, Vol. 18, no. 7, viewed 8 October 2015, http://firstmonday.org/ojs/index.php/fm/article/view/4711/3698.

Ivins, W. M. 1973, *On the Rationalization of Sight: With an Examination of Three Renaissance Texts on Perspective*. Da Capo: New York [first published as *Metropolitan Museum of Art Papers*, No. 8, 1938].

Jacob, C. 1996, 'Towards a Cultural History of Cartography'. *Imago Mundi*, Vol. 48, pp. 192–197.

Krämer, S. 2009, 'Operative Bildlichkeit: Von der "Grammatologie" zu einer "Diagrammatologie"? Reflexionen über erkennendes "Sehen"', in M. Hessler & D. Mersch (eds) *Logik des Bildlichen: Zur Kritik der ikonischen Vernunft*. Transcript: Bielefeld, pp. 94–123.

Latour, B. 2014, 'The More Manipulation, the Better', in C. Coopmans, J. Vertesi, M. E. Lynch & S. Woolgar (eds) *Representation in Scientific Practice Revisited*. MIT Press: Cambridge, MA, pp. 347–350.

Latour, B. 2005, *Reassembling the Social: An Introduction to Actor-Network-Theory*. Oxford University Press: Oxford; New York.

Latour, B. 1990, 'Drawing Things Together', in M. Lynch & S. Woolgar (eds) *Representation in Scientific Practice*. MIT Press: Cambridge, MA, pp. 19–68.

Latour, B. 1987, *Science in Action: How to Follow Scientists and Engineers through Society*. Harvard University Press: Cambridge, MA.

Mitchell, W. J. T. 2004, 'Migrating Images: Totemism, Fetishism, Idolatry', in P. Stegemann & P. C. Steel (eds) *Migrating Images*. Haus der Kulturen der Welt: Berlin, pp. 14–24.

Mukerji, S. 1983, *From Graven Images: Patterns of Modern Materialism*. Columbia University Press: New York.

November, V., Camacho-Hübner, E. & Latour, B. 2010, 'Entering a Risky Territory: Space in the Age of Digital Navigation'. *Environment and Planning D: Society and Space*, Vol. 28, no. 4, pp. 581–599.

Reid, C. 2014, *Roads Were Not Built for Cars*. Appletree Press: Belfast.

Ristow, W. W. 1964, 'A Half-Century of Oil-Company Road Maps'. *Surveying and Mapping*, Vol. 24, no. 2, pp. 617–637.

Ristow, W. W. 1946, 'American Road Maps and Guides'. *Scientific Monthly*, Vol. 62, pp. 397–406.

Rundstrom, R. A. 1991, 'Mapping, Postmodernism, Indigenous People and the Changing Direction of North American Cartography'. *Cartographica*, Vol. 28, no. 2, pp. 1–12.

Santi, S. 1998, 'A Brief History of Rand McNally', in *Collecting Little Golden Books: A Collector's Identification and Price Guide*, Krause Publications: Iola, WI, p. 170.

Stagl, J. 2002, *Eine Geschichte der Neugier: Die Kunst des Reisens 1550–1800*. Böhlau: Vienna.

Star, S. L. 1989, 'The Structure of Ill-Structured Solutions: Boundary Objects and Heterogeneous Distributed Problem Solving', in L. Gasser & M. N. Huhns (eds) *Distributed Artificial Intelligence Vol. II*. Pitman/Morgan Kaufmann: London; San Mateo, CA, pp. 37–54.

Thielmann, T. & Schüttpelz, E. (eds) 2013, *Akteur-Medien-Theorie*. Transcript: Bielefeld.

Verhoeff, N. 2012, *Mobile Screens: The Visual Regime of Navigation*. Amsterdam University Press: Amsterdam.

11 Photographic places and digital wayfaring

Conceptualizing relationships between cameras, connectivities and transformed localities

Sarah Pink

Introduction

In this short chapter I elaborate on two concepts which I have used in my existing work, and that I would consider to be part of a theoretical 'tool box' that digital media scholars might draw on: place and wayfaring. These concepts, although they were not originally developed in the context of media or photography studies, are useful for thinking about how digital photography is at once technological, virtual and material, often played out through human activity in the world, and also part of the actual environment in which we live and act. However, we can also take this further to join up the concepts as a way to consider a framework through which to think about the contemporary digital, material and representational environments in which we play out our lives. This framework also brings together the different areas explored in the chapters in this part of the book, which deal with different themes – transnational families, activism, location and the online/offline – but collectively share some interests across the themes of how the everyday activities through which digital photography becomes part of our lives, the relationships in which these are implicated and the environments in which this happens, and how these environments and relationships are constituted and experienced.

Place

The concept of place is well established across a range of literature, and has been used most consistently in human geography, as well as in anthropology. For me, the most interesting works in this area are by the human geographer Doreen Massey (2005) and the anthropologist Tim Ingold (2008), because they respectively call our attention to the politics and phenomenology of place (Pink 2012). I do not repeat their arguments in detail here; however drawing on these ideas, I would reiterate two points that are important to account for when discussing digital photography.

First, that place should not be confused with locality; locality can be part of place, and of course usually is. In the case of digital photography and its online sharing, for instance, photographs might be produced in localities, they might represent aspects of localities and they might also be viewed in localities. However, if we are considering the digital material world in which digital photography is made, shared and given meaning, then we need to recognize that the configurations of place we are concerned with might be constituted by several different physical localities, as well as different digital platforms, technologies and social relationships.

Second, I emphasize that place is never fixed, but continually changing. Therefore, the configurations of place in or through which we consider digital photography need to be understood as contingent and continually slipping over into an, as yet, unknown future. Such contingency shapes not only the ways in which we find and share images but also the ways in which they are made. As I have also argued, drawing on this work elsewhere:

> Images, thus, are not 'of' places or things. They cannot be, as they are not independent of place and they are contingent on encounters with things. But rather, they are inevitably and unavoidably in places: they are produced by moving through and not over or on environments, and they are not stopping points so much as outcomes of and in movement. This means making a shift in thinking from the commonsense idea that a photograph represents a static moment and thus is a photograph of a place, to the idea that it is in place and in movement.
>
> (Pink 2011a, p. 9)

Recently, some media scholars have started to engage with place as a way of thinking about the way that media become part of the global and local configurations of things and processes in which we live (Couldry & McCarthy 2004; Pink 2012) as well as a way of thinking about the situated nature of our everyday uses of media (Moores 2012; Pink & Leder Mackley 2013) and in relation to mobile media (Wilken & Goggin 2012; Pink & Hjorth 2012, Hjorth & Pink 2014). The important step that these writers take, beyond the initial theoretical discussions of place that have been played out in academic disciplines like human geography and anthropology, has been to begin to explore how the digital and material elements of our worlds are equally part of the same environment. Place, as I have noted above, is not simply locality, we do not need to attend to digital media to acknowledge this, yet, when we do, we are able to use a concept of place through which to consider how the digital and material (which refers to the online and offline, but more than that) come together. However, we should also keep in mind that we cannot understand the relationship between the digital and material without also accounting for other elements of what Ingold would call the 'weather world' (2010), including invisible and intangible elements, to form the environments of which we are also a part. As Tim Ingold reminds us

> We are these days increasingly bombarded with information about what is known as 'the environment' … that we are, I think, inclined to forget that the environment is, in the first place, a world we live in, and not a world we look at. We *inhabit* our environment: we are part of it; and through this practice of habitation it becomes part of us too.
>
> (Ibid., p. 95)

Ingold was not writing about digital photography but, as is often the case, his comments are insightful for generating understandings beyond the contexts he writes about. Here, I suggest taking the idea that we are part of and inhabit our environment as an invitation to consider how we do so with and in relation to digital photography and technologies for producing and sharing them. Here, I do not simply refer to digital content but rather the practice, sharing and viewing of digital images and how this is related to the way in which digital is part of our everyday lives and the invisible architecture of our homes and the streets we walk along.

Digital wayfaring and moving images

The above point brings me to the second concept I wish to discuss – the notion of the digital wayfarer. This concept is discussed in more depth in my writing with Larissa Hjorth (Hjorth & Pink 2014), and used more specifically to discuss camera phone photography. The concept, however, has a wider application as a way to understand how people can be thought to weave their ways through the digital/virtual and material/physical worlds that I have described above. A theory of place focuses on the ways in which configurations of things and processes come together, and the relationality between them, without necessarily privileging the human subjects who are part of place. The concept of the wayfarer, as I develop it here, instead enables us to focus precisely on the question of what people are doing, as they move through the world – that is to put the human subject at the centre of the analysis.

The concept of wayfaring was developed by Ingold in his work on the line (Ingold 2007), to discuss the ways in which we might think of people meandering through the world, attending to what they find on their way and engaging with their environments in doing so. The notion of the digital wayfarer (Hjorth & Pink 2014) developed this to apply the same idea to the ways in which, when we use camera phone photography, we are weaving our way through a digital-material environment. Camera phone photography, as we discuss, is particularly interesting in this respect because people might take photographs of their environments and/or themselves in them, upload them and engage with people in relation to them online. We see how the digital and material elements of people's everyday journeys and activities are entangled in the processes that camera phone photography involves (ibid.). As the chapters in this part show, digital images are made as people are active in and move through the world. As I have argued elsewhere, photographs can be understood as being made as we move forward through the world (Pink 2011b).

It is not only people who move but also images (Pink 2011a). We see examples of this in the chapters in this part of this book, for instance in the case of images related to a contested political event as much as in the case of the photographs of transnational families, or photographs that connect people over geographical distance through web platforms. As images move through the world, they become interwoven in new stories, and those people who engage with them, take them up and journey with them some way, and they become part of new 'stories' (to borrow a term from Massey 2005) as images are implicated in and/or move through different configurations of place, sometimes being pulled in by human actors.

The images in this part of this book are an excellent example: they have not only become part of the stories that the authors of the chapters have narrated to us in their descriptions, but now they also sit with us as readers in a place where they have become academic photographs, entangled not only in the stories that they have emerged from, but also with those of the academic argument made in the narrative of each chapter, and also in the stories that we as readers tell ourselves with them. This scenario is akin to what I have called the 'ethnographic place' (Pink 2009). While I have developed this concept specifically as a way to discuss how sensory ethnographers bring together our research materials, arguments, stories, experiences, writings and more, it can equally be used to think about academic writing about qualitative research more generally. The concept of place can, likewise, be used to consider the configurations of things and processes that come together in academic work, which is also something that is open to change. Our writing and photographs never stop at the texts we present them in, but rather they will always go on new journeys with the readers who pick them up and intertwine their reading with our words and images as they move forward through the world together.

Moving places

Theories of place and theories of movement are commonly brought together. The work of both Massey and Ingold, discussed above, suggests that place is constituted in movement, by moving people, things and processes. Above, I have suggested that we understand digital photography as part of places. I have argued that digital photographs are made and experienced by people in movement. I have also proposed that we see digital images as themselves in movement – as digital artefacts that are not static but always going forward through the world and becoming part of the stories of the people to whom they become related. Digital photography is one of the everyday life, professional and technological practices and activities that are entangled with everyday life, and both photographic technologies and practices become increasingly ubiquitous. It is part of the way in which our worlds are made, experienced and given meaning. The task for us, as digital photography scholars, is to unpick the ways that this is happening, and what it means.

References

Couldry, N. & McCarthy, A. 2004, *MediaSpace*. London: Routledge.

Hjorth, L. & Pink, S. 2014, 'New Visualities and the Digital Wayfarer: Reconceptualizing Camera Phone Photography and Locative Media'. *Mobile Media and Communication*, Vol. 2, pp. 40–57.

Ingold, T. 2010, 'Footprints through the Weather-World: Walking, Breathing, Knowing'. *Journal of the Royal Anthropological Institute*, Vol. 16, supp. 1, pp. S121–S139.

Ingold, T. 2008, 'Bindings against Boundaries: Entanglements of Life in an Open World'. *Environment and Planning A*, Vol. 40, pp. 1796–1810.

Ingold, T. 2007, *Lines: A Brief History*. Routledge: London.

Massey, D. 2005, *For Space*. Sage: London.

Moores, S. 2012, *Media, Place and Mobility*. Palgrave Macmillan: Basingstoke.

Pink, S. 2013, *Doing Visual Ethnography*, revised and expanded 3rd edn. Sage: London.

Pink, S. 2012, *Situating Everyday Life: Practices and Places*. Sage: London.

Pink, S. 2011a, 'Sensory Digital Photography: Re-Thinking "Moving" and the Image'. *Visual Studies*, Vol. 26, no. 1, pp. 4–13.

Pink, S. 2011b, 'Amateur Documents? Amateur Photographic Practice, Collective Representation and the Constitution of Place in UK Slow Cities'. *Visual Studies*, Vol. 26, no. 2, pp. 92–101.

Pink, S. (2009). Doing sensory ethnography. Sage: London.

Pink, S. & Hjorth, L. 2012, 'Emplaced Cartographies: Reconceptualising Camera Phone Practices in an Age of Locative Media'. *Media International Australia*, no. 145, pp. 145–156.

Pink, S. (2009). Doing sensory ethnography. Sage: London.

Pink, S. & Leder Mackley, K. 2013, 'Saturated and Situated: Rethinking Media in Everyday Life'. *Media, Culture and Society*, Vol. 35, no. 6, pp. 677–691.

Wilken, R. & Goggin, G. 2012, *Mobile Technology and Place*. Routledge: New York.

Part III

Camera as the extension of the photographer

12 Exploring everyday photographic routines through the habit of noticing

Eve Forrest

Prologue

The first time it happened to me was whilst I was out with a group of photographers on a quiet Sunday morning; the city streets of Newcastle-upon-Tyne were deserted. I was feeling uninspired even though I had two cameras with me: a newly purchased toy Holga and my trusted 40-year-old Pentax which I wore around my neck. Looking around me, I could see little that I thought was worth photographing. However, one of the photographers beside me suddenly stopped still, then, crouched down. I observed them at work as they moved around: making micro adjustments to their feet, fingers, shoulders and head movements, getting their body in the best position to take the picture. They lingered over what they had seen for a full five minutes taking a variety of different pictures. This episode proved not to be unusual that day: in the few hours I spent with the group, the same thing happened numerous times with other photographers. Despite standing in close proximity to them, what had grabbed their attention had passed me by completely unnoticed. My camera was little used that day and my notebook had one loose scribble underlined: *why can't I see the same way as them and when do photographers start seeing things?*

Introduction – what catches the thread?

Often, when discussions turn to describing the creative process, it is said that something can *catch* the imagination, much like when the singular thread from a scarf snags itself on a nail and begins to unwind itself from its tight weave. In much the same way, imaginative thoughts are pulled through and out of the front of our consciousness, housed deep within the varied interlacing routines of everyday thoughts. As Abraham, McKenna and Sheldrake (2001 p. 36) attest 'motivations in the ordinary psychological sense are not pushing from behind but pulling from ahead … somehow the system … is subject in the present to the influence of a potential future state that hasn't yet come into being'. Quite unexpectedly, something or someone can catch the attention. When this happens, the notional thread can only be grasped and, if desired, the holder follows the potential trail wherever it can lead.

Many have asked, in the course of my fieldwork, what separates a photographer from a person who just carries a camera? What is the nature of that label? It is a difficult weave to unpick. Having spoken with numerous photographers over the course of many years, the common theme in each conversation was the transformative powers of carrying and using a camera every day, be that film, digital or on a mobile phone. They remarked on how they saw the world differently, markedly so from the others around them that did not habitually take photographs. They also noted that after prolonged use, even when they did not take a camera with them, they still saw potential photographs everywhere within their environment. Thanks to the presence of the camera, the imagination of the photographer is often unravelling, on any possible number of everyday hooks.

This chapter gives consideration to how and why this particular kind of imaginative process, or what I term here *noticing strategies*, happens. The phenomenon of noticing is first discussed by David Seamon (1979) in his seminal work *Geography of the Lifeworld*. Seamon (2000, p. 161) later on writes that 'it is impossible to ask whether person makes world or world makes person because both exist always together and can only be correctly interpreted in terms of the holistic relationship, being-in-world.' Using *Lifeworld* as the primary touchstone I will consider the core experiential qualities of photography practice and discover, phenomenologically speaking, how the photographer and their being-in-the-world is affected by the presence of the camera. This work draws from other disciplines too, that whilst initially appearing to be unconnected, are tied together by what could be loosely bracketed as phenomenological threads. The anthropologist Tim Ingold and his ideas on perception (2000) and movement (2008) within everyday life are used to consider noticing strategies online. The work of Terence McKenna, 'anarchist metaphysician' (St John 2011, p. 207) is also worthy of further exploration here, more specifically his work relating to creative consciousness and ontology within everyday life.

The hitherto mentioned conversations were part of a longitudinal ethnographic study of photographers based in North-East England, more specifically, the cities of Newcastle-upon-Tyne and Sunderland. The photographers came from a variety of backgrounds and ages: the only links were geographical location and Flickr, from which they were all enlisted. The photographers presented a mix of abilities (although the traditional labels of amateur and professional, I would argue, are largely outmoded on Flickr and other photography platforms: see Forrest 2013). Often it is now difficult to tell between the quality and styles of images that used to make differentiation more straightforward. I interviewed more than 20 photographers in various locations, both online and face-to-face.[1] At least half of these photographers were then accompanied on an hour-long 'walk and talk' around their local cities of Newcastle-upon-Tyne and Sunderland.

This approach, also known as the guided tour technique, has its roots in what could be widely described as a phenomenological attitude towards thinking about everyday practices such as photography, giving opportunity for the researcher to 'observe their informants' spatial practices in situ while accessing their experiences and interpretations at the same time' (Kusenbach 2003, p. 463). This method emphasizes the 'call to lived experience' (Landau 2004, p. 111) of the photographer, rather than the images they produce, meaning a fuller exploration of the multifarious *doings* of everyday photography, are made possible.

Geography of the Lifeworld

Whilst *Geography of the Lifeworld* (referred to hereafter as *GOL*) has been utilized by a few authors in diverse areas such as urban planning (Wunderlich 2008) and media studies (Moores 2006, 2012; Moores & Metykova 2010) the work is still relatively unknown and underused. It is therefore worthwhile briefly outlining the pertinent themes of *GOL* and how they relate to photography practice. *GOL* is a study of the everyday complexities 'and inescapable immersion in the geographical world' (Seamon 1979, p. 15) via the 'body ballet', a set of integrated gestures, behaviours and actions that sustain a particular task or aim (Seamon 2006). These different forms of gestures and actions connect with the practice approach, as outlined by Lehmuskallio and Gómez Cruz in the introduction to this volume. They argue that the visual is more than representation alone. Practice theory facilitates an exploration into the various routine performances and communicative actions with a camera: a particular dance set to the rhythm of everyday life.

Seamon particularly underlines the impact of habit, drawing attention to factors that structure these various interactions. The distinctive approach of the original text was based in a branch of human geography that came to prominence in the mid-to-late 1970s, through authors such as Relph (1976) and Tuan (1977), which 'shifted analytical focus from social space to lived-in place, seeking to supplant the "people-less" geographies of positivist spatial science with an approach that fed off alternative philosophies – notably existentialism and phenomenology' (Hubbard 2005, p. 42). Seamon particularly utilized the phenomenology of Merleau-Ponty to investigate these everyday actions up close, in relation to the body-subject. Using the technique of themed 'environmental experience groups' he asked his participants to think and observe their patterns of movement and habits in their everyday environments via a theme assigned to them each week. Moores (2006) summarizes that 'Seamon's groups can therefore be thought of, in a certain sense, as having engaged in consciousness-raising ... through the expression of at least some of these tacitly known things that enable the skilful accomplishment of everyday practices'. It is through the outcomes of these group meetings that Seamon persuasively argues that our relationships with place and habitual routines are highly complex and not merely a symptom of automatic reinforcement or a condition of set thought processes. Instead, Seamon (1979, p. 40) believes that everyday interaction and movement 'arises from the body' which is 'at the root of habitual movement' (p. 41). Seamon (p. 55) describes the nature of the everyday body ballet, stating 'Basic bodily movements fuse together ... through training and practice. Simple hand, leg and trunk movements become attuned to a particular line of work or action and direct themselves spontaneously to meet the need at hand.'

The metaphor of dance is particularly useful for thinking about how photographers can vary their everyday movements. When out in groups they waltz in-between one another, so as not to disrupt the image taking of others. Often, of course, they dance solo and, depending on the camera used, they do not just use their feet. They bring their eye close to the viewfinder or hold the screen at arm's length, stretching their muscles out or pulling their elbows in tightly to their body. Even when they are 'still' and watching the world with the camera in hand, they continue to make micro adjustments with their weight, shifting from one foot to the other. Sometimes they even go *en-pointe*, tip-toeing around their subject to gain a better perspective.

These actions, which can be viewed as part of a complex interlacing between body and camera, are being further advanced by new technologies and hardware. Where cameras used to be extensions of the hand and eye, they can now also be integrated into the body through various wearable means, such as clips, mounts and harnesses on the chest (for example GoPro cameras and accessories and the Apple iWatch). Photography practices have, then, become both embodied and an embedded part of everyday life (see Favero, this volume).

One strand of this intricate, embodied ballet is highlighted in Chapter 14, which Seamon (1979, p. 108) names 'Noticing and Heightened contact'. He defines noticing in the following way, 'A thing from which we were insulated a moment before flashes to our attention. Noticing is self-grounded or world grounded ... Incongruity, surprise, contrast and attractiveness (or its opposite unattractiveness) are all characteristics that activate world-grounded noticing.' Whilst Seamon does not specifically tie noticing to image-making practices, I wish to demonstrate, throughout this chapter, that his definition, above, of the particular experiential qualities of noticing, aligns closely with that of the photographer. Importantly, the only instance when photography is mentioned anywhere in *GOL* is in the context of noticing. Seamon (ibid., p. 109) writes that

> One group member, pleased with the photographs he had done, spent an entire afternoon taking more pictures. 'I was noticing more than I usually do', he said 'and it had something to do with the fact that the photographs had come out so well.'

Before moving on to wider discussions on everyday photography, it is interesting, here, to consider the other area that Seamon associates with noticing: heightened contact, particularly in the context of Terence McKenna's statement that more attention should be paid to the 'felt presence of direct experience' within everyday life (McKenna 2012). The unmistakeable transcendental tone of the language Seamon uses in this chapter has more in common with that of McKenna (1991, 1999) and his psychedelic, spiritual and ecological explorations. Seamon (1979, pp. 111–112) notes that through heightened contact 'a feeling of peace and harmony with the world' is possible, that participants noted that everything 'feels more real' in that state of mind and that the person 'feels joined and akin to the world'. This also echoes the writing of Graham St John (2004, p. 21) who, in his exploration of raving, quotes Spurgeon noting that the space of the dance floor becomes 'the space of "awakening ... [raving] is an experience that amounts to rapture"'. In a similar way, Seamon argues that heightened contact involves 'the physical environment beyond the person' (1979, p. 113).

All these aspects are pertinent to discussions relating to everyday photography, particularly the unfolding of movement and space within the urban environment and how photographers engage and reflect on their everyday surroundings. It is worth noting here, too, that the type of equipment used (for example a phone or DSLR camera) as well as the publishing platform that photographers decide to put their photographs on to (such as Flickr or Facebook) may also impact on the different noticing strategies of photographers and, perhaps, with different results, that are discussed within this chapter. All the photographers here used primarily DSLR or film cameras when out 'doing photography', but by the very nature of their primary function they also carried their mobile phones with them too. When they are outside, walking around with the camera, the photographer is acutely aware of the surrounding environment and awakened to its potential. They are aware of themselves, the presence of the camera in their lives and of those who will be looking at the images once produced. Their interaction with both machine and the world around them can often lead to what Abraham Laslow would call a 'peak experience' of creative energy. It is to these various imaginative incarnations that this chapter will now turn.

The various habits of routine noticing

'Who would watch empty streets? Such situations are neutral backdrops and normally do not capture the experience's attention' (Seamon 1979, p. 106).

> When I am going out in Sunderland, I go where I think I am going to get good photos ... you see the world totally differently ... you are keeping an eye out.
>
> (Participant M)

To respond to Seamon's quote, it is the photographer who is always watching whether the streets are empty or filled with people, if the buildings are in light or shade, whether it is warm or damp, afternoon or night. As the hundreds of pedestrians walk along the same paths, allowing the neutral backdrop of the cityscape to merge with their everyday activities, the photographer is noticing. The focused inattentiveness of the urbanites is one part of their natural attitude, like the noise, dirt and architecture which inform their everyday life (Bull 2007). However, photographers here see the city as a space offering an infinite number of sensual opportunities. They interact with its space in complex and enhanced ways, actively engaged in looking for noticeable scenes, people and places. Photographer A2 noted

> I am always thinking with photos in mind; it is kind of an obsession. Once you start taking photographs at a regular level you start to see things through a camera, even if you don't have one.

The camera, then, does not always have to be in hand to instigate noticing. Even when they are without one (although this is rare), photographers are frequently thinking and acting as if they have it with them. Instead of the photographers' awareness 'advancing and retreating like the actions of waves on shore' (Seamon 1979, p. 103) the effect of the camera on their everyday interactions and movement is more permanent. Another photographer (U) also explained

> I walk around, I carry the camera everywhere – that is the best thing about digital, you can take the tools of your trade with you – and, yes, spotting things becomes an annoying habit when you are with other people.

The annoying part inferred to here is that, when photographers notice things, they frequently need to perform a number of different actions. They, first of all, stop, get the body into position and work out the picture they want, pressing the shutter release, whilst often trying different angles. They then review the pictures and then constantly repeat this process until they are happy, by which time the companion they were out with has walked farther on, or complained that they are bored. Other photographers told me similar stories:

> My kids and my wife think I am mad. I will be having a cup of coffee and start staring at something and move my head a bit because I will be interested by a shape, the way the light has hit something, or a reflection, whatever.

(D)

In the above example, noticing happened in an unanticipated way, as, although the photographer was not expecting to find a picture in a coffee shop, something subtly changed in the light or movement. Reacting to changes with small micro-movements, the body instinctively adjusts, as movement 'unfolds instantaneously in one smooth flow' (Seamon 1979, p. 109). Merleau-Ponty (cited in Carman, 2008, pp. 110–111) notes that 'intentionality of perception depends crucially on the normativity of body schema … we have a *feel* for the kinds of balance and posture that afford us a correct and proper view of the world'. In the case of the photographers here, this view is subtly different from the others that they are with. Another photographer explained that

> I'd say I am always photographically aware of my surroundings, carrying a camera or not. It is rare that I am not carrying a camera of some sort; if I was without a camera I would wish I was carrying [one].
>
> (P1)

What does it mean to be 'photographically aware' of surroundings? It differs from photographer to photographer, depending on their preferred subject, but what is important for each of them is habitually and intentionally paying attention to the world around them. The end goal is to find an interesting picture within the overlooked details that are scattered around the everyday environment. Seamon (1979, p. 109) notes that 'training and interest providing some control of noticing … but different people notice different aspects of the same environment'. Certainly, this was true of many of the photographers, as one explained:

> If you are carrying a camera around with you, you are always looking for something to photograph; it's a strange situation. You don't consciously look for a photograph but, when you are wandering along, something will take your eye and you will look at it, move around, you look at it from different angles and all of a sudden you will see a photograph and you will say *I like that, I want to take a picture of it.*
>
> (P2)

Interestingly, the description given above implies that the noticing cannot be forced, even when they carry the camera. The common frustration of the photographers I spoke to is that wandering can often be fruitless, they do not notice anything of interest and nothing comes forth. In this regard I would like to say more about emotion, noticing and photography. When questioned about mood or emotion when taking the camera out with them, participants seemed hesitant to attribute directly one factor to their style of photography on a specific day. However, emotion did have an impact on their photography in general and their noticing strategies in particular. M told me that 'if I am in a bad mood, I won't go out and if I am in a good mood, I will take more risks and go out'. This sentiment was also echoed by other photographers, too, who commented how negative emotion made an impact on their photograph taking:

Yes, I find that if I am not feeling well or in a good mood then I don't take photos. I have to be positive about stuff. I am an upbeat person anyway but if I have a lot on my mind then I don't tend to take as many photographs.

(C)

I have to be in the mood for it. The summer is a bad time for me because of the light [he prefers night photography]. I might go somewhere and something might happen and it will put us off and I will be in a bad mood and I know I will not take decent photos, so I won't bother and just write it off, but definitely have to be in the right frame of mind.

(A2)

Negative emotion does affect the bodily rhythms and processes of the photographer, though it is more difficult to articulate exactly why. One possible reason is that, once fully absorbed in the action of photographing, the mind and body are knotted. Soon, full concentration is given over to photography and the individual becomes entwined in the world, their habitual movements flow, in turn creating more noticing opportunities, leading to further absorption, and so on. In regard to habit, Seamon (1979, p. 40) comments that 'movements occur without or before any conscious intervention', so if there is a negative feeling of frustration, this self-awareness somehow blocks this process from working. Instead of flowing, the body's rhythm stutters as concentration is lost and noticing becomes more difficult. Another responded in different ways when asked about emotion and their photography:

I feel bad if I don't go and take photographs and it can affect my mood if I go out and I might spend all day taking photos and it is the last 10 minutes and I get the unexpected shot. I think people think that it's dead easy but it isn't.

(A1)

The notion that photography is easy to do is a common one within popular discourse.[2] Noticing could also, then, be viewed as a way of the photographer consciously separating themselves as different from (in their opinion) other, less dedicated photographers. One told me

I try and notice things other people wouldn't,

(D1)

which is a common trait amongst many photographers. The 'other people' talked about here were not just those who took the occasional photograph with their mobile phone but also other keen amateurs and professionals.

The skill photographers most appreciate in the work of others is not just the ability to capture a picturesque landscape or portrait, but to see *something* where they have not seen *anything* and create a photographic opportunity through noticing alone. During a walk around, one photographer commented

> the thing on Flickr meets [where online groups meet up offline] is that there is an unofficial competition to see who can get a shot that no one else gets. It is a challenge to get something different to what everyone else is doing.
>
> (D2)

Building on earlier discussions relating to the body schema, it is worthwhile giving brief mention to Bourdieu's ideas surrounding habitus,[3] a blend of 'conditionedness and spontaneity' (Carman 2008, p. 219) in relation to noticing. Tim Ingold (2000, p. 162) explains habitus as 'how people acquire the specific dispositions and sensibilities that lead them to orient themselves in relation to their environment and to attend to its features in the particular ways that they do'. As part of their skill set, photographers become accustomed to looking, in order to find interesting things to photograph, which has subsequently formed into a more solid habit. The photographers below all identified this link:

> I do go about and think, what would be a good image here? So I will look at a street like this … look at the patterns of buildings, the repetition. What I will really look for is a person on the street because that is what I find interesting … you do look for an image.
>
> (A1)

> Before I got a camera, I never looked up so much but there is so much hidden detail that people aren't really aware of around [Newcastle] so I quite like that. It wasn't until I got the camera that I started looking all over at anything, all sorts of different things.
>
> (D3)

> My eyes are everywhere, looking about. I am an inquisitive sort if I am walking around a town. If you look above the shops and on the pavements there is stuff there. I went through a spell of taking pictures of the corners of things … especially when you are cross processing, that enhances the colours of things. I don't plan it, though, I just carry [the camera] and see what happens.
>
> (C)

For Bourdieu (1977, p. 87), habitus lives in the type of noticings described by the participants, above. It is implicit within spatial and body awareness or, in Bourdieu's terms, it can be 'a way of walking, a tilt of the head, facial expressions, ways of sitting and of using implements – all of these, and more, comprise what it takes to be an accomplished practitioner'. Re-enacting the traces of previous bodily movements, the photographer does not necessarily know what they are looking for until they find it; their world unfolds in front of them and they react to it as part of their body's wider intelligence.

What am I *drawn* to? Noticing strategies and movement online

Although the main discussion, here, revolves around photographers and their strategies with the camera offline, noticing also has an important role to play online, too. The folksonomy of Flickr leads to a random ordering system of images, the exploration of which is more akin to a virtual form of what Ingold (2000) terms 'way-finding' (see Pink, in this volume). Users find their own paths to the people, groups or pages they frequently visit on the site. For Ingold (2000, p. 220), places 'exist not in space but as nodes in a matrix of movement ... ordinary wayfinding more closely resembles story telling than map-using'. Ingold has never written about movement in and around online environments. However, his concept of wayfinding very much lends itself to platforms such as Flickr and how users get around or find their way in the space. Discussing navigation and dwelling in physical space, Ingold (ibid., p. 230) believes that people's 'knowledge of the environment undergoes continuous formation in the very course of their moving about in it' so that they 'know as they go' (p. 228). In more ephemeral places, like Flickr (Van Dijck 2011), the knowledge of where things are located, coupled with the unexpected images that can be found in the process of wandering about, means that different paths are continuously forming and disappearing. To this end, Flickr is not a network of points, but a *meshwork* of interactions, a notion also utilized by Pink (2011, this volume), too, in relation to other related photography practices.

Noticing also has a role to play as this part of this navigation strategy. When I observed the photographers[4] accessing their Flickr photo-stream and moving around the site, many used a similar terminology in previous descriptions of how they used the camera and wandered around the city. As they wandered through, clicking from image to image they told me, frequently, how they were 'drawn to' particular photographers and their subjects. They also quickly became absorbed in looking at the images, only making micro-movements with their eyes, and their index finger slightly twitching on the touch-pad to move the cursor. When they saw an image they were interested in, they would often go on to explore that photographer's page, looking at the rest of their images. In other instances when photographers were on Flickr, another repeated movement was that of continually going back and forth between different images, their personal page and groups. Sometimes they would open up multiple tabs to aid these movements and then begin to comment on, favourite or add the chosen photographer as a contact by utilizing different tabs. One participant (T) used continuous quick movements of scrolling down the page, hitting the 'favourite' button multiple times so he could find his way back to the work that 'caught his eye' in the first place.

This happened with other users as well. During our session, one photo-grapher (A1) refreshed the main Flickr 'Explore' page around 20 times, quickly scanning the page and clicking the 'reload' button. In this instance, the hand, eye and computer were synchronized in continued repetitive movement and, with both participants, there was a definite form of con-centrated distraction in their looking practices when exploring Flickr. Other photographers also became absorbed in looking at images. This dis-traction forms part of the complex interaction with the images, and they scanned the screen for an image that they were pulled into, in a similar fashion to the earlier *noticing* strategies. Like wandering in the city, often, when the participants began to explore Flickr, there was no set destination or final place they wanted to get to, so the threads began to weave around one another as they moved across the pages, creating a complex virtual tapestry. This movement was punctuated by noticing, or being drawn to, particular images.

The pages that they navigated around were, of course, deeply familiar to them and they revisited the same places on Flickr in a similar way to their favourite urban sites. Although wandering online, to an extent, is unplanned, ultimately these users are repeatedly exploring the same places (groups and certain features), revisiting the same sites on every visit. There were many overlaps in photographers' online and offline wayfinding strat-egies and the way that photographers know, as they go around Flickr, has parallels to their offline walking. The exploration was built from routine encounter, similarly, in their physical explorations of city spaces. Particip-ants did not tend to seek out the unknown parts of the city, revisiting the same territory, always alert to new opportunities brought about by having the camera in their hand.

Horan (2000, p. 23) writes that 'digital places are new leverage points for creating new experiences and relationships that will profoundly rede-fine our experiences of physical space'. Thanks to the different and varied interactions on Flickr, photographers are also attuned to noticing different things and people around the city, too, inviting other photographers to join them in the process. Flickr has, additionally, become part of the everyday routine for many people, and their habits with the camera are also partially informed by the images they view on the site.

Watching and waiting

Thus far, I have highlighted the complexity of the photographer and their habit of noticing offline and online. However, there is another facet to this strategy that is important in their engagement with the world: watching. Ingold (2000, p. 25) notes that 'perception is grounded in an act of attention' so it is through watching that photographers begin to notice their surroundings or, to paraphrase Ingold (p. 265) it is watching which 'transforms passive looking into active noticing'. The participants in this study stated that they not only enjoyed watching, it was a part of their general strategy when outside with the camera. Some identified that watching was part of their integral personality:

> I am a people watcher I was always interested in what was going on before [without the camera] though!
>
> (R)

> It's getting into [the subject's] head – I have always been a people watcher, even when I go out and have a drink. It is a natural curiosity about the world in general.
>
> (G)

Another expanded on this idea and told me that photography can be

> Quite voyeuristic … I like people watching. I could do that all day, watching people pass by. Sometimes you can tell a story with a photograph, you can choose to show the environment or knock it out of focus and choose to show somebody … I just find it very, very interesting to look at a photo and think *who is that person*?
>
> (A1)

Seamon distinguishes watching from other forms of looking and describes it as 'a situation in which the person looks out attentively upon some aspect of the world for an extended period of time' (1979, p. 105). The photographers, here, detailed how they were pathological in their watching, always on the lookout for their next photograph. When I was out with one participant (R1) he commented that he 'hangs around and waits' so he can see where you get a good view of where people are. Later, when discussing his Flickr photo-stream images, he also noted that he often watched (from a distance) to get the photographs he wants. Seamon (ibid., p. 106) believes 'watching establishes an extended span of attention between person and place. To watch is to pay attention at length to the world at hand – to have one's interest occupied as mutually the world receives that interest.'

Replace the verb 'watching' here with 'photographing' and soon ideas can begin to be formed on the kind of interactions and exchanges which take place between photographer, camera and city. The process of watching also becomes involved in the spontaneous planning of a picture, an evolving process between body, imagination and vision. The photographer makes sure that they move their body correctly, anticipating an upcoming shot.

> When you do have [your camera] you just kind of take things a lot slower, walk places sometimes or even try and look ahead and stand, or I'll move over there, so then that might be something interesting. You can let everything go over you ... sometimes you have to almost create a shot, make sure you get into a position if you can see something developing. Sometimes ... I will walk past someone faster than I normally would and then come back [taking their picture] so they don't notice.
>
> (L)

In this example, the combination of routine watching and movement leads to noticing opportunities. It also points to the idea that noticing is not just a random act but something over which the photographer tries to exert some control and, as Rupert Sheldrake reminds us, development of any kind of skill does 'involve interplay between habit and creativity' (Abraham *et al.* 2001, p. 3). Through watching, noticing can then at times be preempted, especially when the photographer repeatedly revisits a place they know, so, to a certain degree, they can expect what to find. Watching is important to photographers because it means they are always tuned into the possibility of photographic opportunities, taking advantage when a chance presents itself. When discussing a picture that he liked on his photostream, T told me

> I just like all the brick and stone, so many lines. Once I sharpened it, all the lines popped ... there is really nice stuff everywhere you look, all the time, to me at least. It is just a question of translating it into the camera.

For the 'accomplished practitioner' (Ingold 2000, p. 162), the physical presence of the camera assists noticing, too, the weight of the machine on the body leading them through a familiar series of habitual movements as 'your perception of objects is already structured by your body and its sense of its own possibilities' (Carman 2008, p. 106).

Conclusion: noticing as *presence*

'The camera is an instrument that teaches people how to see without a camera' (Dorothea Lange in Meltzer 1978).

I asked, at the beginning of this chapter, what separates a photographer from a person who carries a camera. What is the nature of that label? The category of 'photographer', thanks to numerous technological changes, is now particularly slippery, in an age when most carry some form of image-taking device in their pocket (Hand 2012). However, one could ask the same of other, simpler technologies. If one carries a pen, does that automatically make one a writer? I wear training shoes everyday, but does that make me a runner? The answer to these questions is both 'yes' and 'no'. If I want to run in my trainers, they are designed to support my feet, just as the pen helps elucidate my thoughts on paper. However to be a 'runner' and a 'writer' is a classification beyond the technology that facilitates that process. In this regard, I believe that it is the same for photography. To be a photographer is not always necessarily to do with the *quality* of the images but, instead, the way that the photographers perform photography with their body, their commitment to movement, the habit of noticing and how, through this habit, they observe the world. Tomi Hahn (2007, p. 163), in her work on Japanese dance, considers the knowledge that resides in the intelligent body: that which gives the dancers presence when they perform for an audience. She writes 'I am not certain it is possible to definitively provide a formula for the transmission of presence.' Similarly, I am not precisely sure how or when photographers begin to notice things. Seamon (1979, p. 109) himself concludes that 'the unexpectedness of noticing follows no clear pattern. Different people notice different aspects of the same environment' and there is a certain chaos to the whole process. Terence McKenna, in conversation with Abraham, McKenna and Sheldrake (2001, p. 5), notes that 'chaos, creativity and imagination … each impels and runs the other … and conserves processes caught up in the phenomenon of being'. What draws the photographer to one subject but not another, what leads them to shoot one moment and ignore the rest, still remains somewhat elusive.

Seamon (1979, p. 106) writes that 'at times watching may be more intense as the interest, beauty or excitement of the scene draws the attention and holds it'. However, like Hahn's dancer, it is a skill that cannot be taught and must instead be learned (transmitted) through practice. In a similar way, the photographers who routinely walk around their everyday environment are noticing, but it is also tightly woven into, and directly informs, their habitual camera use. Noticing is a chaotic, complex contradiction, where everyday life has the potential to be somehow transformed through a balance of luck and skill, and it is a 'synergy between understanding and intuition' (St John 2004, p. 216). Noticing is a state awakened within the photographer; it is a form of rapture that can never be shaken off. One photographer (R1) told me

> Eventually, I have become aware about expressing myself: the more you take, the more you look!

Noticing and watching have become a habit and, soon, casual unseen details and the possibilities of everyday life unfurl before the photographer.

The more you take, the more you look, and the more you look, the more you notice. To paraphrase McKenna, it is the felt presence of the camera that makes direct experience of the world heightened for the photographer. From that point, noticing can begin and creativity can blossom every day.

Notes

1 The photographers have been anonymized throughout and are referred to by their first name (or user name) initial only. When photographers have the same initial, a number was added to differentiate them.
2 This also relates to earlier historical struggles for photography to be accepted as an art form within the academy (see Marien 2002).
3 Bourdieu used photographs to link his own concept of 'lived experience' with issues of aesthetics, taste and class (Van House 2011, p. 126). See Bourdieu (1984) for further discussions.
4 This was an extension of the walk and talk method. The browse and talk consisted of participant observation of their movements on Flickr, within a variety of locations, with a laptop.

References

Abraham, R., McKenna, T. & Sheldrake, R. 2001, *Chaos, Creativity and Cosmic Consciousness*. Park Street Press: Rochester, VT.

Bourdieu, P. 1984, *Distinction: A Social Critique of the Judgement of Taste*, trans. Richard Nice. Routledge: London.

Bourdieu, P. 1977, *Outline of a Theory of Practice*, trans. R. Nice. Cambridge University Press: Cambridge.

Bull, M. 2007, *Sound Moves: iPod Culture and Urban Experience*. Routledge: London.

Carman, T. 2008, *Merleau Ponty*. Routledge: London.

Forrest, E. 2013, 'Reflections on Flickr: Everyday Photography Practices Online and Offline'. *Either/And*, viewed 9 October 2015, http://eitherand.org/reconsidering-amateur-photography/reflections-flickr-everyday-photography-practices-/.

Hahn, T. 2007, *Sensational Knowledge: Embodying Japanese Culture through Japanese Dance*. Wesleyan University Press: Middletown, CT.

Hand, M. 2012, *Ubiquitous Photography*. Polity Press: Cambridge.

Horan, T. 2000, *Digital Places: Building Our City of Bits*. Urban Land Institute: Washington, DC.

Hubbard, P. 2005, 'Space/Place', in D. Atkinson, P. Jackson, D. Sibley & N. Washbourne (eds) *Cultural Geography: A Critical Dictionary of Key Concepts*. IB Taurus: London, pp. 41–49.

Ingold, T. 2008, 'Bindings against Boundaries: Entanglements of Life in an Open World'. *Environment and Planning A*, Vol. 40, no. 8, pp. 1796–1810.

Ingold, T. 2000, *The Perception of the Environment*. Routledge: London.

Kriz, J. 1999, 'On Attractors: The Teleological Principle in Systems Theory, the Arts and Therapy'. *POIESIS. A Journal of the Arts and Communication*, pp. 24–29.

Kusenbach, M. 2003, 'Street Phenomenology: The Go-Along as Ethnographic Research Tool'. *Ethnography*, Vol. 4, no. 3, pp. 455–485.

Landau, J. 2004, 'The Flesh of Raving: Merleau-Ponty and the Experience of Ecstasy', in G. St John (ed.) *Rave Culture and Religion*. Routledge: London, pp. 107–124.

McKenna, T. 2012, 'The Felt Presence of Direct Experience', viewed 28 August 2014, www.youtube.com/watch?v=VZGyeALEzuQ.

McKenna, T. 1999, *Food of the Gods*. Rider: London.

McKenna, T. 1991, *The Archiac Revival: Speculations on Psychedelic Mushrooms, the Amazon, Virtual Reality, UFOs, Evolution, Shamanism, the Rebirth of the Goddess, and the End of History*. HarperSanFrancisco: San Francisco, CA.

Marien, M. W. 2002, *Photography: A Cultural History*. Laurence King Publishing: London.

Meltzer, M. 1978, *Dorothea Lange: A Photographer's Life*. Syracuse University Press: Syracuse, NY.

Moores, S. 2012, *Media, Place and Mobility*. Palgrave Macmillan: London.

Moores, S. 2006, 'Media Uses and Everyday Environmental Experiences: A Positive Critique of Phenomenological Geography'. *Participations*, Vol. 3, no. 2, November special edition, viewed 1 July 2013, www.participations.org/.

Moores, S. & Metykova, M. 2010, ' "I Didn't Realize How Attached I Am": On the Environmental Experiences of Trans-European Migrants'. *European Journal of Cultural Studies*, Vol. 13, no. 2, pp. 171–189.

Pink, S. 2011, 'Sensory Digital Photography: Rethinking "Moving" and the Image'. *Visual Studies*, Vol. 26, no. 1, pp. 4–13.

Relph, E. 1976, *Place and Placelessness*. Pion Ltd: London.

St John, G. 2011, 'Spiritual Technologies and Altering Consciousness in Contemporary Counterculture', in E. Cardena & M. Winkelman (eds) *Altering Consciousness: Multidisciplinary Perspectives*. Praeger: Santa Barbara, CA, pp. 203–229.

St John, G. 2004, 'The Difference Engine: Liberation and the Rave Imaginary', in G. St John (ed.) *Rave Culture and Religion*. Routledge: London, pp. 19–46.

Seamon, D. 2006, 'A Geography of Lifeworld in Retrospect: A Response to Shaun Moores'. *Participations*, Vol. 3, no. 2, November special edition, viewed 1 July 2013, www.participations.org/.

Seamon, D. 1979, *A Geography of the Lifeworld*. St Martins Press: New York.

Tuan, Y. 1977, *Space and Place*. Edward Arnold: London.

Van Dijck, J. 2011, 'Flickr and the Culture of Connectivity: Sharing Views, Experiences, Memories'. *Memory Studies*, Vol. 4, no. 4, pp. 401–415.

Van House, N. 2011, 'Personal Photography, Digital Technologies and the Uses of the Visual'. *Visual Studies*, Vol. 26, no. 2, pp. 124–134.

Wunderlich, F. M. 2008, 'Walking and Rhythmicity: Sensing Urban Space'. *Journal of Urban Design*, Vol. 13, no. 1, pp. 125–139.

13 'Analogization'

Reflections on wearable cameras and the changing meaning of images in a digital landscape[1]

Paolo Favero

A long way into the digital era we can, today, start looking back at the debate that has defined our engagement with digital images from a critical distance. This field has been characterized by a certain degree of polarization; on one level we have witnessed celebrations of 'digital utopia' (Rosen 2001, p. 318) where the ever-growing number of images circulating on the net, combined with the bare fact that more and more individuals in the world are actively engaging with images, have been interpreted as signs of a move towards a brighter, more democratic future. Indeed, it is easy to get blinded by the mathematics of this change: today, Facebook contains 10,000 times the number of photos that are present in the Library of Congress in the US. Every two minutes, today, more pictures are taken than throughout the entire 1800s (the century in which photography was invented), and so on. On another level, however, the very same developments have also been read from a perspective where concern and nostalgia meet and mingle. Digital images have, in the latter case, been seen as negations of a truer, more direct, 'more real' experience of the world surrounding us, as a proper detachment from everyday life. Gere (2005) has suggested that the move towards the digital generated a fear for 'the annihilation of physical distance and the dissolution of material reality' (p. 15), Wellman (2001) has maintained that the digital has produced instances of 'net-worked individualism' and Nichols (2000) has famously argued 'the chip is pure *surface*, pure *simulation* of thought. Its material surface is its meaning, *without* history, without depth, without aura, affect, or feeling' (p. 104).

The debate surrounding us today is, therefore, much more nuanced. We seem to have overcome the fear of the death of photography postulated by, among others, Richtin (1990) and nicely summed up by Mirzoeff (1999) with his famous sentence '[a]fter a century and a half of recording and memorializing death, photography met its own death some time in the 1980s at the hands of computer imaging' (p. 86). However, we are still caught up in an interesting and unsolved set of doubts regarding digital images' anchorage in the material texture of everyday life, or, to put it in other words, in 'reality'. Such doubts, I will here suggest, largely depend on the dominance, in the discourse that has characterized the debate on digital practices and technologies, of the notion of digitization and, hence, on the tendency to reproduce (at a discursive and analytical level) the dualism between the material and the virtual.

In this chapter I will attempt to explore these issues by entering the field of digital imaging from an analysis of the changing contemporary scenario of digital technologies at large. In other words, I will foreground the 'digital', identifying leading trends in that context, in order to then look at the specific role played by images in the same scenario. I will open the chapter with a somewhat detailed historical introduction to the core discourses surrounding the birth of the notion of digitization. This passage is needed in order to generate awareness in the reader of the roots (and resilience) of the discourse that has dominated our understanding of digital technologies. In this section, I will also provide a series of glances at contemporary trends in the field of consumer digital technologies. These descriptions will render evident the extent to which we are, today, witnessing the growth of technologies that increasingly close down the gap between technology, the body of the user and the materiality surrounding them. I will suggest that we are in an age characterized not only by digitization but also by what we could call 'analogization' (a process of materialization taking place within a digital environment). I will then proceed to observe the extent to which a similar shift can be detected in the realm of image-making. My analysis of two wearable camera technologies (the 'life-logging' camera Narrative and the action camera GoPro) will lead me to identify the presence of a parallel shift, a 'material turn', which is happening alongside (and probably within) the much-debated 'algorithmic turn' (Uricchio 2011). In the conclusion, I will suggest that such a shift requires from the scholar a capacity to bring the conventional tools of visual culture in contact with elements of digital and material culture and to move away from simplistic dualisms, towards a perspective that integrates the digital with the material (analogue) world. This shift also poses new political and ethical challenges that we must now learn to address.

The digital context

Let me start with a brief historical contextualization. In 1945, Vannevar Bush, an American engineer who had served the US Office of Scientific Research and Development during the Second World War published an article in which he prophesied the birth of a tool capable of functioning like a prosthetic memory (Bush 1945). In times of increasing information flow, Bush suggested, human beings (teachers and scholars in particular) could not be expected to be able to store, categorize, make sense of and use all the information reaching them at an ever-increasing speed. The *Memex* (this is the name of the tool he envisioned) would constitute the solution to this. Built as a memory augmentation system based on microfilm, this was a desk with translucent screens, an engine and a series of basic commands. The precursor of the modern computer, the *Memex* functioned on the principle of association and was immediately identified as a 'personal' tool in which 'an individual stores his books, records, and communications, and which is mechanized so that it may be consulted with exceeding speed and flexibility' (ibid.).

Bush's intuition did, indeed, cover many of the notions that would influence future IT developments. His writings set the standard for much of the understanding of artificial memory and computers that would come in the following decades. In particular, and this is what I would like to draw the reader's attention to, he formulated a lasting association between electronic technologies and miniaturization (a notion that eventually got mixed up, especially in popular discourse, with that of dematerialization). In his article, for instance, he writes:

> The Encyclopoedia [*sic*] Britannica could be reduced to the volume of a matchbox. A library of a million volumes could be compressed into one end of a desk. If the human race has produced since the invention of movable type a total record, in the form of magazines, newspapers, books, tracts, advertising blurbs, correspondence, having a volume corresponding to a billion books, the whole affair, assembled and compressed, could be lugged off in a moving van.

Vanevar Bush's ideas consolidated the notion of digitization that would dominate prevailing understandings of the meaning of digital technologies, up to the present day. His writings clearly identified electronic technologies as tools for making 'virtual' and 'immaterial' that which is actually material and concrete. It anticipated the transposition of books and other paper documents into PDFs, of records into MP3s, films into MP4s, photographs into JPGs, etc.

Popular discourse is, today, to a large extent still influenced by these notions. However, we are already well into an epoch characterized by the opposite movement. A quick look into the market of personal digital technologies reveals that, in fact, we are witnessing a progressive move towards technologies that make possible the translation of visions and abstract ideas into physical items. The 3D printer, to mention one example, is now one of the most popular technologies available in the consumer market. Inverting the principle of digitization, 3D printers provide us with the possibility of giving material shape to abstract ideas. The computer, here, is the vehicle for a process of translation. An idea becomes, first, with the help of 3D design software such as CAD, an image. In the second stage, this image is translated into an STL (Stereolithography) file capable of splitting the image in horizontal layers, hence creating an image/path for each layer. A specific material, called printing ink and looking like a plastic thread but conventionally made up of a variety of different materials (from recycled thermoplastic to wood, salt, cement, nylon, etc.) is, at this point, liquefied, so that it can be progressively dropped to shape up an image, layer by layer.

Designers, artists and a wide variety of other professionals have recently found a passion for this tool. Since 2013, a 3D Printshow has regularly been hosted in various cities of the world.[2] More recently, 3D printers have also been adopted in other fields and, for instance, for the production of three-dimensional biological structures, such as patches for heart muscles, livers, etc. With the help of bioink, which is a paste made up of living cells, companies such as Organovo are, today, successfully creating three-dimensional biological structures that may eventually be transplanted into living human beings. Such advancements help us to discover how the cyborg, the futuristic cybernetic organism resulting from the blending of machine and animal/human qualities, object of many fantasies and films (recently portrayed by Matt Damon in the film *Elysium*) is, hence, no longer a futurist projection but very much a reality. We are probably already living in Donna Haraway's (1991) premonition that 'by the late twentieth century, our time, a mythic time, we are all chimeras, theorized and fabricated hybrids of machine and organism. In short, we are cyborgs' (p. 150).

Going back to a more mundane, day-to-day terrain, it is easy to notice how the electronic consumer market is now flooded with products signalling a move towards an increasing interaction with the body. From heavy, bulky terminals to portable computers, we are moving quickly towards mobile screens and wearable electronics. *The Economist* (2014) recently pointed out the boost in popularity of so-called 'smart clothes' at the January 2014 Las Vegas fair of consumer electronics. Smart clothes, that is, garments containing conductive fibres capable of conveying information to and from the body of the users, have recently invaded the market. Mostly tested in the military (where they have been used for monitoring the health of soldiers and also to create flexible circuit boards, connecting all of the soldiers' equipment), these fabrics have also been employed in the world of sport and, recently, fashion, too. In the world of sports, Adidas has recently commercialized a whole line of gear capable of sending information directly from the body of the athlete to the laptop of the coach, thereby helping the latter to monitor the performance of the former. With the help of elastic conducive fibres, the wearer's breathing or muscular activity can be measured, allowing the trainer to monitor the reactions of the wearer's body during a particular exercise. The same materials can also help to gather other biometric data. They can help to signal the arousal of tensions in the body and, so, helping the athlete to identify moments in which to rest or body parts that need particular attention. Adidas Labs, a sub-brand specializing in this sector, has produced shoes tracking everything the foot does, allowing coach and athlete to envision postural problems, etc.

The overall idea of monitoring the body through wearable technologies has, indeed, also been adopted by creators of other types of gadgets. Among them, mention must be made of the health bracelets (such as Fitbit, Jawbone's Up[3] and Nike's own Fuelband) which have recently taken the market by storm. Aimed at allowing the user to monitor their own performances (the steps taken on a daily basis, the calories burnt, the heart rate etc.) these bracelets have also inspired the birth of smart watches, which I will return to later. Designers have also recently experimented with the creation of clothes capable of detecting and interacting with the changing mood of the wearer. There are shirts available in the market that change colour according to the user's change in mood, jackets sending out soothing music or messages recorded by loved ones in moments of heightened stress (through loudspeakers built into the collar of a shirt, for instance) and jewellery warning the user of too much exposure to the sun, etc.

A further development of these technologies includes the possibility of not only analysing the data but also sending it back in the form of a stimulus, thereby enhancing performance. With the help of a combination of biosensors and actuators connected to smartphones, tablets or computers, smart fibres cannot only take the user's biometric reading, but also analyse it in real time and then send it back to the user as stimuli capable of modifying performance. Electricfoxy Move[4] is, for instance, a garment that corrects the posture of the user during Yoga or Pilates exercises. Gentle 'taps' help them to recognize incorrect postures and suggest how to adjust a movement while it is being executed. Intelligent fibres are also being tested which generate small electrical circuits, activating or deactivating specific muscles.

There is no need to go any further into this for the moment. The products mentioned so far are sufficient to demonstrate the variety of bodily and material engagements realized with the help of digital technologies. However, in order to conclude this section I would like to discuss briefly the launch of Apple's Watch, an event that has, somehow, sanctified this trend.

Apple's recent launch of 'Watch' constitutes the epitome (both in technical, as well as in metaphorical terms) of the process of progressive engagement with the body and with everyday life. The aim of the Apple Watch is, in fact, to engage a continuous dialogue with the body of the user. Meant to be worn all the time (showers included), it synchronizes, thanks to the sensors placed underneath the watch and the band, with the body of the user, constantly gathering information about its functioning. The Watch (which is also armed with an internal GPS tracker) communicates with the iPhone, iPad and the computer, creating a circuit of information that, from the point of view of the user, can be monitored through a series of applications (particularly the 'health application'). These apps, together, collect information regarding the users' eating and sleeping patterns, their biometrics, their fitness habits, their commuting routes, working and relaxation practices, etc.

In line with some of the technologies discussed above, the Watch also uses tactility in order to communicate with the user. Small haptic signals (read 'taps') on the wrist inform the user that it is time to get up, that an SMS has arrived etc. The Watch promises to be the ultimate tool for allowing users to gain control over their own bodies, living habits and health patterns. However, at the same time, it also constitutes the ultimate opportunity for creating the largest database of biometrical data, behavioural and living patterns, shopping and leisure habits, and for putting that data into the hands of market interests.[5] The Watch seems to close a circuit between the body of the user, their phones and computers, and the market[6] in a movement that demands heightened attention from the point of view of both ethics and law. It is not my aim to enter this debate here. Instead, I want to stress how the gradual diminishing of the distance between technology and the body can also be detected in the marketing of the Watch. The leading buzzwords and slogans are 'Our most *personal* device yet', 'A more immediate, *intimate* way to connect', 'intelligent health and fitness *companion*', 'because it *touches* your skin, we were able to add a physical dimension to alerts and notifications' (my italics). We could say that Apple is actively tapping into the trend towards increasing bodily engagements, somewhat sanctioning their present centrality in the context of digital technologies.

The examples cited so far should suffice to show the vast span of bodily engagements that contemporary digital technologies are making possible. Basically, there is a whole market of digital products out there that are directly engaging with our bodies and with the material texture of everyday life, rather that just 'simulating reality'. Such examples may have also shown how technologies and practices that we may still have a tendency to consider avant-garde and futuristic are, today, actually readily available 'out there'. They are affordable for a growing number of citizens who live in the networked parts of the world and who are armed, of course, with the necessary capital.

The visual context

In the field of image-making technologies, there are many examples of the present shift towards an increasing anchorage of images and of the practice of image-making within the materiality, physicality, spatiality and sociality of everyday life. The most obvious example is perhaps that of Google Glass, the first case of wearable vision-based augmented reality technology. The Google Glass allows users to receive 'virtual' data on the lens (thereby overlapping with the direct perception of the world 'out there'), that is, a similar kind of information to that which we conventionally receive on a smartphone screen (such as directions on a map, information about places to visit, incoming calls and messages, etc.). It brings together geolocative (spatial) and geosocial (relational) information in the field of vision, consti- tuting a brilliant example of how images now force us to go 'beyond the frame', as I have suggested in a recent article (Favero 2014). Capable of attracting the attention of critics and scholars from all over the world the Goggle Glass has, however, failed to attract buyers and was recently removed from the market.[7] A recent article in *Time* (Grossman & Vella 2014) which, by the way, is openly flirting with Apple products, suggests that the reason for its failure can be found in its invasive look, which demands attention from bystanders and users alike and therefore interrupts genuine immersion in everyday life.

On a different terrain, an increasing attempt to blur the distance between the image and the sensorial richness of our immediate perceptions can be detected in the growing popularity of multi-sensory cinema halls (the so-called 4D, 5D or even 7D movie theatres). Here, the act of viewing is accompanied by sound, touch and motion related stimuli and, in some cases, also by the use of smells and temperature changes. Also, connecting back to the aforementioned discussion on 3D printing, we could take into consideration the enduring popularity of 3D portraits. Companies like Twinkind, Omote 3D, MiniMe, etc., have recently started promoting the large-scale production of 3D portraits. With the help of a photogrammetry 3D scanner, a technician takes a full 360-degree image of a specific subject. This image is then converted, with the help of a printer, into a small puppet representing the subject. The commercial (and, at times, also tech- nical) fortune of such technologies has indeed been characterized by ups and downs and, for the moment, they seem mostly to constitute gimmicks. However, they contain the seeds of some of the transformations that I am addressing in this chapter, i.e. greater immersion of viewers in images, and of images in the fabric of everyday life.

Such practices constitute a challenge to our conventional way of addressing, for instance, a portrait or visual representation more generi- cally. In the context of, for instance, 3D portraits, we lose the conven- tional, privileged point of observation that photography inherited from Renaissance practices of lifelike depiction (see McQuire 1998; Crary 1990). Let me, however, move on to a couple of more specific examples that will direct our attention not only to the use and consumption of images but to their very production. I will proceed to analyse two popular technologies: one life-logging camera (the Narrative Clip) and one action camera (the GoPro). I will begin with the former.

The Narrative Clip: time, mimesis and monitoring

The Narrative Clip (formerly known as Memoto) is a Swedish-made, small, lightweight, wearable and fully weatherproof camera. Armed with a clip, allowing it to be pinned on a jacket/bicycle, etc., it takes two shots every minute. Such shots are recomposed, with the help of a narrative algorithm, in a time-lapse sequence that the user can view through a dedicated smartphone application. These sequences are divided in discrete blocks (labelled 'moments') that also display GPS and temporal data. The marketing material for Narrative promises the user that they will be able to track specific events happening during the day and then use it, in a McLuhan and Fiore (1967) fashion, as an extension of their bodies and minds. A prosthetic memory, capable of making up for what our mind is not able to do, Narrative produces a kind of visual diary of our day. Devoid of a viewfinder, this camera does, indeed, pose a number of interesting challenges to photography. Primarily, it dissociates the act of image-making from the intentions of the image-maker, that is, from the processes of selection and interpretation that are an intrinsic part of the act of making pictures (choosing the right angle, framing, selecting the moment, etc.). It therefore constitutes a movement towards a somewhat 'purer' form of mimesis.[8]

I must admit that using a life-logging camera is quite a bizarre experience. My main concern, when experimenting with the camera, was really the safety and physics of its positioning. I was concerned about having placed it in the right position and about not losing it. Thus, my expectation of total mimesis and spontaneity was constantly interrupted by such practical concerns. With time, this aspect did, however, improve and I learnt to experiment with different positions. On one occasion, I even ended up forgetting the camera in the lower corner of my coat. Surprised and relieved by having found it, I still had to acknowledge that the material produced from this angle was quite useless.

The material the camera produces requires a set of specific reflections. We are not talking, here, about something different from what the marketing of the product says about good photographs, or just photographs for that matter. Rather, what we bring home with Narrative is, largely, a set of scattered visual impressions (most of the images are underexposed or blurred). With the help of the online mobile phone application, however, the user can choose to view only the images with good light and definition. This, however, brings us to the first problematic aspect of this camera. In order to exploit fully its potential, this camera requires an online subscription (of US$10 per month), which henceforth binds, similarly to the Apple Watch, the user to the market. Detached from that subscription, the user may not access GPS information or share images on social media, etc.

Inserting the act of making images into everyday life, in these somewhat novel ways, life-logging cameras raise a number of ethical and legal concerns. The people in front of the user may not be aware of being photographed by that little tool which looks, more or less, like a tag or a small iPod. On one occasion, for instance, I was able to walk across a metal detector in an airport with my camera 'capturing' the whole process. So, in what way does it distinguish itself from a CCTV camera (for which there are clear principles and laws)? From this point of view, Narrative resembles other technological items, such as the cameras which can be placed on the dashboard of a car and record everything that happens in the traffic and, at times, also the actions of the driver.

I will get back to the political and ethical implications of these technologies in the conclusions. For the moment, let me instead point out the extent to which the features of the Narrative Clip that I have described so far resonate with some of the broader conceptual transformations that have been debated in the context of contemporary image-making practices. In the first place, this camera seems to materialize the instances of bifocality that Peters (1997) described, some time ago, in terms of ongoing dialogues between the local and the global. According to Peters, our experience of the world, today, is constantly mediated by technologies of representation (he uses the examples of the satellite maps used in weather forecasts). Such representations make us constantly aware of who we are in relation to the context in which we live. A phenomenon that is presently embodied by the various forms of emplacement that the integration of image technologies with GPS positioning have made possible (cf. Lapenta 2011: Pink & Hjorth 2012), this aspect is present in the very functioning of the Narrative Clip, which transforms the banality of a regular day at work into an ongoing process of representation. However, pushing Peters' insight further, the Narrative Clip shows us that, in the present age, we are not only constantly being represented but also capable of representing. In fact, while CCTV cameras, satellite imaging and weather forecasts have made us aware of the fact that we are the object of constant monitoring, mobile phone cameras (and ultimately life-logging cameras) stimulate our agency as producers of images, our capacity to 'picture' (Heidegger 1977) and, hence, potentially to dominate the world surrounding us (cf. McQuire 1998).[9] Resonating with one of the fundamental insights on vision (described by, among others, Berger 1972 and Barthes 1977 but also by phenomenological inspired scholars such as Pinney 2001), Narrative reminds us that vision is a reciprocal, dialogical fact and that the act of seeing always corresponds to that of being seen. The Narrative Clip is one of the tools now making us realize that we are, ourselves, part of the visible world.

GoPro: materiality and the opening of the image to the senses

Let me now switch to another technology that embodies a different form of engagement with the mundane. I must warn the viewer that I have now to briefly shift away from photography proper and into that blend of photography and video that characterizes much of image-making in a digital landscape. Action cameras were launched in the world of extreme sports and were originally designed to allow the production of images in conditions and places that would not permit the use of regular cameras. The famous GoPro, for instance, one of the leading companies in the sector and the camera that I will use here to exemplify my reflections, was designed by founder Nick Woodman, in 2002, in order to film the practice of surfing from the point of view of the surfers themselves. It responded to the need to immerse (metaphorically and physically) the camera in a place and a moment that could not be captured otherwise, at least not in the absence of impressive technological and infrastructural investments. Technically, the GoPro produces HD videos and photographs in different formats. It mounts a fixed lens, capable of capturing a 170-degree angle, and can be paired up with another similar device in order to produce 3D images as well. Mounting a shield, protecting it from water (to a depth of 40 metres), scratches and bumps, GoPro cameras can be mounted on the body of the user with the help of straps, thus generating, similarly to the Narrative Clip, an interesting intimacy between body and device.

From being a niche product, GoPro (along with other similar cameras) quickly took the market by storm and became a proper consumer item. Costing between €250 and €450, it is, in fact, available to a quite large proportion of the population today. Combined with its easy functioning (similarly to the Narrative Clip, the user does not need to be a professional) it contributes to the popularization of filming possibilities that were, once upon a time, available only to a limited crowd of specialists. Recently, professional film-makers have increasingly adopted the camera, too, and, among them, Harvard-based ethnographic film-making duo Lucien Taylor and Verena Paravel. Their multiple award-winning documentary *Leviathan* offers a sensorial exploration of the world of open sea fishing. We are offered images of fishermen enduring the hardship of life on the boat, along with an ongoing exploration of the natural world surrounding them. Fishes and men, it could be said, are both equally at the centre of this film and this has been made possible thanks to the use of the GoPro. Taylor and Paravel creatively engaged with the camera (actually, as I was informed by members of the sensory lab, with a large number of GoPro cameras, many of which were lost during filming), inserting it in a variety of different situations. They mounted it on to the bodies of some of the fishermen, thus allowing observation of a set of delicate and potentially dangerous operations that would hardly have allowed for the presence of a cameraperson. They also mounted it on various bars on the boat, to offer us glimpses of the sea and of that thin line separating the sea and the water. In this way, we are offered the opportunity to gaze at the sea, with its wondrous living creatures and, during fishery, also animal debris. In some shots, we see the boat from the perspective of the sea and are invited to, in a way, immerse ourselves in the blood resulting from the first process of cleaning and selecting the fishes. We also follow the fishes from close quarters, as they go through this process of selection, and have some magnificent shots of seagulls following the nets in the hope of finding some food, as well as 'wet', 'hazy' images of the fishermen in the showers. David MacDougall suggested that there is something 'cosmic' about this film.[10]

Basically, we may conclude that the GoPro camera supported Taylor and Paravel in their in-depth, sensorial exploration of open sea fishing. It allowed them to offer a unique window on to a world otherwise out of reach for most human beings (thereby living up to the broader objective of documentary film-making in general). What appealed to me, during a first viewing of *Leviathan*, was the extent to which these cameras allowed the generation of images which went beyond conventions of movement in documentary film-making. Lying there, amidst the fishes or in the sea, the camera is not guided by the intentions of the film-maker but rather by its various engagements with the materiality of the elements surrounding it. This, I also experimented with personally, during my first engagements with this camera. As for most other users, I guess, I felt, right after purchase, immediately compelled to throw the camera straight into the water and experience, by letting it hang with a cord, its way of engaging with water, with sea weed, etc. In *Leviathan*, interesting movements are generated when the camera is mounted on to the fishermen. Here, we are offered images that move according to the needs of the fishermen and not the conventions of cinema (there is, for instance, an overload of canted images in this film).

We are, in other words, offered a series of 'unconventional' yet very revealing point-of-view shots, centring on the fishermen (and also on fishes, the water and on the boat itself). In these moments, the camera functions like an opening, a window on to the other senses. We experience the frailty of balance on a boat oscillating between the waves, the anxiety of the fishermen reflected in their breathing, the sounds that they produce and receive from their own vantage point. We are offered a quite unique sensorial experience of life on a ship. Interestingly enough, the GoPro captured my attention for its capacity to re-produce sounds that are, once again, hardly ever captured with 'prosumer' technologies. This is true for the underwater scenes in *Leviathan*, where our attention is caught by the sound of the water, the squishy noise of the fishes, etc. This was also achieved through my own experimentation with the camera, in an entirely different type of context. I have, in fact, used GoPro cameras in the context on a project focusing on a tennis coach and his teaching methods (see Figure 13.1).

For this project, I mounted cameras on top of players' heads or on their chests whilst they trained. This allowed me to gain a particular perspective on the choices of timing that they make on court (how and when they move in relation to an arriving ball, etc.) and portray one specific activity from the point of view of the subject performing it, that would be difficult to capture in the absence of these cameras. What caught my attention the most, however, was the players' breathing patterns. I have noticed when they inhale and exhale, and when and how they use their voice (shouting) for coordinating their game, etc. The proximity of the camera to the body of the user thus highlights the coming together of the senses, the way in

Figure 13.1 Still from a videoclip taken with a GoPro camera mounted on the head of a player (source: photograph by Paolo Favero, I acknowledge the support of coach Giampaolo Coppo who let me involve his players in my experiments).

which their act of viewing the ball merges with that of touching and feeling it and also with the sounds produced by the body. In the context of a sport such as tennis, GoPro cameras are, in fact, still too bulky and interrupt the spontaneous flow of the body. Nonetheless, they open up a space of exploration, through audio-visual means, that was previously not available to us. In the context of my own work, as in *Leviathan*, the GoPro camera has been functional for opening (to paraphrase MacDougall) a 'pathway to the other senses' (MacDougall 1997, pp. 289). As a tool, it allows us to engage with the materiality of life amidst the most diverse range of situations, closing, by melding with the body of the user, the distance between the image and the sensorial texture of everyday life.

Let me point out that today there are many other tools that offer an opportunity for a closer sensorial exploration of the things surrounding us. Macro and fish eye lenses that can be mounted on top of our smartphones can now be purchased at very cheap prices and reveal to us fascinating aspects that escape the human eye and conventional cameras too. This is the case with the photograph in Figure 13.2, which I took with my iPhone and the help of a mobile cam macro lens.

Conclusions

The discussion above has shown how the Narrative Clip and the GoPro camera constitute two different modalities through which contemporary

Figure 13.2 Photograph of a snail taken with a macro lens mounted on an iPhone 5 (source: photograph by Paolo Favero).

image-making technologies enter the texture of everyday life. I suggest that such technologies (and the practices associated with them) show the extent to which contemporary image-making digital technologies are character-ized by what we could call a 'material turn', that is happening alongside (or, rather, within) what Uricchio (2011) called the 'algorithmic turn'. While the latter (which is more closely connected to the notions of digitiza-tion that I mentioned at the beginning of this chapter) seems to have largely dominated the debate on digital imaging, in the present day we must acknowledge the co-existence of this material shift. This is no longer the age of digitization but that of analogization, of a process of increasing attention and production of material instances that is happening within (and not in opposition to) a digital habitat. Parallel to the variety of algorithm-driven virtual reproductions of the 'real' (see, for instance, the much debated Photosynth software or the Oculus Rift immersive virtual reality goggles), we are now witnessing the 'real' reproduction of the virtual.

Introducing the act of image-making in a context defined by notions of wearability and bodily proximity, the cameras that I have discussed here seem to ask us to suspend some of the conventions that characterize our ways of engaging with (and understanding) the act of making pictures. Devoid of viewfinders, they cut off the intentionalities of the film-maker. Foregrounding mimesis rather than interpretation, they diminish the importance of notions of proper framing, composition, timing, etc., that is, the conventions associated with photography and film-making. This decentring can result, at times, in a creative process offering the image-maker new unexpected perspectives. In fact, the user does not know exactly what they have 'captured' with this camera until we import the images to the laptop. As one film-maker using GoPro told me, 'it feels a bit like going back to the past: you film and only at night you discover what you have actually done'.

In the context of both the GoPro and the Narrative Clip, it is the body of the user that functions as a viewfinder, determining what will be contained and what will be excluded by the image. The body is literally the eye of the camera. In a paradoxical way, rather than functioning as prostheses of our bodies, Narrative Clip and GoPro seem to ask our bodies to become prostheses of the camera, thus inverting the process that Mac-Luhan anticipated decades ago. The manner in which these cameras seem to close down the distance between the image and the world surrounding it (which depends upon a combination of wearability and the use of short lenses) also seems to resonate well with ongoing trends in online digital photography, which are characterized by the increasing portrayal of domesticity, of whatever is in close proximity to the user. Instagram, for instance, is a gallery of coffee mugs, feet and half-eaten dinner plates, etc. As Murray (2008, p. 151) has suggested, photography has started dealing with 'an immediate, rather fleeting display of one's discovery of the small and mundane (such as bottles, cupcakes, trees, debris, and architectural elements'.

There are some major differences between the Narrative Clip and the GoPro. The particularity of the former is that it inserts, through the principle of the time-lapse on which its functioning is centred, the act of picture-taking into everyday life, as a somewhat random activity defined by time. This, too, mirrors another central feature of contemporary digital photography, which can be exemplified by the sharing and viewing practices which characterize common usage of Flickr, Facebook, Twitter and Instagram. Here, photography, rather than appearing as a technology for preserving time or, to use Bazin's (1967) term, for 'embalming' it, serves the purpose of creating a shared simultaneous experience of time, for the creation of what Ito long ago called a 'visual co-presence' (2005). This shift sums up what MacQuire suggested when he wrote that today '[p]hotography is becoming less about capturing "memories" (as Kodak famously phrased it in the 20th century) than about commenting on present events as they are taking place' (McQuire 2013, pp. 226). Similarly to Instagram, Facebook, etc., Narrative Clip foregrounds time as the conceptual centre on which our engagement with images is centred. This happens both at the level of production and of viewing. Besides taking pictures at regular time intervals, the Narrative Clip also forces the viewer to explore the images taken through a time-defined structure. The images are, in the first place, viewed in the form of a video clip made of individual stills.[11] Second, such moments can be posted, similarly to Instagram, Facebook, etc., on the basis of a timeline (with the newest elements on top and the oldest at the bottom), thus foregrounding their 'ephemerality', to use Murray's (2008) term.

The scenario opened up by the GoPro is, instead, characterized by issues of sensoriality and by a playful entanglement between the camera and the material environment surrounding it. The GoPro, as demonstrated through the examples of *Leviathan* and of my own experimentation on the tennis court, allows the image-maker to capture sensorial information that centres on the body of the subjects filmed. Hence, it enters places that were previously out of reach, making accessible to amateur viewers and image-makers alike, a world that was previously out of sight. Through the GoPro (and also the macro lenses that I described above), the act of image-making seems to be given back that magical, transcendental connotation that, according to Benjamin (1931) was at the core of the history of photography. According to him, photographers were, in fact, the descendants of the augurs and haruspices, and the camera a tool for entering the 'optical unconscious', opening up a new perception of the environment surrounding us.[12]

As these lines may have suggested, the technologies I have addressed in this chapter do not only constitute an opportunity to glance towards the future but also to rethink critically the past and to reinsert it in our present analysis. Rather than pulling us out of the history of photography (and film-making) and into an unknown terrain, contemporary technologies seem to bring the notions and debates regarding the meaning of photographs that have lain at the centre of the study of visual culture, back to our attention. I have also shown how such a re-evaluation requires a capacity to bring the analytical tools belonging to this field in touch with those belonging to material and digital culture.

Let me now go back to where I started from, that is, from the world of digital culture. The progressive engagement with the body and with the material texture of everyday life that I have identified in this chapter is mirrored in the cultural history of cybernetics. Hayles (2010, p. 148) has, for instance, suggested how 'Instead of constructing virtual reality as a sphere separate from the real word, today's media have tended to move out of the box and overlay virtual information and functionalities onto physical locations and actual objects.' The present age, she suggests, is characterized by the coming together of the animal, the machine and the human (the fish eye shots of fish eyes and humans contained in *Leviathan* nicely symbolize this). So, as this chapter has hopefully made clear, this is no longer the era of virtualization but one in which the material and the virtual meet and mingle, giving birth to new (at times curious) tools and practices. Besides positing interesting theoretical challenges, this progressive confluence is, however, also raising a series of crucial political and ethical questions. The desire to constantly 'picture' (Heidegger 1977) and explore, in greater detail, the world surrounding us does seem to translate itself, paradoxically, not just into an exercise of freedom (containing the seeds of a future cyber democracy) but also into an act of monitoring the world in which we live.

The disquieting question we must ask is: on behalf of whom is this monitoring enacted? MacLuhan ([1964]/1994) anticipated this question long ago when, commenting upon audio-visual media, he feared that our eyes, ears, hands, etc., no longer belonged to the bodies they were attached to but rather to the multinational companies they are connected to. This is what the Apple Watch seems to represent: a window on to a possibly post-post-modern, decentred Panopticon (or Plenopticon).

In *Discipline and Punish*, Foucault (1977) showed us how, in the passage from Renaissance to modernity, the relation between vision and power had changed significantly. In pre-modern times, the fact of 'being looked at, observed, described in detail ... was a privilege' (p. 191), he suggested. This is nicely embodied by the Hall of Mirrors at Versailles or by the tradition of royal parades (i.e. those moments in which the King would give the people the right to look at him, exercising, simultaneously, his right to be looked at).

In the Modern Age, however, the hierarchy of this relationship was reversed. The act of looking became synonymous with control, monitoring and, consequently, with discipline. This is what Bentham's Panopticon was about. An innovative, more functional and humane way of building a jail, this was a model for disciplining society through vision. In this context, the King no longer had to be looked at but was rather the subject who looked at others. Metaphorically seated at the centre of the Panopticon, he progressively transfigured himself into a kind of Big Brother, seen by no one but able to see everyone. Applying this metaphor to the contemporary context, we may wonder where the King is located and what rights and obligations he has today. No longer the object of a privileged gaze or, himself, an active observer, he (or she? or it?) may, perhaps, be gently leaning back on a throne of big data, relaxing as we monitor and discipline each other in our ongoing playful orgy of visual co-presence.

Notes

1 Research for this chapter has been made possible thanks to the generous grant awarded by the Science Foundation – Flanders (FWO) for the project 'Defying Social Invisibility: A Transnational Study of Empowerment and Social Intervention in the Field of Contemporary Digital Imagining Practices' hosted by the Visual and Digital Cultures Research Center (ViDi), University of Antwerp, Belgium.
2 http://3dprintshow.com/home-2014/, viewed 10 January 2015.

3 Mention should also be made of the way in which US-based company Jawbone used their fitness tracker, a bracelet pedometer/sleep-tracking device, to study the behaviour of people living in the area struck by an earthquake of magnitude 6.0 in Northern California on the 24 August 2014.
4 www.electricfoxy.com/move/, viewed 20 October 2015.
5 This is emblematized by the newly designed payment method that can be easily accessed through the Watch itself.
6 I cannot resist pointing out how the name 'Apple Watch' contains a kind of omen of its desire to control the user, rather than letting them control it.
7 At the time this chapter is going to press, news is spreading that the Google Glass may soon be back on the market again.
8 Foregrounding the habitual movements of the body of the user, as a kind of viewfinder, it also constitutes the final form of disentanglement of the photographer's gaze and that of the camera, completing the transformation that was started by the introduction of LCD screens on digital cameras.
9 As McQuire (1998) suggests, when we photograph from afar we get used to the idea that not only can we take possession of that far away view but, also, that someone else from a far away position can view us and take possession of us through their own view.
10 Personal communication.
11 The viewing of images as moving-image blurs the boundary between photography and video, which is another key characteristic of digital imaging (see Favero 2013).
12 Pinney summed this question up by saying that technology 'suggests the apparatus of the camera and its chemical way of referring to the world. Magic suggests a contagion of qualities and the ability to produce effects beyond the range of ordinary bodies' (Pinney 2001, p. 12).

References

Barthes, R. 1977, *Image Music Text*. Fontana Press: London.
Bazin, A. 1967, *What is Cinema?* Trans. H. Gray. University of California Press: Berkeley, CA.
Benjamin, W. 1931, 'A Short History of Photography', viewed 15 October 2015, http://monoskop.org/images/7/79/Benjamin_Walter_1931_1972_A_Short_History_of_Photography.pdf.
Berger, J. 1972, *Ways of Seeing*. Penguin: London.
Bush, V. 1945, 'As We May Think'. *Atlantic Monthly*, July.
Crary, J. 1990, *Techniques of the Observer: On Vision and Modernity in the Nineteenth Century*. MIT Press: Cambridge, MA.
Favero, P. 2014, 'Learning to Look Beyond the Frame: Reflections on the Changing Meaning of Images in the Age of Digital Media Practices'. *Visual Studies*, Vol. 26, no. 2, pp. 166–179.
Favero, P. 2013, 'Getting our Hands Dirty (Again): Interactive Documentaries and the Meaning of Images in the Digital Age'. *Journal of Material Culture*, Vol. 18, no. 3, pp. 259–277.
Foucault, M. 1977, *Discipline and Punish: The Birth of the Prison*. Random House: New York.
Gere, C. 2005, *Digital Culture*. Reaktion Books: London.
Grossman, L. & Vella, M. 2014, 'How Apple is Ivading our Bodies'. *Time*, 10 September, viewed 18 January 2016, http://time.com/3318655/apple-watch-2/.

Haraway, D. 1991. 'A Cyborg Manifesto: Science, Technology, and Socialist-Feminism in the Late Twentieth Century', in D. Harraway, *Simians, Cyborgs and Women: The Reinvention of Nature*. Routledge: New York, pp. 149–181.

Hayles, N. K. 2010, 'Cybernetics', in W. J. T. Mitchell & M. B. N. Hansen (eds) *Critical Terms for Media Studies*. University of Chicago Press: Chicago, IL, pp. 145–156.

Heidegger, M. 1977, 'The Age of the World Picture', in M. Heidegger *The Question Concerning Technology and Other Essays*. Harper: New York, pp. 115–154.

Ito, M. 2005, 'Intimate Visual Co-Presence', viewed 5 May 2015, www.itofisher.com/mito/archives/ito.ubicomp05.pdf.

Lapenta, F. 2011, 'Geomedia: On Location-Based Media, the Changing Status of Collective Image Production and the Emergence of Social Navigation Systems'. *Visual Studies*, Vol. 26, no. 1, pp. 14–24.

Nichols, B. 2000, 'The Work of Culture in the Age of Cybernetic Systems', in T. Caldwell (ed.) *Electronic Media and Technoculture*. Rutgers University Press: New Brunswick, NJ, pp. 90–114.

MacDougall, D. 1997, 'The Visual in Anthropology', in M. Banks & H. Morphy (eds) *Rethinking Visual Anthropology*. Yale University Press: New Haven, CT, pp. 276–295.

McLuhan, M. [1964]/1994, *Understanding the Media: The Extensions of Man*. MIT Press: Cambridge, MA.

McLuhan, M. & Fiore, Q. 1967, *The Medium is the Massage*. Penguin: London.

McQuire, S. 2013, 'Photography's Afterlife: Documentary Images and the Operational Archive'. *Journal of Material Culture*, Vol. 18, no. 3, pp. 223–241.

McQuire, S. 1998, *Visions of Modernity: Representation, Memory, Time and Space in the Age of the Camera*. Sage: London.

Mirzoeff, N. 1999, *An Introduction to Visual Culture*. Routledge: London.

Murray, S. 2008, 'Digital Images, Photo-Sharing, and Our Shifting Notions of Everyday Aesthetics'. *Journal of Visual Culture*, Vol. 7, no. 2, pp. 147–163.

Peters, J. D. 1997, 'Seeing Bifocally: Media, Place, Culture', in J. Ferguson & A. Gupta (eds) *Culture, Power and Place: Explorations in Critical Anthropology*. Duke University Press: Durham, NC, pp. 75–92.

Pink, S. & Hjorth, L. 2012, 'Emplaced Cartographies: Reconceptualising Camera Phone Practices in an Age of Locative Media'. *Media International Australia*, no. 145, pp. 145–155.

Pinney, C. 2001, 'Piercing the Skin of the Idol', in C. Pinney & N. Thomas (eds) *Beyond Aesthetics: Art and the Technologies of Enchantment*. Berg Publishers: London, pp. 157–179.

Ritchin, F. 1990, *The Coming Revolution in Photography: How Computer Technology is Changing our View of the World*. Aperture: New York.

Rosen, P. 2001, *Change Mummified: Cinema Historicity, Theory*. University of Minnesota Press: Minneapolis, MN.

The Economist. 2014, 'An Uncommon Thread. Conductive Fibres: From Lighter Aircraft to Electric Knickers, Flexible Filaments Raise a Wide Range of Interesting Possibilities'. *The Economist*, viewed 28 March 2014, www.economist.com/news/technology-quarterly/21598328-conductive-fibres-lighter-aircraft-electric-knickers-flexible-filaments.

Uricchio, W. 2011, 'The Algorithmic Turn: Photosynth, Augmented Reality and the Changing Implications of the Image'. *Visual Studies*, Vol. 26, no. 1, pp. 25–35.

Wellman, B. 2001, 'Physical Place and Cyber Place: The Rise of Networked Individualism'. *International Journal of Urban and Regional Research*, Vol. 25, no. 2, pp. 227–252.

14 Photo-genic assemblages

Photography as a connective interface

Edgar Gómez Cruz

Introduction: new photographic practices in everyday life

A few months back I went to a restaurant in London with some friends. The restaurant was a trendy Mexican place in Soho, with colourful walls and tables. We had a lovely dinner and, while we were eating, we noticed how normal it was, for the rest of our fellow diners (and us), to use photography as part of the commensal practices. Some people took photos of the food and posted them on Instagram, I took a photo of the menu to send it to a friend in Mexico and a couple of enthusiastic young women did some 'duckface' selfies and shared them on Facebook. During the dinner, we noticed a sticker on one of the corners of the table. The sticker, a small, colourful QR code surrounded by the words 'scan, type, tap … pay instantly', caught our attention. One of my friends spent some time during the dinner installing and setting up an app[1] on his mobile. When the dinner was over, he took a photo of the QR code with his smartphone and exclaimed 'Done! Let's go!'.

If we observe from the outside, my friend performed exactly the same action as the rest of the people on the other tables: he took his smartphone, pointed it at something on the table and clicked. Nevertheless, the result of this same action was ontologically different. My friend did not capture a nice moment, or share an experience in real time; what my friend was doing, when he 'pressed the button', was paying the bill.

Photography, as we have understood it for more than a century, has radically changed and we are still in the process of those changes becoming stabilized. The restaurant anecdote presents just some of the myriad new ways in which photo-technologies are shaping radically different photo-practices from those of analogue photography in everyday life. The opening point of this chapter is that digital photography is shaping different 'assemblages of visuality' (see Wise 2013) from those of its photo-chemical predecessor. I understand 'assemblage' following Latour's (1990) ideas of a fixed arrangement between technologies, practices and discourses. In the analogue era, the technologies (cameras, film rolls, labs), the everyday practices (photographing special and specific moments and subjects), the discourses about photography ('Holidays are Kodak days', 'all outdoors invite your Kodak', 'The world is mine – I own a Kodak', etc.) and the resulting images (photographs) created a fixed arrangement, an 'assemblage', that we knew as 'Kodak Culture' (see Sarvas & Frohlich 2011). New technologies, practices and discourses regarding digital photography are modelling radically different assemblages from those founded in classical studies of photography, from the social sciences perspective. These new assemblages are still in the process of stabilization and this is important because, following Hand, image-making practices in the digital era had become a 'compelling territory for understanding the dynamics of digital media and society' (2012, p. 4).

It is not uncommon, on any kind of public transport, to see people using the photographic capabilities of phones as mirrors (or taking photos of their faces or hair, in order to share how they look with others), or as a visual notebook (instead of taking notes in class or, in a presentation, using the camera to photograph slides,[2] or taking a quick snapshot of a shopping list). Camera phones, as an 'always-in-sight' instrument, shapes a practice that becomes part of any other experience, on a daily basis (take, for example, concerts, which have become an ocean of small screens harvesting images). It would probably be safe to affirm that, for many people, photography is a more commonly used function of the mobile phone than making a call, and it is equally safe to say that people are taking more photos with mobile phones than with other kinds of camera. The audio capabilities of mobile phones seem to be less important than the visual ones. Photography has gone from being a medium for the collection of important memories to an interface for visual communication. What I want to stress in this text is that vernacular uses of photo-technologies are incorporating practices that move away, not only from traditional uses of photography, but even from representational realms. Photography is increasingly being used as an interface, without even involving an image.[3]

Although there are many accounts of new photography practices and there is still a need for further ethnographic research, this chapter proposes that the 'black box' which vernacular photography used to represent has been opened and not only are photographic practices changing but the entire social meaning of photography is in the process of being reassembled (see also Lehmuskallio, in this volume). It has been clearly stated that we are no longer part of a *Kodak Culture* (see Sarvas & Frohlich 2011; Gómez Cruz 2012). I want to take this argument further and propose that vernacular photography practices are increasingly becoming algorithmic and a source of metadata, while expanding their function as depictions and representations. At the same time, I want to show how this *Kodak Culture*, as one possible assemblage, reinforced the idea that photography always has to be a representation of something.

This chapter looks to analyse some uses of photographic technology, especially with mobile phones (and tablets), that are not based on a semiotic/indexical use of photography but on a photo-algorithm assemblage. I want to describe these practices as 'imageless interfaces'. The ultimate goal of this chapter is to discuss how photographic technologies are increasingly being used not (only) as a representation or performance but as a techno-visual interface between objects, information, networks, environments, databases and people.

This chapter represents the continuation of an ongoing consideration of photographic practices (Gómez Cruz 2012), beyond representation (Gómez Cruz & Ardèvol 2013), that form sociotechnical networks (Gómez Cruz & Meyer 2012), and is based on a new ethnographic study on photography and an emergent project on screen-based cultures and visual mediations. The study and the project both combine visual research, Science and Technology Studies (STS), material culture and practices, focusing on mediation as a key concept.

Before I jump into my central idea, I want briefly to trace two interconnected scenarios that I consider relevant as the bases from which to unfold the central idea of this text. In the first scenario I want to propose a deconstruction of the idea of (vernacular) photography as a single and unique ontology and present it, instead, as a specific assemblage (one of many possible assemblages). The *Kodak Culture* – which is to say a set of practices, a business model and a set of technologies – was a specific stabilization of photography that, almost a century later, has been disrupted due to digital practices. In the second scenario I want to present, equally briefly, the new landscape that digital practices open, focusing on new practices within photography which form the context where the use of photography as interface is taking shape. These two discussions will serve as the basis for my later argument that digital photography practices are forming new visual-digital assemblages that use vernacular 'image-making technologies' for radically different purposes from those of the analogue era. In order to understand this, I propose, following the work of Patrick Maynard, to understand photography as a technology currently under a process of destabilization.[4]

Destabilizing photography: assemblages and practices

'In its new technological environment, photography will be bent to new ends, while it struggles to retain its historically defined purposes' (Lister 2007, pp. 254–255). It is necessary, therefore, to begin by understanding that 'historically defined purposes' of photography were, indeed, the result of several alliances, specific historical contexts and discursive struggles that shaped different practices and technical innovations. To clarify this, I follow the social constructionist position of Hand when he argues that

> The histories, present and futures of every technology – in this case
> photography – are varied, multiple, contested and non-linear in

practice. When technologies do become stabilized, it is in the result of a social process rather than a progressive 'technical' development towards the most superior design, use or interpretation.

(2012, p. 53)

These stabilizations are not necessarily permanent and, specifically in the case of photography, they could be understood as a pendulum movement, constantly swinging through cyclical changes, which comprises knowledge and technologies to afford and constrain certain practices (e.g. higher mobility due to smaller cameras, democratization of photography at the beginning of the twentieth century, when the introduction of film rolls replaced the need for knowledge about chemical processes, etc.: see Gómez Cruz & Meyer 2012). Therefore, while 'new' photographic practices are in the process of becoming stabilized, image-making processes are an important example of how digital culture is being shaped because, following Kember and Zylinska's (2012) work, there are serious implications for how these practices could shape different forms of mediation. Therefore, by analysing the relationship between visuality and digitization, we could have 'the potential to reawaken and rework long-established social and political relations' (Ruppert, Law & Savage 2014).

In his work, Bijker proposes that 'one must study how technologies are shaped and acquire their meanings in the heterogeneity of social interactions' (1997, p. 6). Using this statement as inspiration, I want to use the notion of 'stabilization' to talk about how photography acquired certain meanings in relevant social groups 'in term of the modality's uses and its descriptions' (ibid., p. 87). This deconstruction of photography could aid an understanding of how digital technologies are forming new assemblages, rather than simply reconfiguring digital imagery as a 'new' version of the 'old' photography. This could be helpful, I suggest, to help us understand some wider changes in visual culture, mobility and digital mediations and, moreover, to help us in thinking about our own categories and concepts and their relevance for social scientists.

Photography, from its inception, functioned as a way of representing the world. Since the very beginning, within the context of a scientific, positivist understanding of the world, photography was responsible for preserving the truth of what it depicted and, as a 'new technology', it was understood as a tool to 'reflect' reality objectively. This epistemic connection shaped the different uses of photography but also created a 'trap', within which photography could only ever be an image, following in the wake of painting. As Sontag mentions in her important text 'The subsequent industrialization of camera technology only carried out a promise inherent in photography from its very beginning: to democratize all experiences by translating them into images' (1977, p. 7).

With the introduction of the Kodak camera and the creation of the amateur market for mass photography, different stabilizations formed assemblages that were reinforced through different practices and discourses. Several dichotomies and divisions began to emerge, mutually excluding diverse photographic practices from each other: professional/amateur, photography/snapshots, scientific/vernacular, artistic/documentary, fashion/ everyday, etc. Each of these fields encompassed its own divisions (in photo- graphic art, for example, genres were created: realistic/conceptual/portrait, etc.) and they shaped and were shaped by their own discourses (as the Kodak advertisement made clear: 'a holiday without a Kodak is a wasted holiday')[5] and its particular set of technologies (for example the specialized equipment used in medical or dental photography).

The vernacular use of photography in everyday life, as a memory device, as a 'souvenir' of happy and important moments, shaped that *Kodak Culture*.[6] Photography was considered an assemblage that always gener- ated images (photographs) and these images were recipients of memory and projected a notion of social cohesion by virtue of what they depicted, namely special and unique happy moments in life. As a practice, vernacular photography had clear codes, affordances, constraints and uses that remained more or less stable for almost a century, and that were analysed, in depth, in studies of photography and everyday life (Bourdieu 1990; Chalfen 1987; Hirsch 1997; Rose 2003). Nevertheless, and despite the clear connections with former practices, there have been numerous accounts of how the use of digital technology is transforming the tradi- tional role of photography in everyday life, especially with the emergency of the so-called 'camera phone' (Okabe 2004; Okabe & Ito 2006; Villi 2007; van House *et al.* 2005). What these new practices within digital technology seem to be achieving is the destabilization of photography as it was understood in the *Kodak Culture* (Sarvas & Frohlich 2011).

One of the key technologies in this process of destabilization has been the mobile phone. There is already an important and increasingly relevant corpus of work related to photography and mobile phones. Many common findings had already been reached by the pioneering studies of camera phones almost a decade ago (Villi 2007; Koskinen 2007; Okabe 2004). Okabe and Ito (2006), in an age prior to the introduction of smartphones, pointed out that camera phones were distinct from both cameras and phones, and it seems plausible to think that images produced with camera phones are different as well. Photos from a camera phone, they suggested, tend to be more ephemeral and therefore commonly used for connecting and communicating in real time and not as images to hold memories. One of the most successful photographic apps of recent times, Snapchat, a system used to send photo/video messages that are automatically deleted once they have been seen by the chosen recipient(s), takes this displace- ment as the core of its success. Snapchat has become a successful app by understanding (and pushing) new assemblages of photography as a com- municative device and not as a memory one. In the 'about us' section of the app, they claim 'The image might be a little grainy, and you may not look your best, but that's the point. It's about the moment, a connection between friends, and not just a pretty picture.' Importantly, this connection disappears once it has served its purpose.

Several of the aforementioned studies offered new perspectives from which to regard mobile photography as different from conventional photography, defining it as a 'visual communication' (Villi 2007), as 'connecting images' (Rantavuo 2008) or as 'mobile multimedia' (Koskinen 2007). What all these works have in common is their reflection upon the use of photography for non-traditional purposes, and particularly those related to the real-time temporality of image exchange. The important argument here is that vernacular photography began to change its role, from recording memories to being a connective mechanism. I want to take this argument further and move towards a reflection on the use of photographic technology in everyday life, beyond representation or depiction. I suggest that it would be useful to understand lens-based practices not only as photo-graphies, but as photo-interfaces. However, in order to understand this, we first have to understand photography as a technology.

Photography as a technology

It is surprising, or perhaps it could be understood as a challenge, that probably the biggest corpus of academic research on digital photography, to date, can be found in the informatics/electronics literature. Conferences and journals about human–computer interaction are filled with texts on photography. At the same time, in the social sciences, there is still a lack of studies about photography as a technology. Although there is an increasing interest in the affordances of camera phones in relation to their uses, there seems to be an important gap to be filled. Following Lister's invitation, we have to

> Consider how photography continues to be put to work within a cultural, institutional and even a physical landscape that is pervaded and altered by information and its technologies. It is, I argue; only by attending to change in photography's new technological context that some significant changes in major areas of photographic practice can be understood.
>
> (Lister 2007, pp. 252–253)

Following Lister's call, what this text seeks is to contribute to the understanding of 'the differences between chemical, digital, mobile, and smart … within interconnected histories of image cultures, habits of consumption, systems of production, image manipulation practices, and strategies for market domination' (Chesher 2012, p. 99). In order to do that, once I have presented the idea of photography as a changing assemblage based on innovations and practices, I suggest thinking about photography as a technology.

One of the most important reference points for understanding photography as a technology (or a series of photo-technologies, to be more accurate) is the work of Patrick Maynard. Maynard proposes that 'If the idea of photography as technology seems unfamiliar, the technology of photography is surely very familiar' (1997, p. 3). In his book *The Engine of Visualization*, Maynard also states that 'almost all writing about photography in our own times tends to begin with the alleged nature of the product rather than with its production and use' (ibid., p. 9). That is, 'Photography is understood in terms of *photos*, and photos are invariably understood relationally as being of things' (ibid., p. 15, my italics). What Maynard proposes, instead, is to focus on the photo-technologies and their relation to processes, and not on the resulting 'image', since 'in working toward an understanding of images and thereby of photography in terms of display functions, we are making a slightly stronger claim than that they have to be visible to do their jobs' (ibid., p. 27). Instead, he states 'we shall be investigating photography as a kind of technology for visual display: that is, surface-marking with visual intent' (ibid., p. 34). The move from understanding photography as images/indexes to understanding it as a process for surface-making-detection is key, since, as Maynard suggests, 'image' refers to a certain kind of marked surface, and 'imaging' any method for producing it. This concept will be useful for the purposes of this chapter, since it will allow us to focus our attention on the processes of surface-marking instead of focusing on the 'power of images' as the result of an even more powerful process. By doing this, we can better understand the connection of digital imaging with informational systems, for some of the practices that I will detail are photo based but, instead of resulting in an image, they create a non-depicting connection and function as an interface.

By focusing on image-making, Maynard connects with the primal discourses heralded by the earliest developments in photography, pointing out that 'early inventors and promoters such as William Henry Fox Talbot were prudent to draw attention not so much to a new class of objects [the photos] as to the diverse uses of a new set of technological procedures' (ibid., p. 9). It is interesting to note that, in fact, the process described by Fox Talbot was called 'photogenic drawing'. 'Photogenic', despite the current use of the word, literally means 'produced or precipitated by light', a 'photo-generated' process. This simple connection enables us to see how, in its origins, photography was understood as a process, rather than the result of that process. Images, therefore, were less important than the possibilities of this new technology of visualization. Understanding photography as a process and as a technology freed us from thinking about the photographic image as a semiotic unit and turns our attention to the exploration of the possible processes based on 'photogenic practices'. This is important because it could help us in thinking about the growing importance of the visual, not only as a device for knowledge production, communication, connectivity and the economy of signs, but also in the informational/automatized fabric of everyday life. What I suggest here is that one of the most important processes is precisely the increasing use of photography as an interface.

Photography as interface: QR codes as a case study

Following the anecdote that I used to open this text, I'll introduce the idea of photography as interface around one specific object: the QR Code. QR codes represent a great example of 'triggers or gateways between physical objects or places and the data of the internet' (Jones 2014, p. 40). Also, they are based on the photo-capabilities of mobile phones. QR codes are neither the only example nor the most important but, despite their success (or lack of it), they have two elements that are fundamental to understanding modern digital culture and the role of photo-technologies in it. On the one hand, they signal a growing characteristic of digital culture and are devices which 'mark the world and link it to data' (ibid., p. 40) and therefore, 'they nakedly reveal the gesture of connecting data with the physical world' (p. 46). On the other hand, they 'reveal *the cultural desire to make that gesture*' (p. 46, italics in the original). In this sense, they are probably the first widespread example of a growing trend. QR codes have become extremely common and we can find them everywhere: shopping malls, tourist destinations, information stands, government offices, business cards, delivery boxes, cinema tickets, etc. There are plenty of different examples of how QR codes are being used. I present a few, randomly, with the aim of demonstrating their commonalities.

When I was searching for a place to live in England, besides the usual online search, I walked to neighbourhoods that colleagues had suggested would suit my requirements. I found many 'To let' signs from housing agencies; most of these signs didn't have a phone or a contact address, just a small square with a QR code. My iPhone couldn't 'read' the information contained within the code because I didn't have a data plan. Also, I didn't have an app installed that was capable of 'reading' the 'photo'. Although I could take an image of the QR code with my camera phone, that image was useless for the purpose that the QR code was offering me. As with my friend in the restaurant, the same action with the same device could have results that were ontologically different. The photo-genetic process that connected my mobility and desire for information with the letting agencies was not possible, since I didn't have the right tools.

In a bookstore in San Francisco I saw a book that really interested me. Since I had two more weeks of travelling and had already bought some books, I decided that I wasn't purchasing that one. Nevertheless, since I did want that book, I opened the Amazon app and 'scanned' the barcode of the book. Automatically, I had access to the price, some reviews, etc.

With one click, I bought it. After leaving the book on the shelf, I took a picture of the book's cover and uploaded it to my Instagram/Facebook account with the caption 'buying'. When I got home, a couple of weeks later, the book was waiting for me at my office and I already had several 'likes' and comments on the *image* of the book. The same photo-technology used in both actions (and the same material object) mobilized different sociotechnical networks: one economic-material (buying the book after scanning the barcode) and one 'socio-visual' (sharing the image of the book I was buying).

The university gym updated their exercise machines and the new ones have a QR code that allows my mobile phone to engage in a data exchange between my body's performance with the machine, the overall and historical performance, and the motivational feeling of tracking fitness improvement or lost weight. The route to a 'quantified self' had its seed in an image of a QR code. These are quotidian examples of how

> QR codes *encode* in more than one sense – they stand as signs for an unspoken idea, the idea that the network and its data are connected to the grid of the physical world, and that those connections can be revealed by way of readily available, cheap, and ubiquitous acts of dimensional translation.
>
> (Jones 2014, p. 44)

Interestingly, this translation is based on activating the camera of the mobile phone and 'taking a picture'. In this sense, QR codes represent an important example of how digital photography practices in everyday life are turning into a complex, and sometimes opaque, set of processes (that, at the same time, could open a set of questions about surveillance and control due to geotagging, digital traces, etc.).

If we think about the common words we relate to photography, the QR code completely changes the game, since the camera of the phone did not take a photograph. Instead, what I did was to scan a code with my smartphone. Taking a photograph of a QR code shifts the agency in the encoding/decoding of the image from the user to the algorithm. The QR codes, as images, are obscure to me; they can only be decoded by a combination of an optical system, a sensor, an algorithm and an internet connection. The image from a QR code only becomes meaningful once the machine interprets it and the information is shown in my mobile browser. The result of this process is not a depiction based on a 'real' object, or even an image, it is a direct connection with a digital platform (a webpage, an app, etc.) that does not resemble, in any way, what I was pointing my phone at and seeing through the viewfinder.

Crary, in his influential text, proposes that 'most of the historically important functions of the human eye are being supplanted by practices in which images no longer have any reference to the position of an observer in a "real", optically perceived world' (1992, p. 2). Although Crary is referring more to computer-generated images, this argument could be easily translatable to photographic imagery that acts no longer as an observer or an extension of the eye and memory but as a real translator, aligned more with algorithms and code than with representation and vision per se (see Lehmuskallio, in this volume).

If, as Mitchell suggests, the saturation of images and widespread use of visual codes means that we need to develop new tools to understand this 'pictorial turn' (Mitchell 1995), the latest stage in this process seems to be represented by how camera phones are becoming 'an interface between user events of photography, and a particular set of possible visual and informational processes' (Chesher 2012, p. 98). We could expand this argument and think about how some uses of the smartphone's photo-capabilities are more related, in epistemological terms, to different kinds of images such as radiography or data visualizations, than to traditional snapshots.

Chris Chesher, in his text 'Between Image and Information: The iPhone Camera in the History of Photography', relates the potential combination of photo-technologies to computer processing, especially in the form of apps, and states that modern usage of the camera is going 'beyond its photographic heritage to use it as a data input device, collecting information instead of making conventional photos' (p. 107). By doing this, Chesher implies, the camera phone[7] turns 'into a multi-purpose input device ... in line with many other digital camera applications beyond amateur photography, from the battlefield to security cameras' (p. 111). The photogenic capabilities of the camera phone, Chesher continues, emerged from research in different realms (academic, military, commercial) into image analysis, face recognition and displays (p. 112; see also Kember 2014 on face recognition systems).

This means that photo-technologies are increasingly related to computational processes (Meyer 2008). Chesher himself describes specific apps, as examples, and several more could be described that work on the same principle: the image being an input for a computational process that has an output that is non-directly referential to the object photographed. This way, this photogenic interface enables new forms of mediation, or translators, between information systems and people: face recognition software, scanners (with sign or character recognition), images with GPS metadata, etc. This, inescapably, has broader consequences for knowledge/power systems. If apps such as Snapchat clearly change the idea of vernacular photography as a memory object with success, some other commonly used apps turn the camera into an interface.

Without the intention of creating a taxonomy or fully recounting all the possible apps, just for the sake of giving some examples we could mention successful apps such as *Evernote* (and its use of photos as a note archive), *Textgrabber* (which uses the camera as a scanner with character recognition), *Wordlens* (a translator, in real time, that uses the camera's features without taking any image) and *Instant Heart Rate* (a heart rate monitor that uses the camera to read blood pressure from the finger, as an interface with the body). These are just a few examples of successful apps that use the camera of the mobile phone as an interface.

This spectrum of practices is helpful in two ways. First, they establish a general visual-digital mediation research agenda (along with mobility, material culture, etc.). Second, they help us to consider photo-genic assemblages as part of what constitutes photography practices in everyday life, without focusing on the final image as a semiotic index, or its novelty with respect to past uses of photography.

Everyday photography and techno-visual regimes

Following the argument of understanding photography as an interface, Maynard (1989, p. 264) points out that

> Photographic pictures are an economical and widely used sort of picture, made by means of photographic processes. From this point of view there is no reason to suppose that they must depict at all: there are many which do not. Nor should we assume that, if they do depict, they must depict what they are photographs of.

By understanding photography as an assemblage of 'surface-marking technologies' we move away from a semiotic/indexical understanding of images and could increasingly relate everyday photography with other kinds of image-processes, for example scientific imagery. To understand X-rays or MRIs there's a need for specific expertise. This expertise is held by particular assemblages of people/technologies that turn an image into a 'readable' piece of information. This expertise becomes an elite code attached to knowledge regimes and sustained by power structures (Burri 2013).

Although this chapter is limited in its scope, the analysis of the relationship between image-based processes and knowledge regimes is very relevant and, therefore, it is important to notice how these new photo-genic assemblages could have an important impact on the formation (or further consolidation) of new techno-visual regimes. The relationship between photography and techno-visual regimes is long-standing in specific realms and 'scientific imagery often comes to us with confident authority behind it' (Sturken & Cartwright 2001, p. 279). Although scientific studies have been critical of this idea by showing how 'scientific looking is as culturally dependent as the other practices of looking' (ibid., p. 279), we still need research that relates this with sociotechnical practices of image-making in more vernacular ways. There are two important elements here: the first one, as Sturken and Cartwright suggest, is that the kind of possible knowledge changes with the technologies of mediation. The second important element is that, increasingly, vernacular uses of images require specific codes, not always representational, that reinforce certain power structures through elements such as surveillance or big data.

There is clearly an agenda for a sociology of visuality that goes beyond the representational understanding of depictions and that 'includes the social practices of constructing and using images in its analysis' (Burri 2012). Moreover, I suggest that we engage in understanding photo-technologies not only in relation to images, while, at the same time, we should not think about photographs in relation only to cameras (as Leh-muskallio clearly describes in this volume). This seems to be the key point, to focus on the processes and technologies involved in the creation of images that generate agency but that do not necessarily represent or depict anything. I want to stress the two elements that I consider key in this emerging agenda. The first point is to note that a photograph is not neces-sarily reduced to a mere depiction, and is increasingly inserted into a wider, more complex context, with different temporalities and elements (and this explains many of the current uses of photography in social media). The combination with text, links, mobilities and timing are now part of, or constantly shape, the 'image', while sometimes the specific 'code' used to understand the image is shared only by a specific group of people or technologies (as with X-rays, MRIs or art images). The second element, the one that I have tried to develop in this chapter, is that photo-technologies are increasingly becoming translators (in the literal sense but also in the Latourian one) between material objects, databases, people, etc. This means they are not just representations.

Conclusions

I have used QR codes as one example of how digital photography, com-bined with mobile devices and algorithmic affordances, are signalling new visual interfaces between consumption practices (material, economic, mobile, etc.), informational systems and photo-practices that are becoming increasingly integrated into the fabric of the everyday (see Hand 2012, ch. 2). The bottom-line for these new visual interfaces is that the output result-ing from a 'click' is, increasingly, not just an image but a connection as well – a connection that can be traced, measured and become part of data-bases. These connections are sometimes visual and between people (as the social studies of camera phones demonstrated), but also through codes, sensors and connections. These connections are capable of mobilizing dif-ferent relations, both digital and material. Therefore, these photo-genic practices shouldn't be analysed as a mere resemblance between an object and an image but understood as shared agencies. Photographic technology is forming new digital mediations that are increasingly part of the manage-ment of everyday life.

Although there has been a clear evaluation of how photographs stand for objects, bodies, etc., or of photographs as a material objects in themselves, there is still room to develop theoretical and empirical work on vernacular everyday photographs as techno-visual mediators, as links (or, more accurately, hyperlinks), between physical objects and the digital management of those objects. Such works have, traditionally, been approached in research about the scientific uses of images, but now they seem necessary to understand current practices with photo-technologies.

This is a call to think more about photography as a sociotechnical practice and less about photography as images, representations and depictions. If we think about photography as a sociotechnical practice in constant flux, with new technical affordances, changing environments and discourses about it, then we could save precious time researching how it is stabilized in different contexts instead of engaging in endless discussions about its ontology, its power to resemble the real and, ultimately, the division between analogue/digital or between traditional and new. Ultimately, photography has always been a photo-genetic assemblage with a series of consolidated meanings and practices. We are witnessing the rise of new ones and we should be trying to understand them. This chapter and this book are steps in that direction.

Notes

1 www.flypay.co.uk/
2 As an example, see Allain 2012.
3 Obviously, there remains a question as to whether these practices could still be called photography or not. Although it is a fundamental question, this text's aim is simply to signal how these practices are, indeed, photo-graphic, although non-representational.
4 Or, to be more accurate, a technology currently in the process of forming new stabilizations.
5 This argument could be extended to suggest that corporate discourses, through advertisement, shaped photographic practices.
6 For an historical analysis of how photographic technology was stabilized in different 'moments' see Gómez Cruz and Meyer (2012).
7 Although Chesher's reflections are particularly about the iPhone, nowadays they could be extended to all smartphones.

References

Allain, R. 2012, 'Should Students use Cameras in Class?' *Wired*, 11 May, viewed 9 October 2015, www.wired.com/wiredscience/2012/11/should-students-use-cameras-in-class/.

Bijker, W. E. 1997, *Of Bicycles, Bakelites, and Bulbs: Toward a Theory of Sociotechnical Change*. MIT Press: Cambridge, MA.

Bourdieu, P. 1990, *Photography: A Middle-Brow Art*. Polity Press: Cambridge, MA.

Burri, R. V. 2013, 'Visual Power in Action: Digital Images and the Shaping of Medical Practices'. *Science as Culture*, Vol. 22, no. 3, pp. 1–21.

Burri, R. V. 2012, 'Visual Rationalities: Towards a Sociology of Images'. *Current Sociology*, Vol. 60, no. 1, pp. 45–60.

Chalfen, R. 1987, *Snapshot Versions of Life*. Popular Press: Bowling Green, OH.

Chesher, C. 2012, 'Between Image and Information: The iPhone Camera in the History of Photography', in L. Hjorth, J. E. Burgess & I. Richardson (eds) *Studying Mobile Media: Cultural Technologies, Mobile Communication, and the iPhone*. Routledge: London, pp. 98–117.

Crary, J. 1992, *Techniques of the Observer: On Vision and Modernity in the Nineteenth Century*. MIT Press: Cambridge, MA.

Gómez Cruz, E. 2012, *De la Cultura Kodak a la Imagen en Red: Una Etnografía Sobre Fotografía Digital*. Editorial UOC: Barcelona.

Gómez Cruz, E. & Ardèvol, E. 2013, 'Performing Photography Practices in Everyday Life: Some Ethnographic Notes on a Flickr Group'. *Photographies*, Vol. 6, no. 1, pp. 35–44.

Gómez Cruz, E. & Meyer, E. T. 2012, 'Creation and Control in the Photographic Process: iPhones and the Emerging Fifth Moment of Photography'. *Photographies*, Vol. 5, no. 2. pp. 203–221.

Hand, M. 2012, *Ubiquitous Photography*. Polity Press: Cambridge.

Hirsch, M. 1997, *Family Frames: Photography, Narrative, and Postmemory*. Harvard University Press: Cambridge, MA.

Jones, S. E. 2014, *The Emergence of the Digital Humanities*. Routledge: London.

Kember, S. 2014, 'Face Recognition and the Emergence of Smart Photography'. *Journal of Visual Culture*, Vol. 13, no. 2, pp. 182–199.

Kember, S. & Zylinska, J. 2012, *Life after New Media: Mediation as a Vital Process*. MIT Press: Cambridge, MA.

Koskinen, I. 2007, *Mobile Multimedia in Action*. Transaction Publishers: Piscataway, NJ.

Latour, B. 1990, 'Technology Is Society Made Durable'. *Sociological Review*, Vol. 38, supp. 1, pp. 103–131.

Lister, M. 2007, 'A Sack in the Sand: Photography in the Age of Information'. *Convergence: The International Journal of Research into New Media Technologies*, Vol. 13, no. 3, pp. 251–274.

Maynard, P. 1997, *The Engine of Visualization: Thinking through Photography*. Cornell University Press: Ithaca, NY.

Maynard, P. 1989, 'Talbot's Technologies: Photographic Depiction, Detection, and Reproduction'. *Journal of Aesthetics and Art Criticism*, Vol. 47, no. 3, pp. 263–276.

Meyer, E. 2008, 'Framing the Photographs: Understanding Digital Photography as a Computerization Movement', in M. S. Elliot & K. L. Kraemer (eds) *Computerization Movements and Technology Diffusion: From Mainframes to Ubiquitous Computing*. American Society for Information Science and Technology, Medford, NJ, pp. 173–199.

Mitchell, W. T. 1995, *Picture Theory: Essays on Verbal and Visual Representation*. University of Chicago Press: Chicago, IL.

Okabe, D. 2004, 'Emergent Social Practices, Situations and Relations through Everyday Camera Phone Use'. Paper presented at the *Conference on Mobile Communication*, Seoul, Korea, 18–19 October 2004.

Okabe, D. & Ito, M. 2006, 'Everyday Contexts of Camera Phone Use: Steps Toward Technosocial Ethnographic Frameworks', in J. Höflich & M. Hartmann (eds) *Mobile Communication in Everyday Life: An Ethnographic View*. Frank & Timme: Berlin, pp. 79–102.

Rantavuo, H. 2008, *Connecting Photos: A Qualitative Study of Cameraphone Photo Use*. University of Art and Design: Helsinki.

Rose, G. 2003, 'Family Photographs and Domestic Spacings: A Case Study'. *Transactions of the Institute of British Geographers*, Vol. 28, no. 1, pp. 5–18.

Ruppert, E., Law, J. & Savage, M. 2014, 'Reassembling Social Science Methods: The Challenge of Digital Devices'. *Theory, Culture and Society*, Vol. 30, no. 4, pp. 22–46.

Sarvas, R. & Frohlich, D. 2011, *From Snapshots to Social Media: The Changing Picture of Domestic Photography*. Springer-Verlag: New York.

Sturken, M. & Cartwright, L. 2001, *Practices of Looking: An Introduction to Visual Culture*. Oxford University Press: Oxford.

Van Dijck, J. 2008, 'Digital Photography: Communication, Identity, Memory'. *Visual Communication*, Vol. 7, no. 1, pp. 57–76.

Van House, N., Davis, M., Ames, M., Finn, M. & Viswanathan, V. 2005, 'The Uses of Personal Networked Digital Imaging: An Empirical Study of Cameraphone Photos and Sharing'. Paper presented at the CHI '05 Extended Abstracts on Human Factors in Computing Systems, Portland, OR.

Villi, M. 2007, 'Mobile Visual Communication: Photo Messages and Camera Phone Photography'. *Nordicom review*, Vol. 28, no. 1, pp. 49–62.

Wikipedia. 2015, 'QR code', viewed 26 October 2015, http://en.wikipedia.org/wiki/QR_code.

Wise, J. M. 2013, 'Introduction: Ecstatic Assemblages of Visuality', in H. Koskela & J. M. Wise (eds) *New Visualities, New Technologies: The New Ecstasy of Communication*. Ashgate: Farnham, pp. 1–6.

15 The camera as a sensor

The visualization of everyday digital photography as simulative, heuristic and layered pictures

Asko Lehmuskallio

Introduction

In the course of empirical work on developer visions for networked camera use, I spoke with and listened to people who work with mobile, wearable and remotely controlled camera technology intended for everyday use, in order to learn how they think about a camera and what their understandings are of current and future camera uses.[1] Although some of these developers are particularly interested in photography, video or visual culture in general, others are not. One developer that I talked with, for example, emphasized that he uses cameras as sensors that allow for the recording of optical images that can be computationally transformed, but he was not interested in using these devices to create photographs or videos. Basically, he was interested in using the camera as a sensor among other sensors. He thereby questioned preconceived understandings of what mobile and wearable camera technology may be used for. Nevertheless, by using these cameras he did utilize digital photographic technology as 'an interface or part of a sequential process – in short, as a cue for action' (Elsaesser 2013, p. 241).

Work on media use has historically focused on people and how 'we' make sense of our devices at hand, how we domesticate them as part of our everyday or how we navigate with and around them. This is particularly important work but we need, also, to look at the other side of media use, that is to the ways the media we use is designed, built and implemented to elicit particular responses. Drawing explicitly from work focusing on the specifics of media, and how media play a part in organizing the social relations we take with and through them, we can contemplate the mediated relations we play out during our everyday lives. This perspective calls for understanding media as translators, transformers and modifiers of action, a perspective that does not take images, bodies or media as a given.[2]

From this perspective, the example above calls for looking more closely at the technical devices that are used for everyday photography, particularly since some of those developing this technology do not frame their work in terms of photography or video. How should we, then, understand photography as a mediator, as it is connected to computational devices, networks and developed for an increasing number of different uses? How should we frame the relation between digital photography, as a technology, and that of photographs as particular kinds of pictures? And what difference does it make that these pictures are created with computational technologies, instead of earlier, photochemical ones?

Cameras in mobile camera phones, worn on the body or controlled remotely, are increasingly developed for everyday use. Of these, mobile camera phones have rapidly become nearly ubiquitous already, such that in many places around the globe it is very likely that someone, or even everyone present, is carrying one (Hand 2012; Uimonen, in this volume). Wearable and remotely controlled cameras might, as developers hope, become a similar global success. Even today, camera devices are available that can be clipped to one's clothing, embedded in eyewear such as spectacles or contact lenses or even inserted into the eye.[3] Remotely controlled cameras may be installed in the home, a summer house or the workplace, attached to moving objects, such as flying drones, or placed on the head of a pet or child.[4] Remotely controlled cameras for everyday use are often controlled from a mobile phone, itself a camera device.

Whereas these cameras can be used to create 'film-like digital photographs',[5] they are also used for purposes that we may not immediately recognize as 'photographic'. The cameras are usually attached to devices that carry a range of other sensors, as is the case with mobile camera phones, where the other sensors provide additional information that can be captured during the use of the camera's image sensor, while the image sensor itself can be used for a variety of purposes, not limited to digital photographs. The recorded files can then be used for a host of purposes, including, but not limited to, rendering 'film-like digital photographs'.

Related social scientific work on everyday digital camera use tends to focus mainly on uses of cameras that are related to the idea of 'film-like digital photographs'. In the realm of everyday photography these are often studied as visual artefacts used for social bonding, presenting ourselves or used for memory purposes (Gye 2007). These uses have been stabilized, historically, into particular paths that have taken different form and have by no means been self-evident at the outset (cf. Sarvas & Frohlich 2011). Scholars share a great interest in the photographic pictures taken and shared, along with, as addressed particularly in recent works, the practices in which camera use is embedded (e.g. Larsen & Sandbye 2013). A clear tendency identified in recent analysis suggests the importance of digital photo use for real-time communication (Rantavuo 2008; Villi, in this volume). These studies are of particular importance for understanding uses of everyday digital photography, but they neglect the variety of 'non-film-like' uses that these devices are put to, whilst paying less attention to the diversity in photographic technology.

A practice theoretical perspective, as applied in this chapter, underscores the ways in which a focus on practices necessarily reorients our understanding of bodies and their relation to their environments. As bodies become part of practices, they also become part of particular constellations of objects, environments and understandings of 'how to' (Reckwitz 2002). In discussing the uses of photography, both photographic technology and the images and visualization techniques used provide one such area that plays its part in cueing everyday practices, connecting bodies with particular kinds of 'things'.

To uncover the variety in the technical development of wearable and remotely controlled cameras intended for everyday use, I question the usefulness of letting the idea of 'film-like digital photography' direct our focus. Instead, I suggest a processual description of photography, one that can be used in assessment of developments in wearable and remotely controlled camera technology. This description relies on a distinction suggested by Patrick Maynard (1997, p. 20), between photography as a set of technologies for creating and working with images 'on sensitized surfaces by means of light' and photographs as particular kinds of pictures that are visible to an observer. As I will argue later, photographs possess particular features that, on account of prior experience, we understand to be characteristic of photographs, but we do not always have the diagnostic criteria to hand for distinguishing how these photographs came to be and means of judging whether they have been met.

Turning to a case in point, I look more closely at one crucial aspect of the photographic process, namely, 'making surface markings visible'. Here, I consider the ways in which we get to see pictures created with wearable and remotely controlled cameras, building on the work of Gottfried Boehm (2007) in distinguishing the ways in which they refer to what they depict, in *simulative* or *heuristic* ways. This distinction is particularly useful for drawing attention to the different sets of everyday practices that these visualization techniques call for and thus underscores the roles that visualization techniques play in mediating our attention and subsequent actions. My empirical material on photographic visualizations calls for a third category, one which I call *layered pictures*, since, here, simulative and heuristic information is layered on top of each other. Dealing with heuristic or layered visualizations calls for a different set of everyday practices from the use of simulative pictures, in the following ways:

1   Simulative pictures refer, iconically, to an original setting by modelling a recognizable relation to it. Here, depicted objects are rescaled and particular characteristics are selected for display. This recognizable relation usually looks 'photographic' and the use of these kinds of pictures remains the most studied.

2   Heuristic pictures have an open referent that cannot be entered, which remains invisible or consists of abstractions. Particular relations are worked out by means of the files recorded with the aid of wearable or remotely controlled camera technology. For example, a database of

thousands of recorded images might be used for modelling social networks or geolocation information. Just like simulative pictures, heuristic pictures are rooted in camera technology but they look very different when rendered on a screen.

3　Many visualization techniques in use today frequently operate within a third category, which I call layered pictures, that fuses simulative and heuristic visualizations. These are increasingly commonplace in the use of wearable and remotely controlled camera technology. In this category, a simulative picture refers, iconically, to an original setting, and it is complemented by a heuristic one, providing additional information. These visualizations are often used, for example, for real-time navigational purposes, or when accessing vast image databases.

Dealing with a processual description of photography, alongside consideration of the varying ways in which images may be rendered visible, calls attention to the ways in which the optical images captured and the algorithms used within digital photography are intertwined and, in turn, play their part in reorienting how photography should be used and thought of.[6] *Predictive pictures* are a case in point. Using two examples, of traffic cameras and of face-recognition technology embedded into consumer-grade cameras, I pinpoint the importance of focusing on materiality alongside visuality. A focus on the images alone does not yield information about the range of computational connections the images actually allow for.

When going through the description of the photographic process, we see that each phase can be computationally modelled and, in fact, many developers focus in their work on one part of the process, such as the creation of novel ways of depicting a scene or new methods for displaying the images captured. The focus in development on one part of the process is usually warranted due to the change in practices that developers are seeking. Many are keen on providing their technical solution instead of earlier, already available ones. If successful, the software developed, or the material artefacts constructed, may become pivotal in changing how millions of people 'do photography'.

My perspective has developed in line with recent calls for a material turn in studies of visual culture (e.g. Rose & Tolia-Kelly 2012; Were 2013), and it benefits from discussions with colleagues in numerous disciplines, including those developing digital camera technology within computer science. From this perspective, the focus on medium-specific differences and possible agencies that media[7] take in social interaction are considered important, especially since much of the technology used is black-boxed from lay users of photographic technology as well as from the scrutiny of competing camera developers. In contrast to some recent work on medium-specificity, I maintain that a medium-specific approach should not neglect the role of the image as a nexus that aids us in understanding the production, use and distribution of pictures in the first place (see also Lister and Van House in this volume). Here, I find that images, within the digital realm, can be usefully analysed as interfaces, as is suggested by Thomas Elsaesser (2013) and by Gillian Rose, Monica Degen and Clare Melhuish (2014). Doing so allows us to pay attention to how networked images connect various stakeholders to each other, in a way, coupling particular people and their actions with each other. Similarly, this piece is also a call to take the importance of visuality into account, if one is to understand why pictures are used instead of other modes of communication, such as speech, text or sound. The 'iconic difference' (Boehm 1994), or surplus value of images (Mitchell 2005), has to be considered, as well as the interrelations between images, body and media as they impact on how we live our everyday lives (Belting 2001).[8] A focus on material and visual practices is particularly useful for understanding how various media matter in everyday life (see Rose & Tolia-Kelly 2012 and the Introduction to this volume).

By learning from developers of digital camera technology to look beyond the 'film-like digital photography' frame, one can apply a processual reconceptualization of digital photography that allows discussion of photographic technology as it is empirically found: as a part of complex sociotechnical assemblages in which sensors, algorithms and a range of display media are used in tandem with a camera and the optical images captured. Only some of the pictures thus made visible resemble 'film-like photographs'. People interacting with these technologies routinely are quite varied as actors, with various ways of being able to connect to and make use of particular devices. Although there are important continuities in photographic uses, I want to emphasize, here, the variety that recent developments in digital photographic technologies allow for.[9] This conceptual work might, I hope, help us look beyond the frame of our previous understandings of photography, allowing us to rethink the various social relations we might take with and through it.

In the following discussion, I will argue that thinking about cameras as one type of sensor among many calls for the aforementioned processual reconceptualization. As underpinning my argument, I discuss how commonly applied definitions of photography fall short of taking into account technical developments that become especially visible through digitization. This insecurity linked to the concept of 'photography' is not tied to digitization alone; rather, it is as old as the medium it is claimed to describe, as can be deduced directly from the work of such authors as Geoffrey Batchen and Patrick Maynard. Following this line of argument, I suggest an outline, focusing on the photographic process, that is of assistance for taking into account the variety of phenomena that are connected to photography and the variety of relations we live out through it. Then, presenting examples, I focus on one aspect of the outline, on surface markings made visible, in order to argue that visualizations created with the aid of data originally recorded with digital camera technology do not always look like a 'classic photograph'; they might take simulative, heuristic or layered forms. As they take these diverse forms, they partake in mediating the relations we make through them. Focusing on these individual kinds of visualizations and, particularly, on what they refer to, helps to show that photographs, or surface markings made visible, have a particular pictorial way of providing information. In this way, they provide a visual interface, referring us to possible actions we might use them for. Additionally, they refer to the technical and social processes that stabilized them as images in the first place, be they explicitly visible, or latent behind a fancy picture. Accordingly, images can be analysed both as images and as interfaces; such a perspective allows one to take visual and material characteristics of photographic practices into account.

From 'photographic cameras' to 'sensors'

Image sensors became important, at an early stage, for the development and spread of digital cameras: CCD and CMOS sensors, developed in the 1960s, are still in widespread use in consumer cameras, along with a wide variety of professional domains. They allow the transformation of optical images, created with the aid of a lens and a small opening in front of a dark chamber, into binary digital data. Development in sensor technology has enabled the integration of cameras into ever more devices, including laptops, mobile camera phones, camera devices clipped to the clothing and devices embedded in one's body (such as units in prosthetic eyes).[10] The technical changes facilitated by the introduction of image sensors into cameras have enabled developers of technology to augment human capabilities, as if responding to desires to transcend our human bodies.

Mobile, wearable and remotely controlled devices featuring a camera and image sensor are increasingly developed for everyday use. Often, the devices have a network connection and allow additional information to be added to the images captured. These cameras, though frequently advertised for snapshot photography and the capture of short video clips, afford a variety of usage that cannot be explained with the idea of 'film-like digital photography'. So, how should we understand photography?

What is photography?

The *Oxford English Dictionary* understands photography as '[t]he process, practice, or art of taking photographs; the business of producing and printing photographs',[11] whereas a photograph is understood to be

> a picture made using a camera in which an image is focused on to sensitive material and then made visible and permanent by chemical treatment [and later also] a picture made by focusing an image and then storing it digitally.[12]

The definition seems fairly straightforward at first sight, emphasizing a *picture*, the use of a *camera*, the *focusing of an image* on *sensitive material* and *making the image visible* and *permanent by chemical treatment*. The last part, 'storing it digitally', reveals some insecurity as to the role the digitization of photography plays, since digital techniques are also used for other processes, besides storage.

This definition accentuates the importance of the end result (a photograph) in attempts to understand photography. In so doing, it comes close to the ways in which photography, and, later, digital photography, has been studied in much of social scientific research. Empirical studies of mobile camera phone use, for example, tend to focus on the kinds of photos and videos captured, shared and shown to others, focusing on end products when examining the use of digital devices.

The actual use of the concept of photography has long escaped this narrowing of scope to supposed end results, as the history of the concept shows. The word 'photography', derived from *photos* (φωτός) and *graphos* (γράφος), was used in the nineteenth century by Charles Wheatstone, Sir John Herschel, Johann von Mädler and Hercules Florence, to some extent independently of each other, to describe various processes (Wilder 2006).[13] This became the concept encompassing daguerreotypes, ambrotypes, photogenic drawings and various other forms. It is apparent that, even early on, 'photography' was not tied to any single technique or artefact, and thus not to one specific practice alone.

Fittingly, the idea of fixing images on a light-sensitive surface had captured the Western imagination for decades before photography was officially announced, and ample reference to it can be found in letters, novels and various other narrations (Batchen 1999). The desire for a technique preceded the actual invention of one and, once a technique was found, various others emerged. Sir John Herschel alone is credited with inventing hundreds of photographic processes (Schaaf 1979). Similar desires can be traced for a variety of techniques of today, organized systematically into current photographic technology, replacing, extending or transforming our embodied capabilities (Lehmuskallio 2012, pp. 67–97).

Accordingly, the difficulty of defining 'photography' lies in the variety of actions in which photographic technology is engaged, and, somewhat paradoxically, photography cannot be associated solely with 'photographic cameras' and with pictures bearing particular iconic resemblance to their referents, usually called 'photographs'. Technical development does not halt at certain conceptual understandings of 'photography'.

We can take as an example Autographer, a wearable camera that uses various sensors to determine when to take a picture automatically and store recorded data within each file. It incorporates a magnetometer, a motion detector, an accelerometer, a thermometer, a GPS unit and an image sensor. The company advertises its devices for 'spontaneous, hands-free image capture',[14] but, since the device is used for capturing hundreds and, at times, thousands of sensor readings, including image records, captured image data are not always important in reviewing the data output. Acknowledging the possibilities of sensor readings collected throughout the day, the company suggests that the user '[m]anipulate this data to visualize your life'.[15] These visualizations may look very different from photographs taken with analogue cameras, although they are based on 'using a camera in which an image is focused on to sensitive material and then made visible'. Here, the image sensor inside a camera is only one sensor among many, affording computational transformations of recorded data that may be visualized in various ways.

Photography, as a concept, thus refers to a variety of techniques and artefacts that deal with 'taking and processing photographs', and these are changing, especially as a consequence of digitization (see also Lister 2013; Rubinstein, Golding & Fisher 2013). The concept itself is useful only if it refers to a set of practices that are distinguishable from non-photographic ones.

The photographic process: an outline

A processual approach to photography allows discussion of digital photographic practices in extension of a continuum from historical photographic uses, instead of claiming a strict break with the past. Maynard has worked to extend our understanding of photography and defined it 'in terms of technologies for accomplishing or guiding the production of images on sensitized surfaces by means of light (broadly understood) without necessarily understanding such images as photographs' (Maynard 1997, p. 20). He suggests that one look at the range of practices and technologies that are used to mark surfaces with light, of which only some are used to produce photographs as they are conventionally understood. His work is particularly helpful for understanding the embodied positions we take in relation to photography, without restricting the understanding of photography to only one set of devices that happen to be familiar to us. His definition of photography as 'surface markings made with light' thereby opens a Pandora's box of what had long remained neatly contained.

This approach affords broadening of our understanding of ongoing and possible future developments in mobile and wearable camera technology, without limiting our understanding *ab initio* by focusing only on particular kinds of artefacts, such as stressing the use of CCD and CMOS sensors or their current uses. At the same time, if we are to be able to act empirically, we must carefully choose the artefacts we use as a nexus for understanding photography as surface markings made with light. I do so by referring to empirical work among developers of mobile, wearable and remotely controlled cameras that are intended for everyday use.

In this connection, the *Oxford English Dictionary* definition of 'photograph', cited above, can be outlined sequentially on the basis of the process in which a photograph is taken, fixed, visualized and stored (see Table 15.1).[16] As the empirical work shows, all these parts of the photographic process receive dedicated attention from developers, photographers and entrepreneurs, such that, for example, light sources, light-sensitive materials and ways of sharing photographs are invented, enhanced and developed in novel directions and combinations. Not all parts of the process have to be handled by particular hardware or software in order to count as photographic technology, and, in several cases, we indeed find partial combinations and assemblages.

This outline is intended as a heuristic tool for moving beyond associations of 'film-like digital photography' when discussing 'photographs' and 'photography' in mobile and wearable camera technology. Each of the areas referred to in Table 15.1 (1–10) is a focus of research and development, and this process is reinvented because of digitization in various ways. Some developers, for example, focus mainly on creating novel ways of depicting a scene (item 3 in Table 15.1) – for instance, creating ways of capturing 360° panoramas, stereographic photographs or particularly

Table 15.1 An outline of the photographic process

The photographic process	Example process with a consumer film camera	Example process with a digital mobile camera phone
1 Light	Daylight	Flash
2 A scene to be depicted	Child on a beach	Child on a beach
3 A way to create an image	Optical lens and camera	Optical lens and camera
4 The light-sensitive surface	Film	Image sensor
5 Making surface markings visible	Developing film chemically	Rendering of image file(s)
6 Fixing of the surface markings	Fixing the film chemically	Creating an image file
7 Display of surface markings (the 'image' captured)	Printing on paper	Rendering on the screen as a simulative, heuristic or layered picture
8 Sharing of surface markings	Making a second paper print and giving it to someone	Transmitting – e.g. via the internet (TCP/IP)
9 Convergence of surface markings with additional data	Annotation	Metadata, automatically created and/or manually added
10 Storing of surface markings	Placing in a shoebox	In 'The Cloud' or on a hard drive

detailed gigapixel and terapixel photographs.[17] Others focus mainly on ways to display surface markings (item 7), sometimes in ways that eliminate the need to use any cameras in the first place – for example, when creating software techniques for modelling and rendering pictures that look like photographs.[18] In some cases, particular combinations are of interest, as with Autographer, wherein an image sensor – i.e. a light-sensitive surface (item 4) – is used both for capturing optical images item (3) from scenes to be depicted (item 2) and for its role as a colour sensor for perceiving light and brightness and thereby enabling automatic decisions about when to capture pictures. Importantly, here, the image sensor is only one sensor among many (including a magnetometer, passive infra-red sensor, accelerometer, thermometer and GPS sensor) that are used to determine automatically when to capture pictures.

From the list above, the discussion below focuses on item 5: 'making surface markings visible'. This allows me to present some of the many ways in which images captured with mobile and wearable camera technology are made visible as pictures and, especially, how these call into question some of the assumptions associated with 'film-like digital photography'. As I will show, surface markings are made visible as simulative, heuristic or layered pictures.

Surface markings made visible

The pictures I discuss are based on surface markings made with the aid of mobile and wearable camera technology. I will focus, in particular, on three ways of visualizing pictures, all three of which are of assistance in understanding current and emerging representations created with these cameras, namely simulative, heuristic and layered pictures. These are the types of visualizations that people encounter when acting with and through mobile camera technology and, as such, they provide particular cues for action.

The distinction between simulative and heuristic pictures, made originally by Boehm (2007), with reference to model characteristics displayed in pictures, aids us in considering the role the referent of photographs plays in photographic visualizations.[19] Whereas simulative pictures model what they depict in a recognizable way, showing the kinds of photographic visualizations many of us are used to seeing (often referring to something that 'has been'), heuristic pictures can be visualized by diverse means, within which recognizability is not important. Whilst Boehm discusses model characteristics in pictures in general, here, I am mainly interested in how these come to the fore in pictures made on the basis of recordings with mobile and wearable camera technology. In addition to Boehm's distinction between simulative and heuristic pictures, I suggest considering layered pictures, in which both ways of addressing referents are taken into account. Layered pictures are increasingly popular, for the additional, 'augmented' information they provide, in contrast to plain simulative or heuristic pictures.

The use of this distinction is in line with an understanding of networked camera technology as affording variety of use, including purposes not traditionally considered 'photographic'. For example, wearable cameras can be used to take a photo for a family album but can also be used equally well for eye care, barcode scanning or measurement of distances. The scenes depicted (item 2, Table 15.1) differ significantly from each other from case to case, as do the uses of the images, though in each case the same mobile camera phone can be used for each of the tasks. The affordances of camera technology also have to be activated in particular ways in the visualization of images, for example, as simulative or heuristic pictures.[20] At times, different visualizations converge, as when algorithms are created to take partial agency in deciding what kinds of pictures are to be taken with cameras, in the first place, and on which grounds pictures of any given kind are to be shown, to whom and where (Kember 2014). Taking a closer look at simulative, heuristic and layered pictures aids us in understanding how content captured with mobile and wearable cameras is visualized. By focusing explicitly on variety of use, this perspective is aimed at broadening our understanding of the kinds of visualizations that mobile and wearable camera technology carries into everyday contexts.

Simulative pictures

Many usually recognize visualizations that bear an iconic resemblance to their referents, a resemblance that looks 'photographic'. Following Boehm (2007), I call such visualizations 'simulative pictures', since they refer to an original setting but, as photographs, are detached from it. As Boehm suggests, in his discussion of the simulative models to be found in many pictures, the objects depicted are *rescaled* in relation to the original setting (a mountain in a photograph might be only 10 centimetres high, although the guide book it appears in claims its height to be several thousand metres). *Particular characteristics are selected* for display, which, in photographic visualizations, tend to be focused on visual aspects, neglecting smell, sound, taste and touch. The visualizations, again, are constrained by the photographic apparatus, just as they are by the particular choices a photographer happens to make, such as those of lens, film or exposure time. These simulative models *direct attention* and provide *cues for interpretation*. For these visualizations to fit our understanding of 'photographs', they have to meet our *diagnostic criteria* as to what photographs look like.[21] These are partially derived from our experience of photography.

The simulative pictures, modelling a particular setting with the aid of iconic resemblance, can be created with the aid of a single exposure, through several exposures or purely with computational techniques (Table

15.2). When considering visualizations created with the aid of mobile and wearable camera technology, we can find all of these means applied, along with various combinations of them.

The basic model for 'film-like digital photography' follows the idea of a single camera used in a particular setting to record an optical image (see S1 in Table 15.2). As Table 15.1 outlines, this could be a picture, or several pictures, of a child on a beach. When the image recorded is rendered visible, it is usually expected to look like a simulative picture does, fitting our diagnostic criteria as to how photographs ought to look.

These kinds of simulative pictures may also be created, as with a number of mobile-phone applications, via a camera capturing various images in a particular setting, which are then stitched together to appear as one picture. Here, computational techniques automatically converge images in a manner that shows us one simulative picture, based on various recordings of light *in situ* (see Table 15.2, item S2).

Interestingly, one important criterion for photography, identified time and time again in discussions of photography, is invisible to the human eye and has to be inferred. The *indexicality* of photographs, the fact that photographs, made with a camera, have actually been effected by light *in situ*, in a particular setting, seemed evident from the photographs when photographic techniques were first invented.[22] At that time, the process of photography was used to create particular kinds of visualizations, of which the unique qualities differed from the qualities specific to simulative models known from other visualization techniques of the age, such as oil paintings or drawings. We could take as an example the particular visual characteristics of daguerreotypes. At the time of their invention, no other visualization technique had yet created the kinds of simulative models people saw with the aid of daguerreotypy. The pictures created using the techniques of daguerreotypy looked different from those born of other simulative models, so the particularity of photographs, their trace character, could be inferred merely by observing the visual characteristics evident from the pictures displayed.[23]

Table 15.2 Ways of creating simulative pictures resembling a photo

S1 Capturing a scene once with one camera	Example: single file captured (RAW, DNG, .tiff, .jpg,...)
S2 Capturing the scene(s) several times with one or several cameras	Examples: Pro HDR, 360 Panorama and Mosaic Creator
S3 Creating a scene with a rendering engine	Examples: Maxwell Render, 3ds Max and Terragen software
S4 Any combination of the above	Example: Scalado Remove

Today, however, we often cannot judge whether the diagnostic criteria for distinguishing between visualizations that are indexical and those that are not are met. In fact, several rendering engines are so good at creating the kinds of simulative pictures familiar from photographs taken with cameras that we cannot tell whether they were originally taken with a camera or not. These pictures, created only with computational techniques, proceed from the idea of 'film-like digital photography'. Whereas the indexical photograph has, as its referent, a particular instance, the rendered picture, fully meeting our diagnostic criteria for what photographs look like, is created with reference to the idea of what photographs ought to look like (see S3 in Table 15.2).[24]

For mobile and wearable camera technology, all these ways of creating simulative pictures are of importance. The end result, a picture that refers to a particular setting, tells us little of how it was originally constructed. Its construction may follow any of the ideal types or particular recombinations of these (see Table 15.2, S1–S4). As the empirical research makes evident, for the development of mobile and wearable camera technology, simulative models are clearly of interest, and both developers of rendering software and those working with camera technology envision richer, clearer, fuller simulative models. The desire to represent the seen, or what might possibly be seen as a simulated picture, continues to be important for developments in photography and will surely remain so. Accordingly, developer visions of photographic technology cannot be understood if one fails to account for the role simulative pictures play.

Heuristic pictures

Simulative models have a referent that is visible and identifiable from the visualization, but photographic technology, as digital means emerge, is also increasingly used for visualizations that do not depict a simulative model based on iconic resemblance. Boehm (2007, pp. 116–117) suggests that those visualizations with an open referent can be called *heuristic*. They deal with referents that one cannot 'enter' (as one might imagine doing when looking at simulative pictures), that remain out of sight or that consist of abstractions. As visualizations, they *reduce complexity*, pointing towards relations between/among two or more entities that would be difficult to show with simulative models. These visualizations model particular relations of data points and can be created with diverse information visualization techniques. In the case of pictures taken with cameras, the heuristic visualizations created pick particular pieces of information from photographs, or metadata, and represent them heuristically.

For example, a developer of mobile camera phone software, Risto Sarvas, working with Samuli Kaipiainen, analysed a collection of everyday snapshot photos that Sarvas had taken, consisting of around 23,000 photos, and examined it on the basis of the people depicted. Each photo in which two people appeared at the same time was used to create a link between them, visualized as a line. Instead of visualizing all links to be found, Sarvas and Kaipiainen created a minimum spanning tree, with the intent of optimizing the visualization of the links found (see Figure 15.1). This enabled them to use Sarvas's collection of photos to depict his social network, thanks to him having taken many pictures at home, among friends and at work.[25] The visualization points to a core set of photographs consisting of photos taken with cameras at particular events in Sarvas's life (see Table 15.3, item H2). By focusing on something other than iconic resemblance, one can reveal aspects of the photos taken that would remain invisible if photographs were understood only as simulative pictures. In contrast to simulative pictures that one might imagine entering when

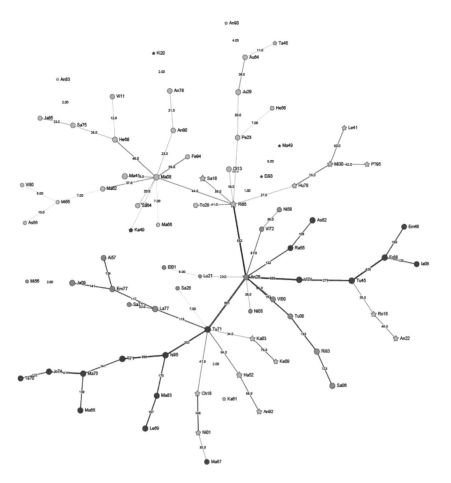

Figure 15.1 A minimum spanning tree based on a social network identified from a collection of approx. 23,000 snapshot photographs (source: courtesy of Risto Sarvas).

Table 15.3 Ways of creating heuristic pictures

H1 Capturing a scene once with one camera	Example: Fourier transform
H2 Capturing the scene(s) several times with one or several cameras	Example: Minimum spanning tree, with points and lines
H3 Creating a scene with a rendering engine	Example: Use of D3.js
H4 Any combination of the above	Example: Use of D3.js

looking at them, heuristic pictures call for other forms of being with pictures.

This example involves photos taken with cameras being visualized in a manner divergent from how many of us think about photographs or what we consider them to be. It shows heuristic pictures, instead of simulative ones. Existing metadata or data collected from image files are used for novel visualizations that shift what we are asked to observe. Sarvas's social network would be difficult to visualize as a simulative picture. A single photograph, the simulative image it might show us, is not necessarily as interesting as the heuristic models we obtain from visualizations of information when working with and synthesizing larger datasets. Whereas this example comes from a research project developing new visualization techniques for photographs, heuristic visualizations are also commonly used in popular photo organization software, such as the Map View in *Adobe Lightroom 4*, which visualizes heuristically large datasets of photographs, based on geolocation information, as icons on a map.

Since heuristic pictures model the relation to what they refer to as information visualizations (graphs, bar charts, maps, points and lines etc.), these models have to be explained by captions or in text. As with simulative pictures, the data used for rendering heuristic pictures may come from a single image file, from several recordings or via computational techniques (see Table 15.3, H1–H3). Here, too, combinations are possible, mainly in relationships between actually captured and computationally generated data.

With the number of pictures that can be automatically collected by means of mobile and wearable camera technology, visualizations of such types are surely going to increase and diversify.[26] Lifelogging cameras, such as Autographer and Narrative, are often used to collect thousands of pictures from a single event, a quantity that people find difficult to capture or work through in day-to-day life. Even if the aim were to pinpoint a particular simulative model, a 'photo', heuristic pictures need to be used in doing so. Heuristic pictures call for different kinds of practices from simulative pictures.

Layered pictures

As we look at the development of mobile and wearable camera technology, we see visualizations develop in both directions, as simulative and heuristic pictures, but especially in various layered forms.

Mobile and wearable camera technology intended to be used in the moment tends to be employed especially in the layering of simulative and heuristic pictures, one on top of the other. In what is often termed 'augmented reality', screens are used for rendering simulative pictures based on images captured in real time, with a camera, and these simulative pictures contain added heuristic information, on navigational cues, nearby restaurants, further information on the objects viewed, etc.

One example among many is iOnRoad, a navigational application that uses a mobile camera phone's camera for object recognition and warns the users of possible sources of accidents. It monitors speed, retains video footage in case of accidents, shows where the user left his or her car and provides users with driving analytics for further research. Many of the metrics from the data collected are visualized on top of simulative pictures, to give users visual cues for driving safely. As is often the case with digital camera technology, in these kinds of applications the distinction between photos and videos becomes blurred.

Now, real-time heuristic models, overlaid on simulative models focusing on iconic resemblance, require computing power and access to databases that provide the information of interest. Whereas simulative models in digital photography already depend on computational techniques for rendering of particular images that we understand to be 'photographic',[27]

Figure 15.2 Using navigational camera software in traffic, visualization layering simulative and heuristic information one on top of the other (source: photograph by Asko Lehmuskallio).

heuristic models are *clearly* based on cultural conventions dictating what is important and what is less so, and, in this way, they help us to understand abstract relations that become significant in everyday practices, such as driving. These conventions are inscribed within computing technology and become part of our day-to-day lives, where they take part in suggesting the focus of our attention. Layered pictures, which tend to draw our attention with the aid of simulative and heuristic visualizations, are becoming commonplace in everyday use of photographic technology, made visible both on the screen, in mobile camera phone applications, and as part of displays used in wearable camera technology.

Nadav Hochman and Lev Manovich (2013) have, in recent years, developed ways of visualizing images in which simulative pictures are organized in accordance with a heuristic model. These layered pictures, which they call 'thick visualizations', are large enough to contain the image data arranged into simulative pictures but also into heuristic visualizations. Instead of layering heuristic information on top of a single simulative picture, they involve crawling of photo-sharing databases for thousands or even millions of recorded image files, which are shown as part of the resulting visualizations. These visualizations rely on very different kinds of computing power than, for example, the aforementioned iOnRoad application does.

Surface markings, algorithms and predictive pictures

Surface markings, created with the aid of light, cameras and light-sensitive surfaces, might become visible in numerous ways, as argued above. In digital environments, the surface markings might be rendered as simulative pictures, as heuristic pictures or as layered pictures, one on top of the other. The latter distinction is useful when one considers the ways in which meaning is visually made available with the assistance of mobile and wearable camera technology. The particularity of pictorial information, in contrast to text or audio, is underscored. We use images for particular purposes and, at times, pictorial information is better at conveying the kind of information we need for the task at hand. Images mediate our relations with the everyday and their particular pictorial characteristics make a difference in how they accomplish this. Different visualization techniques, be they simulative, layered or heuristic, call for particular ways in which we attend to them and take them up as part of our everyday.

The actual surface markings recorded with the aid of mobile and wearable camera technology might remain latent, never made visible as such, as Gómez Cruz discusses in regard to QR codes (see this volume). In fact, digital camera technology relies on conversion of surface markings on image sensors into digital, binary data. Said data, stored in a file, are used as the basis for rendering pictures visible, whether as simulative, heuristic or layered pictures. Since the surface markings are converted to data, the same image sensors, such as CCD and CMOS sensors, can be used over and over again to mark surfaces and convert the new surface markings into digital data. In the capture of several images, these might be stored together and used for creating a simulative picture based on many surface markings (see S2 in Table 15.2).

Since computational techniques can be applied to any part of the photographic process outlined in Table 15.1, their role is crucial for an understanding of how the pictures rendered visible have been created. These techniques are often black-boxed from the end users' scrutiny and are not visible directly from the pictures rendered. Algorithms are used to visualize simulative, heuristic or layered pictures, and these visualizations may be based on a multiplicity of sources, including recorded optical images, metadata and full, rich datasets.

A good example of the importance of computational techniques can be found in what I call *predictive pictures*. I use the term to denote pictures taken on the basis of calculations predicting the capture of particular kinds of photographs. Here, algorithms, prescribing a well-defined set of rules, are used to predict the sorts of situations to be recorded with a camera and then rendered visible on a screen. For example, traffic cameras recording speed violations, for law enforcement purposes, take predictive pictures: the cameras are programmed in advance to take photographs of a predefined scene every time someone's driving speed is above the limit set. Here, the pictorial content to be captured is highly predictable because a particular algorithm is used for capturing just the kinds of pictures desired. If a car exceeds the speed limit, the camera takes a picture of that car. These pictures are often visualized as a layered picture, showing a simulative picture depicting car, licence plate and driver alongside heuristic information, including the time, date and vehicle speed.

Similar algorithms for creating predictive pictures are available for everyday snapshot photography. Scholars studying snapshot photography have shown, over and over, that conventions tend to structure how people take photographs, when and of whom (e.g. Chalfen 1987). In many cases, it is possible to predict the kinds of situations in which cameras are going to be present, the kinds of moments at which people will produce and use them, and the kinds of expressions that are particularly desirable in captured pictures. Digital camera manufacturers, along with developers of mobile and wearable camera technology, have, proceeding from this kind of information, created techniques to capture pictures only when those to be depicted are smiling. Others have developed techniques for automatically synthesizing a simulative picture, blending several frames into one, in an attempt to ensure that everyone in the resulting image is smiling.[28]

These examples are based on automatic face-recognition technologies that are embedded into consumer-grade cameras and photo editing software. The camera embedded with this technology thus awaits and assumes particular kinds of faces in its transformation of depicted faces to ones transmitted via networked cameras. As Kember (2014, p. 185) notes

> [f]ace recognition technology is becoming central to ... everyday control. As a marketing and surveillance-based biometric as well as photographic technology, one of its main advantages over other bio-metrics such as finger printing or iris-scanning is that it operates at a distance and does not require consent or participation.

Networked cameras thus mediate the couplings between humans and material artefacts in complex and multiple mediated ways, that tend to remain opaque to the everyday user.

My empirical work among developers of mobile and wearable camera technology shows that developers are well aware of the necessity to satisfy the needs of a variety of stakeholders, in order to maintain interest in their devices and software. By using a camera, many everyday users continue to frame their practice as taking photographic pictures that can be shown to others. Service developers, again, are less interested in individual photos, but rather in the aggregated data that can be collected with the help of image sensors in camera devices. A focus on the role of algorithms reveals how the cameras used for these practices transform and modify possible subsequent uses of the surface markings created. What we see visualized as pictures in the realm of digital photography does not necessarily tell us much about how it came to be. Conventions inscribed in the development of technology tend to remain invisible.

Conclusions

This analysis suggests that digital photography in day-to-day life, particularly mobile and wearable camera technology, cannot be understood through reliance on the idea of 'film-like digital photography'. If we are to understand the variety in current developments, we need to tease apart, and thereby problematize, accepted understandings of photography. If developers succeed in introducing camera technology that involves taking tens of thousands of pictures, rather than ten or 20, in the span of a few days, they will also succeed in providing different means for relating to visualizations of surface markings, by providing ever more variety. In everyday use situations, people will relate in new ways to both the technologies used and the images created (Van House 2011). How, exactly, this happens is a question for future empirical research.

Thanks to digital cameras, often with a network connection, today's photography can be used for the creation of simulative pictures that look like 'photographs', in the creation of heuristic pictures that do not look at all like 'photographs' do, or in forming layered pictures that contain both simulative and heuristic information. As a complicating factor, when seeing pictures rendered as a simulative picture that looks like a 'photograph', we often do not possess the tools needed, the correct diagnostic criteria, for determining how these pictures have been taken (Is the picture based on a single exposure or several? Was it created with a rendering engine or is it based on combination(s) of these approaches?). Pictures rendered heuristic, again, contain even less certain information on how they were actually created, even though they might be based on one exposure from a particular event.

The necessity of using computational techniques for storing and rendering digital pictures affords a variety of other uses in which the actual images recorded may remain latent. This is the case in a host of settings – for example, when the images recorded are used for understanding consumer behaviour, for providing third-party advertisers with possibilities for targeted marketing or for employing filtering algorithms for purposes of influencing views on 'good taste' and thereby common morals, as is done on some photo-sharing sites.[29] All of these techniques remain invisible if one understands photographs merely as simulative pictures referring to 'that which has been'.

Maynard's suggestion of broadening our understanding of photography is helpful when trying to understand developments in mobile and wearable camera technology. These devices allow, and are developed for, surface markings with light, without necessarily being used for creating simulative pictures that look like 'photographs'. Problematizing the association between photography and a photograph is of particular importance if one wishes to understand the variety of ends to which mobile and wearable camera technology is directed.

Whilst the discussion here has examined primarily pictures made visible, similar analysis could be conducted for other parts of the photographic process. The necessarily limited analysis provided here is an ample starting point, offering material which underscores the need to broaden our understanding of 'photography' in a digital age, and the processual outline provided is of assistance in doing so. In the context of photographic technologies developed for everyday use, the pictures shown to us are rendered as simulative, heuristic or layered pictures. Whereas an understanding confined to film-like digital photographs entails focusing only on simulative pictures that look like photographs, a processual reconceptualization of photography helps us to examine the use of photographic technology as it is found in the development of mobile and wearable camera technology: as a much messier affair.

Notes

1 The empirical work was conducted when I held a post as Visiting Scholar at UC Berkeley School of Information, August 2012 to July 2013. The methods consisted of interviews and participant observation, including attendance of seminars and conferences, visits to companies and research labs, and examination of the available publications. I am thankful especially to Nancy Van House and Coye Cheshire for facilitating my research, to the multitude of people who

shared insights and time, as well as to colleagues in Tampere's 'Hiomo' for constructive critique.

2 A medium is anything that might transport signals, meaning or action, thereby being 'in between'. Whilst media are often taken to be intermediaries, transporting 'meaning or force without transformation' (Latour 2005, p. 39), upon closer scrutiny they usually reveal their work as mediators: 'Mediators transform, translate, distort, and modify the meaning or the elements they are supposed to carry' (ibid.). For discussions of photography and new media, Sarah Kember and Joanna Zylinska (2012) have developed an approach that discusses media in terms of mediation, instead of understanding, for example, a camera or a laptop as concrete objects that are used. My perspective is based particularly on a social scientific reading of Belting's (2001) work.

3 Examples of cameras designed to be clipped to the clothing include brand names such as Narrative and Autographer; for cameras embedded in eyewear or prosthetic eyes, one can look to Google Glass, Google smart contact lenses and Eyeborg.

4 Examples of distal cameras bear brand names such as Elisa Vahti, GoPro and Nixie.

5 'Film-like digital photography' is a term used by computer scientists to distinguish this from other digital camera uses, such as computational cameras, allowing, for example, for creation of multiview radial images or time-of-flight visualizations (Raskar & Tumblin, forthcoming; Nayar 2011). Shree Nayar (2011, p. 2) explains the benefits of computational cameras thus: '[t]he traditional camera performs a very simple and restrictive sampling of the complete set of rays, or the light field, that resides in any real scene'.

6 Scholarship on digitally networked photography pays increasing attention to the various assemblages that the digitization and networked character of photographic technology allow for, see, for example, Lehmuskallio (2012); Lister (2013); Rubinstein and Sluis (2013).

7 I use 'media' as the plural of 'medium'. For 'medium', see Note 2.

8 For a discussion of the relationship between Boehm's and W. J. T. Mitchell's concepts, see Boehm and Mitchell (2009).

9 For a range of earlier empirical work, see Lehmuskallio (2012).

10 An example is found in Rob Spence, who has a prosthetic eye with an embedded wireless video camera, providing unrivalled 'point-of-view' footage (Spence 2009).

11 Search date: 29 October 2014.

12 Search date: 29 October 2014.

13 The source Wilder uses is Schaaf (1979).

14 'Autographer', viewed 1 September 2015, www.autographer.com/.

15 Please see Note 14.

16 In his studies of snapshot photographers, Richard Chalfen has shown the usefulness of a processual understanding of photography. His sociovidistic framework is of particular note (Chalfen 1987, 2001). My outline of the photographic process has been developed based on empirical material collected between August 2012 and July 2013 (see Note 1). I did not limit collection of empirical material to people and companies based in the San Francisco Bay Area only, since it is a rather dynamic environment and particularly well interconnected with many other parts of the world working on computational solutions.

17 An example is the application 360 Panorama, from Occipital; viewed 1 September 2015, http://occipital.com/360/app. Another is the stitched gigapixel photographs by GigaPan, viewed 1 September 2015, http://gigapan.com/.

18 Software such as Maxwell Render and Terragen products provide good examples; see the galleries, viewed 1 September 2015, www.maxwellrender.com/ and http://planetside.co.uk/.

19 Boehm speaks of simulative and heuristic models, but, since I confine my discussion to the pictures rendered visible, I prefer to speak specifically about simulative and heuristic pictures.
20 The understanding of an activation of affordances follows the work of Rose (2010) and Lehmuskallio (2012).
21 The idea of using 'diagnostic criteria' comes from Jukka Häkkinen (personal correspondence), who traces his use of the term to Aude Oliva and Philippe G. Schyns (2000).
22 The term *index*icality is used in photographic writings mostly referring to the notion of a trace, thus neglecting Peirce's broader use of the term.
23 See, for example, an illustrative daguerreotype of Samuel B. Morse, reproduced digitally for the Library of Congress. Morse is credited as the first American to have seen a daguerreotype with his own eyes, viewed 1 September 2015, www.loc.gov/exhibits/treasures/trr089.html.
24 This is sometimes referred to as 'photography after photography' (e.g. von Amelunxen *et al.* 1996).
25 Personal correspondence, with a network image made available by Risto Sarvas.
26 Consider also the recent projects for creation of heuristic models based on thousands of snapshots by Lev Manovich and colleagues (Hochman & Manovich 2013), on the internet (viewed 1 September 2015, http://selfiecity.net/ and http://phototrails.net/).
27 Think, for example, of 'demosaicing' of colour images captured with image sensors patterned in accordance with Bayer arrays.
28 More complex techniques for prediction are being created, so that camera users (or 'photographers'), in the ideal case, do not have to worry about taking pictures at the right moment. The 'secret sauce' of computational algorithms is expected to take care of that part, as an Autographer advertisement expresses by speaking of 'spontaneous, hands-free image capture'. The variety of sensors accompanying the image sensor is used for honing the decision about when to capture photos automatically.
29 Consider, for instance, the case of social networking site Facebook deleting photos that feature breastfeeding (example reference: *BBC News*, 30 October 2014. 'Oswestry Mum's Breastfeeding Photo Deleted by Facebook', viewed 1 September 2015, www.bbc.com/news/uk-29831637).

References

Batchen, G. 1999, *Burning with Desire: The Conception of Photography*. MIT Press: Cambridge, MA; London.

Belting, H. 2001, *Bild-Anthropologie: Entwürfe für eine Bildwissenschaft*. Fink: München.

Boehm, G. 2007, *Wie Bilder Sinn Erzeugen: Die Macht des Zeigens*. Berlin University Press: Berlin.

Boehm, G. 1994, 'Die Wiederkehr der Bilder', in G. Boehm (ed.) *Was ist ein Bild?* Fink: München, pp. 11–38.

Boehm, G. & Mitchell, W. J. T. 2009, 'Pictorial versus Iconic Turn: Two Letters'. *Culture, Theory and Critique*, Vol. 50, nos 2–3, pp. 103–121.

Chalfen, R. 2001, 'Interpreting Family Photography as Pictorial Communication', in J. Prosser (ed.) *Image-Based Research: A Sourcebook for Qualitative Researchers*. Falmer Press Ltd: London; Philadelphia, PA, pp. 214–234.

Chalfen, R. 1987, *Snapshot Versions of Life*. Popular Press: Bowling Green, OH.

Elsaesser, T. 2013, 'The "Return" of 3-D: On Some of the Logics and Genealogies of the Image in the Twenty-First Century'. *Critical Inquiry*, Vol. 39, pp. 217–246.

Gye, L. 2007, 'Picture This: The Impact of Mobile Camera Phones on Personal Photographic Practices'. *Continuum: Journal of Media and Cultural Studies*, Vol. 21, pp. 279–288.

Hand, M. 2012, *Ubiquitous Photography*. Polity Press: Cambridge and Malden, MA.

Hochman, N. & Manovich, L. 2013, 'Zooming into an Instagram City: Reading the Local through Social Media'. *First Monday*, Vol. 18, no. 7, viewed 19 October 2015, http://firstmonday.org/ojs/index.php/fm/article/view/4711/3698.

Kember, S. 2014, 'Face Recognition and the Emergence of Smart Photography'. *Journal of Visual Culture*, Vol. 12, no. 2, pp. 182–199.

Kember, S. & Zylinska, J. 2012, *Life after New Media: Mediation as a Vital Process*. MIT Press: Cambridge, MA.

Larsen, J. & Sandbye, M. (eds) 2013, *Digital Snaps: The New Face of Photography*. I.B. Tauris: London; New York.

Latour, B. 2005, *Reassembling the Social: An Introduction to Actor-Network-Theory*. Oxford University Press: Oxford; New York.

Lehmuskallio, A. 2012, *Pictorial Practices in a 'Cam Era': Studying Non-Professional Camera Use*. Tampere University Press: Tampere.

Lister, M. (ed.) 2013, *The Photographic Image in Digital Culture*, 2nd edn. Routledge: Abingdon; New York.

Maynard, P. 1997, *The Engine of Visualization: Thinking through Photography*. Cornell University Press: Ithaca, NY.

Mitchell, W. J. T. 2005, *What Do Pictures Want? The Lives and Loves of Images*. University of Chicago Press: Chicago, IL; London.

Nayar, S. K. 2011, 'Computational Cameras: Approaches, Benefits and Limits'. Technical Report CUCS-001-11, Columbia University Computer Science Department, New York.

Oliva, A. & Schyns, P. G. 2000, 'Diagnostic Colors Mediate Scene Recognition'. *Cognitive Psychology*, Vol. 41, no. 2, pp. 176–210.

Rantavuo, H. 2008, *Connecting Photos: A Qualitative Study of Cameraphone Photo Use*. Publication Series of the University of Art and Design: Helsinki.

Raskar, R. & Tumblin, J. 2016 [forthcoming], *Computational Photography: Mastering New Techniques for Lenses, Lighting, and Sensors*. A K Peters/CRC Press: Wellesley, MA.

Reckwitz, A. 2002, 'Toward a Theory of Social Practices: A Development in Culturalist Theorizing'. *European Journal of Social Theory*, Vol. 5, no. 2, pp. 245–265.

Rose, G. 2010, *Doing Family Photography: The Domestic, the Public and the Politics of Sentiment*, Kindle edn. Ashgate: Farnham; Burlington, VT.

Rose, G. & Tolia-Kelly, D. P. (eds) 2012, *Visuality/Materiality: Images, Objects and Practices*. Ashgate: Farnham; Burlington, VT.

Rose, G., Degen, M. & Melhuish, C. 2014, 'Networks, Interfaces, and Computer-Generated Images: Learning from Digital Visualisations of Urban Redevelopment Projects'. *Environment and Planning D: Society and Space*, Vol. 32, no. 3, pp. 386–403.

Rubinstein, D. & Sluis, K. 2013, 'Notes on the Margins of Metadata: Concerning the Undecidability of the Digital Image'. *Photographies*, Vol. 6, no. 1, pp. 151–158.

Rubinstein, D., Golding, J. & Fisher, A. (eds) 2013, *On the Verge of Photography: Imaging Beyond Representation*. ARTicle Press: Birmingham.

Sarvas, R. & Frohlich, D. 2011, *From Snapshots to Social Media: The Changing Picture of Domestic Photography*. Springer: London.

Schaaf, L. J. 1979, 'Sir John Herschel's 1839 Paper on Photography'. *History of Photography*, Vol. 3, no. 1, pp. 47–60.

Spence, R. 2009, *Eyeborg*, viewed 19 October 2015, http://eyeborgproject.com/.

Van House, N. 2011, 'Personal Photography, Digital Technologies, and the Uses of the Visual'. *Visual Studies*, Vol. 25, no. 1, pp. 125–134.

Von Amelunxen, H., Iglhaut, S., Rötzer, F., Cassel, A. & Schneider, N. G. (eds) 1996, *Photography after Photography: Memory and Representation in the Digital Age*. G+B Arts: Amsterdam.

Were, G. 2013, 'Imaging Digital Lives'. *Journal of Material Culture*, Vol. 18, no. 3, pp. 213–222.

Wilder, K. 2006, ' "Photography", Etymology of', in R. Lenman & A. Nicholson (eds) *The Oxford Companion to the Photograph*. Oxford University Press: Oxford, viewed 1 September 2015, www.oxfordreference.com/view/10.1093/acref/9780198662716.001.0001/acref-9780198662716-e-1206.

16 Is the camera an extension of the photographer?

Martin Lister

I wish to offer a reading of an image, if only to leave it behind. My reason for doing this – both the 'reading' and the 'leaving behind' is to engage with the idea contained in the title of this part of the book: that the camera can be thought of as an extension of the photographer. It also allows me to mark a current shift in how we are thinking about photography: the turn away from a long dominant preoccupation with photography as representation. The image is Andreas Feininger's 1951 photograph entitled 'The Photojournalist'. It is an image that invites thought about the mechanical extension of the human while hinting at the limits of the idea.

The non-representational turn

The act of finding meaning in a photograph is, of course, to engage with photography as representation. This, in turn (if it is not to be an innocent reading), inevitably entails a measure of academic discipline and methodology: the semiological scrutiny of images treated as texts, with the aim of revealing or interpreting the meanings encoded within them. With regard to photography, this is a developed practice that, over the last 30 years or so, became almost synonymous with photography theory.[1] Now, the ongoing convergence of photography with computing and the rapid development of photography as a networked and computational medium have rendered photography radically more transient, relational, dynamic and polymorphous; we have witnessed a kind of supercharging of what it already was! The sheer degree of this change has rendered the analysis of singular images as discrete artefacts as largely inappropriate; the object of theory has changed.

This transformation in photography has been accompanied by a turn, in theory, to what has been called 'non-representational' or, better (if less common), 'more than representational' theory (Lorimer 2005, p. 84). This is a term that points to a diverse, unsettled (and deliberately unsettling) cluster of approaches to the study of social life and cultural practice, which has been developing for quite some time.[2] Its main home is in the discourse of human geography, but it has strong resonances in science and technology studies, particularly 'actor network theory' (Latour 2005).

The goal of non-representational theory is to shift attention away from the decoding and revelation of the meanings that we take to inhere in representations, and towards the noise, habit, impulse, emotion and unruly activity that surrounds and exceeds them. For the non-representationalist, the world understood as meaningful text, as representation, is a conservative and restricted view and is replaced by a sense of its material and phenomenological richness. Such approaches are interested, therefore, in the embodied and material practices of human social actors and their traffic with non-human things and the physical environments in which they move and meet. Where photography is concerned, this is a challenging project. It asks us to shift our attention away from its products – photographs – and the attention we have traditionally paid to them, to its practices or, as non-representational theorists like to say, to its 'doings' (Larsen 2008, p. 146).

Yet, 'turns' in theory come and go and visual representations do (continue to) tell us things about the world. Radical shifts in photography and photographs, on many levels, do not mean that, with respect to some photographs at least, reading an image as a text cannot still be useful, cannot be 'telling'. For all the important emphases that 'non-representational theory' foregrounds, to eschew representations completely would surely be a bad case of throwing babies out with the bathwater. Andreas Feininger's iconic image, made a little over 60 years ago, is an example in point.

Camera as tool

In Feininger's image we see a Leica camera held close to the photographer's face. The camera's lens and viewfinder are aligned, horizontally, to the photographer's eyes, its body parallels his nose, as his fingers curl around its body. The camera is anthropomorphized; it is depicted as an extension, almost a part, of the photographer's face and head. This is an image that might have been made to illustrate the title of this part of this book.

Feininger's image offers us a certain concept of technology: the anthropological concept of a tool. The camera is pictured as a hand-tool that extends the photographer's body and its sensorium, much in the way that a hammer, a screwdriver or a knife, are seen to extend the body. Such extensions are then held to amplify and refine the body's capacities and, in doing so, they facilitate a human subject's power and intention. Understood in this way, tools are wielded, they are under the control and direction of human subjects. Throughout the twentieth century, the photographic camera, along with the microscope and the telescope, was a paradigm for understanding technologies as extensions of the body, in particular, as extensions of the human eye.

In the era of analogue photography, photographers *used* their cameras. They controlled the work that they did. At the professional and serious

Figure 16.1 Andreas Feininger, 'The Photojournalist', 1951 (source: photo by Andreas Feininger/The LIFE Picture Collection/Getty Images).

amateur end of the spectrum of practice, this was achieved through a mastery and coordination of a number of factors: principally focus, shutter speed, aperture and depth of field. Further, the photographer's choice of film type (what we can now understand, retrospectively, as the analogue camera's 'software') and the manner of its chemical development and printing, gave control of other factors such as tonal contrast, grain, detail and colour. At the level of consumer and snapshot photography, these processes were simplified and automated via a set of simple controls, whose functions were usually announced by small icons on the camera's body. Here, as has been frequently observed, commenced the 'black boxing' and rendering invisible of photographic technology, a process that has developed exponentially as cameras have become software machines (Palmer 2013a, p. 49ff.; Slater 1995, p. 129ff.; Stallabrass 1996, p. 13ff.; Rubinstein & Sluis 2013, p. 25ff.).

In the manner of tools, analogue cameras were discrete and bounded objects. However finely crafted or mechanically ingenious, when not in use, they were inert things. While some auxiliary items could be added to such cameras (for example, a flashlight, a light meter, a motor drive), cameras were discontinuous with other parts of photographic practice or industry, its means of production, storage, distribution and reception. In more concrete terms, the analogue camera was a tool for making a photographic exposure (note to Polaroid) and it required other, often remote, places, institutions and apparatuses for a photograph to be produced: the chemical darkroom and enlarger (where the latent image became visible) and the physical carriers and means of distribution, circulation, display and storage (magazines, newspapers, albums, archives and transport systems of various kinds). While it was already common, from at least the mid-twentieth century onwards, to think of a photograph as a captured 'moment' in time, as something produced in seconds or fractions of seconds, this applied only to the moment of exposure. The full temporal and spatial extent of the analogue photographic process could be considerable, entailing dedicated buildings (darkrooms, laboratories, print shops) and the time and means to travel between these places, across which the division of photographic labour was distributed (Gómez Cruz & Meyer 2012).

However, when in use, the analogue camera was far from inert: it shaped how the photographer looked at the world and how they were positioned to look. Returning to Feininger's photograph, we see that the photographer is looking through a viewfinder that is attached to his Leica camera. Here, human vision is channelled or funnelled and the otherwise mobile and saccadic field of view of the human eye is framed and fixed, it is restricted by the hard metallic edges of the viewfinder's window and it is supplied with a perspectival image constructed by the lens. By these means, the use of a viewfinder also established a distance between the viewer and what or whom they looked at. Scopic power is involved here, as the distance is not only perspectival and optical, it is also physical and psychological. The photographer is set back 'behind the camera' and apart from the world they photograph. A corollary of this distance is the licence or presumed authority to look or gaze at others in an unflinching manner that is hardly possible with the unaided eye (Lutz & Collins 1991).

The networked computational camera

When considering contemporary forms of the camera (the digital camera and the camera phone), Feininger's image of the mid-twentieth century photojournalist ceases to be so instructive. Photographers now view the world on the LCD screens that occupy the full width and height of the camera's slim body, held, with extended arms, away from the photographer's body. As they sweep and scan the environment (the pro-filmic space) the digital photographer watches the world becoming an image, or one image after another, on the camera's mobile screen (see Forrest, this volume). Rather than being distanced or placed outside them, it is likely that the digital photographer will be close to the centre of the events and activities they photograph (see Favero, this volume). Where the viewfinder once conferred a privileged separation on the photographer, the digital screen is likely to prompt a fair degree of social exchange between photographer and photographed, which takes place around the very act of photographing. Moreover, on the same screen, the photographer, and those photographed, can view an almost instantaneous 'playback' of whichever image was chosen. In short, the choosing or conception, the exposure, the storing, and the display and initial reception of an image, all take place within the digital camera. With internet connectivity and the downloading of photographic 'apps' (Palmer 2013b, pp. 157–159) the distribution and, to a degree, the processing of the photographic image can be added to this list.

These capacities of the digital camera mean that it is no longer a discrete tool, passively awaiting its utilization by a photographer. The camera has become a computer – a computer with sensors – and an element, if a key one, within an extended system of connected technologies (see Lehmuskallio, this volume). Photography has become algorithmic and computational (Rubinstein & Sluis 2013, pp. 21–40), and the computer and network technologies of the twenty-first century that now constitute 'digital photography' are no longer discrete, monolithic machines and dedicated places, they are disaggregated and distributed. They pervade our environment, they are ubiquitous, they are 'everyware' (Kember 2013, pp. 56–76). Digital technologies, generally, have become pervasive and embedded in the physical environment we inhabit.

Contemporary cameras, whether in the form of the camera phone or as freestanding digital cameras with wireless connections, exist as devices within a communications network. This network is always active, it is always 'on'. As Rubinstein and Sluis put it, the network observes no holidays or weekends; it exists in a continual present (2013, p. 31). The images that enter this network via such cameras do not follow a linear path: they can be in many places and contexts simultaneously. The singular capture of a latent image in the old 'camera tool', and its subsequent path through the dedicated places and institutions of materialization, distribution and reception, has given way to a process driven and managed online by software. Further, such software does not only dwell within the new cameras themselves, but also within the other computers and online sites to which they are connected and where images are stored, organized and processed.

Edgar Gómez Cruz has argued that we should not understand photography as representation, or solely as technology or object. Rather, photography needs to be understood as the outcome of a complex and changing alignment of technologies, meanings, uses, knowledges, institutions and practices (Gómez Cruz & Meyer 2012, pp. 204, 217; Gómez Cruz, this volume). This is a way to understand photography, in its historical forms as well as in its current condition, as the alignment between this field of actors and agents changes over time. Within this field, the notion that one agent might simply extend another no longer holds. In his thoughts on the current relationship of cameras to software, Daniel Palmer suggests that the 'creative act (of photography) no longer belongs to the photographer alone, if it ever did, but is deferred to software and to increasingly collaborative possibilities (both human and non-human)', and this means that 'the traditional role of individual human agency in photography is changing' (2013b, p. 63).

Maybe a final return to Feininger's photograph is called for, after all, in order to conclude this brief reflection on the changed nature of the camera. In the light of the observations made above, that is, when thinking about digital networked photography, the cyborgian play in Feininger's image, between a body and a machine, between a photographer and a camera, begins to imply something less clear cut and one-directional than my initial reading suggested. It prompts us to invert our title and to consider that the photographer has now become an actor positioned within a dispersed field of non-human agents, to which intelligent and networked cameras give access. In this light, and if the concept of 'extension' is to continue to serve us, we might need to say that, rather than the camera extending the photographer, the photographer has become an extension of the camera.

Notes

1 See, for instance, Burgin (1982), where he influentially argued that a theory of photography should be, mainly, a theory of representation.
2 Even within cultural geography, not to mention its other versions in science and technology studies and philosophy, a bibliography on non-representational theory would be very extensive. However, portals to the field and useful critical and historical reports on non-representational theory are to be found in Haydn (2005 and 2008).

References

Burgin, V. 1982, *Thinking Photography*. Macmillan Press Ltd: London; Basingstoke.

Gómez Cruz, E. & Meyer, E. T. 2012, 'Creation and Control in the Photographic Process: iPhones and the Emerging Fifth Moment of Photography'. *Photographies*, Vol. 5, no. 2, pp. 203–221.

Haydn, L. 2008, 'Cultural Geography: Non-Representational Conditions and Concerns'. *Progress in Human Geography*, Vol. 32, no. 4, pp. 551–559.

Haydn, L. 2005, 'Cultural Geography: The Busyness of Being "More than Repre-sentational"'. *Progress in Human Geography*, Vol. 29, no. 1, pp. 83–94.

Kember, S. 2013, 'Ambient Intelligent Photography', in M. Lister (ed.) *The Photo-graphic Image in Digital Culture*. London: Routledge, pp. 56–76.

Larsen, J. 2008, 'Practices and Flows of Digital Photography: An Ethnographic Framework'. *Mobilities*, Vol. 3, no. 1, pp. 141–160.

Latour, B. 2005, *Reassembling the Social: An Introduction to Actor-Network-Theory*. Oxford University Press: Oxford.

Lorimer, H. 2005, 'Cultural Geography: The Busyness of being "More-than-Representational"'. *Progress in Human Geography*, Vol. 29, no. 1, pp. 83–94.

Lutz, C. & Collins, J. 1991, 'The Photograph as an Intersection of Gazes: The Example of National Geographic'. *Visual Anthropology Review*, Vol. 7, no. 1, pp. 134–149.

Palmer, D. 2013a, 'The Rhetoric of the JPEG', in M. Lister (ed.) *The Photographic Image in Digital Culture*, 2nd edn. Routledge: London, pp. 149–164.

Palmer, D. 2013b, 'Redundant Photographs: Cameras, Software and Human Obsolescence', in D. Rubinstein, J. Golding & A. Fisher (eds) *On the Verge of Photography: Imaging beyond Representation*. ARTicle Press: Birmingham, pp. 49–67.

Rubinstein, D. & Sluis, K. 2013, 'The Digital Image in Photographic Culture: Algo-rithmic Photography and the Crisis of Representation', in M. Lister (ed.) *The Photographic Image in Digital Culture*. Routledge: London, pp. 22–40.

Slater, D. 1995, 'Domestic Photography and Digital Culture', in M. Lister (ed.) *The Photographic Image in Digital Culture*. Routledge: London, pp. 129–146.

Stallabrass, J. 1996, *Gargantua: Manufactured Mass Culture*. Verso: London, pp. 13–39.

17 Outlook

Photographic wayfaring, now and to come

Nancy Van House

This book argues for a practice-theory-based approach to everyday photography, emphasizing people's concrete activities and understandings around photographs, photography and photographic technologies, and how photographs are meaningful in people's social lives. This book is particularly concerned with networked camera devices and the connected interactions they support.[1] This is a good time for a book like this, since technologies-in-the-making are particularly useful for making visible what soon comes to be invisible and taken-for-granted (Latour 2005).

In this chapter, I explore some of the current developments that, I believe, are fundamental to people's experiences of photography and its entanglement with ways of being in the world. Participation in photography has become more extensive and diverse, bringing in new people and transforming practices, especially in association with social media. Images are, in effect, more personal and collective, as well as less durable and more immediate, altering time and place. As images become more public, people don't just see but experience others' points of view. Photos remain important to memory, self-presentation and the enactment of identity, but with important differences. In the second section, I briefly address developments in theory and methods. In the final section I ask what all this means for photography in people's lives and why images are so important.

Significant developments, and a caveat or two

One of the most important current developments associated with networked, digital photography is a massive increase in participation. Participants are critical to practice: without practitioners, there is no practice. Practices and participants change one another. Practices are mutually influential, too, as each person brings together a variety of practice domains.

Currently, a much broader range of people than ever before engage in photographic activity of all kinds, more often, under a greater variety of conditions, making more, and more varied, images. Participants include not just photographers but subjects and viewers, technology designers and producers – anyone who engages in photo-related, photographic-technology-related activities. Many people engage in photography within the framework of social media, which, I argue, torques photographic practices in that direction. Practices are primarily tacit, learned through seeing, doing and talking. Both the persistence of existing practices and the development of new ones require visible, public performance. The practices visible via photographs are of two kinds: photographic practices and the practices made visible *in* photographs. For example, Uimonen's (this volume) Tanzanian mother's photos make visible how she performs her culture's practices of motherhood. Morcate and Pardo (this volume) describe the making and sharing of images of illness, grief and death. These images don't only represent a change in the contemporary photographic practices in Western countries, where such images have been seen as inappropriate. They also depict changes in the practices around illness and death: 'there is no longer a necessity to relegate grief to an intimate environment' (Morcate & Pardo). Put these together and, I argue, we are seeing important implications for photography practice from networked everyday photography. First, it's likely that ongoing photographic practices will have more and more in common with social media and potentially less with traditional photography. Second, I argue that networked photography contributes to more rapid innovation and dissemination in practices in many domains. While this may result in more uniformity across cultures, these chapters give me hope that we will see more diversity in different places and conditions.

Another notable development is that photos have become, paradoxically, both more personal and more collective. Most of the chapters in this volume address the blurring of the boundary between public and private images and the increasing publicness of images. Many chapters describe the immediate, shared uses of networked images and video, up to and including live streaming – what Favero (in this volume) calls 'shared simultaneous experience'. As images (and video) become more collective and immediate, viewers experience more points of view, not just locational but experiential and subjective. We get the visceral experience of seeing (and, with video, hearing) events unfolding in front of our own eyes, even in real time. We see sights usually inaccessible to outsiders, such as from civilians and soldiers in war zones. People publish images and videos online that the mass media cannot or will not publish (Posetti 2014). Furthermore, many shared, online images are indexed or tagged, and thus more easily retrieved than one's own. Why trawl through an unorganized, unlabelled personal collection of digital files when similar images are readily findable online? In fact, some people ask, why make or keep an image when other people, better situated, possibly more skilled, with better equipment, have made better images available?

However, image-capture devices and storage technologies have also become more personal, making some images inaccessible to anyone but the owner. The household camera has been replaced by personal cameras, smartphones and tablets, and even wearable devices. The images in the photo album or box of prints or slides have been dispersed to individuals' cameras, smartphones, hard drives, social media sites and Cloud storage. The massive increase in image-making, not to mention developments like life-logging (Favero, this volume), threaten to bury us in unorganized, undifferentiated images, which are difficult to retrieve (if anyone even cares to try) both logistically and legally after the passing of the owner.

A major traditional use for photos that is threatened, I argue, is personal and collective memory. Blustein (2008), a moral philosopher, goes so far as to say that personal and collective memory is a moral imperative: to know who we are requires that we know where we came from; and we must take responsibility for our past. Bowker (2005) describes how durable memory technologies, objects and practices 'permit both the creation of a continuous, useful past and the transmission *sub rosa* of information, stories and practices from our wild, discontinuous, ever-changing past' (p. 9). He terms 'inaugural acts' (p. 10) disruptions such as the invention of printing that create disjunctions in archives and practices.

The Achilles heel of digital files is durability and retrievability (Van House & Churchill 2008), exacerbated by an emphasis on immediacy and transiency in image making and use. Internet pioneer Vint Cerf has warned of a coming 'digital dark age' (Pultarova 2015) as archiving technologies continue to change and older files become inaccessible. I fear that, as inaugural acts, digital technologies and social media have disrupted our memory regimes and the integrity of personal and collective archives and threaten images' traditional role as memory objects.

My point is not that images are no longer useful or used for memory, collective and individual. Indeed, as more images are made and shared more widely, the visual record is expanding. However, what we can 'remember' via the visual record depends on the images made, archived, indexed and migrated as technologies change. Much is gained, but what is lost with technologies and practices that emphasize immediacy over durability? For example, the Holocaust Museum in Washington, DC, solicits private photos of life in Europe between the Wars to document an important era in European and Jewish history. A box of glass negatives found in a garage proved to be a valuable record of African-Americans' lives in the US Midwest in the 1910s and 1920s. What happens when such images are lost because they are digital files that disappear when they aren't migrated to new storage media, or a Cloud storage service goes out of business? Or are never made because people were relying on others' images?

Finally, I want to comment on networked photography as performance: performance of photographic practices (e.g. Becker, this volume), performance in front of the camera (e.g. Andersen) and, in a different use of the term, performance of self or group, actual or idealized (Blanco; Uimonen; Mota; Villi; Andersen; Thielman), or space (Andersen; Pink; Thielmann; Villi). Even before social media, much of photography was performance for an actual or imagined audience, not just by the subjects but the photographer as well. Photography is never mere representation or transcription: it is performance and enactment by all involved.

Self-aware performance in front of a camera has always made a photo a part of the event being photographed. Crang (1997) argued that travel photography (his particular interest)

> ... sacrifice[s] the immediacy of experience and orientat[es] activities to (future, distant) viewers. Events are framed for the future perfect, to have been ... *We cannot look on the photo as simply recording the event when it is part of that event's very nature.*
>
> (pp. 365–366, emphasis added)

A further hazard of networking is that people may find themselves represented by others, pictured online without their agreement or even knowledge. Becker (this volume) reminds us of the power relations built into networked images. For example, adolescents may agonize every morning over what to wear, knowing that their photos may be taken and posted online. More troubling are the instances where, for example, sexual assaults are filmed and posted online.

Another kind of performance associated with photographs and photography is that of the photographic objects and technologies themselves. The current ontological turn in Science and Technology Studies (STS) means that any entity is multiple. No object or technology is pre-given; it may be enacted in different versions by different people under different circumstances, practices and social and material relations (Law & Lien 2013; Mol 2002, 2013; Woolgar & Lezaun 2013; Van House 2015). These chapters demonstrate many of the different versions, in ontological terms, of photographs and photographic technologies that are enacted currently.

Finally, and perhaps most importantly, there is the performance or enactment of identity. Poletti and Rak say of social media that, from the perspective of auto/biography studies, the self is 'an effect of representation ... rather than one's identity being expressed through online practices ... identity is in fact a product of the writing or composing process' (2014, p. 6). People don't *represent* but *enact* themselves in the process of picturing (literally) themselves online. Elsewhere (Van House 2011) I have demonstrated how the design of social media sites influences the kinds of selves (and places) that can be enacted, are encouraged and supported via the designs and practices of current and developing technologies? What does this mean for who we are and will become? These questions are entangled with the issue of memory: what are the stories that we tell ourselves about our past? That can be told with current technologies? How do these interact with current enactment of identity?

Research theory and methods

This book is also concerned with theory and research methods associated with images, materiality and visuality. Theory, research questions, assumptions and methods are all intertwined.

Research methods

As these chapters demonstrate, practice-based research is largely empirical and qualitative. The downside of qualitative research is that it can only effectively engage with small numbers of people in highly specific situations. Generalization is contrary to the theoretical stance that practices are highly contingent. For example, Uimonen (this volume) shows that Tanzanians' resistance to being photographed by strangers, especially white people, has roots in their country's colonial history and current processes of cultural commodification tied to social inequality.

New empirical research methods take advantage of the large collections of images now available online. Early researchers (e.g. Chalfen 2004; Rose 2003) went into households to see their photos. Now, online services like Flickr and Instagram provide easy access to millions of images, often with metadata and linkages to people and other images. Big data analysis methods are being brought to bear on these collections. Computer vision research, facilitated by these huge corpuses, can recognize elements within photos and even identify faces (a technology that is now filtering down to consumers). Researchers are beginning to use 'big data' statistical analyses to try to understand the content as well as the activity around these images. For example, from a selection of 23 million Instagram images from three million users, Bakhshi, Shamma and Gilbert (2014) concluded that people are more interested in (i.e., they 'like' and comment on) images with faces than those without. These enormous collections of linked images and metadata offer ways to study not just photographs, but the processes of networked photography over time: for example, the kinds of images made, the cameras used and patterns of viewing, linkages, sharing and tags.

From a practice perspective, a major failing of big data research is that it removes images from social contexts and practices. It ignores the situated nature of images. Although such analyses can be useful, it is important to remember what they can and cannot tell us. The inferences computer vision analysis can make are limited. These are only images that owners have put online; access depends on owners' privacy choices and institutional policies. User-supplied metadata such as tags are highly variable both in content and reliability. Many of these corpuses are proprietary. Researchers working for service providers may be the only ones with access to certain collections. Ethical, policy and legal concerns further limit access. We will undoubtedly see a cascade of research on these large collections, but need to understand its limitations.

Theory

The chapters in this volume show influence from a variety of areas of theory, including media studies, geography and communications studies. The editors of a recent *Handbook of Visual Culture* (Sandywell & Heywood 2012) make a strong case for the need for inter- and even transdisciplinary research. They urge their own research community to:

> ... conceptualize 'the visual' less as a discretely bounded domain of study – traditionally occupied by art history, media studies, film studies, and the like – and more as an underlying problematic that informs the disciplinary concerns and research programmes of all the arts, sciences and philosophy. As an intersecting cluster of themes and problems – what we might call a transverse problematic – visual culture lends itself to a multiplicity of theoretical interventions and programmatic inquiries.
>
> (p. 12)

Their advice applies to the research represented in this book as well: to consider what fields like art history, media studies, visual studies and others can offer.

In that same volume, Rose (2012), a cultural geographer who has done extensive empirical research on photographic practices (e.g. Rose 2010; also this volume), argues that the social sciences have much to offer to the field of visual culture. She notes that the discipline of visual culture focuses heavily on the meaning of images derived from the formal qualities of the visual object without discussing audiences or place of production or viewing, and without reflecting on the processes and conditions under which the critic produces claims about meaning. She argues that the field of visual culture can benefit from both theoretical and empirical attention to practices, that is, the kind of research represented by these chapters.

Finally, I want to highlight two noteworthy omissions in current research. First, surprisingly little research addresses high quality, stand-alone, non-networked[1] cameras, except to predict (or celebrate) the death of the point-and-shoot camera. Mirrorless cameras and dSLRs make high quality images and sophisticated functionality readily available to the everyday photographer. Powerful, readily accessible software, from smartphone apps to Photoshop, enable sophisticated image processing. In my experience, while professional photographers and photojournalists are anxious about the future of their professions, many non-professionals are engaged in serious aesthetic and documentary photography, visual narrative and other such activities, previously not part of the everyday photographer's experience. Yet, most of the research on non-professional photography is concerned with more quotidian activity.

Second, a topic currently under-theorized in research on everyday photography is video, especially networked video made by everyday photographers and videographers. Short videos made by mobile devices – we might call them video postcards or video snapshots – are an increasing proportion of networked visual media. In late 2015, Facebook began supporting seven-second videos as profile pictures. However, our understanding of short, networked video is, in some ways, like that of early mobile photography. In this volume, Andersen examines in depth the political uses of video and assumptions about its truthfulness, and Favero discusses the GoPro video device as a window on to other senses. There is much more to be learned about simple consumer-produced video.

As I said at the beginning, innovations and discontinuities help to make visible what has been taken for granted. As video becomes more a part of the ecology of everyday photography, it highlights some of the questions of material mediations raised in this volume. It makes visible some of the interactions among photographic and other kinds of practices, technologies and infrastructure. As infrastructural elements like Facebook and GoPro better support everyday video-making and viewing, uses and practices will emerge. Finally, video, especially live-streaming, raises new issues of ethics and values in design. Video can be more immediate, both temporally and emotionally. Terrorists, for example, display videos of executions online. Just because we can live-stream, should we? Who? When? And when not? Should we watch? (Malik 2015).

Conclusions

Finally, I ask two larger questions about photographic practices and images. The first is about how these developments affect people's lives. The second is about images themselves.

The phenomenological anthropologist Timothy Ingold describes life as wayfaring. People, he says, are in continual movement through the world.

> Along such paths, lives are lived, skills developed, observations made and understandings grown.... To be, I would now say, is not to be in place but to be along paths. The path, and not the place, is the primary condition of being, or rather becoming.... My contention is that way-faring is the fundamental mode by which living beings inhabit the earth. Every such a being has, accordingly, to be imagined as the line of its own movement or – more radically – as a bundle of lines.
>
> (2011, pp. 12–13)

The intersections of these paths of movements he calls meshwork. We all live in a meshwork of our own lines of movement and that of others, human and non-human. Building on Ingold, Pink (this volume) describes people as digital wayfarers, weaving through digital/virtual and material/physical worlds. Images are in movement, too:

> … [Images] are on encounters with things … [Images] are produced by moving through and not over or on environments, and they are not stopping points so much as outcomes of and in movement. This means making a shift in thinking from the commonsense idea that a photograph represents a static moment and thus is a photograph of a place, to the idea that it is in place and in movement.
>
> (Pink 2011, p. 9, cited by Pink in this volume)

Photography, in all its versions, is entangled with people's wayfaring through the meshwork that is the world of living and technology. Ingold says that his field, anthropology, 'is the study of human becomings, as they unfold within the weave of the world' (2011, p. 9). So, too, the study of everyday photography is, in the end, like all social science, the study of human becomings, and how photographic technologies and practices are also in movement (Van House 2015), enmeshed with who we are and are becoming, individually and collectively.

Finally, the question that much of the discussion of photography circles around: why are *images* so important? Why are people so enamoured of photography? Why have new photographic technologies and practices been embraced so enthusiastically even while old ones have remained beloved? David Freedberg (1989, p. xxi) has argued that art history has erred in ignoring the recurring 'unrefined, basic, preintellectual, raw' ways in which people throughout history and cultures have responded to images of all kinds. We should consider

> … the effectiveness, efficacy and vitality of images themselves; not only what beholders do, but also what images appear to do; not only what people do as a result of their relationship with imaged form, but also what they expect imaged form to achieve, and why they have such expectations at all.
>
> (Ibid., p. xxii)

Media theorist W. J. T. Mitchell shares Freedberg's puzzlement.

> Why is it that people have such strange attitudes toward images, objects, and media? Why do they behave as if pictures were alive, as if works of art had minds of their own, as if images had a power to influence human beings, demanding things from us, persuading, seducing, and leading us astray? … How is it, in other words, that people are able to maintain a 'double consciousness' toward images, pictures, and representations in a variety of media, vacillating between magical beliefs and skeptical doubts, naive animism and hardheaded materialism, mystical and critical attitudes?
>
> (2005, p. 7)

Empirical research on the large, diverse and ever-growing domain of everyday photographs – malleable and slippery as they are – and photographic practices and technologies, and the ways that they are entangled in the meshwork of people's lives, may help us further along towards finding answers to these questions.

Note

1 Many of the newest dSLRs are now Wi-Fi capable, but they differ significantly, as networked devices, from the ever-present camera phone.

References

Bakhshi, S., Shamma, D. A. & Gilbert, E. 2014, 'Faces Engage Us: Photos with Faces Attract More Likes and Comments on Instagram', in *CHI 14: Proceedings of the SIGCHI Conference on Human Factors in Computing Systems*, ACM: New York, pp. 965–974.

Blustein, J. 2008, *The Moral Demands of Memory*. Cambridge University Press: Cambridge.

Bowker, G. C. 2005, *Memory Practices in the Sciences*. MIT Press: Cambridge, MA.

Chalfen, R. 2004, 'Snapshots "R" Us: The Evidentiary Problematic of Home Media'. *Visual Studies*, Vol. 17, no. 2, pp. 141–149.

Crang, M. 1997, 'Picturing Practices: Research through the Tourist Gaze'. *Progress in Human Geography*, Vol. 21, no. 3, pp. 359–373.

Freedberg, D. 1989, *The Power of Images: Studies in the History and Theory of Response*. University of Chicago Press: Chicago, IL.

Ingold, T. 2011, *Being Alive: Essays on Movement, Knowledge and Description*. Routledge: New York.

Latour, B. 2005, *Reassembling the Social: An Introduction to Actor-Network-Theory*. Oxford University Press: Oxford.

Law, J. & Lien, M. E. 2013, 'Slippery: Field Notes in Empirical Ontology'. *Social Studies of Science*, Vol. 43, no. 3, pp. 363–378.

Malik, N. 2015, 'If you Watch Isis's Videos you are Complicit in its Terrorism'. *Guardian*, 4 February 2015, viewed 18 October 2015, www.theguardian.com/commentisfree/2015/feb/04/isis-videos-complict-terrorism-death-hostage-killers.

Mitchell, W. J. T. 2005, *What Do Pictures Want?* University of Chicago Press: Chicago, IL.

Mol, A. 2013, 'Mind Your Plate! The Ontonorms of Dutch Dieting'. *Social Studies of Science*, Vol. 43, no. 3, pp. 379–396.

Mol, A. 2002, *The Body Multiple: Ontology in Medical Practice*. Duke University Press: Durham, NC.

Pink, S. 2011, 'Sensory Digital Photography: Re-Thinking "Moving" and the Image'. *Visual Studies*, Vol. 26, no. 1, pp. 4–13.

Poletti, A. & Rak, J. 2014, 'Introduction: Digital Dialogues', in A. Poletti & J. Rak (eds) *Identity Technologies: Constructing the Self Online*. University of Wisconsin Press: Madison, WI, pp. 3–24.

Posetti, J. 2014, 'Is Social Media to Blame for the Increase of Graphic Images in

Media?'. *MediaShift*, 8 August 2014, viewed 18 October 2015, www.pbs.org/mediashift/2014/08/is-social-media-to-blame-for-the-increase-in-graphic-images-in-media/.

Pultarova, T. 2015, 'Digital Data Storage May Leave Future in Dark About Us, Warns Cerf'. *Engineering and Technology Magazine*, 13 February 2015, viewed 18 October 2015, http://eandt.theiet.org/news/2015/feb/vint-cerf-digital-data.cfm.

Rose, G. 2012, 'The Question of Method: Practice, Reflexivity and Critique in Visual Culture Studies', in I. Heywood, B. Sandywell, M. Gardiner, N. Gunalan & C. M. Soussloff (eds) *Handbook of Visual Culture*. Berg: London, pp. 542–558.

Rose, G. 2010, *Doing Family Photography: The Domestic, the Public, and the Politics of Sentiment*. Ashgate: Burlington, VT.

Rose, G. 2003, 'Family Photography and Domestic Spacings: A Case Study'. *Transactions of the Institute of British Geographers*, Vol. 28, no. 1, pp. 5–18.

Sandywell, B. & Heywood, I. 2012, 'Critical Approaches to the Study of Visual Culture: An Introduction to the Handbook', in I. Heywood, B. Sandywell, M. Gardiner, N. Gunalan & C. M. Soussloff (eds) *Handbook of Visual Culture*. Berg: London, pp. 12–31.

Van House, N. 2015 [forthcoming], 'Entangled with Technology: Engagement with Facebook among the Young Old'. *First Monday*.

Van House, N. 2011, 'Feminist HCI meets Facebook: Performativity and Social Networking Sites'. *Interacting with Computers*, Vol. 23, no. 5, pp. 422–429.

Van House, N. & Churchill, E. F. 2008, 'Technologies of Memory: Key Issues and Critical Perspectives'. *Memory Studies*, Vol. 1, no. 3, pp. 295–310.

Woolgar, S. & Lezaun, J. 2013, 'The Wrong Bin Bag: A Turn to Ontology in Science and Technology Studies?' *Social Studies of Science*, Vol. 43, no. 3, pp. 321–340.

Index

Page numbers in **bold** denote figures or illustrations, those in *italics* denote tables.

3D printing technology: 3D portraiture 215; and Haraway's cyborg premonition 212; medical uses 212; printing of biological structures 212; and the translation of visions 211
9/11 (September 11th terror attacks) 142

Abraham, R. 193, 206
actor network theory 143, 267
Adidas 212
Adobe Lightroom 4 257
affordances, the concept of 53
Africa: historical perspective of photography 21; mobile modernity and photographic practice 20–2; use of photo montage 27
Akerman, J.R. 163, 176
algorithmic turn 210, 221
algorithms: filtering 262; and predictive pictures 259–60; QR codes and the shifting of agency from the user to 236–7; role of in creating images 253, 260; wearable technologies and the shifting of agency to 253
Alzheimer's disease: awareness raising 74; caregiver groups' image-sharing practices 74; examples of caregivers' blogs 75–6; and the importance of visibility 74; intimacy and the representation of mental health in social networks 73–4; and motivation for sharing images 75; the need for companionship 76–7; selfies 74; sharing experiences of through blogging 74, 76; tags, importance for sharing experiences 74

amateur photography, and understanding of conflict 142
ambrotypes 249
analogue photography, and the camera as tool 268, 270
Andén-Papadopoulos, K. 87, 100, 153–4
Andersen, R.S. 280
Apple Watch 213, 224
archiving technology, technological change and retrievability of digital files 276
Arevalo, C.L. 75
art history, Freedberg's argument 281
Atlanta Olympics 92
Augé, M. 108
augmented reality navigation: historical basis 160; photo-auto guides, integration of media 160
augmented reality technology, wearable 214
Autographer life-logging camera 249, 252, 257
automobile maps, photographic *see* photo-auto guides; Rand McNally guides
awareness-raising: blogging and 75; image sharing and 73–4

Barredo, P.A. 75–6
Barthes, R. 111
Batchen, G. 247
Baudrillard, Jean 88, 94
Bauma, Jeff 90
Bazin, A. 222
beauty pageants 30

Beck, U. 128
Beck-Gersheim, E. 128
Behrend, H. 22
Belting, H. 55
Benjamin, W. 223
Bentham, J. 224
Between image and information: the iPhone camera in the history of photography (Chesher) 237
Bieber, Justin 36
big data: analytical power 92–3; as a panopticon 224; *see also* surveillance
Bijker, W.E. 231
Bildwissenschaft 6, 55
bioinks 212
Blandford, A. 77
blogging: and awareness-raising 75; fashion blogging 42; sharing experiences of Alzheimer's disease through 74, 76
Blustein, J. 276
body, monitoring the *see* monitoring the body
Boehm, G. 245, 252–3, 255
Boston Marathon bomb attack, real-time coverage 86
Boston Marathon bombing investigation: and the Baudrillardian notion of fragmented hyperreality 88; 'crowdsourcing' 86, 88, 90; false rumours and unconfirmed information 91; journalism by social media 87–8; official investigation by law enforcement 90–2; and the power of big data 92–3; primary social media sources 88–9; themes of *Boston Globe* social media 89; traditional media reporting 90; various roles of images and the use of social media 88–92
Bourdieu, P. 28, 54, 201
Bowker, G.C. 276
Boyd, D. 45
brand creation, Facebook closet shops and 47–8
breastfeeding mother, Facebook deletes photos of 264n29
Brorson Church eviction: activists' strategies 154; the camera as an inscription device 145–6; church location 141; digital imagery, social networks and political protest 148–50; image performativity as network effect 151–3; and the

importance of visual media in shaping understanding and resistance 142–4; overview 144–6; police strategies 154–6; screen captures from citizen recordings of police **141, 147, 156**; the unlikely main character 146–8; visual translations of political conflict 153–6
Burgess, J. 47
Burgin, V. 272n1
Bush, V. 210–11

camera: depiction as tool 268–70; the networked computational camera 270–2
camera as sensor: heuristic pictures 255, 257; integration of cameras into ever more devices 248; layered pictures 258–9; life-logging cameras 249–50, 252, 257; looking beyond 'film-like photography' 243–8; navigational applications 258–9 (*see also* navigational applications); from 'photographic cameras' to 'sensors' 248–50; the photographic process 250–2; predictive pictures, algorithms and 259–61; simulative pictures 253–5; surface markings made visible 252–9; understanding photography 248–50; *see also* wearable technologies
camera phones 107; Chesher's implications 237; and the destabilization of photography 230–3; and digital wayfaring 188 (*see also* digital wayfaring); ephemeral nature of photographs taken with 232–3; location awareness *see* location-awareness of camera phones; pioneering studies 232–3; range of sensors 244 (*see also* camera as sensor); and the transformation of photography 232; ubiquity of 244; use of as mirrors 229; vernacular uses 229; *see also* mobile phone cameras; mobile phone photography
camera technology, Sontag on the industrialization of 231
cameras, ubiquitous nature 1
Camgirls: Celebrity & Community in the Age of Social Networks (Senft) 44
Campbell, D. 143, 155
Cartwright, L. 238
Castells, M. 112

CCD and CMOS sensors 248, 250, 260
celebrities, visual social media practices
  36
celebrity culture: consumption and
  42–6; the expansion of 48; Facebook
  closet shops and 42–6; outfit selfies
  and 43; pervasiveness 44; webcams
  and the concept of microcelebrity
  44–5
Cerf, Vint 276
Chalfen, R. 4, 132
Charlie Hebdo 87
Chesher, C. 237
children, concerns about sharing digital
  photographs of 128
Christensen, M. 102
cinema, multi-sensory 215
citizen journalists, and news on the
  Arab spring 94n1
citizen-created photos, reliability as
  source for professional journalism 87
CMOS sensors 248, 250, 260
commemoration/tribute websites: for
  babies or stillbirths 79–80; collective/
  historical memories 79; *Dear
  Photograph* 77–9; for elderly people
  79; as enablers for talking about grief
  and death 79; function 77;
  grandparents 78; *Much Loved*
  79–80; parents or siblings 78; pets 79
commercial photography, co-existence
  of mobile photography with 28
commercial transactions, photographs
  as evidence for 39
communication: digital photography as
  tool for 52; digitally networked
  cameras and 124; families' use of
  photography to keep in touch 123;
  importance of digital photo use for
  real-time communication 244;
  importance of photography as an
  instrument of 36; mobile
  photography as visual
  communication 233; social networks
  and mobile communication 22;
  through photographs 107
computing, convergence of
  photography with 267
conflict, the importance of amateur
  photography in understanding 142
connective interfaces: camera phones
  and the destabilization of
  photography 230–3; examples of
  successful apps 237–8; new

photographic practices in everyday
  life 228–30; photography as a
  technology 233–5; QR codes 235–8;
  restaurant experience 228
'Conspicuous and Authentic'
  (Marwick) 42
control: image sharing and challenges
  for 133; over distribution of images
  21; risk of mobile theft and loss of
  30–2
Cook, T.E. 150
Cordero, I. 75
Côte d'Ivoire, Förster's study of online
  and mobile displays of portrait
  photographs 21
Crang, M. 277
Crary, J. 236–7
creative agency, digital editing and
  26–7
creative process: and imagination 193;
  mobile phone photography's
  facilitation 26
Cross, K. 100
cyborgs, Haraway's premonition 212

daguerreotypes 249, 254
dance: heightened contact and 197; and
  photographers' variation of their
  everyday movements 196
dashboard cameras 217
de Souza e Silva, A. 108–9
Dear Photograph commemoration
  website 77–9
death: acceptability as photographic
  subject 70; commercialization 70;
  historical perspective of photographic
  representation 70; *see also* illness,
  death and grief
Degen, M. 247
dementia, exploring through digital
  photography 73–7; *see also*
  Alzheimer's disease
democratization of photography 231;
  see also Kodak Culture
demosaicing 264n27
Denmark, Brorson Church eviction *see*
  Brorson Church eviction
destabilization of photography,
  assemblages and practices 230–3
digital culture, image-making processes
  and the shaping of 231
'digital dark age' 276
digital editing, creative agency and
  26–7

digital media: anthropological perspective 21; changing technology and retrievability of older files 276; digital photographs as postcards 116; and identity/ownership 21
'digital natives', and 'digital immigrants' 56, 58, 65–6
'digital refugees' 103
digital wayfaring: the concept 188; photographic places and 190
digitization: concept of 'photography' and 247; Vannevar Bush's prediction 210–11
Discipline and Punish: the Birth of the Prison (Foucault) 224
distribution of images, mobile phone photography and control over 21
Dods, J.P. 176
driving, photographic navigational aids *see* photo-auto guides; Rand McNally guides
drones 1, 143, 244

editing software, and creative agency 26–7
Edwards, E. 100
Electricfoxy Move posture correction garment 213
Elsaesser, T. 247
empowerment, the selfie as source of 36
Engine of Visualization, The (Maynard) 234
environment, Ingold on the 188
ethnographic research: ethnographic analysis of photography 54; ethnographic approach to seniors and digital photography 54–5; ethnographic approach to transnational family photography 125; Facebook as fertile area for 37; Facebook closet shops 38; guided tour technique 195; photographers in Newcastle-upon-Tyne and Sunderland 194; in urban Tanzania 19
Evernote (app) 237
everyday life: the monitoring of 223–4; new photographic practices in 228–30; visual documentation of 35
everyday photography, and techno-visual regimes 238–9
everyday routine: exploring through the habit of noticing 193 (*see also* noticing); Flickr as part of 203

exchanging snaps, importance of reciprocity 123
execution videos, ethical perspective of watching 280
exhibitionism, in celebrity digital culture 36
exploitation, mobile phone photography and fears of 21, 29–30

face-recognition technology: advantages over other biometrics 261; and the Boston Marathon bombing 92–3, 99; embedding in consumer grade cameras 260
Facebook 19, 23–4, 133; and the Boston Marathon bombing 89–90; comparison with the Library of Congress 209; deletes photos of breastfeeding mother 264n29; and everyday surveillance 102; Iranian 'Facebook revolution' 102; number of photos 209; number of users worldwide 37; Portugal, number of users in 37; premise 37; scope of application 24; as space for selling second-hand goods 37 (*see also* Facebook closet shops)
Facebook closet shops: 'Ana's Glam Closet' 41–2; and brand creation 47–8; Catarina's closet shop 38–9; and commercial image culture 43; comparison with fashion blogging 42; consuming and playing for celebrity 42–6; ethnographic research 38; function of photography 39, 42, 48; and the illusion of being backstage 45; Maria's closet shop 46–7; 'Marta's Bargain Closet' 43; microcelebrity and 37 (*see also* microcelebrity); outfit selfies, shopping haul snaps and closet stories 37–42; owners 37; and popular media discourse 44; Portuguese closets 38; presentation and quality of photography 38; and the promotion of celebrity 45–6; self-imaging practices, personal branding and the marketplace 46–9; social dynamic 47; socio-economic background of owners 37; 'Sofia's Closet' 39, 41; Sofia's outfit selfie 40; and visual consumption 42
Facetime 1
families, use of photography to keep in touch 123

family composition, and social media choices 24
family pictures, circulation of 24
family relations, mobile phone photography and relational objects for memory making 22–4
fashion blogging: and conspicuous consumption 42; Marwick's analysis 42
Favero, P. 275, 280
Feininger, A. 267–8; *see also* 'The Photojournalist' (Feininger)
female empowerment, the selfie as source of 36
Fields, B. 77
'film-like digital photography' 244–5, 247–8, 251–2, 254–5
Find My Friends (app) 110
Fiore, Q. 216
Fitbit health bracelet 213
Flickr 71, 74, 194, 201–3, 222, 278
Florence, Hercules 249
food, photographing 228
Förster, T. 21
Foucault, M. 224
Foursquare (app) 107, 110, 113, 117–18
Fox Talbot, William Henry 234
fragmented hyperreality 88
Franklin, S. 128
Freedberg, D. 281
Friedberg, A. 102
Fuelband health bracelet 213

Gabb, J. 128
Gartner, S.S. 92
Geography of the Lifeworld (Seamon) 194, 195–7
Gere, C. 209
glass negatives, as invaluable record 276
Gleick, James 87
Goffman, E. 45, 73
Gómez Cruz, E. 259
Google Glass 214–15
GoPro action camera 217–20; video still **220**
Gordon, E. 109
Grabbe, Lauren 93
Gram, S. 36
grassroots-level information, sources of 86
Green, J. 47
grief, exploring illness, death and *see* illness, death and grief

Guantanamo Bay 142
guided tour technique, of ethnographic research 195

habitual movement, Seamon's belief 196
habitus 54, 201
Hahn, T. 206
Hand, M. 229–30
Haraway, D. 212
Hayles, N.K. 223
head movements 193
health bracelets 213
Hearn, A. 47
Herschel, Sir John 249
heuristic pictures: definition 245–6; distinction between simulative pictures and 252
Hirsch, M. 77
HIV/AIDS 142
Hjorth, L. 115, 188
Hochman, N. 259
Holocaust Museum, Washington DC 276
hyperreality, fragmented 88

identity, the enactment of 277
identity construction, role of contemporary media 44
identity formation, networked photographs and 36
illness, death and grief: awareness-raising, image sharing and 73; changing attitudes to photographic representation 71, 73; commemoration/tribute websites 77–80 (*see also* commemoration/tribute websites); exploring dementia through digital photography 73–7 (*see also* Alzheimer's disease); historical perspective of photographic representation 70; mental health, digital photography and the representation of 73; post-mortem photography 70; the real need behind sharing pictures 76; sharing images of 72–3; study methodology and ethical context 71
image sharing *see* sharing images
image-making: mobile phone cameras and the spontaneity of 20–1; and the shaping of digital culture 231
imageless interfaces 230
images: 'double consciousness' towards

281; exposure to in Western culture 35; German visual sociological approaches to interpretation 55; 'iconic difference' 247; the importance of 281; social and cultural role 35; surplus value 247; wearable cameras and the changing meaning of 224 (*see also* wearable technologies)
imagination, and the creative process 193
inaccessibility, of older files 276
indexicality of photographs: as guarantee of presence 117; invisibility 254
industrialization of camera technology 231
Ingold, T. 186–8, 194, 201, 204, 280
inscription device, definition 145
Instagram 110; and everyday surveillance 102; food photographs 228; increasing portrayal of domesticity 222; launch 1; motivations for sharing images related to Alzheimer's disease 75; scope of application 24; and sharing images of illness 74
Instant Heart Rate (app) 238
interfaces, connective *see* connective interfaces
intermediality of portraiture in Cote d'Ivoire, Förster's study 21
internet access, and the availability of mobile networks 20
interrelatedness of things 108
'interveillance' 102
intimacy, and the exchange of photographs 28
iOnRoad (navigational application) 258–9
iPhone 5, snail taken with a macro lens **221**
Iran, 'Facebook revolution' 102
Iraq war, and visual media 142
Ito, M. 112, 232

Jeffries, L. 43
Jones, T. 77

Kaipiainen, S. 255–6
Kardashian, Kim 36
Kellner, D. 44
Kember, S. 231, 261
Kennedy, L. 143

Kenya, panic accompanying the rise of digital photography 22
Khomeini, Ayatollah 102
Kindberg, T. 115
kinship, and transnational family photography 128, 135
Kodak Culture: Chalfen's identification 4; definition 229; disruption 230, 232; introduction of the Kodak camera 231; shaping of 232

La trahison des images (Magritte) 145
Laboratory Life (Latour/Woolgar) 145
Laslow, Abraham 197
Latour, B. 145, 150, 163–5
Law, J. 145
layered pictures: definition 246; function 252; using navigational camera software in traffic **258**
Lehmuskallio, A. 195, 229, 237, 239
Leibovitz, A. 72
"Leviathan" (documentary) 218–20, 223
Library of Congress, photographs, comparison with Facebook 209
Licoppe, C. 110
lifestyle association, of mobile phones 22
Linnemann, T. 86
Lister, M. 98, 144, 233
locality, place vs 187
localization services 110
location: the concept of 108; importance in social and networked interactions 109; place and non-place 108
location-aware technologies, description 107
location-awareness of camera phones: context 107–8; examples of uses 109; Finnish study 113–17; geotagging 110; and mediated presence 110–12; 'phonespace' and 'photospace' 112–13; popularity of location-based services 108; and the re-localization of mobile communication 108–10; 'sending the place' 107
locative media, definition 107–8

MacDougall, D. 219–20
McKenna, T. 194, 197, 206
McKinnon, S. 128
McLuhan, M. 216, 222, 224
McNally, Andrew 164

Madianou, M. 102, 134
Magritte, René 145
manipulation of photographs, Reuters' rules 94n3
Männistö, A. 99, 102
Manovich, L. 259
mapping, through photography *see* photo-auto guides; Rand McNally guides
Maragall, Pasqual 74
Marwick, A. 42–3, 45
Massey, D. 112, 186
material and visual practices, focusing on 7–8
Maynard, P. 230, 234, 238, 245, 247, 250, 262
mediated presence: the concept 108, 138n8; examining the mediation of place 108; location-awareness of camera phones and 110–12; photo messaging and 28, 116; photographic re-localization and 110
mediation theory, photo-auto guides and 163–4
medium-specificity 246
Melhuish, C. 247
'MeMedia' 36
Memex memory augmentation system 210–11
memory making: everyday photography and 244; mobile phone photography and 22–4
mental health, scientific representation through photography 73
Merleau-Ponty, Maurice 195, 199
metadata: and the Boston Marathon bomb attack 94; carried by digital photo files 7; and everyday surveillance 102; and the use of big data analysis 278; using for novel visualizations 257; value of 93–4; vernacular photography as source of 229
microcelebrity: and audience management 45; definition 45; enablement through digital technology 45; Mota's identification 101; the seeking of 48
Miller, D. 102
minimum spanning tree, of a social network **256**
Mirzoeff, N. 209
Mitchell, W.J.T. 3, 6, 145, 162, 237, 281

Mobile Image (Koskinen *et al.*) 114
mobile multimedia 233
mobile phone cameras: scholarly interest 20; social uses of personal photography 23; and the spontaneity of image-making 20–1; and the spread of vernacular photography 20; ubiquitous nature 20; *see also* camera phones; location-awareness of camera phones; mobile phone photography
mobile phone photography: access to technology 20; circulation practices 22–4; and control over distribution 21; creative agency and digital editing 26–7; cultural significance of the family 23; ethnographic research in urban Tanzania 19; facilitation of creative image making 26; fears of commercial and sexual exploitation 29–30; as a genre in its own right 22; lifestyle association of mobile phones 22; and location-aware technology *see* location-awareness of camera phones; materiality in display and circulation 27–8; mobile phone ownership in Tanzania 19; mundanity and ubiquity of photographic practices 29; normative boundaries and crazy pictures 28–9; performing selfhood 24–6 (*see also* selfies); personal nature 31; and relational objects for memory making and family relations 22–4; as relational practice 21; risk of theft and loss of control 30–2; snail taken with a macro lens **221**; Tanzanian telecom penetration statistics 20; versus conventional photography 233
mobile phones: and the communication of location 107; multifunctional nature 22; risk of theft 30; as status symbol 22; use of to display photographs 27; *see also* camera phones
monitoring the body: through wearable technologies 213–14; using a phone app 238
Moores, S. 124, 195
Morcate, M. 275
Mota, S.P. 99–101, 277
motorists, photographic navigational aids *see* photo-auto guides; Rand McNally guides

Much Loved tribute website 79–80
Murray, S. 222–3

Narrative Clip life-logging camera
  215–17, 257
navigational applications: iOnRoad
  (app) 258–9; using in traffic **258**; *see
  also* photo-auto guides; Rand
  McNally guides
net locality 109
networked everyday photography,
  implications 275
networked journalism 87, 93
networked video 280
Newcastle-upon-Tyne and Sunderland,
  ethnographic study of photographers
  in 194
Nichols, B. 209
non-place: the concept of 108;
  examples of non-places 108;
  transformation of non-places into
  telecommunicative spaces 113
non-representational theory 3, 268
non-representational turn, 'The
  Photojournalist' and the 267–8
noticing: the habits of 197–202; habitus
  and 201; and heightened contact 197;
  mood/emotion and 199–200;
  movement and 198, 202–3, 205; as
  presence 205, 207; and the presence
  of the camera 198–9; and publishing
  platforms 197; Seamon's definition
  196; as skill 200–1; the
  unexpectedness of 206; watching and
  waiting 204–5

Oculus Rift immersive virtual reality
  goggles 221
Okabe, D. 112, 232
Omote 3D 215
Organovo 212
outfit selfies: and celebrity culture 43;
  the sharing process 46; Sofia's outfit
  40; staging 43; *see also* selfies

Panopticon, Bentham's 224
Pantti, M. 153
Paravel, V. 218
Pardo, R. 275
participation in photography: massive
  increase 274; participants and
  approaches 274–5
Pasqual Maragall Mira (Maragall &
  García) 74

performance, networked photography
  as 276–7
performance of photography,
  multisensory nature 101
personal and collective memory, threats
  to 276
personal photography: the digital turn
  and 35; diversity of modes 64–5; the
  personal nature of mobile phone
  photography 31; social functions 23,
  52
Peters, J.D. 217
'phatic communities' 137n7
photo collage, homemade **129**
photo messaging 20, 28
photo montage, African use of 27
photo-auto guides: analysis of guides
  between 1905 and 1909 164–74; and
  augmentation 183; and the Blue
  Book model 176; Chicago to
  Milwaukee **172–3**; conceptual flaws
  169; form of production 176–81;
  groundwork 164–5; historical
  context 160, 164; integration of
  media 160; and mediation theory
  163–4; navigational practices 175–6;
  objects of analysis 164–5;
  performative cartography and
  operative images 160–3; and the
  Railroad Guide 164; Rand McNally
  examples and comparative analyses
  166–74; short lifespan 183; similarity
  to nineteenth-century military
  cartography 167; 'social media'
  design 160; Southbend to Chicago
  178–9; structuring 166–8; *see also*
  Rand McNally guides
photogenic, literal meaning 234
photogenic connective interfaces *see*
  connective interfaces
photographic practices, Tanzanian
  examples 22–3
photographic process, outlined 251
photographs: as certificate of presence
  111; communication through 107; as
  evidence for commercial transactions
  39; Reuters' rules on manipulation of
  94n3; storage options 31
photography: camera phones and the
  destabilization of 230–3;
  conceptualizing as *pictorial* practice
  54–5; conceptualizing as practice
  53–4; convergence with computing
  267; difficulty of defining 248–9;

photography *continued*
ethnographic analysis 54; importance as instrument of communication 36; Maynard's definition 250; OED definition 248–50; outline of the process 250–2; performativity of 21; as professional and leisure activity 99; as social act 36; social functions, global similarity 21; as 'surface markings made with light' 250; as a technology 233–5; traditional use 36; understanding 248–50, 272

'The Photojournalist' (Feininger) **269**; and the changed nature of the camera 270–2; depiction of the camera as tool 268–70; and the non-representational turn 267–8; a reading of the image 272

Pickering, M. 52

Pink, S. 108, 115, 280–1

place: bringing together of theories of place and movement 189–90; Castells *et al* on the redefinition of 112; the concept of 108; examining the mediation of 108; Ingold on the environment 188; and the interrelatedness of things 108; literature review 186–9; locality vs 187; online and offline places 112; theoretical focus 188

point-and-shoot camera, prediction of demise 279

Poletti, A. 277

police, screen captures from citizen recordings, Brorson Church eviction **141, 147, 156**

political protest and the digital camera: importance of amateur photography in understanding conflict 142; the visual translation of protest 145–6; *see also* Brorson Church eviction

polymedia 102

Ponzanesi, S. 134

popular media discourse, and Facebook closet shops 44

Portugal: number of Facebook users 37; popularity of social networking sites 37; the second-hand goods market 37

post-mortem photography: historical perspective 70; *see also* death

postcards, digital photographs as 116

power relations 102

practice-based approaches: benefits of 4–6; need for 2–4

practices, definition 53

predictive pictures, examples 246

QR codes: restaurant experience 228; and the shifting of agency from the user to algorithms 236–7; ubiquity 235

Railroad Guide 164

Rak, J. 277

Rand McNally guides: Chicago to Lake Geneva **161**; criteria for choice of route 166; objects of analysis 164–5; origins 164, 166

raving, and heightened contact 197

reality television 39, 44, 48

reciprocity, importance of in exchanging snaps 123

reflexivity, performance and 101

relational objects, photographs as 24

Relph, E. 195

remotely controlled cameras, examples of uses 244

research: the downside of qualitative research 278; noteworthy omissions 279–80; theory and methods 278, 280; *see also* ethnographic research

restaurants, use of photography in 228

Reuters, rules concerning news photo manipulation 94n3

Ritchin, F. 209

Rose, G. 123, 134, 247

Rubinstein, D. 271

Sartre, J.-P. 48

Sarvas, R. 255–7

Schroeder, J. 35

Science in Action (Latour) 163

scientific imagery 238

Scifo, B. 114–15

Scoville, Georges 90

'screen practices' 102

Seamon, D. 194–6, 204, 206

self-representation, networked photographs and 36

selfies: and Alzheimer's patients 74; challenge to narcissism narrative 49n1; the concept 36; as everyday practice 123; scholarly interest 36; selfie culture 26, 112; young women's use of 36; *see also* outfit selfies

Senft, T.M. 44–5, 47–9, 101

seniors and digital photography: Bertl's image **59**; and the concept of digital natives and immigrants 56, 58, 65–6; conceptualizing photography as *pictorial* practice 54–5; conceptualizing photography as practice 53–4; diversity of modes of personal photography 64–5; and ethnographic approaches 54–5; generational perspective 56–7; movie production 61–4; and the perception of seniors using computers 57–8; personal photography as a hobby 58–61; photo editing training course 57–8; pictures provided by participants **59, 62**

sensor, the camera as *see* camera as sensor

September 11th terror attacks (9/11) 142

sharing images: Alzheimer's caregivers' practices 74; awareness-raising through 73–4; concerns about sharing digital photographs of children 128; and creation of a 'shared simultaneous experience' 222, 275; enabling participation in family events through 132–3; of illness, death and grief 72–3; motivations for sharing images related to Alzheimer's disease **75**; outfit selfies, the sharing process 46; photo-sharing circles in transnational families 125–8; the real need behind 76; social media and 20; tags, importance for sharing experiences 74; and trust 39

sharing photographs, and gendered norms in visual culture 25

Sheldrake, R. 205

Shepherd, L.J. 142

Shipman, B. 128

Silva, Steve 90

simulative pictures: creating 253–4; definition 245, 253; distinction between heuristic pictures and 245, 252, 257; ways of creating 254

Skype 1, 122–3, 130, 132–3

Slater, D. 100

Sluis, K. 271

small-talk, photographs as 112

Smart, C. 128

"smart clothes" 212

smart watches, the birth of 213

smartphones: and the use of the internet to store photographs 31; using to pay the restaurant bill 228

smiling, and camera technology 260

snail, photographed with a macro lens using an iPhone 5 **221**

Snapchat 1

social bonding, everyday photography and 244

social cohesion, projection of by the depiction of important moments 232

social media: explaining current uses of photography in 239; and the instant sharing of images 20; and participation in photography 274; reporting role 88; as source of information 86–7 (*see also* Boston Marathon bombing investigation)

social networks: minimum spanning tree **256**; and mobile communication 22

social presence 111–12, 117

social relations: embedding of photographs in 24; place and 108

soldier photography, Kennedy's work 157n2

Søndergaard, Christina 146–9, 151

Sonesson, G. 110

Sontag, S. 72, 111, 231

souvenirs, photographs as 232

space, Massey's definition 112

spontaneous image-making, mobile phone cameras and 20–1

St John, G. 197

Stelmaszewska, H. 77

storage options for digital photographs 31

Sturken, M. 238

surface markings made visible, using mobile and wearable technology 252–9

surveillance: everyday 102; face recognition technology and 261; and the 'lie of safety' 102; and power 239; QR codes and 236; *see also* big data

synchronous gaze 116

tags, importance for sharing experiences 74

Taylor, L. 218

techno-visual regimes, everyday photography and 238–9

technology: photography as a connective technology 233–5; wearable *see* wearable technologies

'tele-cocooning' 135

telepresence 115
text messaging, vs sending photographs 115–16
Textgrabber (app) 237
time, a 'shared simultaneous experience' of 222
traffic cameras 246
transformation in photography, and the non-representational turn 267–8
transformation in photography and, and the non-representational turn 267
translation, and the digital camera 145, 149–50
transnational family photography: and the concept of *affordances* 133–4; concerns about sharing photographs of children 128; contextual analysis 122–4; and controlling access 133; enabling participation in family events through sharing of photographs 132–3; ethnographic approach 125; homemade photo collage **129**; incorporating relatives into children's everyday life 130–1; keywords associated with 134; kinship and 128, 135; multiple media, use of 128–32; Pedro and Maria's 'circle of reference' **127**; photo-sharing circles 125–8; place-making event **131**; practices and places 125–34; research design *126*; 'tele-cocooning' 135
trust, sharing photographs and 39
Tuan, Y. 195
Turner, G. 44
Twinkind 215
Twitter: as an 'awareness system' 87; and the Boston Marathon bombing 87, 89–92; and the Charlie Hebdo attack 88

Uimonen, P. 20, 22, 24, 27, 30, 99, 102, 275–6, 278
United States, 'Kodak Culture' 20; *see also* Kodak Culture
Up health bracelet 213
uprisings in the Middle East, and citizen journalism 94n1
Uricchio, W. 221

Van Dijck, J. 23, 52, 123
Van House, N.A. 22, 24
vernacular photography: the concept 100–1; research challenges 102; research requirements 238–9; role change 233, 237; and the shaping of *Kodak Culture* 232; social cohesion and 232; as source of metadata 229
Versailles Hall of Mirrors 224
viewfinder, the body as 222–3
Villi, M. 123, 138
virtual date-nights 123
'visual chitchat' 111
visual communication, mobile photography as 233; *see also* communication
visual consumption, Facebook closet shops and 42
visual culture, calls for a material in studies of 246
visuality, the role of in digital photographic practices 6–7
von Mädler, Johann 249
voyeurism, in celebrity digital culture 36

Wall, T. 86
"war on terror", and visual media strategies 142–3
war zones, 'shared simultaneous experience' 275
watches, smart 213
way-finding, Ingold's concept 202
wayfaring, the concept of 186, 188; *see also* digital wayfaring
wearable technologies: algorithms and agency 253; Apple Watch 213; the body as viewfinder 222–3; and the changing mood of the wearer 213; and the collection of biometric data 212; the digital context 210–14; examples 244; Google Glass 214–15; GoPro action camera 217–20; GoPro camera video still **220**; health bracelets 213; life-logging cameras 215–17, 249–50, 252, 257; and the metaphor of dance 196; military uses 212; monitoring the body through 213–14; Narrative Clip life-logging camera 215–17; the photographic process 250–2; posture correcting 213; and sensor technology development 248 (*see also* camera as sensor); "smart clothes" 212; smart watches 213; sports uses 212; and trends in online digital photography

222; variety of usage 248; vision-based augmented reality technology 214; the visual context 214–15
Web 2.0 44, 47
Webcamming (Senft) 42
Wellman, B. 209
Weston, K. 128
Whatsapp: scope of application 24; and transnational relationships 122, 123
Wheatstone, Charles 249

women, mobile photography and the fear of sexual exploitation 30
Woodman, Nick 218
Woolgar, S. 145
Wordlens (app) 237
Wulff, H.B. 137n7

YouTube, beauty community 42–3

Zylinska, J. 231

Taylor & Francis eBooks

Helping you to choose the right eBooks for your Library

Add Routledge titles to your library's digital collection today. Taylor and Francis ebooks contains over 50,000 titles in the Humanities, Social Sciences, Behavioural Sciences, Built Environment and Law.

Choose from a range of subject packages or create your own!

Benefits for you
- >> Free MARC records
- >> COUNTER-compliant usage statistics
- >> Flexible purchase and pricing options
- >> All titles DRM-free.

REQUEST YOUR **FREE** INSTITUTIONAL TRIAL TODAY

Free Trials Available
We offer free trials to qualifying academic, corporate and government customers.

Benefits for your user
- >> Off-site, anytime access via Athens or referring URL
- >> Print or copy pages or chapters
- >> Full content search
- >> Bookmark, highlight and annotate text
- >> Access to thousands of pages of quality research at the click of a button.

eCollections – Choose from over 30 subject eCollections, including:

Archaeology	Language Learning
Architecture	Law
Asian Studies	Literature
Business & Management	Media & Communication
Classical Studies	Middle East Studies
Construction	Music
Creative & Media Arts	Philosophy
Criminology & Criminal Justice	Planning
Economics	Politics
Education	Psychology & Mental Health
Energy	Religion
Engineering	Security
English Language & Linguistics	Social Work
Environment & Sustainability	Sociology
Geography	Sport
Health Studies	Theatre & Performance
History	Tourism, Hospitality & Events

For more information, pricing enquiries or to order a free trial, please contact your local sales team: www.tandfebooks.com/page/sales

 Routledge Taylor & Francis Group | The home of Routledge books | **www.tandfebooks.com**